Geocriticism and Spatial Literary Studies

Series Editor
Robert T. Tally Jr.
Texas State University
San Marcos, TX, USA

Geocriticism and Spatial Literary Studies is a new book series focusing on the dynamic relations among space, place, and literature. The spatial turn in the humanities and social sciences has occasioned an explosion of innovative, multidisciplinary scholarship in recent years, and geocriticism, broadly conceived, has been among the more promising developments in spatially oriented literary studies. Whether focused on literary geography, cartography, geopoetics, or the spatial humanities more generally, geocritical approaches enable readers to reflect upon the representation of space and place, both in imaginary universes and in those zones where fiction meets reality. Titles in the series include both monographs and collections of essays devoted to literary criticism, theory, and history, often in association with other arts and sciences. Drawing on diverse critical and theoretical traditions, books in the Geocriticism and Spatial Literary Studies series disclose, analyze, and explore the significance of space, place, and mapping in literature and in the world.

More information about this series at
http://www.palgrave.com/gp/series/15002

Christian Beck
Editor

Mobility, Spatiality, and Resistance in Literary and Political Discourse

palgrave
macmillan

Editor
Christian Beck
University of Central Florida
Orlando, FL, USA

Geocriticism and Spatial Literary Studies
ISBN 978-3-030-83476-0   ISBN 978-3-030-83477-7   (eBook)
https://doi.org/10.1007/978-3-030-83477-7

© The Editor(s) (if applicable) and The Author(s), under exclusive licence to Springer Nature Switzerland AG 2021
This work is subject to copyright. All rights are solely and exclusively licensed by the Publisher, whether the whole or part of the material is concerned, specifically the rights of translation, reprinting, reuse of illustrations, recitation, broadcasting, reproduction on microfilms or in any other physical way, and transmission or information storage and retrieval, electronic adaptation, computer software, or by similar or dissimilar methodology now known or hereafter developed.
The use of general descriptive names, registered names, trademarks, service marks, etc. in this publication does not imply, even in the absence of a specific statement, that such names are exempt from the relevant protective laws and regulations and therefore free for general use.
The publisher, the authors and the editors are safe to assume that the advice and information in this book are believed to be true and accurate at the date of publication. Neither the publisher nor the authors or the editors give a warranty, expressed or implied, with respect to the material contained herein or for any errors or omissions that may have been made. The publisher remains neutral with regard to jurisdictional claims in published maps and institutional affiliations.

This Palgrave Macmillan imprint is published by the registered company Springer Nature Switzerland AG.
The registered company address is: Gewerbestrasse 11, 6330 Cham, Switzerland

SERIES EDITOR'S PREFACE

The spatial turn in the humanities and social sciences has occasioned an explosion of innovative, multidisciplinary scholarship. Spatially oriented literary studies, whether operating under the banner of literary geography, literary cartography, geophilosophy, geopoetics, geocriticism, or the spatial humanities more generally, have helped to reframe or to transform contemporary criticism by focusing attention, in various ways, on the dynamic relations among space, place, and literature. Reflecting upon the representation of space and place, whether in the real world, in imaginary universes, or in those hybrid zones where fiction meets reality, scholars and critics working in spatial literary studies are helping to reorient literary criticism, history, and theory. *Geocriticism and Spatial Literary Studies* is a book series presenting new research in this burgeoning field of inquiry.

In exploring such matters as the representation of place in literary works, the relations between literature and geography, the historical transformation of literary and cartographic practices, and the role of space in critical theory, among many others, geocriticism and spatial literary studies have also developed interdisciplinary or transdisciplinary methods and practices, frequently making productive connections to architecture, art history, geography, history, philosophy, politics, social theory, and urban studies, to name but a few. Spatial criticism is not limited to the spaces of the so-called real world, and it sometimes calls into question any too facile distinction between real and imaginary places, as it frequently investigates what Edward Soja has referred to as the "real-and-imagined" places we experience in literature as in life. Indeed, although a great deal of important research has been devoted to the literary representation of certain

v

vi SERIES EDITOR'S PREFACE

identifiable and well known places (e.g., Dickens's London, Baudelaire's Paris, or Joyce's Dublin), spatial critics have also explored the otherworldly spaces of literature, such as those to be found in myth, fantasy, science fiction, video games, and cyberspace. Similarly, such criticism is interested in the relationship between spatiality and such different media or genres as film or television, music, comics, computer programs, and other forms that may supplement, compete with, and potentially problematize literary representation. Titles in the *Geocriticism and Spatial Literary Studies* series include both monographs and collections of essays devoted to literary criticism, theory, and history, often in association with other arts and sciences. Drawing on diverse critical and theoretical traditions, books in the series reveal, analyze, and explore the significance of space, place, and mapping in literature and in the world.

The concepts, practices, or theories implied by the title of this series are to be understood expansively. Although geocriticism and spatial literary studies represent a relatively new area of critical and scholarly investigation, the historical roots of spatial criticism extend well beyond the recent past, informing present and future work. Thanks to a growing critical awareness of spatiality, innovative research into the literary geography of real and imaginary places has helped to shape historical and cultural studies in ancient, medieval, early modern, and modernist literature, while a discourse of spatiality undergirds much of what is still understood as the postmodern condition. The suppression of distance by modern technology, transportation, and telecommunications has only enhanced the sense of place, and of displacement, in the age of globalization. Spatial criticism examines literary representations not only of places themselves, but of the experience of place and of displacement, while exploring the interrelations between lived experience and a more abstract or unrepresentable spatial network that subtly or directly shapes it. In sum, the work being done in geocriticism and spatial literary studies, broadly conceived, is diverse and far reaching. Each volume in this series takes seriously the mutually impressive effects of space or place and artistic representation, particularly as these effects manifest themselves in works of literature. By bringing the spatial and geographical concerns to bear on their scholarship, books in the *Geocriticism and Spatial Literary Studies* series seek to make possible different ways of seeing literary and cultural texts, to pose novel questions for criticism and theory, and to offer alternative approaches to literary and cultural studies. In short, the series aims to open up new spaces for critical inquiry.

San Marcos TX USA   Robert T. Tally Jr.

Acknowledgments

When we first began this endeavor in the fall of 2019, there were the typical political dramas unfolding across the world: climate change was making itself more visible, the voices of young people were beginning to be heard, and everyone was living their daily lives as best they could. Enter COVID-19. Most of the world goes on lockdown. Confined to our homes, our worlds seemingly became detached; connected only through our screens, spaces shrunk, movement ceased, and political engagement became solitary and digital. There were new personal and professional pressures that affected everyone. Then armed protests against lockdown restrictions sprung up around the USA. Then came the murder of George Floyd Jr. Black Lives Matter protests and marches were organized around the world amid a pandemic, which is testament to the urgency of the message. Then there were more deaths. More protests. A general election in the USA whose results were disputed by the sitting president. More protests. January 6 insurrection of the US Capital. Deaths. Arrests. Protests.

Typically, in an Acknowledgments section you would thank everyone who helped making the project come together. But given the rather extreme nature of the last year and a half, the people that need to be thanked are unnamed precisely because I don't know their names. They are the partners, spouses, children, parents, friends, and colleagues of all the contributors of this volume. Everyone that participated in this collection read, wrote, and edited (on top of their other work responsibilities) with their families in (very) close proximity. The support afforded by those around us is what allows a project like this to be completed in a time such as now. Therefore, it is with a very sincere "Thank You" that I would like

viii ACKNOWLEDGMENTS

to dedicate this book to all of our families and friends—that network of people who have and continue to support us in whatever way possible. Thank you to Rob and all the wonderful editors at Palgrave Macmillan for their understanding and patience (indeed, all of you were dealing with the same issues). In the end though, it is those that we surround ourselves with that deserve so much credit for the role they play in our writing and thinking. Thank you all.

CONTENTS

1 Introduction: Movement, Space, and Power in the
  Creative Act   1
  Christian Beck

Part I   Mobility   21

2 Colonial Advertising and Tourism in the Crosscurrents of
  Empire   23
  Scott Cohen

3 The Chivalrous Nation: Travel and Ideological Exchange
  in *Sir Gawain and the Green Knight*   57
  Ruth M. E. Oldman

4 Conjuring Roots in Dystopia: Reconciling
  Transgenerational Conflict and Dislocation Through
  Ancestral Speakers in Nalo Hopkinson's *Brown Girl in the
  Ring* and Edwidge Danticat's *Brother, I'm Dying*   73
  Zeba Khan-Thomas

5 Mobility, Incarceration, and the Politics of Resistance in
  Palestinian Women's Literature   91
  Leila Aouadi

ix

x CONTENTS

6 Matriarchal Mobility: Generational Displacement and
Gendered Place in Marilynne Robinson's *Housekeeping* 115
Marisa Stickel Higgins

Part II Spatiality 135

7 Interiorized Imperialism in Native American and
Japanese American World War II Narratives 137
Olivia Hulsey

8 Turning the Earth, Changing the Narrative: Spatial
Transformation in Frances E. W. Harper's *Iola Leroy; or,
Shadows Uplifted* (1892) 163
Mike Lemon

9 Woolf in the Background: Distance as Visual Philosophy,
Then and Now 185
Amy A. Foley

Part III Radical Positions 207

10 A New Cartographer: Rabih Alameddine and *An
Unnecessary Woman* 209
François-Xavier Gleyzon

11 Vulnerable Erotic Encounters: A Chronotopic Reading
of the Bus-Space in Chicu's *Soliloquy* 233
Prerna Subramanian

12 Anti-capitalism and the Near Future: In Mohsin Hamid's
Exit West and Louise Erdrich's *The Future Home of the
Living God* 257
Jessica Maucione

CONTENTS xi

13 Frantz Fanon, Chester Himes, and a "Literature of Combat" 281
David Polanski

Part IV Conclusion 299

14 Resisting a Wilting Society: *To Blossom* 301
Christian Beck

Index 313

Notes on Contributors

Leila Aouadi is Associate Professor and holds tenure at the University of Tunis, Tunisia; she is teaching in Qatar. Aouadi specializes in Victorian literature and Middle-Eastern women's writing in English.

Christian Beck is Associate Lecturer of English at the University of Central Florida, USA. He has written on a wide array of topics ranging from medieval English literature to graffiti and hacktivism. His scholarship can be found in *Medievalia*, *The Journal for Cultural Research*, and *Contemporary Women's Writing*. His most recent book is *Spatial Resistance: Literary and Digital Challenges to Neoliberalism* (2019) and he is working on his next monograph, *The Figure of the Vigilante: Concepts for Political and Social Justice*.

Scott Cohen is Associate Professor of English and Founding Director of the Digital Innovation Lab at Stonehill College, Easton, Massachusetts, USA, where he teaches courses in modernism, modernity, and digital humanities. He is working on a book project that examines the role broadcasting has played in transforming narrative during the twentieth century.

Amy A. Foley is Instructor of Modern Literature and Philosophy at Providence College, USA, and recipient of a postdoctoral research fellowship from the American Association of University Women. Some of her scholarly work can be found in *Modern Language Studies*, *Irish Studies Review*, the *Virginia Woolf Miscellany*, and *Chiasmi International*. Her completed manuscript under review, *On the Threshold: Modernism, Doorways, and Building with the Body*, studies the doorway in modernist

xiii

fiction as a politicized experience. She continues to write about fiction, philosophy, architecture, and modernism in a global context.

François-Xavier Gleyzon is Associate Professor of English at the University of Central Florida, USA, and the Series Editor of Anthem Studies in Renaissance Literature and Culture. He is the author of *Shakespeare's Spiral* (2010) and *David Lynch in Theory* (2011), along with a number of peer-reviewed articles on English Renaissance literature and visual arts. His publications include *Shakespeare and Theory I & II* (2013), *Reading Milton Through Islam* (2015), *Shakespeare and the Future of Theory* (2016), and *Deleuze: Spaces of Change and Challenges* (with Christian Beck), along with an essay on "Deleuze and the Grandeur of Palestine: Song of Earth and Resistance" (2016). His latest publication is "Minoring Shakespeare: Deleuze's Storm, Caliban or the Last of the Palestinians" (2019) and he is working on his next monograph: *New Perspectives on Religion and Politics in Early Modern Literature*.

Olivia Hulsey holds a Ph.D. in Literary and Cultural Studies from the University of Memphis, USA. She is revising her dissertation, "Novel Perspectives of the Iraq War," for publication. Hulsey teaches literature and composition courses at Christian Brothers University, Memphis, Tennessee, USA.

Zeba Khan-Thomas is Assistant Professor of English at Tennessee State University, Nashville, Tennessee, USA. She specializes in Black diasporic literature, critical race studies, Black feminist thought, Black radical thought, and popular culture and music studies.

Mike Lemon received his Doctorate from Texas Tech University, USA, where he teaches composition and literature courses. His research explores nineteenth-century regional American literatures, ecocriticism, and representations of race and gender in American comic books.

Jessica Maucione is Professor of English and Powers Chair of the Humanities at Gonzaga University, USA. Her teaching and scholarship engage in intersectional explorations of race, place, and displacement.

Ruth M. E. Oldman is an Independent Scholar living in Latrobe, Pennsylvania, USA.

David Polanski is an independent scholar whose work explores the manner in which the prominent themes and tropes of ancient Near Eastern literature have been repurposed by the proponents and opponents of capitalist development.

Marisa Stickel Higgins is a doctoral candidate at the University of Tennessee, USA, where she specializes in twentieth-century American literature and feminist studies, with interests in modernism, embodiment, dance studies, and spatial theory. Her work explores the 19th Amendment, modern dance, and how embodiment and expressive movement can be used as a feminist revisionist tool for modernist literature.

Prerna Subramanian is a Ph.D. Candidate in Cultural Studies at Queen's University, Kingston, Ontario, Canada (situated on the lands of Anishinaabe and Haudenosaunee people). She is working on politics of sanitation and transgender representation in contemporary Indian cultural production. She has interests in feminist geographies, specifically cultural materialist analysis of gender and space.

LIST OF FIGURES

Fig. 2.1	Austin Reed advertisement from *The Sphere* [London] (May 4, 1935): 200	44
Fig. 2.2	The Atlas Service from *Travel* [New York] (January 1910): 195	51
Fig. 12.1	Tomás Saraceno, "Cloud Cities/Air-Port-City" Tonya Bonakder Gallery, 2012 https://www.artforum.com/print/reviews/201208/tomas-saraceno-38835	259
Fig. 14.1	Tatyana Fazlalizadeh, *To Blossom* (2016). Located at PS 92 in Harlem, NY. (Used with permission of the artist.)	303

CHAPTER 1

Introduction: Movement, Space, and Power in the Creative Act

Christian Beck

The effects of postcolonialism, technology, and neoliberalism have high-lighted the importance of spatial analysis, particularly in literary and cultural studies. This so-called spatial turn has brought significant attention to the ways in which spaces and places construct identities, behaviors, expectations, communication, and politics. Attention to geographical, cultural, and sociological spaces in literature introduces readers to the realities of many identities that are overlooked, underrepresented, or oppressed. Similarly, spatial analysis has also been linked to issues surrounding movement and mobility, as well as studies of resistance to dominant and oppressive power. However, more can be said about literature's role in illuminating new and diverse spaces, mobility studies, and a politics of resistance. Specifically, literature can be an avenue toward political and social action through its spatial awareness, production, and potentiality.

While offering interpretations of literature, this collection seeks to show how literary spaces contribute to understanding, changing, or challenging notions of mobility and physical spaces of our lived world. Literature has

---

C. Beck (✉)
University of Central Florida, Orlando, FL, USA
e-mail: christian.beck@ucf.edu

© The Author(s), under exclusive license to Springer Nature
Switzerland AG 2021
C. Beck (ed.), *Mobility, Spatiality, and Resistance in Literary and Political Discourse*, Geocriticism and Spatial Literary Studies,
https://doi.org/10.1007/978-3-030-83477-7_1

1

always entertained the "what if" questions to a society's issues, but this volume looks beyond the fictional and attempts to identify the effects of space on mobility and resistance in our lived experience. Bill Richardson writes, "In literature, as in life, we regularly experience a capacity to simultaneously live within a place and to be aware that the place we are in forms part of a more extensive—potentially infinite—spatial context."[1] From these possibly infinite spatial contexts, literature possesses the possibility of affecting social change through spatial awareness and analysis. As such, Michel Foucault's claim that our time will be "above all the epoch of space" marks an epistemological transition that ushers in new forms of literary and cultural analyses of the spatial scaffolding that engenders hegemonic institutions.[2] This project draws from various disciplines—such as geography, sociology, political science, gender studies, and post-structuralist thought—to posit the productive capabilities of literature in examining the politics of movement and spatial transformations and at the same time shows how literary art offers alternatives to oppressive institutions, practices, and systems of thought. In this way, this book is more than a collection of essays interpreting pieces of literature, it gestures outward to our space and encourages the creation of new spaces that meet the needs and desires of people, not institutions determined to control our movement, actions, ideologies, and thought.

In *The Production of Space*, the first extended study on socially constructed space, Henri Lefebvre identifies three distinct types of space: conceived, lived, and perceived. Conceived space represents space that is developed by those with the power and ability to produce space for a particular reason and use (i.e., urban planning). Lived space refers to the ways in which ordinary people think of space for daily living. Perceived space is socially constructed space.[3] There is significant overlap among these categories of space, but what is embedded in these definitions is the importance of social relations. Lefebvre contends that instead of treating space as a "passive receptacle" we should focus on "uncovering the social relationship (including class relationships) that are latent in spaces" and "concentrat[e]

---

[1] Bill Richardson, "Mapping the Literary Text: Spatio-Cultural Theory and Practice," *Philosophy and Literature* 42, no. 1 (2018), 77.

[2] Michel Foucault, "Of Other Spaces," trans. Jay Miskowiec, *Diacritics* 16 (1986): 22.

[3] The spaces in this conceptual triad are actually referred to as "Spatial Practice," "Representations of Space," and "Representational Spaces." I chose to use less confusing monikers, but the language is taken from Lefebvre's description. See Henri Lefebvre, *The Production of Space*, trans. Donald Nicholson-Smith (Oxford, UK: Blackwell, 1991), 38–39.

1 INTRODUCTION: MOVEMENT, SPACE, AND POWER IN THE CREATIVE ACT 3

our attention on the production of space and the social relationships inherent to it."[4] As Foucault's entire catalogue of work suggests, space and power are intimately linked.[5] Thinking Lefebvre vis-à-vis Foucault, we should attend to the power relations that are manifest in spaces and how social relationships are constructed through power's effect on spaces. Power not only informs space and spatial construction, but mobility as well.

As an area of study, mobility is concerned with large-scale movements of people, animals, objects, information, and capital, as well as more localized forms of movement, such as public transportation, infrastructure for bike and pedestrian lanes, and overall accessibility for all people. Mobility concerns individuals and nation-states, social institutions, and neoliberal globalization. "Mobility," Tim Cresswell writes, "is a fact of life. To be human, indeed, to be animal, is to have some kind of capacity for mobility. We experience the world as we move through it. Mobility is a capacity of all but the most severely disabled bodies. Unlike the division between public and private space, mobility has been with us since day one."[6] However, precisely because mobility is a fact of life, it is a site of control, power, protection, liberation, opportunity, subversion, and resistance.[7] While often seen by privileged persons as effortless, quick, and clean, mobility is actually, as Mimi Sheller states, "full of friction, viscosity, stoppages, and power relations."[8] Mobility, like space, is "a thoroughly social facet of life imbued with meaning and power."[9] Power, then, not only connects how we understand spatiality and mobility, but also unites the various analyses in this volume. Every chapter, directly or indirectly, engages with the effects of power—particularly biopower—and given the topics, themes, and social awareness of these essays there is an undercurrent of resistance that saturates the volume. And as we know from Foucault's famous statement, "Where there is power, there is resistance."[10]

---

[4] Lefebvre, *The Production of Space*, 90.

[5] For a discussion of Foucault and spatial analysis, see Robert T. Tally Jr., *Spatiality* (New York: Routledge, 2013), 119–128.

[6] Tim Cresswell, *On the Move: Mobility in the Modern Western World* (London: Routledge, 2006), 22.

[7] See Cresswell, *On the Move*, 1–2.

[8] Mimi Sheller, *Mobility Justice: The Politics of Movement in an Age of Extremes* (New York: Verso Books, 2018), 10.

[9] Cresswell, *On the Move*, 4.

[10] Michel Foucault, *The Will to Knowledge. The History of Sexuality, Volume 1*, trans. Robery Hurely (London: Penguin Books, 1998), 95.

4   C. BECK

Power for Foucault is ubiquitous and diffuse, always moving and changing as society and social institutions change. Power is very much the shifting sands under our feet that invisibly shape our environments, identities, and society writ large. Power's pervasiveness and invisibility not only mark a problematic for resistance, but also makes resistance itself diffuse and changing. Nevertheless, power and resistance are linked together, as Foucault's comment makes clear. Brent Pickett expands on this relationship:

> Foucault sees resistance as the odd element within power relations. Resistance is what eludes power, and power targets resistance as its adversary. Resistance is what threatens power, hence it stands against power as an adversary. Although resistance is also a potential resource for power, the element or materials that power works upon are never rendered fully docile. Something always eludes the diffusion of power and expresses itself as indocility and resistance.[11]

Resistance escapes the grasp of power and uses this "freedom" to limit the domination of power. Power creates the very thing it seeks to control, but through its systemic institutions, power also creates the very thing that comes to resist it. Indeed, power and resistance are inextricably linked, so much so that it leads some critics to see power and resistance as not only the same thing, but ontologically similar. As Kevin Heller writes, "At the heart of [Peter] Dews's interpretation is the unjustified assumption that power is, for Foucault, ontologically different from resistance. Power and resistance are no more than two different names Foucault gives to the same capacity—the capacity to create social change. [...] Power and resistance are, for Foucault, ontologically correlative terms."[12] Ostensibly, this fits directly into Foucault's articulation of power and resistance: they are two sides of the same coin and only from a particular perspective can one side be labeled "power" and the other "resistance."

In a 1982 interview, however, Foucault makes a rather provocative claim about the relationship between resistance and power:

> If there was no resistance, there would be no power relations. Because it would simply be a matter of obedience. You have to use power relations to

---

[11] Brent L. Pickett, "Foucault and the Politics of Resistance," *Polity* 28, no. 4 (1996): 458.

[12] Kevin Jon Heller, "Power, Subjectification and Resistance in Foucault," *SubStance* 25, no. 1 (1996): 99.

1 INTRODUCTION: MOVEMENT, SPACE, AND POWER IN THE CREATIVE ACT 5

refer to the situation where you're not doing what you want. So resistance comes first, and remains superior to the forces of the process; power relations are obliged to change with the resistance. So I think that *resistance* is the main word, *the key word*, in this dynamic.[13]

In this comment, Foucault seemingly inverts what we have previously thought about the power/resistance relationship: resistance creates the power relations that become oppressive and dominant. As Marco Checchi writes, "it is only at the very moment when resistance increases or decreases its intensity, that power is obliged to change and to adapt it accordingly. Therefore, resistance is the dynamic and active element in power relations and this confers to it its primacy over power."[14] This conceptual change to the power/resistance relationship does more than institute a reversal in primacy; according to Checchi, it functionally changes the ontology of resistance to be different than power. The ontological shift of resistance is reinforced by Gilles Deleuze's assessment of Foucault's thought.[15]

In his book on Foucault, Deleuze analyzes Foucault's understanding of power and thought. Deleuze writes that power is, simply put, the relations between forces or rather that "every relation between forces is a 'power relation.'"[16] Force, for Deleuze, is a concept he employs to discuss how change occurs—this is often done in reference to speed and movement—and as a type of "strength" (*puissance*) that exerts control over an entire social order.[17] Deleuze writes, "An exercise of power shows up as an affect, since force defines itself by its very power to affect other forces (to which

---

[13] Michel Foucault, "Sex, Power, and the Politics of Identity," in *Ethics: Subjectivity and Truth*, ed. Paul Rabinow (New York: New Press, 1997), 167. Emphasis original.

[14] Marco Checchi, "Spotting the Primacy of Resistance in the Virtual Encounter of Foucault and Deleuze," *Foucault Studies* 18 (2014): 199.

[15] Cesare Casarino reaffirms the ontological difference between power and resistance and the primacy of resistance by tracking Deleuze's idea of resistance back to his work on Spinoza. In a very subtle and deliberate reading of Spinoza's *Ethics*, Casarino argues that while Spinoza did not speak about resistance as such, his use of the word *conatus* shares, if not allows for, the conceptual framework of resistance and makes resistance "the main word, *the key word*." See Cesare Casarino, "Grammars of *Conatus*. Or, On the Primacy of Resistance in Spinoza, Foucault and Deleuze," in *Spinoza's Authority: Resistance and Power in Ethics, Volume 1*, eds. A. Kiarina Kordela and Dimitris Vardoulakis (London: Bloomsbury, 2018), 57–85.

[16] Gilles Deleuze, *Foucault*, trans. Seán Hand (Minneapolis: The University of Minnesota Press, 1988), 70.

[17] For a detailed explanation of force see Kenneth Surin, "Force" in *Gilles Deleuze: Key Concepts*, ed. Charles J. Stivale, Second Edition (Cambridge: Acumen Press, 2011), 21–32.

6   C. BECK

it is related) and to be affected by other forces. [...] At the same time, each force has the power to affect (others) and to be affected (by others again), such that each force implies power relations: and every field of forces distributes forces according to these relations and their variations."[18] As these forces act upon other forces (and are acted upon) the power relations that connect them begin to create a network, a structure, a *diagram*. The diagram presents the ways in which these (ever changing) forces take shape at a particular moment. An example of such a diagram would be Foucault's deployment of the Panopticon: unlike the physical structure of the Panopticon prison, the function of the Panopticon traverses a multiplicity of institutions (education, care, punishment, production) and particulars (students, the sick, prisoners, soldiers) and presents a way of viewing the navigation of power through a social order. Simply put, the diagram is "the presentation of the relations between forces unique to a particular formation" and "the distribution of the power to affect and the power to be affected."[19] However, because forces are always shifting, changing, and escaping (they are "in a perpetual state of evolution"), "this means that the diagram, in so far as it exposes a set of relations between forces, is not a place but rather 'a non-place': it is the place only of mutation."[20] The diagram, and the power relations it presents, cannot be precisely plotted for the same reason the forces are not visible: they are always changing. Nevertheless, the diagram obviously communicates with the material world and its expression of this power. The diagram remains apparent through its interaction with the fixed structures of the social order. At the same time, the diagram communicates with the unstable forces that give the diagram its shape. Because of its position between the stable and the unstable, "the diagram always represents the outside of the strata."[21]

The "outside" is the site of mutation, the area in which forces act and are acted upon, the "different dimension" that allows for the "emergence of forces."[22] This outside is productive insofar as it produces the diagram,

[18] Deleuze, *Foucault*, 71.

[19] Deleuze, *Foucault*, 72–73. There is a third component to Deleuze's definition of the diagram ("it is the mixing of non-formalized pure functions and unformed pure matter"), but I chose to omit this particular formulation for reasons of space within the article. Pure functions and pure matter serve an important role in the establishment and function of the diagram, but for the current purposes, these terms exceed the scope of this introduction.

[20] Deleuze, *Foucault*, 85.

[21] Deleuze, *Foucault*, 85.

[22] Deleuze, *Foucault*, 86.

but the diagram does not ever merge with the outside; only new diagrams are produced and may be associated with other diagrams. The outside is always oriented toward the future: there is a perpetual creation of new (interlocking and related) diagrams by the mutation of forces. As Deleuze says, "nothing ends, since nothing has begun, but everything is transformed."[23] The emergence of forces, the continued change in trajectory, the new drawings, and the persistent transformation allow the outside (and the forces found there) to be a site of potentiality. The potentiality of the forces opens another avenue, "which presents itself as the possibility of resistance." Deleuze continues, "the final word on power is that *resistance comes first*, to the extent that power relations operate completely within the diagram [as the fixed form of a set of power relations], while resistances necessarily operate in direct relation with the outside from which the diagrams emerge."[24] Resistance is the surprise that no one expects; resistance is the unforeseen event that transforms power relations and the institutions that maintain them; resistance comes from the outside to create a mutation that carries lasting effects beyond the immediacy of the initial event. Marco Checchi writes, "resistance is never entirely predictable, and this reveals the fundamental impotency of power."[25] In one of the more creative examples of how resistance might function, Checchi imagines a chess match in which a player throws a frog onto the board and declares the rules of this particular play. He writes, "The event, as radically unexpected resistance, compels power to improvise its counter-action: it is unprepared to control and defy a frog on the chessboard. Thus, power relations are more likely to be reversed once resistance catches power by surprise, namely when power is unprepared as it was not able to anticipate the occurrence of that resistance."[26] While offering a chuckle at the thought of slapping a frog down on a chess board, Checchi's example shows that effective resistance is unexpected and, to a certain degree, does not want to be recognized as resistance—that is, a planned protest against police brutality is not resistance, but simply a visible disagreement; this act is done from within the established relations of power and, indeed, sanctioned by the power structure in place. Effective, influential resistance that comes from the outside possesses creativity; it is an act that is spontaneous,

[23] Deleuze, *Foucault*, 89.
[24] Deleuze, *Foucault*, 89. Emphasis original.
[25] Checchi, "Spotting the Primacy of Resistance," 208.
[26] Checchi, "Spotting the Primacy of Resistance," 209.

8   C. BECK

yet impactful, an event that is strategic, yet instrumental in provoking power to divert its scope and control. In other words, resistance to the dominant powers that structure our world, language, and desires must come from multiple fronts, be presented in a novel fashion, and create gaps in the pervasiveness of power's control.

Later in his career, and after the Foucault's death, Deleuze builds upon these ideas of resistance. In "Postscript on Societies of Control," he portends the emergence of a new type of society, not one of confinement and discipline, but one that is less visible, less hands-on. A control society is more malleable and less susceptible to the direct opposition to power. Deleuze writes, "Control is not discipline. You do not confine people with a highway. But by making highways, you multiply the means of control. I am not saying this is the only aim of highways, but people can travel infinitely and 'freely' without being confined while being perfectly controlled. That is our future."[27] This is to say, unlike a disciplinary society like Foucault analyzes, a control society does not rely upon *enclosure* as a means to exert power over a social order. For Deleuze, information in a control society is monitored and regulated through a particular set of order-words. Information can and must be communicated in a particular form, a form that is authorized by power structures—speak freely, but you cannot communicate effectively unless it takes the form of these order-words. There can be counter-information that combats the information disseminated by the control society, but this does not necessitate resistance. Rather, a work of art, which bears no resemblance to information or communication as such, becomes a form of resistance. Art, like resistance, comes from the outside: "art resists, even if it is not the only thing that resists."[28] Deleuze continues, "Every act of resistance is not a work of art, even though, in a certain way, it is. Every work of art is not an act of resistance, and yet, in a certain way, it is."[29] While Deleuze claims that he does not know what the "mysterious relationship" between a creative act and an act of resistance is, we can begin to decipher this connection.[30]

---

[27] Gilles Deleuze, "What is the Creative Act?," in *Two Regimes of Madness: Texts and Interviews 1975–1995*, ed., David Lapoujade, trans. Ames Hodges and Mike Taormina (New York, NY: Semiotext(e), 2007), 327.

[28] Deleuze, "What is the Creative Act?," 328.

[29] Deleuze, "What is the Creative Act?," 328.

[30] Deleuze, "What is the Creative Act?," 328.

1 INTRODUCTION: MOVEMENT, SPACE, AND POWER IN THE CREATIVE ACT   9

Art is full of potentiality and this potentiality arises from outside of the diagram. Much like resistance, art emerges often as an unforeseen event whose full meaning and effects are not immediately known or realized. Art presents the familiar in uncertain terms and surprises power when it arrives as a mutation. Art may be, very literally, a frog on a chess board. Not all art has this effect—"Every work of art is not an act of resistance, and yet, in a certain way, it is"—but art's potentiality can be realized if we look at it from a different perspective, at a different angle perhaps, through a different type of configuration, or by uniting unsuspecting, seemingly divergent pieces of art together. Art is also, Deleuze claims, a resistance to death—here he cites Malraux who claims that art is the *only* thing that resists death.[31] In his book on Foucault, Deleuze doubles down on this, but from a different angle, "Life becomes resistance to power when power takes life as its object. [...] When power becomes bio-power resistance becomes the power of life, a vital power that cannot be confined within species, environment or the paths of a particular diagram. Is not the force that comes from outside a certain idea of Life, a certain vitalism, in which Foucault's thought culminates?"[32] When power seeks to objectify life, confine and control life, life itself becomes resistance. Much like the mysterious relationship between art and resistance, the relationship between life and resistance is forged by forces, but unknowingly. Art, resistance, and "a certain idea of Life" all come from the outside. These independent concepts are interconnected; they draw new maps, new diagrams that intersect, but are not a part of the diagrams of power. Art and resistance, then, share an ontological similarity insofar as they emerge from outside the diagram of power relations. In "Postscript on the Societies of Control," Deleuze writes, "There is no need to fear or hope, but only to look for new weapons."[33] It is at the intersection of concepts of art and resistance that we can begin to find "new weapons" to resist the controlling powers that seek to make life its object. The mapping of possible avenues of art and resistance is the basis for this volume.

As a cohesive unit, *Mobility, Spatiality, and Resistance in Literary and Political Discourse* has literature as its focal point and the site on which discussions of the politics of movement and space emanate. By taking literature as its focus, this collection necessarily concerns itself with art and,

[31] See Deleuze, "What is the Creative Act?," 328.
[32] Deleuze, *Foucault*, 92–93.
[33] Gilles Deleuze, "Postscript on the Societies of Control," *October* 59 (1992): 4.

subsequently, finds itself with a foot outside the diagram of power relations—only one foot because we are still very much within the systemic control of academic writing and publishing. Nevertheless, we are placing ourselves firmly in the realm of art and potentiality. In other words, literary art presents the possibility of something new emerging from the outside and affecting the power relations we are embedded within. But the art as such, alone does not affect power; there must be an engagement with it, there must be an *active* participation, not simply a passive reception of the potentiality. The avenues literature presents begin within the texts, but the effects of literature must be dialogic between the reader and the text. In this way, literature functions as a type of map that allows us to navigate new or unfamiliar perspectives, identities, places/spaces, conflicts, emotions, and/or ideas. But literature is more than just a map laid out in front of us; we must actively decipher the map, and determine how we understand and "read" the map.[34] The second critical term of this volume, "spatiality", relates not just to the spaces found within literature, but also to the ways in which we navigate the cartographic model literature presents to us. By actualizing (one or some of) the possibilities that an art work contains, we create a new map of how a specific piece of literature relates to our world, can change our world, through challenging elements of control vis-à-vis resistance. The chapters contained in this volume, through their engagement with issues of mobility, space, and power relations, discuss works of art as sites of resistance, as maps toward resistance. These works need to be explored to overcome "fear or hope," and as a way "to look for new weapons." We expend a lot of energy hoping for something to happen, to change the trajectory of our path. We fear what happens if we stay on this same path, but also fear the unknown of what will be on a new line. Art allows us to see in new trajectories, new lines of flight; it helps us to find action—which is to say resistance—where power does not think to look. Art is not, itself, weaponized, but the weapons to combat oppressive or nefarious forms of power emerge from art and the outside. If resistance comes first, then we already have the weapons at our disposal; we just need to find them. This collection serves as another type of map that plots new routes to gender, sexual, class, racial, mobility, and spatial justice.

As I have argued, resistance opposes the forces that shape the power relations that seek to confine and "control" our lives. These acts of

---

[34] Robert T. Tally Jr. thoroughly develops the ideas of "Literary Cartography" and "Literary Geography" in his book *Spatiality*.

1 INTRODUCTION: MOVEMENT, SPACE, AND POWER IN THE CREATIVE ACT

resistance must come from multiple fronts and create a singularity so as to redirect the forces that map our diagrammatic knowledge, which is to say power relations that structure our thoughts, actions, norms, and cultural mores. To put a finer point on the issue, resistance stands opposed to racism, sexism, misogyny, poverty, transphobia, homophobia, classism, empire, colonialism, capitalism, and the ways in which these ideologies infiltrate our spatial lives. All of these types of oppression are connected through the spatial practices of omission, restriction, and policing. They are also connected through the desire to keep and maintain power through the preservation of the status quo. In other words, power relations run directly through these types of oppression; they are part of the diagram, they effectively make up the diagram and have, in their various manifestations, sustained the diagrammatic power so many societies are founded upon. Resistance on one front is a resistance on all fronts; and all fronts must be populated by various forms and approaches to the problems confronting our societies. The chapters that follow may seem desperate and unrelated, but this approach is necessary in order to show how the issues that affect one group are connected to and can be addressed by other (if not all) groups. Resistance, ontologically speaking, is not owned by or meant to benefit any particular group or identity and as such, the strategies and tactics of resistance ought to be shared, replicated, changed, and allowed to mutate as needed. Our goal in this volume is to outline, diagram, and map the ways in which literature informs resistance. The grouping of these chapters could take multiple routes—along with no grouping at all—but I have chosen the following three territories that, I believe, put our thinking on a particular trajectory toward a means of thinking about mobility, space, and resistance in a productive and novel way. These chapters could be dis- and reassembled in any number of ways and each time produce a new line on the plane of resistance—not unlike the plateaus of Deleuze and Guattari and as my nonsequential discussion of the chapters evinces below. Nevertheless, at this particular interval, the organizational principles of "Mobility," "Spatiality," and "Radical Positions" will function as literary spaces resistance.

MOBILITY

Mobility often presupposes ableism, social liberty, and a financial capacity—which is not to say "security." Mobility, specifically, gestures toward a means of traversing and experiencing space that many take for granted or are forced to endure due to social, governmental, or environmental concerns. It is something that allows us to change our perspective, to remove ourselves from harm or unwanted experiences, to gain individual liberty, to manipulate our environment, to communicate to the world beyond our contained, immediate surroundings. In a similar way, mobility, precisely because it is assumed, offers a unique site of resistance. Movement and the ability to move at one's will is a perceived hallmark of individual freedom, so when it is restricted, impeded, curtailed, or even simply policed, individual mobility becomes a contested site. On a larger scale, when issues of mobility affect more than just an individual and encompass an entire cross-section of a population (i.e., women, people of color, immigrants), power exposes itself and shows how it operates and what it values. Even more macroscopically, mobility is within the domain of control (consider Deleuze's comment on highways multiplying the means of control). The desire to control the ways and means not just of individual movement, but the mobility of an entire social order posits the possible threat mobility possesses to institutions of governance, power, and domination.[35] By recognizing the ways in which control and mobility interact, we can begin to see the ways to use mobility to resist these mechanisms of control. For example, in Chap. 6, "Matriarchal Mobility: Generational Displacement and Gendered Place in Marilynne Robinson's *Housekeeping*," Marisa Stickel Higgins explores the category of "womanhood" in reference to the space of the home. Through this approach, the expectations and social determinations of women's role in the home highlight how women are expected to move. In her analysis, Stickel Higgins identifies how the heteronormative space of the home leads to a resistance of confinement and the breaking of normative social expectations. While Stickel Higgins explores the confines of a particular home and its reflection of social norms, Leila Aouadi looks toward mobility as a form of resistance in a Palestinian context in Chap. 5, "Mobility, Incarceration, and the Politics of Resistance in Palestinian Women's Literature." Aouadi shows mobility for Palestinians is resistance—a direct result of the colonial project of Israel and the forced removal of Palestinians from their lands in 1948. This push into a different form of existence becomes, for Palestinian women, a site of resistance. In the texts Aouadi explores, the Palestinian women's

---

[35] Paul Virilio's analysis of speed in his various books always addresses, even if obliquely, the issue of mobility. See for example, *Speed and Politics*, *The Original Accident*, *A Landscape of Events*, and *The Administration of Fear*, to name but a few.

1 INTRODUCTION: MOVEMENT, SPACE, AND POWER IN THE CREATIVE ACT   13

experience with mobility becomes cross-generational and transfers to other members of their families, which coalesces into action and a life of resistance against Western colonial endeavors, specifically Israel. Both of these chapters explore not just mobility, but specifically female mobility, and each in a different type of environment. Each highlights the normative expectations foisted upon women, but, as their topics suggest, these norms emanate from different places and affect the women's spaces in dramatically different ways. As such, their experiences, awareness, and approaches to mobility manifest in different forms of resistance. These chapters point to the compelling elements of state and social control, and not just a subversion of female expectations. When these concerns are paired with the other chapters in this section, we gain a better view of how societies seek to control the ways people move.

Travel, unlike mobility, is not perceived as an individual liberty, but rather more of a "luxury," a privilege of the monied classes. Travel, however, is not always desired, luxurious, or a privilege, as Zeba Khan-Thomas demonstrates in Chap. 4, "Conjuring Roots in Dystopia: Reconciling Transgenerational Conflict and Dislocation through Ancestral Speakers in Nalo Hopkinson's *Brown Girl in the Ring* and Edwidge Danticat's *Brother, I'm Dying*." In two texts that deal with migrant and immigrant experiences, travel to new places is fraught with cultural change that challenges the characters' assumptions and identities. The metropolitan spaces these characters must navigate only underline the loss of their socio-political agency that they once embraced in their former country of residence. Their resistance is not against their new spaces, but to the isolation of the immigrant/migrant experience. Finding a place, a new "home" in a foreign land means understanding the norms and expectations of the culture—a tiring and difficult task indeed, particularly if there is a language difference involved. The challenges of inclusion and acceptance are only highlighted by the immigrant/migrant experience—what Khan-Thomas designates as "dystopian." Therefore, the resistance of these narratives takes the shape of defying the underlying nationalist and racist fabric of US culture. These forms of oppression are in place precisely to keep people of color (not just immigrants and migrants) from positions of power or even acquire access to a locus of power. These forms of oppression and discrimination function as deterrents and merely by maintaining a continued presence in the face of these "dystopian" elements is a form of resistance. Similarly, though in a radically different time period, Chap. 3, "The Chivalrous Nation: Travel and Ideological Exchange in *Sir Gawain and the Green Knight*" by Ruth M. E. Oldman, offers a positive view of how travel can transform perspectives on inclusivity. By using a medieval text to show how language and poetics can transform views of minority cultures, poetic form, itself, becomes a mode of negotiation and cultural unity. By attending to the poetics of *Sir Gawain and the Green Knight*, the Alliterative Revival, and the travels of Gawain himself, Oldman argues that the poem posits an ideological exchange that overcomes a "counter-stance," to use Gloria Anzaldúa's term. Oldman's approach reveals the ways that poetics and art emerge from the outside to create not just resistance, but also a path toward resolution. In a similar approach, Chap. 2, "Colonial Advertising and Tourism in the Crosscurrents of Empire," by Scott Cohen shows the fissures and fractures in established travel narratives. Using Jean Rhys's novel *Voyage in the Dark* (1938), Cohen argues that travel's spaces of origin and destination are undone by the voyage itself. More precisely, in his analysis of Rhys's novel, the elements of travel resist narration precisely because they cannot account for the differences compounded by the travelers. This is to say, the dominant travel narratives propagated by empire (then and now) are undercut by highlighting the complexity of travel and the movement through and in space—space that is created and recreated through not just travel/tourism, but by the narration of the movement. In this instance, resistance emerges from the trajectories of travel, spatial construction, and narrative. By showing the fragility of the established travel narrative, Cohen opens an avenue of resistance to Empire itself. Cohen's analysis shows what travel brings to bear on the failures and fractures of a desired neoliberal, "globalized" world, even before this ideology has taken hold.

Travel and mobility are conceptual approaches to space that are, as these chapters show, sites of potential resistance. These various methodologies and analyses form alternative routes to understand, contain, and challenge the multivalent forms of power. As mentioned earlier, resistance must come from multiple fronts, from unexpected areas of intervention. The territories resistance takes for its own are not always easily visible—and they ought not be. Mobility and travel are routes toward resistance, as shown through power and control. By (re)claiming these concepts in the face of control, they provide openings for future actions by means of analysis and art. They are necessarily spatial and artistically rendered in literature. As such, they come from the outside; they can surprise power in their effectiveness and location.

1 INTRODUCTION: MOVEMENT, SPACE, AND POWER IN THE CREATIVE ACT

Spatiality

Whereas the previous section deals specifically with movement, this section investigates space and how it is conceptually, visually, and physically organized. Our sight lines might move from the background to the foreground of a painting or in order to find the exterior of a concept or space, we might move from the interior to the exterior (or vice versa—exterior to interior/foreground to background). In this seemingly binary function of sightlines, horizon lines, conceptual and architectural structures, spatial boundaries, thresholds, limitations, and clearly defined sites of knowledge, backgrounds and interiors are necessarily in direct dialogue with their conceptual opposites. In other words, these spatial and conceptual sites combine to form a composite sketch of possible spaces where power can exercise control—again we are confronted with a diagram that creates lines into the most visible of places (exteriors/foregrounds) and penetrates into places of limited visibility if not invisibility (interiors/backgrounds). Controlling either side of this binary leads to control of the other half, thus creating dynamic control over movement, sight, and knowledge. Resistance to this control *en totum* means attempting to maintain a comprehensive grasp on the functions of both sides of the binary. However, due to the interconnected and dynamic nature of these binaries, disrupting one side of the binary destabilizes the entire diagrammatic power/ control structure. Chapter 9, "Woolf in the Background: Distance as Visual Philosophy, Then and Now," by Amy A. Foley exemplifies this approach. In this chapter, Foley explores the ways in which the background not only informs Virginia Woolf's own writing, but also the visual paradigms of contemporaneous theatrical and performance artists. Foley argues that Woolf's attention to background serves as a counter-visual space that becomes a value of the 1920s and manifests as a form of digital vision that serves as an emergent site of resistance in present-day digital culture. By drawing the visual background into the forefront of a discussion of resistance, Foley's chapter seeks to highlight the ways "sighting" functions in artistic and digital cultures. In a more temporal understanding of "background," Chap. 8, "Turning the Earth, Changing the Narrative: Spatial Transformation in Frances E. W. Harper's *Iola Leroy; or, Shadows Uplifted* (1892)" by Mike Lemon, investigates the ideological and foundational relationships between the American frontier landscape of the early nineteenth century and reconstructed spaces of the American south. The background of the American south rests not on the transgression and surpassing of physical borders, but rather on the liberation of African Americans and their ability to determine their own spatial independence. By transforming former plantations into functioning homesteads, African Americans overwrite land with a new narrative; but much like a palimpsest, the background of the previous narrative can never completely disappear. In his analysis of Harper's late nineteenth-century novel, Lemon shows how the transformative space of the American south is a resistance against the background of Black enslavement through spatial agency. However, precisely because this background is ushered into the foreground, the novel must make an argument for inclusion of African Americans into the US citizenry and the imagined spatial community. In effect, Lemon argues that this novel's overwriting of spatial narratives seeks to make the background of African enslavement and liberation part of the interior and internal narrative of US history.

Interiors, as a spatial concept, are contained, controlled, and part of the mechanisms of power. Resistance, as I have argued, comes from *outside* the diagrams of power, so when we consider interiors, we are necessarily discussing the *inside* of the diagram. Or so it would seem. In fact, interiors are spaces that while part of a larger conceptual or physical entity can still form nodes of resistance that change or challenge the power that gives the space its shape—this is how the old adage "change from the inside" gains traction. However, the interiors the authors discuss in this section function in dynamic ways. Olivia Hulsey in Chap. 7, "Interiorized Imperialism in Native American and Japanese American World War II Narratives," looks toward the US colonization of the interior through the internment of Japanese Americans and the confinement of Native Americans to reservations. By attending to the colonized interior of the US and by analyzing narratives of two internment memoirs and two novels of the Native American Renaissance, Hulsey looks to resist simple categorization of literature based on (at times divisive) identity politics and argues for a comparative multicultural literature that offers a more holistic and inclusive examination of American imperialism. In this sense, the interiors of the American experience afford avenues resistance to the dominant perspectives of US history.

Backgrounds and interiors are spatial categories that surprise diagrammatic power precisely because they come from the "outside." These dynamic aspects of spatiality produce new ways of viewing not only literary fiction, but also categories of spatial resistance. By seeking alternative forms of functionality, backgrounds and interiors create possibilities of

1 INTRODUCTION: MOVEMENT, SPACE, AND POWER IN THE CREATIVE ACT   17

new socio-cultural affiliation from the inside by producing resistance from the outside. Literature affords us new perspectives of interiors and backgrounds precisely because our knowledge and cultural understanding are founded on these spatial elements and all too frequently we take them for granted or bypass them all together. These chapters seek out the nuances of literature's spatial foundations to show the aporias in the dialogic between interior/exterior and background/foreground. In a similar fashion, the next group of chapters utilize spatial positions in unanticipated ways to highlight the problematics of normative spaces and the viability of new, radical spatial positions.

Radical Positions

Political positions are assigned spatial designations: conservatives are on the "right" and liberals are on the "left." These designations of "right-wing" or "left-wing" politics emanate from the spatial organization of the French National Assembly in 1789: the supporters of King Louis XVI and the aristocratic order organized and sat together on the right side of the assembly hall and the anti-royalist, social revolutionaries sat on the left side of the hall. From this point onward the political ideologies held by conservatives and liberals are given over to the territorial language of right and left, respectively. However, there remain voices that are not represented or heard by the territories of right and left. These political positions are often marginalized, pushed to the periphery and not a part of the normative political discussions. All too often, these voices are criticized for being too far-fetched for the "realpolitik" of the day. These positions are marked as "radical" and pushed to the outside of political machines of power. Once again, we are presented with the outside, but in this instance these radical positions are precisely where they want to be so that they may challenge not just the effects of power, but the very structure of power and control. The radical positions discussed in these chapters form a constellation of probabilities and geographies, from the remapping of a city through a fictional account of a female body to the rearticulating of community values through anti-capitalism and the remaking of Harlem through a "literature of combat." Each of these chapters highlights spatial possibility through the analytic deterritorialization of ideologically informed spaces.

In Chap. 11, "Vulnerable Erotic Encounters: A Chronotopic Reading of the Bus-Space in Chicu's *Soliloquy*," by Prerna Subramanian, the everyday space of the bus becomes something more, something transformative.

By reading erotic fiction geocritically, Subramanian argues that new configurations of the body, the spaces of intimacy, and interpersonal relations transform and challenge normative relations in common spaces. By showing the radical possibility of exploring the intimacy in new spaces, Subramanian produces a new map for creating socio-spatial relationships that allow us to create new forms of social interaction. Effectively, we are invited to navigate a new topography of spatial existence. Similarly, in his analysis of Rabih Alameddine's text *An Unnecessary Woman*, François-Xavier Gleyzon—Chap. 10, "A New Cartographer: Rabih Alameddine and *An Unnecessary Woman*"—creates a new map of Beirut. More than simply allowing the text to determine movement in the city, Gleyzon argues that Alameddine becomes a cartographer that through the navigation of the city-body, he creates new avenues in thought and writing. This remapping of the city, body, and text resists normative daily life by forging new sensibilities, a means for a new consciousness. In their investigations of new spaces, new cartographic creations, Gleyzon and Subramanian are proposing more than challenges to existing ways of thinking and behaving; they are radically departing from normative positions to point us toward new ways of becoming, to show us the possibilities inherent in novel spatial relations that emerge from reimagining literary space.

In Chap. 13 "Frantz Fanon, Chester Himes, and a 'Literature of Combat,'" David Polanski shows how the Harlem-based crime fiction of Chester Himes possesses a similar literary liminality with the "Israel" of the Bible. Polanski argues that Himes creates a new space as a means for social reorganization. Hime's Harlem becomes "unsettled" and the inhabitants are free to reorganize as they see fit. Polanski continues by showing how Franz Fanon's idea of "literature of combat" is realized in Hime's construction of Harlem and becomes a site of resistance to capitalism and neo-colonialism. Effectively, Polanski brings together the resistance of Palestine with forms of resistance that could be effectively employed in places like Harlem. In this particular case, literature decidedly reconstructs space as a means to overlay sites of resistance onto the lived world as a means to create a new site of resistance against oppressive forms of power found in capitalism and neo-colonialism. Chapter 12, "Anti-Capitalism and the Near Future: In Mohsin Hamid's *Exit West* and Louise Erdrich's *The Future Home of the Living God*," by Jessica Maucione, also advocates resistance to capitalism by attending to literary texts that imagine an anti- or post-capitalist world. The chapter analyzes Mohsin Hamid's *Exit West* and Louise Erdrich's *The Future Home of the Living God* as a means to

1 INTRODUCTION: MOVEMENT, SPACE, AND POWER IN THE CREATIVE ACT   19

show how literature can register the savagery of late-capitalism and offer a form of radical hope that forges "the means for another consciousness and another sensibility."[36] This chapter, like all the chapters in this section, takes a position that is neither right, nor left, but someplace beyond typical, normative political positions. From these radical positions, new forms of resistance, as imagined or derived from literature, can begin to take shape in our lived world.

Radical positions can be numerous and multifaceted. The power of a radical position, much like resistance, comes from a place not often noticed, it surprises dominant power, and yet, it is connected to other radical events, situations, and actions. The concluding chapter of the volume, Chap. 14 "Resisting a Wilting Future: *To Blossom*," shows not only how a radical position functions in the lived world, but also utilizes the critical categories of mobility and spatiality. Through an analysis of Tatyana Fazlalizadeh's mural of a young Black woman reading, placed on the side of Harlem Public School 92, I bring together the three conceptual frames of the collection and argue for this image's social importance by showing the potentiality of a new future. In my conclusion, the various threads found in the preceding chapters are brought together through a singular image, which acts as an insurgent that dismantles the mechanisms of control and liberates spaces so that communities might be free to reorganize themselves, unbound by the ideologies connected to diagrammatic knowledge, the diagram of power, and mechanisms of control.

Works Cited

Casarino, Cesare. "Grammars of *Conatus*: Or, On the Primacy of Resistance in Spinoza, Foucault and Deleuze." In *Spinoza's Authority: Resistance and Power in Ethics, Volume 1*, edited by A. Kiarina Kordela and Dimitris Vardoulakis, 57–85. London: Bloomsbury, 2018.

Checchi, Marco. "Spotting the Primacy of Resistance in the Virtual Encounter of Foucault and Deleuze." *Foucault Studies* 18 (2014): 197–212.

Cresswell, Tim. *On the Move: Mobility in the Modern Western World*. London: Routledge, 2006.

Deleuze, Gilles. *Foucault*. Translated by Seán Hand. Minneapolis: The University of Minnesota Press, 1988.

———. "Postscript on the Societies of Control." *October* 59 (1992): 3–7.

---

[36] Gilles Deleuze, *Essays Critical and Clinical*, trans. Daniel W. Smith and Michael A. Greco (London: Verso, 1998), 17.

20   C. BECK

———. *Essays Critical and Clinical*. Translated by Daniel W. Smith and Michael A. Greco. London: Verso, 1998.

———. "What is the Creative Act?" In *Two Regimes of Madness: Texts and Interviews 1975–1995*, edited by David Lapoujade and translated by Ames Hodges and Mike Taormina, 317–329. New York: Semiotext(e), 2007.

Foucault, Michel. "Of Other Spaces." Translated by Jay Miskowiec. *Diacritics* 16, no. 1 (1986): 22–27.

———. "Sex, Power, and the Politics of Identity." In *Ethics: Subjectivity and Truth*, edited by Paul Rabinow, 163–173. New York: New Press, 1997.

———. *The Will to Knowledge. The History of Sexuality, Volume 1*. Translated by Robert Hurley. London: Penguin Books, 1998.

Heller, Kevin Jon. "Power, Subjectification and Resistance in Foucault." *SubStance* 25, no. 1 (1996): 78–110.

Lefebvre, Henri. *The Production of Space*. Translated by Donald Nicholson-Smith. Oxford: Blackwell, 1991.

Pickett, Brent L. "Foucault and the Politics of Resistance." *Polity* 28, no. 4 (1996): 445–466.

Richardson, Bill. "Mapping the Literary Text: Spatio-Cultural Theory and Practice." *Philosophy and Literature* 42, no. 1 (2018): 67–80.

Sheller, Mimi. *Mobility Justice: The Politics of Movement in an Age of Extremes*. New York: Verso Books, 2018.

Surin, Kenneth. "Force." In *Gilles Deleuze: Key Concepts*, edited by Charles J. Stivale, 21–32. Second Edition. London: Routledge, 2011.

Tally Jr., Robert T. *Spatiality*. New York: Routledge, 2013.

PART I

Mobility

CHAPTER 2

Colonial Advertising and Tourism in the Crosscurrents of Empire

Scott Cohen

From her first novel, *Quartet* (1928), to her last, most well-known novel, *Wide Sargasso Sea* (1966), Jean Rhys demonstrates the turbulence of social, emotional, and spatial displacements. For almost two decades, post-colonial critics have seen Rhys's *Wide Sargasso Sea* as a provocative over-haul of Western literary traditions. Adding First World feminist politics to the catalog of the novel's critical interventions, Gayatri Spivak has convincingly argued that in Rhys's novel we learn how "so intimate a thing as personal and human identity might be determined by the politics of imperialism."[1] While her later novel remains a touchstone for understanding mid-century postcolonial reckoning, Rhys's 1934 novel, *Voyage in the Dark*, offers a powerful rendering of the confluence of personal identity

[1] Gayatri Chakravorty Spivak, "Three Women's Texts and a Critique of Imperialism," in *"Race," Writing, and Difference*, edited by Henry Louis Gates, Jr. (Chicago: University of Chicago Press, 1986), 269.

S. Cohen (✉)
Stonehill College, Easton, MA, USA
e-mail: scohen@stonehill.edu

© The Author(s), under exclusive license to Springer Nature Switzerland AG 2021
C. Beck (ed.), *Mobility, Spatiality, and Resistance in Literary and Political Discourse*, Geocriticism and Spatial Literary Studies, https://doi.org/10.1007/978-3-030-83477-7_2

24   S. COHEN

and empire's global geography. Presenting the conditions of exile and liminality in devastatingly personal detail, Rhys's novel registers the trauma of immobility and spatial dislocation on global and local scales.

Through its first-person narrative of Anna Morgan, an eighteen-year-old Creole woman from Dominica who comes to England to tour provincial towns as part of a vaudeville show, Rhys's novel tells a tale of immense loneliness and despair. Living on the margins of London's respectable society, Anna leaves the unfriendly but familiar group of traveling chorus girls when she becomes the mistress of Walter Jeffries, a London businessman. When Walter breaks off the affair, promising a modest pension on which she might survive, Anna is heartbroken and decides to take up lodgings above a manicure parlor where she eventually begins working as a prostitute. This is a story of a young woman fallen between the cracks of empire, living alone in her ancestors' native country. Rhys fleshes out the position of the exiled colonial, illuminating the difficult position of a single woman of the laboring classes with an ambiguous racial identity. Located betwixt and between the currents of empire, Anna obliquely confronts—if her awkward orientation toward empire's signs, attitudes, and structures can even be called a confrontation—the forces of empire. Her world is filtered through a double vision, where her bright Caribbean past is contrasted with the gray of prewar London. Against the interminable cold of the city, Anna's memory of a warmer place persistently intervenes, offering moments of comfort as well as unremitting reminders of an unrecoverable world: "Sometimes I would shut my eyes and pretend that the heat of the fire, or the bed-clothes drawn up round me, was sun-heat."[2] In capturing the difficulty of traveling to the imperial center as a colonial outsider, *Voyage in the Dark* stands as a clue for a tendency in modern fiction that anticipates concerns typically associated with the postcolonial moment. Urmila Seshagiri rightly contends that Rhys "unravels the violent cultural epistemologies that give form to such much experimental modernism, thereby reimagining English fiction along a new—and inevitably transnational—axis."[3]

Most critical discussions focus on the geographical poles of the novel, the trajectory from the pleasant West Indies to the alienating city of

---

[2] Jean Rhys, *Voyage in the Dark* (London: Norton, 1982), 8. References hereafter are cited parenthetically from this edition.

[3] Urmila Seshagiri, "Modernist Ashes, Postcolonial Phoenix: Jean Rhys and the Evolution of the English Novel in the Twentieth Century" *Modernism/modernity* 13, no. 3 (2006): 489.

London.[4] To accept this plotting is to accept a particular notion of space that prioritizes destination and origin over intermediate designations, leaving the agonizing in-betweenness that permeates nearly every line unexplored. While the tragic arc between home and away is the prevailing obsession of the narrative voice, it hardly accounts for the unending, tedious, and variegated effects of Anna's real and imagined journeys. I would argue, by contrast, that the novel hinges on the complexity and indeed painfulness of movement and mobility when the designations of origin and destination are suspended or denied. As Dorreen Massey has illustrated, space "is created out of the vast intricacies, the incredible complexities, of the interlocking and the non-interlocking, and the networks of relations at every scale from local to global."[5] Anna embodies this finely knitted notion of space with all its difficulties. *Voyage in the Dark* is less about the transition between spaces than about illustrating the lasting effects of the voyage by showing how, under the specific conditions of empire, certain types of travel resist narration.

In order to illustrate this fluid type of space and its relation to representations of the West Indies, this chapter scrutinizes the many geographical dimensions of *Voyage in the Dark*. My analysis aims to uncover a more flexible understanding of the production of space as a real and imaginative endeavor. Indeed, in Rhys's fiction, the West Indies and Europe are constituted in relation to one another through nexuses of memories, historical events, and mass cultural influences. By focusing on the construction of these poles, her fiction ultimately undoes their strict difference. In her novel about a young Creole woman in London, Rhys charts the transition

---

[4] The colonial outskirts are drawn in lush and brilliant colors, where spaces are familiar, maps are the accrual of childhood memories, and one is warmed by a sun that never sets. Conversely, the city is regarded as dull and dangerously synthetic, where alienation amidst uniformity is the rule, one can become lost without directions or a cab, and the grayness of day nearly indistinguishably fades into a darker gray of night. As Elaine Savory has put it, "Anna reads her world as dualist, the West Indies versus England, which signifies many subordinate oppositions." See Elaine Savory, *Jean Rhys* (Cambridge: Cambridge University Press, 1998), 91. Lucy Wilson suggests, "counterpoint is the main structuring device employed in the novel." Lucy Wilson, "European or Caribbean: Jean Rhys and the Language of Exile," in *Literature and Exile*, edited by David Bevan, (Amsterdam: Rodopi, 1990), 79. See also, for example, Thomas Staley, *Jean Rhys: A Critical Study* (Macmillan Press, 1979), 61. Also see Urmila Seshagiri, *Race and the Modernist Imagination* (Cornell University Press, 2010), 77–139.

[5] Doreen Massey, *Space, Place, and Gender* (Minneapolis: University of Minnesota Press, 1994), 265.

26   S. COHEN

and indeed the overlapping of three enduring tropes that have come to define the West Indies: first as an exotic place of discovery and encounter, then as a location integral to the European colonial system, and ultimately as a tourist destination for leisure and escape. Rhys utilizes all three conceptions to great effect, sketching the backdrop for a global subjectivity that would only become apparent later in the twentieth century. Anna's geographical imagination locates her within three corresponding negative positions: as a castaway, yet in an inverted position and without the resources to organize her new experiences; as a colonial import who is at once a metaphor for and an example of the commodity in circulation; and as a tourist for whom typical narratives of travel fail to account for her voyage.

By examining how these fields—the colonial encounter, the colonial system of trade and settlement, and the culture of tourism—intersect, I hope to shed light on the radical geography of mobility and immobility. To see Rhys's work involved with these three cross-historical tropes, to investigate the weaving and residues of these currents, and to recognize the disconcerting mobility of circulation which foregrounds the difficulty of identity in an imperial world is to discover a novel that has close ties to colonial and postcolonial Caribbean Anglophone literature, namely a modern novel that registers transitions in mass visual culture and bridges the aesthetics of shock with the routines of everyday life.[6] In the character of Anna, Rhys offers a narrative subjectivity that is able to articulate that which is not visible until the postcolonial moment: a new form of global subjectivity and a dramatic rendering of a tortured clash with cosmopolitan ideals. Rhys's novel participates in a sea change in how the Caribbean was represented. If in large part empires existed to produce certain types of movement and circulation, Rhys's writing serves to thematize some of the most disconcerting and untoward experiences stemming from the

[6] If in its hostility toward empire's presumptive cultural values and geographical centering *Voyage in the Dark* stands as a postcolonial prefiguration, as I shall endeavor to show here, it is also a novel that consolidates a range of modernist concerns. As its very title indicates, *Voyage in the Dark* offers an uncanny conflation of Virginia Woolf's *A Voyage Out* and Joseph Conrad's *Heart of Darkness*. Much like both earlier texts, Rhys's novel forges a complex relationship between home and away through a narrative of human alienation that explores the limits of literary representation and psychological rendering. Yet almost as if set against the work of these literary giants with whom Rhys maintained an uneasy creative relationship, *Voyage in the Dark* constructively picks up on the real and implied elliptical breaks within these novels.

flows of people and objects among colonial locations, illustrating how mental journeys into the past and across vast spaces can produce injurious effects, and ultimately demonstrating the bruising of national cultures in transit.

Anna's Global Imagination

The extent to which *Voyage in the Dark* responds to transitions in global imagery during the last decades of the formal British empire can be seen in how images of global space enter the novel, become entwined with local experiences, and ultimately emerge as a form of geographic consciousness. Contrasting England with the imperial backwaters from which Anna has come, Rhys inverts the dominant imperialist mode of understanding the world which dictates that civilizing light emanates from the metropole outward to the hinterlands. While Anna is essentially shipped to England as part of her aunt's mission to civilize her, it is the imperial city in its cruel, cold grayness that requires civilizing. From the first lines, Anna's narrative registers a radical newness of place: "It was as if a curtain had fallen, hiding everything I had ever known. It was almost like being born again. The colours were different, the smells were different, the feeling things gave you right down inside yourself was different. Not just the difference between heat, cold; light, darkness; purple, grey. But a difference in the way I was frightened and the way I was happy" (7). The transformation described here determines every aspect of her life. Even though the narrator positions herself as a performer with particular attention to the atmospherics of lighting through the rhetoric of the stage, such a theatrical entrance does not utterly shut out the past. Instead, the world that Anna imagines takes on a reality just as vivid as her current environment in England: "sometimes it was as if I were back there and as if England were a dream. At other times England was the real thing and out there was the dream, but I could never fit them together" (8).

Unable to make these two realms correspond even in the most basic way, Anna compensates by developing a remarkably attuned if volatile sense of space. In London, she rarely narrates details of her excursions outside—"You were perpetually moving to another place which was perpetually the same" (8)—but instead she describes interior spaces with great precision. From the reputable Judd Street house to the seedy Bird Street "manicurist" studio, the boarding rooms that Anna inhabits figure as locations that forge her identity and also chart her dissolution.

28   S. COHEN

Recognizing what Massey calls the "power geometry" of the arrangement of physical space—that is, how a particular space is dynamic in its production, how it "is by its very nature full of power and symbolism, a complex web of relations of domination and subordination, of solidarity and cooperation"—affords a glimpse into how local spaces feed into the global spaces of the novel.[7] An old print on the wall, a linen table cloth touched by a ray of sunlight, a breakfast tray cluttered with unpalatable pabulum, a tilted wine glass framed by a warm fireplace: Anna cathects onto the accouterments of various shabby rooms, and her understanding of a location can be determined by a single object. The spaces of buildings and rooms are tied to national and economic registers. Anna thinks, "*This is England, and I'm in a nice, clean English room with all the dirt swept under the bed*" (31).

It is difficult to distinguish the physical spaces of the novel from Anna's perception of her relationship with Walter Jeffries, her lover and benefactor in London. Her emotional states bleed into her perception of real geographical features of the city. Thus the physical geography is catapulted back and forth between subjective and objective realms. Anna coordinates her perception of their relationship—which is clearly founded on a dynamic of submission if not outright servitude—with her understanding of geographical space: "[fear] filled me and it filled the whole world" (96). Momentary local events threaten to engulf the world. For instance, Anna exhibits a seismic response to Walter's mischaracterization of the tropics: "Sometimes the earth trembles; sometimes you can feel it breathe" (54). This global imagination is as volatile as it is precarious. In response to the insinuating glances of waiters, she globalizes their scowls calling them "Brothers Pushmeofftheearth" (20). Ultimately, the worlds of England and the Caribbean are imagined in tectonic terms whose transection can only be jarringly violent. In this planetary scheme of discontinuity, Anna is an outlander, if not entirely an unearthly being, a fact made clear when she wonders whether the servant is thinking, "where on earth did [Walter Jeffries] pick her up?" (49).

Yet Anna Morgan is of this earth: a global laborer *avant la lettre*. Despite what appears as an insurmountable gulf between that which is familiar (memories of home) and unfamiliar (everyday life in London), Rhys's narrator possesses a keen sense of geography. At moments the world can be summarized in the simple if painful binary of home and away

---

[7] Massey, *Space, Place, and Gender*, 265.

2 COLONIAL ADVERTISING AND TOURISM IN THE CROSSCURRENTS... 29

as it is articulated by Anna's homesickness and amplified by others' attention to her racial difference. But still at other times the novel reveals a geographical specificity that functions to position Anna in a familiar if surprisingly pedantic planetary schema. "Lying between 15° 10′ N. and 61° 14′ and 60° 30′ W. 'A goodly island and something highland, but all overgrown with woods,' that book said" (17), Anna's thoughts intervene early in the first chapter with the geographical specificity found in a schoolbook or guidebook. For instance, Thomas Atwood's early study, *The History of the Island of Dominica* (1791), begins with a similar recitation of coordinates. This early text, which was written for audiences like Anna Morgan's family (and Jean Rhys's) who set sail for Dominica at the end of the eighteenth century, shares with Rhys's novel a common desire to survey one of the lesser-known West Indian islands. Atwood's study, like many others that would follow, maintained that "although the island of Dominica is so very capable of being rendered one of the chief, if not the best, the English have in the West Indies; yet, from a want of knowledge of its importance, or inattention, it is at this time almost as much unsettled as when it was ceded to Great Britain, near thirty years ago."[8] The adopted rhetoric of discovery narratives mingles with Anna's utterly idiosyncratic mappings of space. In this respect, the novel offers a composite account in which personalized imagery quickly follows rote recitation: "And all crumpled into hills and mountains as you would crumple a piece of paper in your hand—rounded green hills and sharply-cut mountains" (17). Still, one cannot help but ask what use do these coordinates have? It is unclear whether they make Anna feel closer to home or farther away, whether they soothe or aggravate her unremitting homesickness. Insofar as they reduce the distance that stands between England and Dominica to a numeric spatial abstraction, precise coordinates represent a considerably less painful orientation than counting the weeks a return journey would take.

The ability to make distinctions—between England and the West Indies, between others' perception of the tropics and reality, between a textbook rendering of the colonies and her affection for its lush landscape and diverse population—is an important even radical activity for Anna, who otherwise finds herself in the semi-debilitated state of following the vaudeville tour, resting in boarding rooms, or wandering London alone.

---

[8] Thomas Atwood, *The History of the Island of Dominica* (London: J. Johnson, 1791, reprinted London: Frank Cass, 1971), iii. See also Thomas Coke, *A History of the West Indies* (London: A. Paris, 1810), especially 332–383.

As such, the geographical consciousness that allows her to recall and perhaps even invent events from her childhood represents the primary form of agency Rhys furnishes her protagonist. This provides some relief in a novel that offers a considerably bleak treatment of its heroine who seems to walk into every trap set for her. The optimism found in the mere possibility of travel—"Anywhere will do, so long as it's somewhere that nobody knows" (100)—constitutes her only sense of safety and security. Later Anna's desire to escape London becomes more urgent, but going home is not immediately part of the plan: "For several days ... I kept on planning to leave London. The names of all the places I could go went round and round in my head. (This isn't the only place in the world; there are other places. You don't get so depressed when you think that.)" (159). This hopeful vision is tempered by the utter lack of specificity of destination. As much as Anna desires to be other places—"I kept telling myself, 'You've got to think of something. You can't stay here. You've got to make a plan'" (150)—she can hardly muster the words to name the location of her deliverance. Instead, Anna immediately returns to the mental game of trying to remember the pathway to her family's home in Dominica: "It's funny how well you can remember when you lie in the dark with your arm over your forehead. Two eyes open inside your head. ... You ride in a sort of dream, the saddle creaks sometimes, and you smell the sea and the good smell of the horse. And then—wait a minute. Then do you turn to the right or the left? To the left, of course" (150–151).

Anna's geographic consciousness of the recurrent return, as frustrating as it might seem, is far from inconsequential. Her most jejune meditations about an escape to the spaces of the past exhibit what might be termed an affirmative geography, following Herbert Marcuse's reflections on the stultifying effects of poeticizing the individual soul. But in Anna's case, instead of cultural materials leading to imaginary solutions that ultimately become a refuge in the face of mounting material problems, it is the very promise of travel and imagined voyages home that result in her rarely leaving her room. Through Anna's embrace of geography as a quasi-spiritual experience, Rhys illustrates that, as Marcuse would say, even "the most cramped surroundings are large enough to expand into an infinite environment for the soul."[9] Thus the reader is left to puzzle over whether Anna's penchant to take refuge in imagined voyages back to the West

---

[9] Herbert Marcuse, *Negations: Essays in Critical Theory*, trans. Jeremy Shapiro (Boston: Beacon Press, 1969), 110.

2 COLONIAL ADVERTISING AND TOURISM IN THE CROSSCURRENTS... 31

Indies might very well heighten her alienation and contribute to the inevitability of her tragic arc. The text hints that Anna might even be culpable for her circumstances when Walter's cousin notes the advantages of reading books: "It makes you see what is real and what is just imaginary" (93). This advisory resonates with something Anna's father once told her: "don't get tangled up in myths" (53). Neither of these impugning male voices offer a solution other than to question the protagonist's whimsical approach to the serious and apparently masculine business of travel.

Accordingly, Rhys's novel actively reads against the geographical grain, foregrounding both the liberating and oppressive aspects of history and geography. While her vivid geographical consciousness sets Anna apart and in many cases furthers her alienation from any semblance of community, it nevertheless becomes the space for Anna's creative energy and critical thought. Just as Walter cannot fathom living in the tropics, at one point noting "I don't like hot places much" (54), there is something remarkably audacious in Anna's distaste for London: "this is London—hundreds thousands of white people white people rushing along and the dark houses all alike frowning down one after the other all alike all stuck together—the streets like smooth shut-in ravines and the dark houses frowning down" (17). To imagine traveling around the world, whether it is a return to her home or simply travel elsewhere, Anna seizes on a conception of herself that is markedly different from how others perceive her. In the clutches of the Orientalist logic of the city, as it is represented by Walter and others who view Anna as an exotic import from the colonies, Anna is marked by racial difference, a designation that is charged with erotic excitement. Yet to imagine leaving the city is quite outside of this logic, which hardly endows her with agency. Similarly, each voyage back to Dominica is a historical return as much as an imagined spatial return. As such, Anna charts a rough history of the Caribbean that stands to contradict colonialist ideology which insisted that history began with the arrival of Columbus.[10]

V. S. Naipaul has seen the geographic consciousness that informs Anna's experiences as one of the distinguishing characteristics in Rhys's writing, grafting it onto the author's biography:

By the 1920s, when Jean Rhys began to write, the Caribbean and the Spanish Main belonged to antique romance; and the West Indian needed to

---

[10] Anna notably offers a thumbnail account of the genocide of the Caribs. See page 105.

32   S. COHEN

explain himself. Jean Rhys didn't explain herself. She might have been a riddle to others, but she never sought to make her experience more accessible by making it what it was not. It would have been easy for someone of her gifts to have become a novelist of manners; but she never pretended she had a society to write about.[11]

Naipaul concludes, "Rhys thirty to forty years ago identified many of the themes that engage us today: isolation, an absence of society or community, the sense of things falling apart, dependence, loss."[12] Naipaul's take on the prevailing tropes associated with the West Indies during the first part of the twentieth century is revealing.[13] Archives suggest the romantic notion of the West Indies—of pirates and buccaneers—was hardly the only or even most dominant, if persistent, understanding of the region for Rhys's audience. Contrary to Naipaul's assertion that Rhys was a different kind of expatriate, one whose "journey had been the other way around, from a background of *nothing* to an organized world with which her heroines could never come to terms," Rhys's writing in *A Voyage in the Dark* has a different aim.[14] In fact, Rhys's long career saw several different emerging understandings of the Caribbean. The unfolding of meaning in her novels depends on portraying the West Indies as a space in constant transition at the hands of competing imperial powers and never a blank slate upon which one can construct imaginary universes. The slow transition in metropolitan thinking about the West Indies—from a world of romance, to a world of colonial balance sheets, to a world of the tourist's fantasy—must be seen in the context of the radical geographic and political imagination in Rhys's fiction which holds these elements in tension. Much like Simon Gikandi's compelling argument that Caribbean writers contest colonial ideologies through "a discourse of alterity which is predicated on a deliberate act of self-displacement from the hegemonic culture and its central tenets," Anna's escape to fantasies of home is a form

[11] V.S. Naipaul, "Without a Dog's Chance," *The New York Review of Books* 18, no. 9 (1972): 29.

[12] Naipaul, "Without a Dog's Chance," 29.

[13] Seshigiri develops aspects of Naipaul's observation to offer a more compelling frame for Anna's "literary successors" who "move through former capitals of imperial power undaunted by their historical status as empire's second-class citizens. Racial hybridity, cultural multiplicity, and geographical restlessness no longer hold life-narratives hostage, but instead illuminate the mercurial labyrinths of national and familial history." Seshigiri, "Modernist Ashes, Postcolonial Phoenix," 501.

[14] Naipaul, "Without a Dog's Chance," 29.

of resistance.[15] Anna's peculiar geographical imagination exists in relation to the portrayal of the West Indies in colonial discourses. The political import of Anna's compulsive escape to the memories of her West Indian home on Dominica is apparent when seen competing with other representations of the Caribbean.

REVERSE CASTAWAY

In one of the inaugural texts of colonial discourse studies, *Colonial Encounters: Europe and the native Caribbean, 1492–1797*, Peter Hulme describes the formative position of the Caribbean in Western discourse: "discursively the Caribbean is a special place, partly because of its primacy in the encounter between Europe and America, civilization and savagery, and partly because it has been seen as the location, physically and etymologically, of the practice that, more than any other, is the mark of unregenerate savagery—cannibalism."[16] The colonial construction of the Caribbean follows the terms of classic Orientalist representation where encounters between Europeans and indigenous peoples are founded on varying degrees of desire and repulsion. Hulme's historicized account of the colonial encounter finds its literary sources in the encounter narratives of Prospero and Caliban, John Smith and Pocahontas, Robinson Crusoe and Friday, and Inkle and Yarico.

As a large body of Rhys criticism has demonstrated, the logic of the encounter and its often violent consequences can also be read throughout *Voyage in the Dark*. Seeing Anna as a character who is overwhelmed with self-doubt, Margaret Paul Joseph contends that Anna is a Miranda figure who "looks into a mirror and sees Caliban."[17] An element of what Hulme calls "the ideal of cultural harmony through romance" that defines the John Smith and Pocahontas encounter myth exists in Anna's "soppy"

---

[15] Akin to the escaped slave (Maroon) culture, Anna's retreat offers a powerful autonomy. As Gikandi explains, "like the slaves fleeing into the hills to establish autonomy, the modern Caribbean writer seeks to rework European forms and genres to rename the experience of the 'other' American." See Simon Gikandi, *Writing in Limbo: Modernism and Caribbean Literature* (Ithaca: Cornell University Press, 1992), 20.

[16] Peter Hulme, *Colonial Encounters: Europe and the native Caribbean, 1492–1797* (London: Methuen, 1986), 3.

[17] Margaret Paul Joseph, *Caliban in Exile: The Outsider in Caribbean Fiction* (New York: Greenwood Press, 1992), 28.

34   S. COHEN

thinking about Walter (44).[18] However, this ideal of self-sacrifice and eternal love is quickly shattered by the novel's starkly pragmatic voice of Maudie: "Only don't get soppy about him. ... That's fatal. The thing with men is to get everything you can out of them and not care a damn" (44). Similarly, Walter's seduction and eventual dismissal of Anna, leaving her to a desperate life of prostitution, exhibits certain similarities with the native girl Yarico's fate after taking the shipwrecked Englishman Inkle as a lover, only for him to sell her into slavery at the first opportunity. In each case, the seeds of exploitation and the economy of exchange are planted early in the ostensibly ideal relationship only to be fully realized once the relationship withers.

When all three narratives of colonial encounter are revisited by Rhys in *Voyage in the Dark*, individual agency, especially when it is coded as feminine, is thwarted; racial status can be seen trumping emotional attachment; and, as if to emphasize that the colonial encounter contains irrevocable brutality, Anna cannot shake off her first brush with England— "oh I'm not going to like this place I'm not going to like this place I'm not going to like this place" (17). This sentiment remains familiar to Anna long after her arrival, contributing to a sort of narrative detachment that occurs under the pressure of her recurrent returns home. Anna's perpetual colonial encounter is complicated by a number of factors. She is both a colonizer (she comes from a family of slave-owning colonial settlers) and colonized (she finds herself regarded as an exotic import within the imperial metropolis). Even though Rhys powerfully blurs distinctions, Anna's geographical imagination constantly reinstates the spatial difference that produces this distinction. It is this very tendency that contributes to making elements of Anna's story resonate with the Robinson Crusoe narrative. Both Anna and the shipwrecked Crusoe face seemingly insurmountable obstacles and must negotiate a hostile environment in order to survive. Like the Crusoe settler fable, *Voyage in the Dark* entails surviving the radically defamiliarizing experience of being thrown onto a strange, albeit intense and populated island. On the island, the castaway's new life is defined by loss. The approach to survival stands as an allegory for the recovery of the virtues of home, civilization, and connections of empire. Like Crusoe who swims out to the ship's wreckage to salvage materials for his new island home, Anna dredges up memories of the past which serve as the flotsam that sustains her.

[18] Hulme, *Colonial Encounters*, 141.

2 COLONIAL ADVERTISING AND TOURISM IN THE CROSSCURRENTS... 35

Thus within the cultural and geographic logic of imperialism, Anna represents a noteworthy reversal of the conditions ordinarily associated with the castaway. Although she is at the heart of empire with civilization around her, she nevertheless (and perhaps even more decisively) finds herself in the position of Crusoe, marooned on the shores of distant and unfamiliar island with only the memories of her former life to sustain her. This helps to explain her affinity for the indigenous Caribs themselves made castaways in their own territories. Relegated to a corner of Dominica, their last refuge remains Anna's obsession. At times Anna's narrative reads like a chronicle of events authored by the shipwrecked journalist who writes for no one but herself. In this case, her writing reflects a horrifying version of rugged capitalism: Anna tallies her income and few possessions, finally drawing on the only resource she can imagine, her own body. Just as the survivor of a shipwreck dreams of the mainland, fittingly Anna dreams of islands, dreams that only offer the frustrating "climax of meaninglessness, fatigue and powerlessness, and the deck was heaving up and down, and when I woke up everything was still heaving up and down" (164).

The reverse castaway figure does not serve as a mere reversal of cultural icons. Much like *Wide Sargasso Sea* would nearly forty years later, *Voyage in the Dark* embodies a study of differences. As with many postcolonial novelistic revisions—not to be confused with the postcolonial novel in general—particular deviations from the course of a familiar colonial narrative, whether it is J.M. Coetzee's rendition of Friday as mute or Aimé Césaire's depiction of Caliban as a mutinous potential revolutionary, constitute the political thrust of the narrative, seductively sliding the rewrite into the well-worn grooves of literary history. A similar re-visionary structure guides Rhys's novel which depicts a range of experiences with a variety of encounters as Anna navigates her new island and maps the new territory while she confronting metropolitan natives.

Across the unfamiliar landscape of England, advertisements figure as prominent features for Anna, functioning as landmarks that effectively both center her and reaffirm her position as an outsider. Commercial slogans mingle with Anna's thoughts, shaping the novel's form and oozing into the narrative as unattributed lines within the markedly economical use of language. For instance, when confronting her aunt, Anna glances at a Bourne's Cocoa advertisement which suddenly becomes the vehicle for her ruminations: "I kept wondering whether she would ask me what I was living on. 'What is purity? For Thirty-five Years the Answer has been

36   S. COHEN

Bourne's Cocoa.' Thirty-five years. ... Fancy being thirty-five years old. What is Purity? For Thirty-five Thousand Years the Answer has been" (59). The marketing catchphrase blends with her anxious self-assessment. Again, when anxious about her clothes for her meeting with Walter, she thinks, "It was a pity about my clothes, but anyway they were black. 'She wore black. Men delighted in that sable colour, or lack of colour'" (22), as if reciting an advice column from a fashion magazine.

Colonial advertising is particularly significant in the novel because it helps to establish specific geographic terms, modeling the translation of spaces that occurs through the associative work of selling a product through the imagining of place. The global traffic represented in colonial advertising traveled far beyond the products they marketed. What Anne McClintock calls "commodity racism," which "in its capacity to expand beyond the literate, propertied elite through the marketing of commodity spectacle," saw its appeals reproduced on a global scale.[19] The most significant instance of the novel's interlacing of colonial advertising and geography occurs at Bird Street where Anna is working as a manicurist (who doesn't know how to manicure) for her landlady Ethel. Looking at a print over the bed, Anna recalls a different image, an advertisement for "Biscuits Like Mother Makes, as Fresh in the Tropics as in the Motherland, Packed in Airtight Tins" (149). Anna reveals a deep affinity for this image that she describes in detail:

> The white furniture, and over the bed the picture of the dog sitting up and begging—*Loyal Heart.* I got into bed and lay there looking at it and thinking of that picture advertising the Biscuits Like Mothers Makes, as Fresh in the Tropics as in the Motherland, Packed in Airtight Tins, which they stuck up on a hoarding at the end of Market Street.
> There was a little girl in a pink dress eating a large yellow biscuit studded with currants. ... And a high, dark wall behind the little girl.
> Underneath the picture was written:
> *The past is dear,*
> *The future is clear,*
> *And, best of all, the present.*
> But it was the wall that mattered.
> And that used to be my idea of what England was like.
> 'And it is like that, too,' I thought. (148–159)

---

[19] Anne McClintock, *Imperial Leather: Race, Gender and Sexuality in the Colonial Contest* (New York: Routledge, 1995), 209.

2 COLONIAL ADVERTISING AND TOURISM IN THE CROSSCURRENTS...   37

Anna's analogy is telling not only for her ironic take on a triumphant slogan of modernity, but for her imagining of England as a dark and imposing wall. Andrea Lewis rightly reads this passage as an instance of Anna's recognition of her economic and racial difference and apparent inferiority, adding, "the wall symbolizes to her the over-protected infantile femininity and patriotic masculinity of England that walls her out, and suggests the impossibility of completely crossing national boundaries."[20] Just as surely, Anna's meditation on this advertisement for a colonial object is informed by her own experience in the metropolis as a commodity.

This advertisement, like the actual biscuit tins it promoted, represents a lasting and popular form of colonial nostalgia. Notably, within the circuit of Anna's thinking, England is thrice removed—a gloomy print in England inspires the memory of a backdrop to an advertisement for a British product once viewed in the West Indies. The kind of commercial traveling done here in the realm of the symbolic is even more significant considering the advertisement's specific claims that a product that can effortlessly travel across the globe without bruising, crushing, or ruining.

Yet for Rhys's protagonist's reverse voyage the opposite is true. When the colonial is brought to the imperial center the bruising is traumatic, mothers are lost, if not altogether forgotten, and homelands remain behind a veil of fading memories. The falsity of the advertising prophecy—*"The past is dear,/The future is clear,/And, best of all, the present"*—stands in painful contrast to Anna's perspective from her Bird Street quarters, where London is stale and the streets are monochromatic. Strikingly, in the logic of imperialism both colonial subject and biscuit are products to be consumed. It is therefore fitting that the advertisement haunts Anna's thoughts offer an allegory for her own in voyage in reverse, imported fresh from the tropics for consumption in the metropolis.

THE BODY GEOGRAPHIC

If in its treatment of Anna as a reverse castaway *Voyage in the Dark* illustrates the complicated status of the colonial subject by inverting the tropes of the island encounter, then the question of colonial settlement—as characterized by British plantations and imported products—also animates

---

[20] Andrea Lewis, "Immigrants, Prostitutes, and Chorus Girls: National Identity in the Early Novels of Jean Rhys," *Journal of Commonwealth and Postcolonial Studies* 6, no. 2 (1999): 89.

much of the novel. Unlike the experience of the castaway, which is largely defined as an individual's struggle with nature and the lonely task of reproducing a former culture, in a colonial settlement a much more global economy of the mass transmission and rationalization of British culture is involved. I want to turn now to some more abstract concerns involved with the mythology of the West Indies as a colonial space in order to show how *Voyage in the Dark* confronts these enduring ideas about the Caribbean. The relevance of West Indian colonial possessions can be traced back to the beginnings of modern European empires and the systems of colonial rule and exploitation that developed during the eighteenth and nineteenth centuries. Always a tinderbox for continental rivalry, the West Indies of the twentieth century cannot be separated from the historical facts of the Caribbean region during this earlier period. This history harkens back to the very existence of modern imperialism, including the triangle of exploitive trade among Europe, Africa, and the Caribbean.[21] By the twentieth century, the Caribbean was better known for its banana and lime trade; however, even these patterns of resource extraction were rapidly changing in light of the decline in sugar prices and the realignment of trade agreements. This contributed to the general perception that the region was an imperial backwater, a site of past colonial ventures that rested in ruin. As Anna takes on the character of a colonial import, her identity cannot help but be articulated in the context of this history and these enduring channels of exploitation.

It is therefore significant that Rhys unites her protagonist's exploitation with colonial tropes discovery. Anna's sexual coming of age represents the transition from a series of encounters to a state of colonization and commodification. The scene of the sexual encounter exemplifies the use of the colonial woman's body as a site of discovery and exploitation. Imperial domination is complicated by Anna's in-between status which allows her to participate in a kind of mimicry that, as Homi Bhabha has helpfully elaborated, results in "at once resemblance and menace" to imperial authority: "the excess or slippage produced by the ambivalence of mimicry (almost the same, but not quite) does not merely 'rupture' the discourse, but becomes transformed into an uncertainty which fixes the colonial subject as a 'partial' presence."[22] Yet in Rhys's thematization of mimicry, this

---

[21] See Alvin Thompson, *The Haunting Past: Politics, Economics and Race in Caribbean Life* (New York: M. E. Sharpe, 1997).

[22] Homi K. Bhabha, *The Location of Culture* (London: Routledge, 1994), 86.

nearly visible existence takes on the phantom qualities we might associate with the packaging or branding of the commodity. This is startlingly clear in a scene that has many similarities to the logic of packaging apparent in the biscuit advertisement above. The moment that Anna realizes she too is packaged occurs during a conversation with her friend and fellow vaudeville performer Maudie. Looking at Anna's closet Maudie says, "Very ladylike. I call that one very ladylike indeed. And you've got a fur coat. Well, if a girl has a lot of good clothes and a fur coat she has something, there's no getting away from that" (45). It suddenly dawns on Anna that her relationship with Walter has unceremoniously escorted her into the realm of exchange value. Making light of this possibility, Maudie continues, "'D'you know what a man said to me the other day? It's funny, he said, have you ever thought that a girl's clothes cost more than the girl inside them?'" (45). Though she is immediately reviled by the assertion which she slightly deflates with her nervous laughter, Maudie continues, recounting the man's insistence and her ultimate concurrence:

> 'Well, it's true, isn't it? You can get a very nice girl for five pounds, a very nice girl indeed; you can even get a very nice girl for nothing if you know how to go about it. But you can't get a very nice costume for her for five pounds. To say nothing of underclothes, shoes, etcetera and so on.' And then I had to laugh, because after all it's true, isn't it? People are cheaper than things. And look here! Some dogs are more expensive than people, aren't they? And as to some horses. (46)

Anna retorts, "'Oh, shut up. ... You're getting on my nerves'" (46). For Anna, who has purchased these garments with the money Walter gave her, the equation is abundantly clear. The clothing that draws the attention of her landlady also becomes the focus of Maudie's interest as she tries to measure her younger friend's success at "swanking."

At the same time, clothing figures as a refuge for Anna: "You look at your hideous underclothes and you think, 'All right, I'll do anything for good clothes. Anything—anything for clothes" (25). Not only is Anna her happiest when shopping—she immediately shops for dresses when she finds Walter's money for the first time, thinking "*This is a beginning. Out of this warm room that smells of fur I'll go to all the lovely places I've ever dreamt of. This is the beginning*"—but she understands that consumption

40   S. COHEN

has its own time-space rhythm (28).[23] For instance, one day while window shopping on Oxford Street, Anna reflects on women passing by as well as the dresses clinging to mannequins:

> The clothes of most of the women who passed were like caricatures of the clothes in the shop-windows, but when they stopped to look you saw that their eyes were fixed on the future. 'If I could buy this, then of course I'd be quite different.' Keep hope alive and you can do anything, and that's the way the world goes round, that's the way they keep the world rolling. So much hope for each person. And damned cleverly done too. But what happens if you don't hope any more, if your back's broken? What happens then? (130)

Shifting her gaze from the vacant eyes of the mannequin to the living women on the street around her, Anna elegantly unfolds the logic of consumption, notably drawing on a metaphor of global mobility. From Oxford Street, Anna takes a taxi to Bird Street where she arranges for a room with Ethel. After a short time here, the window shopping no longer serves as a refuge. As a castaway in the imperial metropolis she turns to camouflaging herself as a respectable local, though she clearly signals otherwise with clothing beyond her means. Her fur coat comes to symbolize this, first by Maudie's explanation of this economy of women in London and later by her xenophobic neighbor Ethel. Ethel sees the coat as collateral for a room and a stake in her manicure business; for Anna, the coat figures as her last vestiges of respectability. Anna holds on to the coat, "I don't want to sell my coat. ... And I don't know how to manicure" (112). By emphasizing the role of clothing as a form of advertising, marketing, and packaging, the novel places Anna into seemingly infinite circulation along with various commodities.

The terrifying association of the value of clothing with the value of the female body has even greater significance in light of Anna's unique colonial status and ambiguous racial identity. Like the masking effect of clothing, Anna's difficult position of being an outsider leads her to desire a more stable identity. Veronica Gregg comments:

> [T]he novel simultaneously historicizes the subjectivity of the white West Indian woman showing the effects of colonization even as it attempts to

---

[23] See Nancy Harrison, *Jean Rhys and the Novel as Women's Text* (Chapel Hill: The University of North Carolina Press, 1988) 81–82.

2 COLONIAL ADVERTISING AND TOURISM IN THE CROSSCURRENTS... 41

forge another subjectivity out of memory, senses, and the imagination. The 'dream' of the West Indies stands for a refusal by the white Creole of absorption into the ideology that constitutes Englishness and an attempt to valorize ... a 'structure of feeling' grounded in the West Indies.[24]

Anna occupies an interstitial position, circulating among positions and affiliations. Much of this stems from her aunt's brutal language: "I tried to teach you to talk like a lady and behave like a lady and not like a nigger and of course I couldn't do it. Impossible to get you away from the servants. That awful sing-song voice you had! Exactly like a nigger you talked—and still do" (65). At the heart of her harangue is the not-so-subtle suggestion that Anna's mother was black. The evidence is not so much located in her mother's racial identity as it is in Anna's behavior, what her aunt calls her "unfortunate propensities" (65).

Rhys is reluctant to locate her protagonist in any essential racial scheme.[25] However vehemently Anna argues for her mother's whiteness, she also desires the stable identity she imagines would be hers were she actually black: "I wanted to be black, I always wanted to be black" (31). This assertion coupled with her claim to be a "real West Indian" (55) indicates her willingness to embrace what Frantz Fanon would call the "The Fact of Blackness" as being "overdetermined from without" and "the slave not of the 'idea' that others have of me but my own appearance."[26] As designations like "Hottentot" and "nigger" float by her, Anna desires to occupy these intentionally disparaging terms. She is decidedly not interested in the romantic and fetishized way her lover deploys these terms—"let's go upstairs, you rum child, you rum little devil"—but rather she seeks a legible form of alterity that might lead to community and

---

[24] Veronica Marie Gregg, *Jean Rhys's Historical Imagination: Reading and Writing the Creole* (Chapel Hill: University of North Carolina Press, 1995), 132–133.

[25] Thomas Stothard's *The Voyage of the Sable Venus from Angola to the West Indies* represents a contemporaneous perspective of how the mass migration of blacks to the West Indies was depicted. Its accompanying ode cites Botticelli's *Birth of Venus* and unites the two figures through the metaphor of sexual conquest: "The loveliest limbs her form compose./Such as her sister VENUS chose./In FLORENCE. where she's seen:/Both just alike, except the white./No difference. no—none at night./The beauteous dames between." Quoted in Neville Connell, "Colonial Life in the West Indies as Depicted in Prints," *Antiques* 99, no. 5 (1971): 732.

[26] Frantz Fanon, *Black Skin, White Masks* (New York: Grove Press, 1967), 116.

possibly help her recover the past (55).[27] Ultimately the novel details the difficulty of *indeterminacy from without*. In this case, what Fanon recognizes as the "real dialectic" between the body and the world becomes the real problem, bringing us back to the geographic disjunction from her origins (111).

Anna faces the double subordination of a woman and an outsider. Without any recognizable community to which she might attach herself, she desires to be invisible but also is unavoidably the object of spectacle and desire. Seamlessly becoming a product and reified in a way that alienates her from others, Anna is unstable in any identity construction because its very terms are produced by the whims of the spectator. An important fact is revealed when she attempts to stop her own circulation, which she accomplishes only by not leaving her room. Once Anna stops going out and is just looking forward to sleeping, the terms of her escape become clear: "Really all you want is night, and to lie in the dark and pull the sheet over your head and sleep, and before you know where you are it is night—that's the one good thing. You pull the sheet over your head and think, 'He got sick of me,' and 'Never, not ever, never.' And then you go to sleep" (141). Resembling a funeral pall or more interestingly a veil, the sheet affects the type of time travel that shopping once offered Anna, but with the new implications of the exotic Other. Both the sheet-veil and clothing figure as a form of masking that offers only transient refuge for the wearer, but remains as an indelible sign for the spectator. As Sara Suleri points out in a different context, "the veil is figuratively transferred from the colonized female body to the colonizing discourse itself; rage and hiding become the impulsions of an ethnography that knows it cannot see the full implications of its association in the racial repulsion that it seeks to transcribe."[28] This helps explain Anna's fascination with images in the metropolis. Since she finds herself embodying elements of what Suleri calls the "colonial picturesque," that is, "a mode of perceiving racial bodies as though they were pictures before the act of representation," any investigation into the production and reception of images is ultimately an attempt at self-knowledge.[29] As Deborah Cherry, drawing on Suleri and Rey

---

[27] See Andrea Lewis, drawing on Sander Gilman's work on nineteenth-century sexuality and medicine, "Immigrants, Prostitutes, and Chorus Girls," 86.

[28] Sara Suleri, *The Rhetoric of English India* (Chicago: University of Chicago Press, 1992), 109.

[29] Suleri, *The Rhetoric of English India*, 108.

2 COLONIAL ADVERTISING AND TOURISM IN THE CROSSCURRENTS... 43

Chow's work on the visual imagery of the Other, has suggested: the "colonizing desires to translate opacity into visibility, to search behind the veil for the secrets of the orient, were played out on the bodies, faces and pictorializing images of "Oriental" women."[30]

Although Anna is unable to assert any particular origin because of competing racist and Orientalist perspectives, she is nevertheless inspired to search for such a community.[31] Anna wants to assert that she is a "real West Indian," but empire and capital do not allow for this (55). Instead, much of *Voyage in the Dark* is dedicated to exploring how empire effectively strips such designations. Rather, as Anna recognized in the biscuit tin advertisement, the problem of origins can be resolved in the consumer's gaze that has a global reach, a fact that manufacturers seeking support for imperialist policies were always quick to point out. This is especially true during the years surrounding the First World War when the Empire Marketing Board, under the influence of Leo Amery's "Buy from the Empire" campaign, placed renewed importance on the colonial origins of products imported into the metropolis and sent throughout the empire (Fig. 2.1).

Such is the case in Austin Reed's full-page color advertisement featured in a 1935 issue of the appropriately named magazine *The Sphere*. Here a global perspective is articulated as both an advertisement for a clothier and a lesson in colonial geography. The material for the shirt (manufactured elsewhere) travels the length of an ocean to arrive at Regent's Street but retains its origins, legible in the perceived quality of its label. Enmeshed with this myth of the global and the triumph of modernity, the import

---

[30] Deborah Cherry, "Algeria In and Out of the Frame: Visuality and Cultural Tourism in the Nineteenth Century" in *Visual Culture and Tourism*, eds. David Crouch and Nina Lübbren (Oxford: Berg, 2003), 46.

[31] Paul Gilroy has shown how tradition can figure as a source of power in the face of subaltern conditions: "The discourse of tradition is thus frequently articulated within the critiques of modernity produced by blacks in the West. ... However, the idea of tradition is often also the culmination, or centre-piece, of a rhetorical gesture that asserts the legitimacy of a black political culture locked in a defensive posture against the unjust powers of white supremacy. ... In these conditions ... the idea of tradition can constitute a refuge. It provides a temporary home in which shelter and consolation from the vicious forces that threaten the racial community (imagined or otherwise) can be found." See Paul Gilroy, *The Black Atlantic: Modernity and Double Consciousness* (Cambridge: Harvard University Press, 1993), 188–189. So far as Anna attempted refuge is driven by what Gilroy discusses as the grasping at the discourses of tradition, it is also indicative of a remarkable failure in attempt to develop double-consciousness.

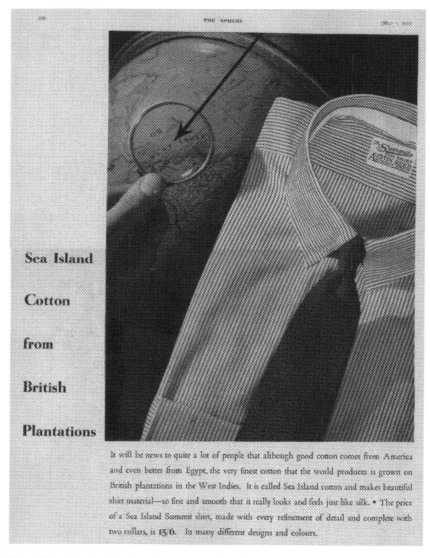

Fig. 2.1 Austin Reed advertisement from *The Sphere* [London] (May 4, 1935): 200

advertisement is founded on colonial nostalgia. The antique globe and magnifying glass foreground the longing for clear origins and authenticity, as if the shirt itself announces, *"I am a real West Indian."*

This vivid manifestation of the colonial system filtered through nostalgia can be seen as parallel to Anna's geographic imagination as well as her status as colonial import. Promising colonial authenticity to an urbane, metropolitan audience, the shirt advertisement is founded on a similar symbolic economy as the advertisement for biscuits Anna remembers seeing, only in the opposite direction. Not only does the Austin Reed advertisement stand as an example of the metropole's rendering of the West Indies, but it illustrates how the rhetoric of colonial advertising articulates a fantasy of origins and promulgates a form of geographical consciousness. Whether it is biscuits from an English oven or cotton from a colonial plantation, under empire's global exchanges, space is traversed without effort. Juxtaposed as they are here, the two advertisements—one textual, the other contextual—go to explain Anna's attraction to the rhetoric of colonial advertising and the formative position it occupies in her vague attempts to settle in England. Anna lives in the precarious space between the trajectories described in the biscuit advertisement channeling Englishness outward and the shirt advertisement bringing its colonial cousin inward.

TOURING THE EMPIRE

The specter of tourism haunts *Voyage in the Dark*. It is in this context that the novel frames the disconcerting mobility of a young woman on *tour* as a performer and eventually circulating as commodity in the city. At a very basic level, Anna encounters any number of bad hosts. But more to the point, if we see tourism and colonial visual culture as intimately related, then it helps to explain the dominant imagery as less an oppositional binary of England-West Indies and rather an experience more akin to the structure of tourism. During the twentieth century, a subject position would evolve, in that of the global leisure tourist, that could stand in the crosscurrents of empire as described here, luxuriating in the interstitial space between the voyage in and the voyage out. While Rhys was composing *Voyage in the Dark*, tourism to West Indies was still an inchoate industry, though by the time the novel was published in 1934 tourism was

46 S. COHEN

showing signs of becoming the mass commercial sector that it is today.[32] Although the Caribbean would ultimately become inextricably linked with white sand beaches and palm trees, during the first decades of the century tourism was largely tied to the imperial enterprise.[33]

Intimately related to the mobility and ideology embodied by the colonial system, tourism offered a different structure of feeling from that of settlement or entrepreneurial visits. Most early accounts of sightseeing opportunities in the Caribbean follow in the mold of James Froude's 1888 travelogue *The English in the West Indies: Or, the Bow of Ulysses*, where tourism is heralded as one step short of colonial settlement and a precursor to economic or (ideally) personal investment in the colonial enterprise.[34] The pioneering spirit of tourism is celebrated in the special 1910 edition of the *Times* which included the instructive article, "How to See the Empire: Some Notes for Travellers." Among other things, the *Times* observed that the region's moderate temperatures offered relief from cold winters and that its friendly and faithful West Indian Negro constituted "a people in the making."[35] The local folk culture was the region's primary attraction, as Algernon Aspinall, the Secretary of the West India Committee, noted, "To study these kindly folk would alone be worth a visit to the West Indies."[36] The implication for the audience reading the *Times* was that cultural refinement made some islands less hospitable to British tourists: some islands "(especially Grenada, Antigua, and Dominica) ought to be prepared to cater more adequately than they do at present for the requirements of the more luxuriously inclined and, therefore, best

---

[32] If tourism in Jamaica is taken as an indicator, then the increase in tourism between 1919 and 1922 and 1937 was tenfold. See Frank F. Taylor, "The Tourist Industry in Jamaica, 1919–1939," *Social and Economic Studies* 22, no. 2 (1973): 205–228.

[33] We need not agree with all the conclusions of anthropologists like Dennison Nash, who investigates the ways in which tourism is a form of imperialism and find suggestive similarities between metropole-periphery relations and the host-guest dynamic that characterizes touristic systems. Dennison Nash, "Tourism as a Form of Imperialism," in *Hosts and Guests: The Anthropology of Tourism*, edited by Valene L. Smith (Philadelphia: University of Pennsylvania Press, 1989). See also Taylor who recounts debates about public and private land and the evolution of tourism in Jamaica. Taylor, "The Tourist Industry," 213–215.

[34] See James Froude, *The English in the West Indies: Or, the Bow of Ulysses* (New York: Scribner's Sons, 1888).

[35] "A People in the Making," *The Times*, May 24, 1910, 37.

[36] Quoted in Taylor, "The Tourist Industry," 207.

2 COLONIAL ADVERTISING AND TOURISM IN THE CROSSCURRENTS... 47

paying class of visitors."[37] Elsewhere in the *Times* special issue, the "Special Correspondent with the Royal Commission" is quick to note that the tourist might be surprised by how isolated some islands remain. But even this is not without its advantages:

> The visitor can hardly fail to be struck by the absence of any sense of what may be called West Indian nationality. That between some of the islands ... there should be positive jealousy is perhaps unavoidable and as an incentive to emulation in commerce and self-improvement, such jealousy might well be a wholesome thing if it was softened by a more intimate feeling of a common destiny. Not only on political grounds would it be better for all this islands if they could draw closer together so as to act as a unit within the Empire, but in more material ways, also, they would assuredly be better able to push and to protect their own commercial interests if they were more ready to turn to each other for joint action in a common cause.[38]

The gap between colonial and tourist interests is bridged by Allister Macmillan's encyclopedic *The West Indies Illustrated* which synthesized the entangled history of the region, the principal European mythologies regarding its inhabitants, and the most minute details concerning commercial opportunities. As with many other surveys of the Caribbean, here past triumphs and the ultimate survival of the empire are located in the region.[39] This point is illustrated by Macmillan's introductory verse, "The Isles of the West":

> Of all the beauty spots of the Earth the fairest and the best
> Are the jewels of the Caribbean, the Islands of the West,
> Where Nature in profusion great her choicest gifts bestows
> In land and sky, in temperature, in everything that grows.
>
> ...
>
> Perchance among these lovely isles great things will yet be done;
> Perchance, when least expected, too, the trying days will come
> When, in the Caribbean Sea, Great Britain's fate once more

---

[37] "How to See the Empire: Some Notes for Travellers," *The Times*, May 24, 1910, 48. Tourists from the United States likely carried Frederick Ober's popular *Guide to the West Indies and Bermudas*, which appeared in several editions beyond the first 1908 edition.

[38] "The British West Indian Islands: Impressions and Views," *The Times* May 24, 1910, 34.

[39] See, for example, A. S. Forrest and John Henderson, *The West Indies* (London: Adam and Charles Black, 1905) and Henry Albert Phillips, *White Elephants in the Caribbean: A Magic Journey Through all the West Indies* (New York: Robert McBride & Co., 1936).

48 S. COHEN

Will tremble in the balance, as it often did before.

...

And in the coming time of dread, when over all the world
Great Britain's battle pennons will be fatefully unfurled,
Supreme she'll still be on the sea if in the awful test
Men fight for her like those who won her Islands of the West.[40]

A less portentous but no less patriotic tone is struck in Stephen McKenna's articles on the "Hospitable Islands" published in the *Times*. By 1923 when the series appeared, McKenna could record progress in the development of British tourism, suggesting that the visitor would feel very much at home in the tropics: "Nature has done more than art for [Barbados]. The blistered, ramshackle houses and pitted roads are monotonous; but, after months of flowerless winter and weeks of landless seas, the red and purple, bougainvillea make you hold your breath in ecstasy of gratitude."[41] By the 1930s, advertisements for British shipping lines to the West Indies appeared alongside the more popular advertisements for European and Mediterranean tours, and what might be called a mass tourism industry had developed enough to warrant the establishment of tourist bureaus throughout the Caribbean.

Within the discourses and imagery of Caribbean tourism there is a fusion of romance and adventure with the emerging possibility of regular leisure travel. The mythology of pirates, cannibalistic natives, and rugged wilderness is kept in check but arguably not entirely effaced by tourists' belief in modernity's assertion of time-space compression, imperialism's pacifying ability, and colonialism's importation of British civilization. To be sure, there is a rather clear equation that determined the perceived hospitality of the West Indies as a tourist destination: the extent to which potential travelers from the metropolis had faith in their availability to acquire British goods around the globe combined with their understanding of geopolitics. Significantly, both elements were largely formed through a lifetime of acts of consumption from within the metropolis— whether in the form of purchasing products marked by their colonial source or witnessing imperialist pageantry at exhibitions. Therefore, the

---

[40] *The West Indies Illustrated: Historical and Descriptive[,] Commercial and Industrial[,] Facts, Figures, & Resources*, edited and compiled by Allister Macmillan, 1st Edition (London: W. H. & L. Collingridge, 1909), 11.

[41] Stephen McKenna, "Hospitable Islands: IV Protean Jamaica," *The Times*, April 23, 1923, 9.

2 COLONIAL ADVERTISING AND TOURISM IN THE CROSSCURRENTS... 49

bi-directional traffic that is apparent in the juxtaposition of the biscuit company's guarantee of fresh Britishness and the global imagery involved with showcasing raw materials for a business shirt reveals some aspects of the visual culture related to the development of tourism.

Ease of passage, relative luxury, certain trappings of civilization, and the need to see the activity of travel as outside the realm of labor were four factors that distinguished the privileged enterprise of tourism from other types of travel. In this regard, it is worth noting that the specifics of Anna's island home in Dominica make it one of the less popular tourist destinations.[42] The island's unique position is central to the novel, not only for the protagonist's emotional history, but for historical and political reasons. If the West Indies was a colonial backwater under immense pressure from emerging independence movements and competition from the United States—pressures which ultimately would set the stage for the later century's transition from an exploited resource economy under the colonial system to an arguably equally exploitive economy of tourism—then the tiny island of Dominica occupied a position even further removed from the currents of imperial thought.[43] In *The Book of the West Indies*, A. Hyatt Verrill's description of the capital city is particularly scathing: "Picturesque to a degree, marvelously neat and clean, yet Roseau is scarce more than a town of hovels. ... and until that time, Roseau will remain as it is—an eyesore, an ulcer, and a disgrace."[44] Conversely, in a short dispatch from Dominica, "the Gem of the Antilles," the American magazine, *Travel*, focused on the island's pristine beauty—its "green undulating slopes," its "magnificent" mountains "with their volcanic peaks," and its "stately palms, and somberhued wood of tamarind and mahogany."[45] The primitive

---

[42] See Patrick L. Baker, *Centering the Periphery: Chaos, Order, and the Ethnohistory of Dominica* (Montreal: McGill-Queen's University Press, 1994); J. H. Parry and P. M. Sherlock, *A Short History of the West Indies* (London: Macmillan, 1971), esp. 133–139; Jan Rogozinski, *A Brief History of the Caribbean: From the Arawak and the Carib to the Present* (New York: Facts on File, 1999), esp. 356–357; John Bryden, *Tourism and Development: A Case Study of the Commonwealth Caribbean* (Cambridge: Cambridge University Press, 1973). See also Robert Myers's extraordinary three volume bibliography on writing about Dominica, *A Resource Guide to Dominica, 1493–1986*, 3 vols. (New Haven: Human Relations Area Files, 1987).

[43] When Rhys returned to the island of Dominica in 1936, Tourist Information Bureau had been open for ten years. See Peter Hulme, *Remnants of Conquest: The Island Caribs and their Visitors, 1877–1998* (Oxford: Oxford University Press, 2000), 204–243.

[44] A. Hyatt Verrill, *The Book of the West Indies* (New York: Dutton, 1919), 74–75.

[45] J. M. Cheney, "Dominica, The Gem of the Antilles," *Travel*, January 1910, 191–193.

50   S. COHEN

Roseau—where "natives from the country swarmed into town to buy, sell, dicker, and beg" and where a "moving throng, composed of the sick, the lame, the halt, the beggar, the outcast and the knave"—is surveyed from the secure position beyond the fray with a police escort.[46] Finally, Dominica's preindustrial status is encapsulated by a single fact: "As there are no wheeled vehicles on the island, ponies furnish the only transportation for the tourists"[47] (Fig. 2.2).

The postcard-length account of the day-visitor to primordial Dominica is contrasted in the same issue with an advertisement for Jamaica. Towering palm trees shade a late-model motorcar stopped to take in a scenic bayside vista; the heading proclaims "Now is the time to visit Jamaica with its sublime scenery and perfect climate."

The comparison of islands based on the vague but deeply ideologically laden term "hospitality" is evident in *Wide Sargasso Sea*, set more than a quarter of a century earlier than any of these accounts. When Antionette and her unnamed husband return to her family estate in the Windward Islands, the lush vegetation sagging under a heavy rainstorm helps to add an ominous tone to the couple's honeymoon: "A cool and remote place ... And I wondered how they got their letters posted," the unnamed bridegroom remarks.[48] Like *Voyage in the Dark*, *Wide Sargasso Sea* is fascinated with retracing the experience of arrival and return. In one exchange, Antionette asks her new husband whether "England is like a dream," as she had been told by a friend whose story reveals remarkable similarities to Anna's: "Because one of my friends who married an Englishman wrote and told me so. She said this place London is like a cold dark dream sometimes. I want to wake up." To this the Rochester figure responds, "that is precisely how your beautiful island seems to me, quite unreal and like a dream."[49] Rhys cultivates the unfamiliarity of locations to suggest that certain elements of relocation are common no matter what the new location might be. Both the idea of an unreal city and the idea of a ghostly island are disconcerting for the visitor, and the dreamlike qualities of these places are dangerously close to being nightmares. Such universalizing of the experience of travel to new places, however, fails to create a common

---

[46] Cheney, "Dominica," 192.
[47] Cheney, "Dominica," 192.
[48] Jean Rhys, *Wide Sargasso Sea* (New York: Norton, 1982), 76.
[49] Rhys, *Wide Sargasso Sea*, 80.

Fig. 2.2 The Atlas Service from *Travel* [New York] (January 1910): 195

52   S. COHEN

bond between characters; for characters who seem uncomfortable in their own skin, alienation ultimately prevails.

In *Voyage in the* Dark, language about travel to the West Indies does not resemble the marketing-inflected language seen in other contexts that pepper the novel. Accordingly, Anna finds it difficult to verbalize the very place she compulsively returns to in her thoughts. Nearly the midway through the first part of *Voyage in the Dark*, an important exchange between Anna and Walter centers on the two geographical poles in the novel:

> "I wish you could see Constance Estate," I said. "That's the old estate—my mother's family's place. It's very beautiful. I wish you could see it."
> "I wish I could," he said. "I'm sure it's beautiful."
> "Yes," I said. "On the other hand, if England is beautiful, it's not beautiful. It's some other world. It all depends, doesn't it?"
> Thinking of the walls of the Old Estate house, still standing, with moss on them. That was the garden. One ruined room for roses, one for orchids, one for treeferns. And the honeysuckle all along the steep flight of steps that led down to the room where the overseer kept his books. (52)

In her mind, her West Indian home is in ruin but still in bloom. Significantly, Anna's abbreviated syllogism reveals precisely how the dyadic relationship between England and the West Indies is in fact much more complicated. Not only does Anna place the binary into question, but her relativistic response—"It all depends"—is a brief but powerful rejoinder to Walter's earnest celebration of pastoral England (52).[50]

Tourism relies on clear narrative events—of departure, arrival, and return. *Voyage in the Dark* explores the difficulties of description and recounting such events. Thus the novel is preoccupied with the failure of narration as tourism would have it, a fact the title quite clearly indicates. The resulting narrative is disconcerting, as if to show how traveling has no guarantees, voyages are not prefigured, and memory might fail the traveler. Having been pensioned off by Walter to live in London alone, Anna dreams of leaving: "Anywhere will do, so long as it's somewhere that nobody knows." (100). By the same token, in a novel of relentless new arrivals and recurring fantasies of return, Anna occupies the position of a

---

[50] But it is also about knowledge and experience of the West Indian island that Anna holds closely to her as her only possession. She will not allow Walter to violate this last realm despite her momentary lapse into wishing he could see it.

negative tourist, travel is torturous, arrival is anything but hospitable, and nothing is outside the realm of work.

On the other hand, being exactly neither colonial nor metropolitan, Anna is compelled to occupy the position of the visitor. Thus, to see Anna's journey as a pilgrimage, with all its connotations of spirituality, inevitability, and even its ancient spatial form, is only to heighten the sense of her disappointment with England. Tourism is a template for a particular type of travel that Anna simply cannot undertake. Nevertheless, Anna desires to be transient, to be a tourist, to have the privilege of leaving: "This isn't the only place in the world; there are other places. You don't get so depressed when you think that" (159). At its core, all varieties of tourism are forms of escape from the ordinary or everyday. In this respect, the plight of Anna is even more distressing, for she cannot escape the sameness that inspires fear in her: "I was thinking, 'I'm nineteen and I've got to go on living and living and living" (109). In this tortured novel of becoming, the mingling of desire and geography means her imaginative journeys consist of constant arrivals and returns, a point made clear in the novel's final lines: "I lay there and watched [the ray of light under the door] and thought about starting all over again. And about being new and fresh. And about mornings, and misty days, when anything might happen. And about starting all over again, all over again" (188). The ability to start all over again implies an end to the migrations that have been her obsession. Seen at the intersection of the flows of labor, materials, and ideas in which Anna is caught, tourism—that very activity that is supposed to be a compelling benefit of these interwoven networks—as it is portrayed here ends up frustrating imperialist visions of mobility. Nevertheless, it is the tantalizing possibility of becoming a tourist one day that distinguishes Anna's experience from that of just trading one island home for another.

This economy of island trading that is predicated on loss neither begins nor ends with Rhys. In his introduction to *The Lonely Londoners*, Kenneth Ramchand draws an apt comparison between Rhys's novel and Sam Selvon's narrative of West Indian immigrants in London during the middle decades of the twentieth century.[51] It is not stretching the point, I think, to see *Voyage in the Dark* as a touchstone for the writing of transnational identity, a novel that might be read as a lens through which other Caribbean writers that follow, including C.L.R. James, George Lamming,

[51] Kenneth Ramchand, introduction to Samuel Selvon, *The Lonely Londoners*, (New York: Longman, 1985), 3–20.

54   S. COHEN

V. S. Naipaul, Sam Selvon, and Earl Lovelace, come into focus. I am not making the case, however, for including Rhys in the canon of writers who contribute to a broader Caribbean poetics.[52]

Instead, *Voyage in the Dark* might be seen in an even more contemporary transnational context. It is not difficult to see Anna in the faces of women who travel the world today as global laborers. The Filipina maid working in Saudi Arabia, the Nigerian girl struggling to survive after finding herself laboring as a sex worker in Italy, the Mexican nanny assisting a Canadian family—"women are on the move as never before in history," as Barbara Ehrenreich and Arlie Russell Hochschild write in their introduction to *Global Woman: Nannies, Maids, and Sex Workers in the New Economy*.[53] In the utterly uneven yet utterly interconnected phenomena of First World women traveling for leisure and business and Third World women migrating for work and survival we can recognize a variety of voyages in the dark and the traces of the untoward passages that Rhys detailed.

WORKS CITED

"A People in the Making," *The Times*, May 24, 1910.

Atwood, Thomas. *The History of the Island of Dominica*. London: J. Johnson, 1791, reprinted London: Frank Cass, 1971.

Baker, Patrick L. *Centering the Periphery: Chaos, Order, and the Ethnohistory of Dominica*. Montreal: McGill-Queen's University Press, 1994.

Bhabha, Homi K. *The Location of Culture*. London: Routledge, 1994.

Bryden, John. *Tourism and Development: A Case Study of the Commonwealth Caribbean*. Cambridge: Cambridge University Press, 1973.

Cheney, J. M. "Dominica, The Gem of the Antilles." *Travel*, January 1910.

---

[52] Silvio Torres-Saillant has compellingly set the groundwork for a unified West Indian literary tradition that might only include Rhys in a limited way: "Caribbean writers present themselves thematically and formally in contradistinction to their counterparts in the Western metropolises. In their attitude to the West, in relation to which they exist as marginal writers, and in their attitude to the local setting, in relation to which they function as spokespersons, Caribbean writers practice a *modus scribendi* whose uniqueness corresponds to their unique world." Silvio Torres-Saillant, *Caribbean Poetics: Toward an Aesthetic of West Indian Literature* (Cambridge: Cambridge University Press, 1997), 91.

[53] Barbara Ehrenreich and Arlie Russell Hochschild, eds. *Global Woman: Nannies, Maids, and Sex Workers in the New Economy* (New York: Metropolitan Books, 2002), 2. See also Rhacel Salazar Parreñas, *Servants of Globalization: Women Migration, and Domestic Work* (Stanford: Stanford University Press, 2001).

Cherry, Deborah. "Algeria In and Out of the Frame: Visuality and Cultural Tourism in the Nineteenth Century." In *Visual Culture and Tourism*, edited by David Crouch and Nina Lübbren, 41–48. Oxford: Berg, 2003.

Coke, Thomas. *A History of the West Indies*. London: A. Paris, 1810.

Connell, Neville. "Colonial Life in the West Indies as Depicted in Prints." *Antiques* 99, no. 5 (1971): 732–737.

Ehrenreich, Barbara and Arlie Russell Hochschild, eds. *Global Woman: Nannies, Maids, and Sex Workers in the New Economy*. New York: Metropolitan Books, 2002.

Fanon, Frantz. *Black Skin, White Masks*. New York: Grove Press, 1967.

Forrest, A. S. and John Henderson. *The West Indies*. London: Adam and Charles Black, 1905.

Froude, James. *The English in the West Indies: Or, the Bow of Ulysses*. New York: Scribner's Sons, 1888.

Gikandi, Simon. *Writing in Limbo: Modernism and Caribbean Literature*. Ithaca: Cornell University Press, 1992.

Gilroy, Paul. *The Black Atlantic: Modernity and Double Consciousness*. Cambridge: Harvard University Press, 1993.

Gregg, Veronica Marie. *Jean Rhys's Historical Imagination: Reading and Writing the Creole*. Chapel Hill: University of North Carolina Press, 1995.

Harrison, Nancy. *Jean Rhys and the Novel as Women's Text*. Chapel Hill: The University of North Carolina Press, 1988.

"How to See the Empire: Some Notes for Travellers," *The Times*, May 24, 1910.

Hulme, Peter. *Colonial Encounters: Europe and the native Caribbean, 1492–1797*. London: Methuen, 1986.

———. *Remnants of Conquest: The Island Caribs and their Visitors, 1877–1998*. Oxford: Oxford University Press, 2000.

Joseph, Margaret Paul. *Caliban in Exile: The Outsider in Caribbean Fiction*. New York: Greenwood Press, 1992.

Lewis, Andrea. "Immigrants, Prostitutes, and Chorus Girls: National Identity in the Early Novels of Jean Rhys." *Journal of Commonwealth and Postcolonial Studies* 6, no. 2 (1999): 82–95.

Macmillan, Allister, ed. *The West Indies Illustrated: Historical and Descriptive[,] Commercial and Industrial[,] Facts, Figures, & Resources*. 1st Edition. London: W. H. & L. Collingridge, 1909.

Marcuse, Herbert. *Negations: Essays in Critical Theory*. Translated by Jeremy Shapiro. Boston: Beacon Press, 1969.

Massey, Doreen. *Space, Place, and Gender*. Minneapolis: University of Minnesota Press, 1994.

McClintock, Anne. *Imperial Leather: Race, Gender and Sexuality in the Colonial Contest*. New York: Routledge, 1995.

McKenna, Stephen. "Hospitable Islands: IV Protean Jamaica." *The Times*, April 23, 1923.

Myers, Robert. *A Resource Guide to Dominica, 1493–1986.* 3 Volumes. New Haven: Human Relations Area Files, 1987.

Naipaul, V.S. "Without a Dog's Chance." *The New York Review of Books* 18, no. 9 (1972): 29–31.

Nash, Dennison. "Tourism as a Form of Imperialism." In *Hosts and Guests: The Anthropology of Tourism,* edited by Valene L. Smith, 37–52. Philadelphia: University of Pennsylvania Press, 1989.

Parreñas, Rhacel Salazar. *Servants of Globalization: Women Migration, and Domestic Work.* Stanford: Stanford University Press, 2001.

Parry, J. H. and P. M. Sherlock. *A Short History of the West Indies.* London: Macmillan, 1971.

Phillips, Henry Albert. *White Elephants in the Caribbean: A Magic Journey Through all the West Indies.* New York: Robert McBride & Co., 1936.

Ramchand, Kenneth. Introduction to *The Lonely Londoners,* 3–20. Text by Samuel Selvon. New York: Longman, 1985.

Rhys, Jean. *Voyage in the Dark.* London: Norton, 1982.

———. *Wide Sargasso Sea.* New York: Norton, 1982.

Rogozinski, Jan. *A Brief History of the Caribbean: From the Arawak and the Carib to the Present.* New York: Facts on File, 1999.

Savory, Elaine. *Jean Rhys.* Cambridge: Cambridge University Press, 1998.

Seshagiri, Urmila. "Modernist Ashes, Postcolonial Phoenix: Jean Rhys and the Evolution of the English Novel in the Twentieth Century." *Modernism/modernity* 13, no. 3 (2006): 487–505.

———. *Race and the Modernist Imagination* (Cornell University Press, 2010).

Spivak, Gayatri Chakravorty. "Three Women's Texts and a Critique of Imperialism" In *"Race," Writing, and Difference,* edited by Henry Louis Gates, Jr., 262–280. Chicago: University of Chicago Press, 1986.

Staley, Thomas. *Jean Rhys: A Critical Study.* Macmillan Press, 1979.

Suleri, Sara. *The Rhetoric of English India.* Chicago: University of Chicago Press, 1992.

Taylor, Frank F. "The Tourist Industry in Jamaica, 1919–1939." *Social and Economic Studies* 22, no. 2 (1973): 205–228.

"The British West Indian Islands: Impressions and Views," *The Times,* May 24, 1910.

Thompson, Alvin. *The Haunting Past: Politics, Economics and Race in Caribbean Life.* New York: M. E. Sharpe, 1997.

Torres-Saillant, Silvio. *Caribbean Poetics: Toward an Aesthetic of West Indian Literature.* Cambridge: Cambridge University Press, 1997.

Verrill, A. Hyatt. *The Book of the West Indies.* New York: Dutton, 1919.

Wilson, Lucy. "European or Caribbean: Jean Rhys and the Language of Exile." In *Literature and Exile,* edited by David Bevan, 77–90. Amsterdam: Rodopi, 1990.

CHAPTER 3

The Chivalrous Nation: Travel and Ideological Exchange in *Sir Gawain and the Green Knight*

Ruth M. E. Oldman

The Middle Ages saw alliterative poetic tradition flourish across the British Isles, though not in a singular, unified form. Variations in the form emerged depending upon geographical, cultural, and political variables, and many texts reveal a sense of strong regional pride. A theme of nationalism also became prominent as the British Isles began to define which geographical areas were part of its nation. While some scholars believe these two elements are mutually exclusive, I argue that the "Alliterative Revival" is not strictly indicative of regional and local literary pride or of thematic nationalistic fervor. Rather, the poetry of this Revival contributes many voices to an overarching national narrative through the alliterative style.

Sir Gawain and the Green Knight, one of the most defining examples of the medieval alliterative poetic resurgence, provides a complex and

R. M. E. Oldman (✉)
Independent Scholar, Latrobe, PA, USA

© The Author(s), under exclusive license to Springer Nature
Switzerland AG 2021
C. Beck (ed.), *Mobility, Spatiality, and Resistance in Literary and Political Discourse*, Geocriticism and Spatial Literary Studies,
https://doi.org/10.1007/978-3-030-83477-7_3

57

58 R. M. E. OLDMAN

innovative perspective on travel and ideological exchange in England during the Middle Ages. Written in a North Midlands dialect, several moments in the poem provide commentary on relations between the royal court of Richard II and the provinces of the North West Midlands. While the poem reveals moments of regional pride, through the use of the alliterative style and the rhetorical execution of Sir Gawain's final punishment, this poem reveals a commentary on the overarching English national identity of the time, giving voice to minority groups. Sir Gawain's travels lead him through Wales and North West England, allowing him to experience these traditions and lifestyles, which differ from the royal tradition he is used to. Through the use of language and alliteration within certain key scenes, the ideological exchange that occurs between minority and majority cultures in *Sir Gawain and the Green Knight* contributes to a commentary on how the court should treat its minority groups and gentry.

Written in the late fourteenth century, *Sir Gawain and the Green Knight* comes from a time in England's history that was internally divisive with shifting social and political ideologies. In the mid-fourteenth century, England was overwhelmed by the bubonic plague. Paula Arthur's analysis of pre- and post-Black Death peasantry mortality numbers demonstrates the sheer devastation of the pestilence on rural areas. For instance, in Alverstoke, where in the previous year "one death was recorded ... had eighty-five deaths during 1348–1349. The same story of an exponential rise in deaths also occurs for the manor of Hambledone where previous records reveal an average annual death rate of nine; this figure had increased to an extraordinary 138 by 1348–1349."[1] While these numbers are devastating alone, it is critical to note that "only the names of those peasants responsible for the payment of rent, and performance of labour services and charged with the maintenance of their buildings and land were recorded."[2] Thus, it is not an exaggeration to say that the death toll was likely much higher and had a much greater impact on the numbers of laborers than recorded.

In addition to the reduction in the peasantry, England was also going through a change in leadership and identity. The country was in the midst of the Hundred Years War and while the first phase of the conflict seemed to bode well for England, success eventually ebbed. Importantly, however,

---

[1] Paula Arthur, "The Black Death and Mortality," in *Fourteenth Century England VI*, ed. Chris Given-Wilson (Woodbridge, UK: Boydell, 2010), 70.

[2] Arthur, "The Black Death and Mortality," 72.

"English military success, proclaimed throughout the country in the first phase of the war, ensured Edward III's aspirations became those of the English political class as a whole, and this now was a group that had widened as a result of the national mobilization of men and resources."[3] This is especially important within the context of *Sir Gawain and the Green Knight*: as English military success against France would unify the country and formulate a cohesive national identity, particularly since the "growth of chivalric and military orders, the central role of the monarchy and the importance of language, especially the increasing use of the vernacular, have also been identified as contributing to a new or at least an enhanced sense of national identity."[4] These elements are explicitly seen in *Sir Gawain and the Green Knight*, as will be extrapolated further below. However, despite the unifying context of the Hundred Years War, instead of being a celebration of national identity, the poem's author utilizes these elements—the use of vernacular, a chivalric tradition, conversations about the monarchy—to critique England's inability to sow a cohesive national identity.

The Black Death's effects on the peasantry and, therefore, England's economy were not fully realized until after the deaths of Edward the Black Prince and Edward III. According to William A. Pelz, tensions started brewing as early as 1351 with the passage of the "Statute of Laborers," which

> demanded that common people work for the same price as before the Plague's onset, and allowed landowners to insist on payment in the form of labor instead of money. As prices rose, many [peasants] were squeezed by stagnant income and an ever higher cost of living. This situation continued for a generation, with various minor but significant scrimmages between lords and serfs, rich and poor. In 1377, the burden of England's military campaigns in France caused the government to introduce a head tax. Payable by all adult males in cash not produce, this new tax was seen as a real hardship by many commoners. Within a few years, men often hid from the tax collectors, leading to a decline in revenue. In spring 1381, the Royal Council, worried by the drop in income, ordered a new round of tax collections with collectors charged to obtain the full amount due.[5]

---

[3] David Green, "National Identities and the Hundred Years War," in *Fourteenth Century England VI*, ed. Chris Given-Wilson (Woodbridge, UK: Boydell, 2010), 117.

[4] Green, "National Identities," 117.

[5] William A. Pelz, *A People's History of Modern Europe* (London: Pluto, 2016), 13.

60   R. M. E. OLDMAN

The tax—in addition to the reduction in workforce—created an unsustainable system, particularly regarding funding the wars with France. The peasantry felt the financial and social pressures from the upper echelon, and the skirmishes escalated, coming to a head with the Peasants' Revolt of 1381.

Although the Peasants' Revolt itself demonstrated a splintering between the court of Richard II and the peasantry, the aftermath of the event also revealed the growing tensions between the nobility and the lesser gentry. W. A. Ormrod explains that while Richard II offered lip-service to the rebels, his advisors were much more concerned with the wars with France than the demands of peasants. However, the real challenge came from the gentry represented in the Commons who "now decided to take advantage of the king's precarious financial situation and to press for certain reforms. ... To put down a proletarian rising was one thing, but to quell unrest among a substantial and influential section of political society was altogether more difficult."[6] As Ormrod succinctly states, "The Peasants' Revolt exposed Richard II's minority government for what it really was: an insecure, hesitant, and mediocre regime."[7] Tensions between the upper and lower estates reveal a divisiveness that was evident throughout the nation. As such, definitions of national identity and what was the "true England" varied: nationalists supported the crown and the identity that sprung out of London, considering this identity as the overarching and superior character of the country. The royal court and government decided what was definitive of England. Regionalists were concerned with regional characteristics, focusing on local matters and minority pride, and resisting the imperial implications of an overarching national narrative.

The tension between the regional and national identities manifests itself in *Sir Gawain and the Green Knight* in multiple ways. Most important are the commentary the author provides on the chivalric code through the actions of Sir Gawain and the use of the alliterative tradition. These elements contribute to the national narrative and support what I believe is the author's belief that ideological exchange could effectively occur between the court and nobility, despite the historical tension between the two. As Christine Chism addresses, the poem is written in a North Midlands dialect and provides a commentary on "a royal court becoming

---

[6]W. M. Ormrod, "The Peasants' Revolt and the Government of England," *Journal of British Studies* 29, no. 1 (1990): 23.

[7]Ormrod, "The Peasants' Revolt," 30.

increasingly alienated from traditional seigneurial modes of chivalry and a conservative and insecure provincial gentry, whose status, livelihoods, and careers were increasingly coming to depend on careers at the royal court."[8] Specifically, "[t]he poem constructs its central characters to invoke and amplify contemporary tensions between the royal court and the provinces of the North West Midlands."[9] While Chism draws specific and intricate parallels between Arthur and Richard II and Bertilak/Green Knight and the North Midlands gentry, the tensions between the general settings of court and country provide enough evidence to indicate the poet's regional pride as well as a nationalist commentary.

To conclude that Arthur's court is a representation of the *Gawain* poet's contemporary royalty is reasonable: Arthur represents King Richard. In the poem's opening, Arthur is surrounded by his closest companions, those he trusts the most. Richard II was an absolutist king, surrounding himself with a close circle of aristocrats who worked as advising councils to the king. After the Peasants' Revolt of 1381, in which the estates' status quo was drastically challenged, and several power grabs throughout the end of the fourteenth century by those within his inner circle, Richard II was suspect of any potential or inferred challenge of the crown. When the Green Knight appears and challenges the honor of Arthur's court, the reaction of Arthur and the Knights reveals similarities to Richard's reactions to confrontations he experienced during his fourteenth-century reign. The poet included this moment to reveal the ideological issues between the royal court and the nobility.

The parallel between Arthur and Richard II, however, is further illustrated through the emphasis on Arthur's age. Richard II was a teenager in 1381 and his anger was well-documented: A popular political poem from the Middle Ages contains a rhymed couplet reading:

> The ax was scharpe, the stoke was harde,
> In the xiiii yere of Kyng Richard.[10]

---

[8] Christine Chism, *Alliterative Revivals* (Philadelphia: University of Pennsylvania Press, 2011), 66.

[9] Chism, *Alliterative Revivals*, 68.

[10] The axe was sharp, the stock was hard, In the fourteenth year of King Richard. John H. Pratt, "The 'Scharpe Ax' of 'Richard II,'" *Neuphilologische Mitteilungen* 77, no. 1 (1976): 80.

John H. Pratt explains that although the Roman numerals in these types of poems typically refer to the years of Richard's rule, in this case it would be referring to Richard's age, making him roughly fourteen years old and the poem's subject refers to the events of 1381.[11] Arthur shares Richard's youth in the opening lines of *Sir Gawain and the Green Knight*. Prior to the Green Knight entering, Arthur's mood is described as "sumquat childgered"[12] as he could not sit still "so bisied him his ȝonge blod and his brayn wylde"[13] (89). Here, Arthur is shown to be acting in a childish manner, a departure from the traditionally stoic King of Camelot that had been established in the Arthurian canon thus far. When the Green Knight enters, the similarities between Arthur and Richard II are deepened as the Green Knight refers to Arthur and the Knights as "berdlez chylder"[14] (280), a sharp dichotomy from the hypermasculinized Green Knight who has just entered Camelot. The language used to describe Arthur's physical attributes and behavior offer stark contrast to the typical medieval depictures of King Arthur as well as The Green Knight, creating a rhetorical link to Richard II. However, in comparing Arthur to Richard II, The Green Knight, then, becomes a representative of those who opposed Richard. The Green Knight, then, represents the rural gentry and landowners.

Additionally, the "scharpe ax" poem referenced by Pratt helps solidify the similarities between Arthur's Camelot and Richard II's Court. During the Peasant's Revolt, Richard left the Tower of London to speak with the commoners to grant concessions. The next day, he left again, "with a sizable armed guard. ... There, encircled by royal forces and hidden from his followers, [Wat Tyler, leader of Tyler's Rebellion] was killed ... he accompanied Tresselian throughout the southern counties and watched the executions [of other rebel leaders]."[15] Although the beheading game illustrated in Part I of *Sir Gawain and the Green Knight* is not identical to the situation created by Richard following the Peasants' Revolt, the similarities in tone are evident, particularly when taking into consideration Arthur's boyish behavior and Richard's insouciant decisions regarding the

---

[11] Pratt, "The 'Scharpe Ax,'" 80.

[12] Somewhat childish. *The Poems of the Pearl Manuscript: Pearl, Cleanness, Patience, Sir Gawain and the Green Knight*, eds. Malcolm Andrew and Ronald Waldron, 5th edition (Liverpool: Liverpool University Press, 2016), 86. All citations of *Sir Gawain and the Green Knight* are line numbers and will henceforth be parenthetical.

[13] So busy his young blood and his wild brain.

[14] Beardless children.

[15] Pratt, "The 'Scharpe Ax,'" 83.

3 THE CHIVALROUS NATION: TRAVEL AND IDEOLOGICAL EXCHANGE... 63

rebels. As the Green Knight taunts the Knights, at one point Arthur becomes enraged and leaps at him,

> Now hatz Arthure his axe and þe halme grypez
> And sturnely sturez hit aboute, þat stryke with hit þoʒt.[16] (330–1)

The brash reaction from Arthur, as well as his lunging for the axe, creates a clean linguistic parallel between Camelot and Richard's court. Although it is Gawain who ends up swinging the Green Knight's axe and decapitating him, he does so as a representative of Arthur. This initial scene in which the chivalry of Arthur's court is challenged creates the stark dichotomy between the court and the rural gentry, demonstrating the depth of the conflict that England had to overcome.

While it is clear that conflict existed between the court and lesser gentry, the poet shows this tension by sending Gawain as far from Camelot as possible, forcing him out of his comfort zone and into an "othered" setting. When Sir Gawain begins his travels and encounters different places:

> Now ridez þis renk þurʒ þe ryalme of Logres ...
> Til þat he neʒed ful neghe into þe Norþe Walez.
> Alle þe iles of Anglesay of lyft half he haldez
> And farez ouer þe fordez by þe forlondez;
> Ouer at þe Holy Hede, til he hade eft bonk
> In þe wyldrenesse of Wyrale.[17] (691–701)

The author provides Gawain's perspective in this scene, demonstrating a desperation and courtly attitude toward "other" places, revealing the dichotomy between court and rural gentry. However, to allude to the court-gentry tensions during the fourteenth century, the author provides contextual clues that Sir Bertilak is specifically representing the gentry of the North Midlands through geographical indicators. The author provides contextual clues and geographic indicators to Sir Bertilak's location. As Gawain gets closer to Bertilak's castle,

---

[16] Now has Arthur his axe and the haft grips, And sternly stirs it about, thinking of striking with it.

[17] Now he rides his array through the realm of Logres ... 'Til he had wandered full nigh into the North of Wales. All the Isles of Anglesey are to his left and follows as he fares the fords by the coast over at the Holy Head, 'til he had entered into the Wilderness of Wirral.

64   R. M. E. OLDMAN

> Into a forest ful dep, þat ferly watz wylde,
> Hiȝe hillez on vche a halue an holtwodez vnder
> Of hore okez ful hoge, a hundredth togeder.
> Þe hasel and þe haȝþorne were harled al samen,
> With roȝe raged mosse rayled anywhere,
> With mony bryddez vnblyþe vpon bare twyges,
> Þat pitosly þer piped for pyne of þe colde ...
> Þurȝ mony misy and myre, mon al hym one[.][18] (741–9)

These indicators, in addition to the physical mentions of North Wales and Logres, are physical representations of the landscape of the Northwest Midlands. The location significantly differs from Camelot—and thus "civilization." Additionally, the Northwest Midlands are one of the farthest points in England from London. For the poet to remove Gawain from the comforting and familiar halls of Camelot and putting him in a place of cultural and physical alterity, illustrates the strain between the regionalists and nationalists during the time of composition.

The duel, conflicting ideological identities of regionalism versus nationalism, court versus gentry, are challenged when Gawain arrives at Bertilak's castle and his attitude toward "other" places begins to change. Instead of finding a place that seems completely foreign, Gawain feels at home almost immediately. He is in the presence of "fine company" (928) and finds the lady of the house "even lovelier than Guinevere" (945). When Bertilak discovers Gawain is a member of the Round Table, he "laughed loudly, delighted with his luck" (909). With its cordiality and culture, the scene at Bertilak's castle mirrors that of the Christmas feast at Camelot. Gawain, although in an "othered" location, is exposed to familiar lodgings within the castle and the usual activity of the feast. While this demonstrates a cordiality that could exist between regional and national ideologies, it also initiates a challenge to the chivalric code of Arthur's and, thus, Richard II's courts: "In the controlled environment of his manor, so familiar and desirable to Gawain, Bertilak proposes an exchange of winnings, which like the preceding exchange of blows is a test of courtliness, predicated on persuading his guest to set aside his practical concerns and jump right

---

[18] Into a forest full deep, that was feral and wild, High hills on each side, and hoar woods below, Huge old oaks by the hundred together, The hazel and the hawthorne were snarled altogether, with rough ragged moss raveled everywhere, With many birds unblithe upon bare twigs, That piteously piped there for pain of the cold. ... Through many a marsh and mire, a man alone.

in."[19] This test reveals the decline and faltering of the chivalric code within the late fourteenth-century court. By the time *Sir Gawain and the Green Knight* was written, chivalry was no longer a code of conduct but instead a suggested guideline. For instance, Edward the Black Prince did use the chivalric code when dealing with his enemies. However, during military campaigns against France he would use the chevauchée strategy, which could be described as "political destabilisation and economic attrition."[20] Much of the chevauchée style involved burning and pillaging, which directly violated the chivalric code. Thus, a challenge of a knight of the Round Table's chivalry is a challenge of the modern court's chivalry by the Gawain-poet.

Although not a direct parallel between the poem's plot and the happenings in fourteenth-century England, the fact that *Sir Gawain and the Green Knight* is a poem that discusses the failings of the chivalric system cannot be ignored. While this demonstrates a cordiality that could exist between regional and national ideologies—Bertilak provides Gawain with great hospitality—when Gawain fails to give the green girdle to Sir Bertilak, the event reveals the decline and faltering of the chivalric code within the late fourteenth-century court. As explained by Martin:

> chivalry was ultimately no more than the circle of its own careful delineation, a cipher marking an empty space, a signifier without a determinable essence, meaning, or goal. In the minds of its proponents, of course, chivalry was always directed toward the satisfaction of honor; but as Patterson points out, "the term 'honor' became its own verbal symbol, a shorthand for motives that would not bear further inspection." Whatever its specific form, origin, and aim, chivalry was whatever its enthusiasts wanted it to be, accommodating and ennobling all sorts of martial action, no matter how objectless, imprudent, or predatory.[21]

It does not seem, however, this was an attempt by the Gawain-poet to reverse the hierarchy. Instead of creating a strictly pro-regional text, the climactic scene in which Gawain receives his final punishment presents a solution to the tensions between nationalist and regionalist ideologies.

---

[19] Carl Grey Martin, "The Cipher of Chivalry: Violence as Courtly Play in the World of *Sir Gawain and the Green Knight*," *Chaucer Review* 43, no. 3 (2009): 318.

[20] Clifford J. Rogers, "Edward III and the Dialectics of Strategy, 1327–1360: The Alexander Prize Essay," *Transactions of the Royal Historical Society* 4 (1994): 85.

[21] Martin, "The Cipher of Chivalry," 323.

66   R. M. E. OLDMAN

When the Green Knight reveals himself as Sir Bertilak and confronts Gawain for not sharing his winnings of the green girdle, he absolves the knight:

> I halde hit hardily hole, þe harme þat I hade;
> Þ*o*u art confessed so clene, be-knowen of þy mysses.[22] (2389–91)

This act of forgiveness reveals author bias in regard to regionalism, or at least to the flaws evident in the court's chivalric code of conduct. The language identifies the fault of the courtly figure, drawing attention to the "mysses" committed by the imperial figure.

The challenge of the court's chivalry and ethos proved successful, and Gawain is given the green girdle to keep. He proclaims:

> Þat wyl I welde wyth good wylle, not for þe wy*n*ne golde,
> Ne þe saynt, ne þe sylk, ne þe syde pendau*n*des,
> For wele, ne for worchyp, ne for þe wlonk werkke3,
> Bot i*n* sy*n*gne of my surfet I schal se hit ofte.[23] (2430–2433)

This moment reveals the culmination of the Gawain-poet's commentary on royal and regional relations: Gawain's flaws are brought to his attention and instead of responding violently or defensively, he accepts he has committed wrongdoing. Turning back to the historical context of the late fourteenth century, the Gawain-poet provides a solution through forgiveness and acceptance. If Richard practiced humility and recognized that his response to the disruption of the status quo and the challenges to his decisions was an indication on the effectiveness of his actions and policies, more could be accomplished. The Gawain-poet also demonstrates that forgiveness by those wronged by harmful royal decrees is a necessity and that engaging in these negotiations would result in a cooperative socio-economic situation, creating a unified English national identity.

The shift from an absolute binary of regionalism and nationalism to one of cooperation is best understood through Gloria Anzaldúa's theory of *la mestiza*, specifically overcoming "counterstances." She recognizes that the

---

[22] The harm that I have had, I hold it quite healed. You are so fully confessed, your misses known.

[23] That will I wield with good will, not for the pure gold, Nor the belt, nor the silk, nor the beautiful pendants, Nor for wealth, nor for worldly state, nor for the fine workmanship, But as a sign of my surfeit I shall remember often.

3 THE CHIVALROUS NATION: TRAVEL AND IDEOLOGICAL EXCHANGE...

traditional treatment of interactions between two opposing forces in terms of dichotomies and hierarchies is not the solution:

> [I]t is not enough to stand on the opposite river bank, shouting questions, challenging patriarchal, white conventions. A counterstance locks one into a duel of oppressor and oppressed; locked in mortal combat, like the cop and the criminal, both are reduced to a common denominator of violence. The counterstance refutes the dominant culture's views and beliefs, and, for this, it is proudly defiant. All reaction is limited by, and dependent on, what it is reacting against. Because the counterstance stems from a problem with authority—outer as well as inner—it's a step towards liberation from cultural domination. But it is not a way of life. At some point, on our way to a new consciousness, we will have to leave the opposite bank, the split between the two mortal combatants somehow healed so that we are on both shores at once and, at once, see through serpent and eagle eyes. Or perhaps we will decide to disengage from the dominant culture, write it off altogether as a lost cause, and cross the border into a wholly new and separate territory. Or we might go another route. The possibilities are numerous once we decide to act and not react.[24]

Both modes of thought need to engage with, not against, one another in order to move forward. For Anzaldúa, cultural progress is not modernity triumphing over tradition or vice versa. It is the collaboration of the two modes of thought. Within the context of *Sir Gawain and the Green Knight*, this occurs when The Green Knight reveals himself as Bertilak and Morgan Le Fay as Lady Bertilak:

> Ho is euen þyn aunt, Arþurez half-suster,
> Þe duches doȝter of Tyntagelle ...
> Make myry in my hous: my meny þe louies
> And I wol þe as wel, wyȝe, bi my faythe,
> As any gome vnder God, for þy grete trauþe.[25] (2465–70)

This passage is important for two reasons. First, Bertilak extends hospitality once more to Gawain and explains that they are both men of faith. Second, the presence of Morgan Le Fay—Arthur's half-sister and Gawain's

---

[24] Gloria Anzaldúa, *Borderlands/La Frontera* (San Francisco: Aunt Lute, 2008), 100–01.

[25] She is your own aunt, Arthur's half-sister, The Duchess's daughter of Tintagel. ... Make merry in my house: my men love you And I wish you as well, sir, by my faith, As any man under God, for your great righteousness.

aunt—creates a familial bridge between Camelot and the Green Chapel. Although, canonically, the family relationship between Arthur and Morgan Le Fay is typically fraught, the emphasis on hospitality and faith draws attention to the unification of these two ideologies, rather than the counterstance that exists between them. Thus, *Sir Gawain and the Green Knight* closes out with a demonstration of the ways in which regionalists and nationalists could bridge the conflict that had divided them up to this point in history.

While the plot of the poem illustrates a negotiation of regional and national identities, the use of the alliterative tradition is what emphasizes and encourages this interpretation. The Green Knight, when he first enters Camelot, states that "here is kydde cortaysye, as I haf herd carp,"[26] a subtle jab at the court's chivalry (263). When Gawain leaves Bertilak's castle, he comments "[h]ere is a meyny in þis mote þat on menske þenkke3,"[27] revealing the courtesy and chivalry present in the gentry (2052). These instances reveal a regional pride but also contribute to a nationalist narrative. As Larry D. Benson notes, "the influence of alliterative verse is … to be found throughout England" and that alliteration "to a sophisticated fourteenth-century audience the opening stanza of *Sir Gawain* would seem … an astonishing display of the author's command of the most fashionable poetic idiom."[28] Although the dialect used in *Sir Gawain* is from the North Midlands, the use of a popular English poetic style adds the regional voices to a national narrative. In much of the alliterative literature that emerged from this period the status quo began to be questioned and a variety of voices started contributing to literary and historical narratives. In the case of *Sir Gawain and the Green Knight*, the evident regional pride contributes to a commentary on how the court should treat its gentry and how regional ideologies can contribute to a unified national identity. The alliterative poem provides a type of nationalist literature insofar as a minority group from within the nation is awarded the opportunity to contribute to the national narrative through regional and local pride narratives.

Authors in the Middle Ages also recognized alliteration as a complicated oral literary tool and that mastery of this device reveals mastery of literature. Thus, authors who used alliteration effectively within their

---

[26] And here is chivalry, as I have heard told.

[27] Here is a many in this castle that thinks about courtesy.

[28] Larry D. Benson, *Art and Tradition in Sir Gawain and the Green Knight* (New Brunswick, NJ: Rutgers University Press, 1965), 123, 125.

3 THE CHIVALROUS NATION: TRAVEL AND IDEOLOGICAL EXCHANGE... 69

poetry were respected. This includes the Gawain-poet whose use of the poetic style places *Sir Gawain and the Green Knight* within the alliterative canon, indicating that the poem is worthy of praise and preservation within the cultural mindset. From this also comes the preservation and popularization of its message. Benson addresses that alliteration was attractive to poets: "as an oral tradition alliterative verse was a sophisticated medium, demanding an experienced audience that could understand its specialized diction and syntax."[29] These experienced audiences would have been members of the upper estate, who had access to education. Since alliterative poetry was immensely popular, as well as Arthurian romance, *Sir Gawain and the Green Knight* and its message of national and regional identity negotiation would have been easily available to these audiences.

This is not to say it was strictly meant for this audience, however. There are many examples of alliterative texts whose audiences may not have had the education or awareness to appreciate the grammatical and poetic intricacies provided by alliteration. As such, Middle English alliterative authors were aware of the need for both aurally and visually pleasing literature, as there was need for both oral and literate types of poetry. Many of the texts draw attention to this. For instance, Benson notes that in *Sir Gawain and the Green Knight*, the author says:

> I schal telle hit as-tit as I in toun herde,
> wyth tongue,
> As hit is stad and stoken
> In stori stif and stronge,
> Wyth lel letteres loken,
> In londe so hat͡ʒ ben longe.[30] (31–6)

However, Benson neglects to mention line 30 in which the author states "If ͡ʒe wyl listen þis laye bot on little quile,"[31] which draws direct attention to the author's intent that this retelling of the tale is designed for oral recitation as well as "letteres loken" (35). *Sir Gawain and the Green Knight* also demonstrates itself as an prosodic evolution of Old English alliterative line in that it owes its basic patterning to Old English, though in Middle

---

[29] Benson, *Art and Tradition*, 123–124.

[30] I shall tell it as I heard it in town with tongue, as it is said and spoken in story stiff and strong, with letters locked in this land so long.

[31] If you will listen to this lay but a little while.

English "the meter is purely accentual, the alliterating syllables more frequent, and the rhythm predominantly rising, iambic and anapestic in movement ... rather than falling, trochaic and dactylic, the usual movement in Old English verse."[32] I attribute this to the poetic need to appeal to an oral and literate audience. When the Green Knight appears in *Gawain*, the author describes:

> Wel gay wat3 þis gome, gered in grene,
> And þe here of his hed of his hors swete.
> Fayre, fannand fax umbefoldes his schuldres.[33] (179–81)

Not only does the alliteration allow the text to be aurally appealing, it also draws the reader's eyes across the line, illustrating alliteration's importance in balancing the two traditions.

Thomas Cable reflects upon the meaning of "tradition" and explains "though perceived as a single entity by those who join or define it, [it] is upon closer examination a set of discontinuous parts, sequenced only by time. The tradition must be created anew."[34] Although similarities are evident throughout the course of literary history, the alliterative tradition has evolved and adapted in order to thrive. Many authors recognize alliteration as an intricate and complex poetic device. More so, these authors recognize the lasting impression of this poetic style. To participate within the alliterative tradition is to be a part of literary heritage. In the case of *Sir Gawain and the Green Knight*, the use of the poetic style was a way to illustrate the unity of a nation. During a time when political divisiveness dictated how identity was formed, alliteration provided the Gawain-poet a way to bridge these rifts between regionalist and nationalist ideologies. Rather than fueling the dichotomy, the poet leaves the audience with a sense of hope and that change within the court is possible, that the impact of a minority culture on a majority one could create social change that would appreciate each identity and create a strong, united English nation.

---

[32] Benson, *Art and Tradition*, 112.

[33] Very gay was this man, geared in green, and the hair of his head sweet like that of his horse. Fair, fanned locks enveloped his shoulders.

[34] Thomas Cable, *The English Alliterative Tradition* (Philadelphia: University of Pennsylvania Press, 1991), 133.

WORKS CITED

Anzaldúa, Gloria. *Borderlands/La Frontera*. San Francisco: Aunt Lute, 2008.

Arthur, Paula. "The Black Death and Mortality." In *Fourteenth Century England VI*, edited by Chris Given-Wilson, 49–72. Woodbridge, UK: Boydell, 2010.

Benson, Larry D. *Art and Tradition in Sir Gawain and the Green Knight*. New Brunswick, NJ: Rutgers University Press, 1965.

Cable, Thomas. *The English Alliterative Tradition*. Philadelphia: University of Pennsylvania Press, 1991.

Chism, Christine. *Alliterative Revivals*. Philadelphia: University of Pennsylvania Press, 2011.

Green, David. "National Identities and the Hundred Years War." In *Fourteenth Century England VI*, edited by Chris Given-Wilson, 115–30. Woodbridge, UK: Boydell, 2010.

Martin, Carl Grey. "The Cipher of Chivalry: Violence as Courtly Play in the World of *Sir Gawain and the Green Knight*." *Chaucer Review* 43, no. 3 (2009): 311–329.

Ormrod, W. M. "The Peasants' Revolt and the Government of England." *Journal of British Studies* 29, no. 1 (1990): 1–30.

Pelz, William A. *A People's History of Modern Europe*. London: Pluto, 2016.

Pratt, John H. "The 'Scharpe Ax' of 'Richard II.'" *Neuphilologische Mitteilungen* 77, no. 1 (1976): 80–84.

The Poems of the Pearl Manuscript: Pearl, Cleanness, Patience, Sir Gawain and the Green Knight. Edited by Malcolm Andrew and Ronald Waldron. 5th edition. Liverpool: Liverpool University Press, 2016.

Rogers, Clifford J. "Edward III and the Dialectics of Strategy, 1327–1360: The Alexander Prize Essay." *Transactions of the Royal Historical Society* 4 (1994): 83–102.

CHAPTER 4

Conjuring Roots in Dystopia: Reconciling Transgenerational Conflict and Dislocation Through Ancestral Speakers in Nalo Hopkinson's *Brown Girl in the Ring* and Edwidge Danticat's *Brother, I'm Dying*

Zeba Khan-Thomas

Edwidge Danticat's *Brother, I'm Dying*, and Nalo Hopkinson's *Brown Girl in the Ring* showcase the ways in which Black immigrant groups use spiritual systems and storytelling traditions to perform narrative elegies for lost loved ones using ancestral speakers and their elders. In Danticat's and Hopkinson's texts, both heroines (Danticat and Ti-Jeanne) come to embody the personal hardships and dystopic conditions of the Western metropolises in which they reside. Danticat and Hopkinson narrate their heroines' coming-of-age stories within the framework of these Western metropolises and their promises for a better life through their parents' life stories and their struggles to integrate their cultures and spiritual customs

---

Z. Khan-Thomas (✉)
Tennessee State University, Nashville, TN, USA
e-mail: zkhantho@tnstate.edu

© The Author(s), under exclusive license to Springer Nature Switzerland AG 2021
C. Beck (ed.), *Mobility, Spatiality, and Resistance in Literary and Political Discourse*, Geocriticism and Spatial Literary Studies,
https://doi.org/10.1007/978-3-030-83477-7_4

as Black immigrants in these spaces. Danticat's memoir, *Brother, I'm Dying*, centers on her early recollections of Haiti through her father's immigration story. In the text, Danticat explores the conflicts that she and her family experienced while trying to transition from Haiti to America. On the other hand, Hopkinson's fictional, Afrofuturistic text *Brown Girl in the Ring* seeks to pay homage to the Black immigrant stories of Jamaican born Canadians like herself through emphasizing the African spiritual practices and systems that they summon and retain after integrating to Western metropolises. In *Brown Girl in the Ring*, Hopkinson highlights a Caribbean Black immigrant family's effort to fend off evil spirits within their family, as well as shield themselves from corrupt political forces in Toronto that seek to keep them oppressed as second-class citizens because of their desire to maintain their cultural roots. Danticat's memoir and Hopkinson's Afrocentric, speculative fiction novel present visions of dystopian displacement within North American and Canadian metropolises.

CARIBBEAN CONNECTIONS

In their texts, Danticat and Hopkinson consider the similarities and nuances of Black immigrant experiences in Western metropolises and give special consideration to families that are native to the Caribbean. The Black immigrant families centered on in these texts share the common desire to seek social, political, and economic stability, which contrasts to that of their home nation. The differences between the two heroines' in these texts are revealed through their coping and survival methods within the Western metropolises that they occupy, which is further highlighted through their connections with the extended family and their cultural roots. In the introduction of her book, *Searching for Safe Spaces: Afro-Caribbean Women Writers in Exile*, Myriam J.A. Chancy argues that "The condition of exile crosses the boundaries of self and other, of citizenship and nationality, of home and homeland; it is the condition of consistent, continual displacement; it is the radical uprooting of all that one is and stands for, in a communal context, without loss of the knowledge of those roots."[1] In *Brown Girl in the Ring*, Afro-Caribbean writer Nalo Hopkinson develops an intersectional discussion about Black immigrant struggles

---

[1] Myriam J. A. Chauncy, *Searching for Safe Spaces: Afro-Caribbean Women Writers in Exile* (Philadelphia: Temple University Press, 1997), 1.

4 CONJURING ROOTS IN DYSTOPIA: RECONCILING TRANSGENERATIONAL... 75

with nationality, cultural retention, and dislocation from home in her text. In Hopkinson's *Brown Girl in the Ring*, the protagonist Ti-Jeanne's role as the Black immigrant "middle generation" places her at the center of her familial conflict in the story. Both Hopkinson's and Danticat's texts apply conscious and fantastical elements of ventriloquism through performance and embodiment of ancestral speakers by the "middle generation" of Black immigrants and their children. The synchronization of struggles in the past and present highlights Danticat's and Hopkinson's desire to work across differences and create more inclusive societies where reconciliation of transgenerational conflicts is attainable. Through channeling the ancestral speaker, each heroine performs an elegy that overlaps past and present life histories. The heroines reflect on their familial connectivity and relativity to others who share their immigration stories as they all try to survive dystopic conditions within Western metropolises. Danticat and Hopkinson pay homage to those who came before them by recognizing their ancestors' tenacity and histories, and by literally summoning their heroines to "speak" them into existence. In the end, Danticat and Ti-Jeanne struggle to make peace with that which has been relayed and spoken "*In Living Memory.*"

In *Brother, I'm Dying* and *Brown Girl in the Ring*, Danticat and Ti-Jeanne conjure the voices of their Black immigrant ancestors, as the "middle generation" of Black immigrants seeking to reclaim and protect their "Caribbeanness" while navigating between metacognitive realities and metropolitan dystopia. At the beginning of each text, readers learn that Danticat's and Ti-Jeanne's families suffer displacement from their native homes, and they also fight to retain the memory of their communities through family and the performance of cultural traditions. As they attempt to resist the cycle of social death and cultural erasure, Danticat and Ti-Jeanne channel ancestral speakers to reconcile their transgenerational conflict through conjured parental wisdom and experience. Ti-Jeanne learns her grandmother Gros-Jeanne's supernatural power to shield her from evil spirits and death within "the Burn" (Toronto, Canada). Hopkinson describes "The Burn" in *Brown Girl in Ring's* prologue as "half-mired in muddy water" where the poor are "othered" as mere bodies to be preyed upon as organ donors and left to fend for themselves in "Muddy York."[2] Her characterization of "the Burn" as Toronto's dystopic core, rampant with decay and social unrest, comes to be embodied by

---

[2] Nalo Hopkinson, *Brown Girl in the Ring* (New York: Warner Books, 1998), 3–4.

Ti-Jeanne's grandmother, Gros-Jeanne, and the rest of her immediate family. Consequently, Gros-Jeanne's embodiment of the gang violence and corrupt political conditions in the Burn force her to develop a protective maternal instinct through the performance of rituals to keep the Calabash duppy (Mi-Jeanne) and other evil spirits, which Rudy (Ti-Jeanne's grandfather) has summoned, from harming her or others in their dystopic enclave:

> When Ti-Jeanne had been a child living with her mother and grandmother in the apartment building on Rose Avenue, Mami Gros-Jeanne would regularly go off in the evenings dressed in all white and carrying food for some king of religious celebration. ... Mami was soon leading regular rituals in the chapel. At nights, people dressed in white would troop past the front door of their house, carrying food and drums. ... Many nights Ti-Jeanne would lie on her little cot, awake and restless from the compelling sound of drumming and singing coming from the back house. The occasional screams, grunts, and moans frightened her.[3]

Gros-Jeanne and her family attempt to preserve their metaphysical selves from the dystopic conditions of the Burn by implementing their spiritual rituals as a community in the evenings. These rituals were practiced by Gros-Jeanne's family and their community to fight the potential embodied dystopia that they might experience after city officials fled to the suburbs, abandoning them to reside in a lawless city-center rampant with poverty, homelessness, and gang violence. Hence, Gros-Jeanne's rituals re-center and relocate her family using the spiritual systems and traditions of their ancestors as they attempt to avoid embodying the dystopic conditions of their physical environment.

Gros-Jeanne's family's susceptibility to embodied dystopia while living within the Burn resembles the exploitive socio-political systems and violent environmental landscape that Danticat and her family encounter and seek to escape as they immigrated from Haiti to the United States. Within a few lines of Danticat's memoir, *Brother, I'm Dying*, she mentions her ailing father who had just been diagnosed with pulmonary fibrosis while residing in New York. Sherly Vint's "'Only by Experience': Embodiment and the Limitations of Realism in Neo-Slave Narratives" examines the notion of embodiment in Octavia Butler's *Kindred* and Toni Morrison's

---

[3] Hopkinson, *Brown Girl in the Ring*, 86–87.

4 CONJURING ROOTS IN DYSTOPIA: RECONCILING TRANSGENERATIONAL... 77

Beloved, but could also be linked to Danticat's embodiment of dystopia from her father's storytelling of some of his memories in Haiti. Vint's application of embodiment to Butler's and Morrison's texts suggests that neo-slave narratives commemorate their ancestral foremothers by reflecting on trauma from a collective standpoint. Vint articulates embodiment as an ancestral intervention to perform a kind of ventriloquism that preserves the dead through the living. Danticat further renders her embodiment of dystopia in the chapter "The Return." This chapter includes Danticat's father's descriptions of the violence in New York's Haitian community. His story recalls an incident where a woman who was once robbed, opted to carry a knife to protect herself thereafter. Unfortunately, the woman fell victim to an attempted robbery a second time, wherein she ended up stabbing her assailant who turned out to be her son. Danticat's recollection of her father's story illustrates how embodied dystopia transfers and emanates within a family. Both Danticat and her father indirectly experience the trauma of the woman who mistakenly stabbed her son through memory and storytelling and are left vulnerable to the same unstable environment in Haiti unless they seek refuge in a perceived "promise land" like the United States. Furthermore, Vint's recognition of embodiment as a type of intervention between Black descendants and their ancestors is also conveyed through Hopkinson's intermingling of Gros-Jeanne's, Ti-Jeanne's, and Mi-Jeanne's consciousnesses and individual efforts to survive dystopic conditions in the Burn. By being dispersed across different urban metropolises, Black immigrant parents like Gros-Jeanne Hopkinson's novel and Mira and Uncle Joseph in Danticat's memoir struggle with the idea of integration; their alien statuses in a new territory perpetuate their dislocation from home, leaving them desolate and desperate to find comfort within dystopic centers.

In *Brown Girl in the Ring*, Ti-Jeanne serves as a literal visionary and channeler of spirits, whereas Gros-Jeanne's spiritual instructions provide her with prophetical knowledge to protect her and their family from the consumptive nature and evil spirits in the Burn conjured through her grandfather, Rudy's, spells. To illustrate Gros-Jeanne's spiritual influence on Ti-Jeanne, Hopkinson writes, "Ti-Jeanne could see with more than sight. Sometimes she saw how people were going to die. When she closed her eyes, the childhood songs her grandmother had sung to her replayed in her mind, and dancing to their music were the images. ... Never peaceful deaths. Ti-Jeanne hated the visions."[4] Ti-Jeanne's visions appear clearer through her embodiment of Gros-Jeanne's wisdom and ritualistic practices. Hence, Gros-Jeanne's conjuring of the Eshu's and orishas garners their support from the spirit-world into the physical realm to provide Ti-Jeanne with the tools necessary to overcome the dangers that haunt in her dystopic location. In a "Conversation with Nalo Hopkinson," Jené Watson-Aifah poses a question to Hopkinson regarding the writer's effort to subvert the science fiction/fantasy genres to accommodate the multidimensional perspectives she explores through cultural hybridity and the African diasporan experience. Hopkinson responds to Aifah's question by stating, "The kind of signifying I do as a Caribbean person is different from what a black American person would do, but I recognize that it has the same historical roots. ... And as a black and Caribbean person, I have my own cultural references for the magical or futuristic."[5] Hopkinson's insistence on using her ancestral background and imagination to cultivate familiar stories reflecting Caribbean diasporic people is what makes *Brown Girl in the Ring* a multi-voiced and multidimensional commemoration of Black immigrants' histories covering similar experiences across various terrains.

As a work of speculative fiction, *Brown Girl in the Ring* has been classified as science fiction in Laura Salvini's "A Heart of Kindness." However, Hopkinson's intentional imagining the supernatural through West African traditions and spiritual systems categorizes *Brown Girl in the Ring* as more speculative than science fiction. Hopkinson asserts, "When *Brown Girl in the Ring* came out, a lot of people who are used to conventional science asked me why I was mixing science fiction and fantasy. My answer has always been that that's what you do in everyday life."[6] In other words, Hopkinson's curation of *Brown Girl in the Ring* within the speculative fiction genre offers her a space to develop Ti-Jeanne's coming-of-age story through Gros-Jeanne's fantastical persona as the maternal medicinal woman, who, even in death, pronounces herself as the Brown Girl in the Ring that regenerates, guides, and protects her descendants even in the afterlife.

---

[4] Hopkinson, *Brown Girl in the Ring*, 9.

[5] Jené Watson-Aifah and Nalo Hopkinson, "A Conversation with Nalo Hopkinson," *Callaloo* 26, no. 1 (2003): 167.

[6] Watson-Aifah and Hopkinson, "A Conversation with Nalo Hopkinson," 168.

Metaphysical Conflict in Dystopia

Dystopia is realized through the internal and external conflicts people face in their environments, which is compounded with the conflicts of others that travel with them spiritually. We are not privileged to assume the fate of our lives without addressing the uncanny factors of reality and the selected incidences of self-inflicted chaos that account for our suffering in one way or another. Much like the medieval "wheel of fortune," one minute we find ourselves on top of the world with all the chips stacked in our favor and in the next, we may find ourselves "six-feet under," literally or figuratively dead. Several existential questions surround Black dystopian novels, fiction or creative-nonfiction, including the question of safety and inclusion. When Black immigrants migrate to urban metropolises, they often have to confront oppressive systems and racist practices that seek to keep "aliens" out. The Western practice of "weeding out" Black immigrants through isolation and alienation is addressed in Danticat's chapter "Alien 27041999." In the chapter, Danticat conveys how traumatic the U.S. immigration interrogation process was for her uncle Joseph, which led to his incarceration at the Krome Detention Center in Miami, FL:

> At 1:30 a.m., I received my phone call. At 4:20 a.m., my uncle and Maxo were transported to the airport's satellite detention center, which was in another concourse. By then my uncle was so cold that he wrapped the woolen airplane blanket he was given tightly around him as he curled up in a fetal position on a cement bed until 7:15 a.m. ... Maxo was handcuffed, but asked if my uncle would not be handcuffed because of his age. The officer agreed not to handcuff my uncle, but told Maxo to tell my uncle that if he tried to escape he would be shot.[7]

Uncle Joseph's detention experience showcases the way in which Black immigrants are forced into a dystopian reality. These traumatic events reveal the specter of death for Black immigrants by inciting fear and paranoia, which can foster perpetual transgenerational implications. For many Black immigrants dispersed throughout the world, the memory of home (where the heart and family are located) is the only place where they can find refuge when they are subject to public ridicule and possible violence.

In "Home Is Where the Heart Is: Danticat's Landscapes of Return," Elizabeth Walcott-Hackshaw writes, "The place we call home may be a

---

[7] Edwidge Danticat, *Brother, I'm Dying* (New York: Vintage, 2007), 221.

80   Z. KHAN-THOMAS

fixed location, offered rooted security, grounding, a continual reference point or point de repere, or it can be ambiguous, enigmatic, shifting space that destabilizes and promotes feelings of transience."[8] Walcott-Hackshaw suggests that the necessity of transferring familial security through spiritual protection occurs through multi-voiced conscious and subconscious embodiments. In Hopkinson's *Brown Girl in the Ring*, Gros-Jeanne's heart infiltrates Premier Uttley's subconscious state to invoke a sense of integrity in her decision to continue the Porcine Harvest Organ program, and a desire to restore ethics in the Burn. After Uttley receives Gros-Jeanne's heart though a transplant, she becomes more conscious of the Burn's citizens' humanity and can use her position as a government official to affect their well-being—for the people of the Burn, alienation and dislocation from home and their cultural roots seemed unending. In this sense, Uttley's literal embodiment of Gros-Jeanne's heart and spirit helps citizens of the Burn fight the socio-political turmoil and corruption of Rudy's posse. Hopkinson's text interrogates Black mortality in urban metropolitan cities that deny children their innocence and protection by their local government officials. Hopkinson showcases how the constant threat of state violence and poverty can prevent Black immigrant families from being hopeful and optimistic about their migration to supposed "promise lands." The specter of death as a prescribed condition for Black immigrant families like Danticat's and Ti-Jeanne's foreshadows their inability to survive socio-political struggles in those spaces without the help of family and the community.

Politicizing Identity, Nationality, and "Home"

In many instances, the narrators and authors of Black dystopian works emerge as types of litigators of the urban metropolis system, which "others" Black immigrant bodies to the point where they become unrecognizable to themselves or their loved ones. Hopkinson's text seeks to provide a counter-narrative to the cosmopolitan reputation of Toronto and other Western societies that are driven by capitalism and a notion of inclusion. Stories like Danticat's and Ti-Jeanne's magnify the incidences of erasure and societal desensitization that Black immigrants often experience within Western metropolises as they are seeking refuge or the promise of a better

---

[8] Elizabeth Walcott-Hackshaw, "Home Is Where the Heart Is: Danticat's Landscapes of Return," *Small Axe* 12, no. 3 (2008): 71.

life for their descendants in those dystopian spaces. These individual and collective stories often reveal the chronic pessimism and hopelessness of Black immigrants who desire better lives for themselves and their children, but nonetheless suffer in Westernized territories due to systemic oppression and anti-Black sentiment. Often Black immigrants, who are perpetually disenfranchised and displaced by the greed inherent in imperialist societies, feel the pressure to assimilate through abandoning their nativity and indigenous cultures. Danticat's and Hopkinson's stories offer testimonial perspectives on the Black dystopian experience, and how Black immigrants find ways to succeed despite arriving in foreign places as alien bodies. These texts also showcase how Black immigrants might find ways to rise above their circumstances through channeling their ancestors' and spiritual guides' wisdom and resilience.

Frantz Fanon's "On National Culture," from *The Wretched of the Earth*, explores the ways in which indigenous groups struggle against the impeding demand and infiltration of colonialist and imperialist values on their culture. Fanon's objection to imperialism and its consequences reflect Danticat's sentiments about her uncle's socio-economic condition in Haiti prior to being detained at Krome Detention Center. As Uncle Joseph's health continues to decline, Danticat recognizes how the U.S.'s invasion of Haiti had left her uncle vulnerable to gang and street violence. Uncle Joseph's church was even destroyed due to the social unrest that transpired as a result of the U.S.'s infiltration. In the chapter "Hell," Danticat recalls a story Granmè Melina told about a man who fell asleep and woke up in a foreign land where he did not know anyone. Granmè Melina's story precedes Danticat's account of Uncle Joseph's detainment at Krome to reflect his continued strife while living in Haiti and later as he was trying to flee from death. Danticat's retelling of Granmè Melina's story reiterates Fanon's sentiment on the struggle that many Black immigrants may face when trying to retain their nationality within imperial, Western metropolises. Within the essay, Fanon further suggests that native intellectuals, like Danticat, become personally troubled and impacted by colonial presences in their indigenous spaces like Haiti. Fanon writes, "Perhaps unconsciously, the native intellectuals, since they could not stand wonderstruck before the history of today's barbarity, decided to back further and to delve deeper down; and let us make no mistake, it was with the greatest delight that they discovered that there was nothing to be ashamed of in the past, but rather dignity, glory, and solemnity."[9] Thus, Granmè Melina emerges as an ancestral speaker through whom Danticat can convey the traumatic circumstances of Black immigrants, which parallel her uncle Joseph's struggle to make it through the U.S. immigration process.

Danticat unpacks memories of her childhood and young adulthood experiences, having lost two father figures to health issues and the U.S. immigration system. Danticat writes her memoir as an outspoken activist and human rights advocate for Haitian people and other Black immigrants venturing to the United States seeking a better life through the abandonment and sacrifice of their former lives.[10] At the end of her memoir, Danticat's narrative elegy about her uncle Joseph and father indulges inquiries on the afterlife as a way to explore possible ways to reconcile the memory of these important father figures after they have passed. She writes, "I wish I were absolutely certain that my father and uncle are now together in some tranquil and restful place, sharing endless walks and talks beyond what their too-few and too-short visits allowed."[11] The uncertainty of Uncle Joseph's and Mira's access to peace in the afterlife haunts Danticat, as she tries to imagine them together in reconciliation of all the experiences and setbacks in their respective lives that remain lost in translation. In overlapping their past and present consciousnesses through her memory, Danticat's elegy for her uncle Joseph and father becomes her memoir, given as a peace offering to assure them that their stories will not "go" untold. As a text, *Brother, I'm Dying* should be categorized as creative non-fiction, autobiography, and memoir. Danticat applies several techniques that confer her multi-voiced and conversational approach to telling her family's story through the experiences of two father figures. Danticat's creative chapter titles, dialogue, and non-linear plot make her story come "alive" in a vivid way. Moreover, Danticat's text functions as memoir and political commentary in the way she reflects upon her conflicting familial history, which is marked by dystopian realities rooted in socio-political displacement and death.

In "Empathizing with the Rights of Others: Reading Jamaica Kincaid's *My Brother* and Edwidge Danticat's *Brother, I'm Dying* as Humanitarian

---

[9] Frantz Fanon, "National Culture," in *The Post-Colonial Studies Reader*, eds. Bill Ashcroft, Gareth Griffiths, and Helen Tiffin, 2nd edition (New York: Routledge, 2006), 119–120.

[10] Roseanna L. Dufault, "Edwidge Danticat's Pursuit of Justice in *Brother, I'm Dying*," *Journal of Haitian Studies* 16, no. 1 (2010): 95.

[11] Danticat, *Brother, I'm Dying*, 268.

Narratives," Lourdes López Ropero suggests that both Kincaid's and Danticat's works are humanitarian narratives, which emphasize sameness, vulnerability, and the deprivation of human rights.[12] Danticat's utilization of memoir allows her to recall interviews and conversations between family members to synchronize their collective consciousness and spiritual essences. In "Fictions of Displacement: Locating Modern Haitian Narratives," J. Michael Dash writes, "Edwidge Danticat attempts to give voice to that imagined community that inhabits in-between sites. ... The strength of Danticat's writing is to give voice to reap a harvest of testimony from fluid people of borderlands, the displaced victims of the vagaries of history."[13] Thus, *Brother, I'm Dying* functions as Danticat's familial, narrative elegy following the traumatic deaths of her uncle and their mutual embodied dystopia due to the strain of U.S. and Haitian political relations. Through the memoir genre, Danticat is able to face her childhood grief and also reflect on her uncle's and father's tragic endings.

Conjuring Ancestors and Spiritual Messengers

Both Danticat and Hopkinson rely on ancestral forces to relay didactic messages through the Black immigrant adult speaker and their children to manifest their spiritual embodiment. In doing so, Danticat and Ti-Jeanne embrace their ancestors and parents' embodiment as a means to survive various dystopian landscapes and personal adversities. In "A Heart of Kindness" Laura Salvini suggests that "Legbara appears as the Eshu" for Ti-Jeanne to assist her with completing Gros-Jeanne's ritual to protect the family from evil spirits.[14] Gros-Jeanne's spiritual conjuring begins with her filling up a basket with various items "three bunches of dried herbs ... two white potatoes ... a margarine tub into which she had poured cornmeal; some of her homemade hard candy; her sharpest kitchen knife; a pack of matches; and a cigar"[15] Later, Ti-Jeanne learns that the basket was prepared to summon Eshu and the other spirits to protect the family from

[12] Lourdes López-Ropero, "Empathizing with the Rights of Others: Reading Jamaica Kincaid's *My Brother* and Edwidge Danticat's *Brother, I'm Dying* as Humanitarian Narratives," *Concentric: Literary and Cultural Studies* 42, no. 2 (2016): 85.

[13] J. Michael Dash, "Fictions of Displacement: Locating Modern Haitian Narratives," *Small Axe* 12, no. 3 (2008): 40.

[14] Laura Salvini, "A Heart of Kindness: Nalo Hopkinson's *Brown Girl in the Ring*" *Journal of Haitian Studies* 18, no. 2 (2012): 181.

[15] Hopkinson, *Brown Girl in the Ring*, 83.

Rudy's Calabash duppy (Mi-Jeanne) and his gang sent to kill Gros-Jeanne. As the power of Gros-Jeanne's supernatural ritual unfolds, Ti-Jeanne's child, named Baby, embodies the spirit of Legbara and rejects his father Tony when he tries to reunite with the family; Baby senses that he carries a bad spirit that jeopardizes the family. Following Baby's rejection of Tony, Gros-Jeanne tries to assure Ti-Jeanne that Baby has been selected to reveal Legbara's presence and disposition because the ancestral spirit shows preference toward children. Legbara is also identified by Gros-Jeanne as a trickster figure, like the West African spider figure, Anansi, who warns of the presence of evil spirits using game-playing. Hopkinson's utility of obeah and other Western African spirits in *Brown Girl in the Ring* performs ritual and commemoration of the ancestor's power to protect Gros-Jeanne's distressed and endangered family in Toronto's urban dystopia. Hopkinson highlights Ti-Jeanne's appreciation for her African heritage through observation of Mami in the novel:

> As ever, Ti-Jeanne marveled at Mami's trim strong body. … Mami said to start off, it have eight names you must know. She ticked them off her fingers. Shango, Ogun, Osain, Shakpana, Emanjah, Oshun, Oya, and Eshu. Ti-Jeanne tried to memorise the sounds. … The African powers, child. The spirits. The loas. The orishas. The oldest ancestors … Them is the ones who does carry we prayers to God Father, for he too busy to listen to every single one of we on earth talking at he all the time.[16]

Likewise, Danticat's chapter "Angel of Death and Father of God" recalls a story passed down from Granmè Melina to Tante Denise. Danticat embodies Granmè Melina's story as being "told to keep death away."[17] In the story, Granmè Melina relays that Father God and the Angel of Death strolled through neighborhoods knocking on doors and requesting water. One day, they arrived at a woman's house, where Father God gestured that he was "parched" and in need of something to quench his thirst. The woman denies Father God's request and states that she will only give the water rationed for herself and family to the Angel of Death. Her response, of course, astonished Father God, wherein he proposes that the woman would fulfill his request if she knew who he was. In the end, the woman shares why she acquiesces to the Angel of Death by suggesting that he

---

[16] Hopkinson, *Brown Girl in the Ring*, 126.
[17] Danticat, *Brother, I'm Dying*, 143.

does not "play favorites" when it comes to who dies and who suffers.[18] The woman believed that hopelessness and powerlessness conferred in faith was the true crime of humanity, made apparent by those who suffered socio-political injustices in Bel-Air. Granmè Melina's lesson on faith and justice emphasizes the indiscriminate nature and reality of death. Subsequently, through Granmè Melina's story, Danticat learns that she must come to terms with her uncle Joseph's and father's deaths to avoid falling victim to those same circumstances.

By the end of *Brown Girl in the Ring*, Ti-Jeanne is reunited with her mother Mi-Jeanne after years of silence and abandonment. Hopkinson shares Ti-Jeanne's struggle to express what it feels like to be reunited with someone she had buried deep down in her memory: "Ti-Jeanne was finding it awkward having her mother back. There was a lot between them that Ti-Jeanne would have preferred to be left unspoken, but after twelve years of silence, Mi-Jeanne was eager to unburden herself."[19] Ti-Jeanne's silence implicates Toni Morrison's essay "Unspeakable Things Unspoken," which emphasizes the phrase "Quiet as its kept" as it was rendered in *The Bluest Eye*. In the essay "Unspeakable Things Unspoken," Morrison repurposes the phrase to offer a critique on how white American literary traditions neglect to acknowledge African American writers' nuance and complexity, and then contextualizes the reference to her novel. Morrison's insistence on African diasporic folkloric traditions desire to obscure, or "quiet," translates as a method for writers, such as Danticat and Hopkinson, to be able to deal and cope with incidences of transgenerational conflict in dystopic conditions. For Morrison, Pecola's "quiet" hides the resentment and shame of her own Blackness and rape by her father in *The Bluest Eye*. In Hopkinson's *Brown Girl in the Ring*, Gros-Jeanne's silence about her failed marriage to Rudy literally haunts her throughout the story, until she is killed for her heart and Ti-Jeanne is forced to confront him and the Calabash duppy (Mi-Jeanne) who had abandoned her for most of her life. Morrison's adaptation of "quiet" in "Unspeakable Things Unspoken" and *The Bluest Eye* is appropriately employed in Danticat's and Hopkinson's Black immigration stories through breaking the silence of their elders' trauma and displacement. Danticat and Hopkinson implicate the conventions of "quiet" to reconcile that which has been deemed as "unspeakable" about their familial histories and requires telling through the

[18] Danticat, *Brother, I'm Dying*, 144.
[19] Hopkinson, *Brown Girl in the Ring*, 241.

coming-of-age stories of their heroine's and ancestor's metacognitive revelations. In this way, Danticat's and Ti-Jeanne's narrative elegies contrive their ancestors' wisdom to protect them from incurring the silences that once were. Their resistance to "quiet" in these stories reveals their ancestors' and parental guardians' desire to be heard and embodied as spiritual keepsakes. Furthermore, through emphasis on the "unspeakable" Danticat and Hopkinson conjoin younger and elder spirits to perform storytelling as a method of reconciling the "quiet" and silenced voices of the past and present. And yet, Morrison's notion of "quiet" probes us to consider what unspeakable things we so desperately want to conceal about ourselves in the illumination of events that have passed through our own present as readers of these types of stories.

SACRIFICING FOR FAMILY AND OPPORTUNITIES

Danticat and Ti-Jeanne's stories commemorate the Black immigrant sacrifices to migrate to foreign lands to obtain "better" opportunities for their families at the expense of death. Miguel De Unamuno's chapter "The Hunger for Immortality" from his book *Tragic Sense of Life* meditates on society's hunger to obtain immortality. Unamuno repeatedly chastises the idea of an afterlife, citing parental sacrifices for children as the primary method used to pass on cultural and historical inheritances. He writes, "Sacrifice yourself to your children! And sacrifice yourself to them because they are yours, part and prolongation of yourself ... a sterile sacrifice by which nobody profits."[20] Unamuno's existential implication of parents translates to his desire to see children learn from what their parents have endured through shared wisdom and personal sacrifice. Furthermore, Unamuno implies that conflict ensues when children are reluctant to use the tools they have been afforded through the sacrifices of their parents. Unamuno seems to mock the idea of transgenerational inheritances, spiritual or otherwise. However, with further deliberation of Unamuno's background as a socialist and positivist one must question whether his implication of "sterility" in the passage above is a broader critique of our familial conflicts and values being infiltrated by outside forces. Unamuno's emphasis on the word "sacrifice" emerges as "the way of life" in many West African traditions, including those imparted by Gros-Jeanne to

---

[20] Miguel De Unamuno, *Tragic Sense of Life* (New York: Dover Publications, 1954), 46.

Ti-Jeanne reflecting her grandmother's own personal sacrifice to protect her and their family.

To Unamuno's point on the act of "sacrifice," Mi-Jeanne's, Rudy's, and Premier Uttley's dispassion for the welfare of others is what fosters most of the conflict in Hopkinson's *Brown Girl in the Ring*. These characters take from others, rather than compromise their selfish agendas, for the good of their family and community. Hopkinson hones in on both sides of Unamuno's implication of parents' "sterile" sacrifice for their children through Gros-Jeanne's continued physical and spiritual sacrifice to fight the evil spirits that possess Rudy, Mi-Jeanne, and Tony and to protect Ti-Jeanne and Baby, which ultimately contribute to her death. Mami (Gros-Jeanne) sacrifices herself to teach ancestral rituals to Ti-Jeanne, who consistently resists her power to embody the ancestor's spirits. Hence, Gros-Jeanne's sacrifice becomes key to the novel's optimistic ending where the Burn's system of justice can be restored and Baby can be named, signifying hope for the future. For Ti-Jeanne, summoning a spirit is one thing, to embody one is entirely another. Toward the end of the text, Ti-Jeanne is confronted by her mother, Mi-Jeanne, who attempts to rationalize why she had abandoned her. She claims Ti-Jeanne was "eating up her whole life"[21] as a baby, and her father Rudy became disappointed with her decision to conceive in the first place. Alice Walker's chapter, "One Child of One's Own" from *In Search of Our Mothers Gardens* reiterates Mi-Jeanne's reluctance to become a mother: "The Child is perceived as threat, as danger, as enemy. In truth, society is badly arranged for children to be taken into happy account. ... I like many other women who work ... was terrified of having children."[22] Walker explains how the extension of one's legacy as a maternal figure involved the transference of rituals, values, and cultural traditions as well as sacrifice. Walker explores the expectations of motherhood in the same way that Mi-Jeanne confronts her own at the end of *Brown Girl in the Ring*. Walker laments on her mom's advice that she should conceive her second child right after her daughter Rebecca was born. For Walker, having a child "hurts" and overthrows her feminine power and her will to do with her body as she pleased. Although Mi-Jeanne adopts Walker's stance, Gros-Jeanne knows better. In acting as a maternal elder to Ti-Jeanne and the community, Gros-Jeanne is elegized as the loving grandmother that put her life on the line to reconcile her familial

---

[21] Hopkinson, *Brown Girl in the Ring*, 242.
[22] Alice Walker, *In Search of Our Mothers' Gardens* (HBJ Books: New York, 1984), 362.

conflict and restore justice for the Black immigrant community in the Burn. Hopkinson concludes, "Thank God for Mami's flock, eager to teach Ti-Jeanne their rituals,"[23] revealing that Gros-Jeanne's ritualistic practices and sacrifices were felt even after she had reincarnated into a spirit.

Danticat's *Brother, I'm Dying* also invites an uncomfortable, yet resonate inquiry on the topic of mortality and the afterlife in the first chapter of the text, "Have You Enjoyed Your Life?" Once the narrator receives diagnosis of her father's terminally ill condition, they proceed to have a family meeting with her siblings and mom to discuss what should happen next and after he passes away. Bob, Danticat's brother, asks their father the question that titles the chapter during their family meeting to discuss his health and future; wherein, Mira responds:

> I don't know what to say about that. ... I don't—I can't remember ever moment. But what I can say is this. I haven't enjoyed myself in the sense of party and glory. I haven't seen a lot of places and haven't done that many things, but I've had a good life. ... You, my children, have not shamed me...You all could have turned bad, but you didn't. I thank God for that. I thank God for all of you. I thank God for your mother. ... Yes, you can say I have enjoyed my life.[24]

Mira's response applies an existential understanding of how legacy is conferred through children. Danticat's and Ti-Jeanne's children become the primary benefactors of these stories as they can reflect on their parents' sacrifices to provide them with better opportunities and safety from harm. Nonetheless, the significance of this question posed to Mira by Bob raises the general question as to whether life could be enjoyable without the connection and sustenance of family.

RECONCILING TRANSGENERATIONAL DISPLACEMENT THROUGH STORYTELLING AND SPIRITUAL PRACTICE

The multi-voiced ancestral speakers in *Brother, I'm Dying* offer past and present reflections on severing family ties from migration experiences that begin and end in death. Likewise, Hopkinson's *Brown Girl in the Ring* contributes to the issue of Black immigrant struggle through its ancestral

[23] Hopkinson, *Brown Girl in the Ring*, 242.
[24] Danticat, *Brother, I'm Dying*, 21.

speaker, Gros-Jeanne, and her attempt to prevent transgenerational conflict from haunting her family. Gros-Jeanne's supernatural intervention on Rudy and Premier Uttley's conspiracy to "feed" on the city saves her family and the collective community in the Burn. By the end of Danticat's and Hopkinson's stories, readers must come to terms with the fact that life is too short to only retain what can be seen and possessed tangibly. The opportunity for reconciliation between those that have passed and those who live in the present is made possible by descendants who share what they have learned from their ancestors through spiritual, cultural, and intangible practices. Danticat and Hopkinson collectively emphasize that the denial of one's ancestral history results in an internalized state of trauma and chaos. Thus, the narrative elegies of Black immigrant's revere those who walk hand in hand into other worldly places, commemorating ancestors whose journeys ended too soon in dislocation from their homes.

Works Cited

Chancy, Myriam J. A. *Searching for Safe Spaces: Afro-Caribbean Women Writers in Exile*. Philadelphia: Temple University Press, 1997.

Danticat, Edwidge. *Brother, I'm Dying*. New York: Vintage, 2007.

Dash, J. Michael. "Fictions of Displacement: Locating Modern Haitian Narratives." *Small Axe* 12, no. 3 (2008): 32–41. https://muse.jhu.edu/article/252588

Dufault, Roseanna L. "Edwidge Danticat's Pursuit of Justice in "Brother, I'm Dying." *Journal of Haitian Studies* 16, no. 1 (2010): 95-106. http://www.jstor.org/stable/41715469

Hopkinson, Nalo. *Brown Girl in the Ring*. New York: Warner Books, Inc., 1998.

Fanon, Frantz. "National Culture." In *The Post-Colonial Studies Reader*, edited by Bill Ashcroft, Gareth Griffiths, and Helen Tiffin, 119–122. 2nd ed. New York: Routledge, 2006.

López-Ropero, Lourdes. "Empathizing with the Rights of Others: Reading Jamaica Kincaid's *My Brother* and Edwidge Danticat's *Brother, I'm Dying* as Humanitarian Narratives." *Concentric: Literary and Cultural Studies* 42, no. 2 (2016): 85–104. https://doi.org/10.6240/concentric.lit.2016.42.2.06

Salvini, Laura. "A Heart of Kindness: Nalo Hopkinson's *Brown Girl in the Ring*." *Journal of Haitian Studies* 18, no. 2 (2012): 180–93. http://www.jstor.org/stable/41949211

Simpson, Hyacinth M. "Fantastic Alternatives: Journeys into the Imagination: A Conversation with Nalo Hopkinson." *Journal of West Indian Literature* 14, no. 1/2 (2005): 96–112. http://www.jstor.org/stable/23020014

Unamuno, Miguel de. *Tragic Sense of Life*. New York: Dover Publications, 1954.

Vint, Sherryl. "'Only by Experience': Embodiment and the Limitations of Realism in Neo-Slave Narratives." *Science Fiction Studies* 34, no. 2 (2007): 241–61. http://www.jstor.org/stable/4241524

Walcott-Hackshaw, Elizabeth. "Home Is Where the Heart Is: Danticat's Landscapes of Return." *Small Axe* 12, no. 3 (2008): 71–82. https://muse.jhu.edu/article/252592

Walker, Alice. *In Search of Our Mothers' Gardens.* New York: HBJ Books, 1984.

Watson-Aifah, Jené, and Nalo Hopkinson. "A Conversation with Nalo Hopkinson." *Callaloo* 26, no. 1 (2003): 160–69. http://www.jstor.org/stable/3300638

CHAPTER 5

Mobility, Incarceration, and the Politics of Resistance in Palestinian Women's Literature

Leila Aouadi

The correlation between mobility and borders in the Palestinian-Israeli context frames people's lives and their artistic production. Movement despite imposed borders in the Palestinian Occupied Land is a political statement against colonial oppression and incarceration; it engenders a deep sense of self and community, struggling against siege and colonialism—an everyday reality that determines the inhabitant's existence. Boundaries forge identities and their ubiquity as edifices of the colonial grip's stifling presence resonates in Palestinian literature, which foregrounds borders' physical, cultural, and emotional debilitating impact on colonized subjects, fractured land, and jeopardized wildlife. However, the landscape, despite its mutilation, offers possibilities of negotiation between the opposing parties and ways to resist the proliferation of checkpoints,

---

L. Aouadi (✉)
University of Tunis, Tunis, Tunisia

© The Author(s), under exclusive license to Springer Nature
Switzerland AG 2021
C. Beck (ed.), *Mobility, Spatiality, and Resistance in Literary and Political Discourse*, Geocriticism and Spatial Literary Studies,
https://doi.org/10.1007/978-3-030-83477-7_5

road-blockades, and the separation wall.[1] All these forms of colonially engineered methods of control and subjugation made the occupied territories and Gaza "the world's largest open-air prison," according to the artist and activist Robert Bransky.[2] Israel has established and sustained systematic control over many Palestinians' daily movements and basic activities, aiming at protecting its borders and citizens from "terrorists."[3] Israel's foundation on Historical Palestine, now absent from the official world map, and its control over the West Bank and Gaza have an insidious effect on people's livelihood, creating complete economic dependence on Israel and pushing Palestinians into poverty and squalor.[4] The bond that knits Palestinians to the land of Palestine is strong, especially for those still living inside Palestine/Israel.

Avran Bornstein, an Israeli architect, writes in *Crossing the Green Line between the West Bank and Israel* that Israel's surveillance mechanism in the West Bank is powered by checkpoints, prisons, and walls.[5] However, these forms of incarceration are intensified and solidified by the introduction of more devices such as control-checks, random arrests, verbal and physical abuse, siege as collective punishment, the ongoing building of settlements, land confiscation, eviction, prison, torture, to mention only a few forms of control and coercion utilized by Israel. Building settlements that tower over Palestinian villages in the West Bank and constructing roads that cut through farm lands in order to link the settlements with Israel serve to dominate and control what is left of Palestine and its people. This plethora of incarceration devices is dramatized in Palestinian art, whereby the narrative becomes a political statement against colonialism, poverty, and injustice. Many literary works and movies engage Palestinian

---

[1] Israel began the construction of the separation wall, sometimes called the Apartheid Wall, in 2002 on confiscated Palestinian lands to separate the West Bank from Israel.

[2] Robert Bransky, *Wall and Piece* (London: Century, 2005), 111. He calls the wall, Segregation Wall and adds that Palestine has become "the ultimate activity holiday destination for graffiti artists," thanks to the wall. He includes nine of his famous works of graffiti in his book. Branksy, *Wall and Piece*, 111.

[3] These so-called terrorists may be called freedom fighters for they are fighting to liberate their land from colonization.

[4] The building of the wall claimed "more than 10 percent of Palestinian lands. Bearing in mind that the West Bank and Gaza constituted 28 percent of the area of Mandate Palestine." Zahi Zalloua, *Continental Philosophy and the Palestinian Question: Beyond the Jew and the Greek* (London: Bloomsbury, 2017), 98.

[5] Avram Bornstein, *Crossing the Line between the West Bank and Israel* (Philadelphia: Pennsylvania State University Press, 2002), 106.

border crossing to Israel or reckoning with checkpoints in the West Bank. Ido Haar's *9 Star Hotel* (2008) and Suad Amiry's *Nothing to Lose but Your Life: An 18-Hour Journey with Murad* (2010) exemplify the plight of Palestinian illegal workers in Israel whose journey into the world of illegal work at construction sites exposes the brutality of colonialism, the dismal failure of Palestinian national leaders, and the dire conditions of workers. Art functions to "pull the clandestine out of his existential parentheses" and in doing so the text becomes an index to reality as a discursive reproduction of the lives of characters.[6] The effort to document the Palestinian plight attempts in order to bear witness to silenced voices and neglected histories of pain and suffering is central in Palestinian art.

Resistance Literature in Occupied Palestine 1948–1966 by the Palestinian political activist and prolific writer Ghassan Kanafani (1938–1972)[7] is a trailblazing work in Arabic literature for coining the concept of resistance to identify and explore the role of literature in the fight against colonization. Arguing that the power of words is as penetrating as the power of bullet in the fight against occupation and injustice, he unsurprisingly was assassinated by the Mossad (the Israeli Secret Service) for his words and actions. In the introduction of his book, Kanafani divides Palestinian literature into two major parts: "exile literature," written by those who left Palestine and were exposed to Arab and international trends of literary innovation, and "inside literature," written under Israeli colonialism. He detects six foundational factors in the shaping of resistance literature inside what he calls the occupied land (modern day Israel); cardinal among them is "the cultural colonial siege."[8] The total dismantling of the Palestinian way of life, the redistribution of land and its confiscation by Jews who came after the Second World War to settle in Palestine, and of course the declaration of the state of Israel on Arab lands in 1948, sent shockwaves across Palestinian communities.

For Kanafani, art is intrinsically bound with resistance and poetry more than any other genre took center stage as the prevalent genre of the

---

[6] Magali and Pieprzak 2007, 120.

[7] Kanafani was born in Accra, North of Palestine, before the Nakba of 1948—the date that marked the partition of Palestine and the expulsion of many Palestinian from their homes and villages. He was assassinated by the Mossad in Beirut with his niece on July 8, 1972. I refer to the Arabic text not to the translated version, *Adab al Mouqawama* in Arabic means resistance literature.

[8] Ghassan Kanafani, *Adab Al Mouqawama fi Falstin al Mohtala: 1948–1966* (Cyprus: Rimal Books, 2015), 12.

94   L. AOUADI

post-partition era. In his 1987 lecture "What is the Creative Act," Gilles Deleuze explores the connectedness of art to resistance by highlighting the power of art to resist death and hegemony. For Deleuze, a work of art is an act of resistance that takes shape notwithstanding erasure and control. His ending remarks analogize people's struggle to artistic creation and ponders such affinity: resistance and art don't exist in vacuum; they have a cause and a message.[9] Kanafani argues, and long before Deleuze theorized the interplay of sociopolitical dynamics in art and people's struggle, both poetry and resistance happen in a given space and subsist well beyond the limitations of its context. Kanafani was aware of the significance of art not only to document resistance but also to actively fight colonialism and displacement. In the preface to the book, Kanafani reminds his readers that the composition does not and cannot claim "cold subjectivity" and colonial brutality and dispossession informs both art and its theories.[10]

In the 1940s (before and during the birth of Israel), poetry was "shaped by the preponderance of peasantry oral tradition, which drew heavily on Palestinian folk culture, and embedded in the peasant argot, sustained by the ' long-lasting love for the land."[11] After the departure of the urban litterateurs and the occupation of Palestinian towns and cities by new settlers and immigrants, popular poetry has become a venting space to mourn the cataclysmic loss of Palestine. Alliterative verse poems, written in Palestinian peasant dialect, rely on ornamental sound effects to maximize the impact of words in order to be easily recited and memorized. Palestinian bards who were invited to social gatherings helped to turn such gatherings into manifestations against the soldiers of the newly declared state of Israel by rallying people against colonialism.[12] Kanafani's trailblazing theories on the instrumental role of art, be it written or oral, in fermenting resistance and rallying masses to stand against colonial presence are unprecedented in Arabic literature. He ushered in a new literary trend that characterized Palestinian

---

[9] See Gilles Deleuze, "What is the creative act?," in *Two Regimes of Madness: Texts and Interviews 1975–1995*, ed., David Lapoujade, trans. Ames Hodges and Mike Taormina (New York, NY: Semiotext(e), 2007), 312–324.

[10] Kanafani, *Adab Al Mouqawama*, 8. This is echoed in Edward's Said preface to *Orientalism*, when he addressed the charges against the personal tone of the book by maintaining the importance of the personal in his theories—by personal he simply meant Palestine.

[11] Kanafani, *Adab Al Mouqawama*, 18.

[12] Kanafani, *Adab Al Mouqawama*, 18–19.

literature—a literature conceived under the dire colonial violence and informed by its context—and proved to be his enduring legacy.[13]

Palestinian literature within the occupied territory and Israel has undergone great changes after the partition of the land in 1948 and the 1967 defeats, signaling the colonization of the remaining Palestinian territories, a major setback that proved to be enduring. The historical juncture during which Kanafani wrote and published is characterized by a strong unwavering conviction that Palestinians will return to their lost homes and the newly founded state of Israel will not survive. This, of course, proved to be wrong and the defeat of 1967 triggered new foreboding emotions that are interlaced within artistic productions, including Kanafani's own novels. Poetry, though prominent in the Palestinian literary scene, is no longer the most prevalent genre. Numerous literary genres, namely autobiographical and testimonial writing, have become a major platform to mount resistance to Israeli colonial presence and other major concerns. A significant number of Palestinian women, writing in Arabic and English, are contributing to new forms of resistance literature. Writing from inside or from exile, Palestinians weave their national plight into all forms of writing, including literary theory. As such, this essay studies mobility as resistance in the works of two Palestinian female authors: Suad Amiry's *Golda Slept Here* (2014) and the debut novel of Salma Dabbagh, *Out of It* (2011). The two texts fall within the category of resistance literature, and are shaped by the current politics of colonialism, which features the geography of Palestinian suffering. Both narrative forms, the novel and the architectural diary of pre-1948 Palestinian houses, charter the experience of people whose lives are in constant flux and whose land is consistently being redrawn with the arbitrariness of colonialism.

GOLDA SLEPT HERE (2014) AND COLONIAL ARCHITECTURE

In *Golda Slept Here or Palestine: The Presence of the Absent*, Suad Amiry writes about the architecture of the colonialized land by utilizing her professional knowledge to explore architecture—a tool to finalize dominance and colonial authority—and engage subaltern narratives that counter the hegemony of the colonial settler state of Israel. *Golda Slept Here* catalogs

---

[13] Barbara Harlow uses the term "resistance literature" to refer to third world literature that engages the political and positions itself as a changing force within society. She employs Kanafani's theories to frame and sustain her argument in *Resistance Literature*.

the histories of Arab Palestinian houses in West Jerusalem whose owners were forced to leave in 1948. The writer, who resides in Ramallah,[14] is involved in preserving the cultural heritage of Palestinian building and restoring many old houses, and is also an activist, a university teacher, and the founder of the Centre of Architectural Conservation, a non-governmental organization for the preservation of Palestinian heritage. The use of the name Golda has an intended effect to underscore the illegality of Israel as a state created by a British mandate order.[15]

Golda Slept Here laces the artistic with the political and reflects on the presence of the land from the standpoint of its legitimate owners, the dispossessed Palestinian. The diary is a documentation of the stories of Palestinian houses in West Jerusalem through the lenses of Huda al-Imam, her eldest cousin Nahil, and Gabi Baramki, the son of "the first Palestinian architect."[16] They are, along with the writer, the protagonists of this architectural border diary where the loss of her parent's house left a lasting affect; she never "had the emotional courage to visit [her] own family's house in Jaffa."[17] The book's first part relates the story of the author's parents, and the second is about Andoni whose monumental buildings marked Palestinian architectural revival before 1948 and whose houses were lost in 1948 and 1967. The third part is devoted to Huda, and the last part of the narrative is a homage to the author's mother-in-law who lost her home in Jaffa in 1948 and settled in Ramallah until her death in 2005, refusing to leave even during the curfew and the Israeli incursion of 2002. On the cusp of architecture, trauma, and testimony, the writing about lost houses is cathartic and palliative for both author and her protagonists as they face their own fear and frustration about the loss of family homes, and, by implication, their country. The history of Palestinian houses in West Jerusalem still haunts the exilic lives of Palestinians inside the occupied land and in exile. The text revolves around making the authorial apostrophe, "Ah, if only buildings could tell their stories" and endeavors to animate them by unearthing their past, a symbolic act of bringing Palestine back to life.[18]

---

[14] Ramallah is also known under the name of West Bank, colonized after the 1967.

[15] Golda Meir (1898–1978) was an Israeli prime minister from 1969 to 1974.

[16] Suad Amiry, *Golda Slept Here: Palestine: the Presence of the Absent* (Doha: Bloomsbury Qatar Foundation Publishing, 2014), 4.

[17] Amiry, *Golda Slept Here*, 5.

[18] Amiry, *Golda Slept Here*, 19.

East Jerusalem, where the author sneaks to meet her friends, is part of Palestinian land that remains under Israeli occupation. Its Arab inhabitants are under constant threat of losing their homes or of being deported because of the growing number of house confiscations and Jewish immigration. For the author to sneak "illegally" to East Jerusalem and then to West Jerusalem is as serious a crime as a Palestinian "sans papiers" can commit.[19] The author and her friends' trip to their old houses shows how spatial resistance to colonial presence is still possible despite the passage of time and the legal maze that Israel creates to stamp out Palestinian presence. The movement across land and the artifices characters invent to cross checkpoints such as smoking, listening to "a Lady Gaga CD" while in the car waiting for security clearance capture the absurdity of life under colonialism and the randomness of subjugation.[20] With humor and ridicule, the diary caricatures such moments, namely crossing "illegally" in one's own country and being checked, stopped, or searched at any moment; for without laughter the pain of enduring colonial grip and the "unfairness of the present" becomes unsurmountable.[21]

The interplay of the legal and illegal in the text exposes the unfairness of the legality that underpins international and colonial laws. In the text, Amiry records the legal theft of Palestinian houses and properties that fell, according to the United Nations, under the territories that formed the state of Israel in 1948. The theft, that of slicing a large part of Palestinian lands, destroying towns, and erasing villages in order to form Israel, has never been acknowledged or even condemned because it is legal under international law. The text highlights seminal moments in the history of Palestine by switching from narrative prose to free verse poetry. For example, "They [the British] Missed Mama's Cooking" narrates the tragedy of "4 May 1948" in the most plausible and mundane way possible: "Having fulfilled their promise/A Jewish state over Palestine/The British packed up and went home."[22] International law—a tool in the hands of colonial powers—is the law of the powerful as they coerce the weak into forced acceptance, engineered by great political players regardless of the human and environmental cost. Amiry's text opens a new conversation from the victims' perspectives, the people whose lives have been shattered, and pro-

[19] Amiry, *Golda Slept Here,* 75.
[20] Amiry, *Golda Slept Here,* 76.
[21] Amiry, *Golda Slept Here,* 77.
[22] Amiry, *Golda Slept Here,* 14.

vides intimate insights into Palestinian lives as impacted by international legal decisions, namely the creation of Israel.

The legality of appropriating Palestinian houses by Israel, an extension of British colonial laws, is another focal point the text examines by delineating the lives of the protagonists as they grapple with the absurdity of the Israeli legal system. The space occupied by *homo sacer* in Roman jurisdiction is analogous to that of Palestinians living in Israel, Gaza, and the West Bank. Employed to design outcasts who are killed with impunity but without sacrificial values, the concept captures the devalued Palestinian lives.[23] Therefore, the question of legality and illegality cannot be applied to Palestinians who inhabit the in-between space that the Muselmann occupied in Auschwitz, a term used by Agamben to refer to Auschwitz's prisoners, the living dead of the camp: they are "the human that cannot be told from the inhuman."[24] In other words, the law, aimed at stripping Palestinians of their humanity, resists seeing the unhoused as victims. The composition exposes this by mapping the sufferings of those whose existence have been reduced to nullity. Amiry's text narrates her two-day trip to East and West Jerusalem with two of her friends as they cross the Green Line on an illegal trip to Israel.[25] The documentation of the trip is meant to humanize the Palestinian suffering by reviving intimate memories and evoking the pain of those who lost their homes. Their loss becomes more acute when they are treated by Israel's judiciary system as absentees—the closest term to *homines sacri* and *Muselmann*.[26] Despite being physically present in court and having all the necessary documentation to prove the ownership of their houses, Palestinian are still considered "absent" and are treated as living dead.

Andoni Baramki, a pioneering Palestinian architect who lost his two houses during the wars of 1948 and 1967, tried many times to plead his

---

[23] Zalloua, *Continental Philosophy and the Palestinian Question*, 44.

[24] Georgio Agamben, *Remnants of Auschwitz*, trans. Daniel Heller-Roazen (New York: Zone Books, 1999), 81–2.

[25] In *Crossing the Green Line between the West Bank and Israel*, Avram Bornstein defines the Green Line as "Jordanian-Israeli armistice line that separates the West Bank from Israel" and "shape[s] everyday life, more than ever, in the opportunities to make a living." Also called the 1949 Armistice Line and recognized by the United Nations as the official border of Israel, the Green Line fell under Israeli control in 1967. Avram, *Crossing the Green Line*, ix.

[26] Absentees Property Law is a law designed by Israel to confiscate Palestinian properties. See the law provisions, pdf retrieved from The Knesset, accessed: September 15, 2020, https://www.knesset.gov.il/review/data/eng/law/kns1_property_eng.pdf

case in Israeli courts and failed because he is an absentee. His experience bears witness to how colonialism operates in an absurd world of illegitimate legality. The judge explains: "Mr Baramki; there are hundreds of thousands of Arabs who are considered absentees, just like you. All Palestinian refugees, whether present or absent, are considered absentees."[27] The boundaries between logic and illogic are not only blurred but Israel employs nonsensical sophistry to deny the presence of Palestinians: "Needless to say, in a country where nothing makes sense only crazy acts do."[28] The legal maze that Baramki has to deal with until his death, causing his continuous laughter, articulates how the concept of victimhood is manipulated and distorted by Israel to favor Jewish immigrants at the expense of Palestinians. The case of Baramki is representative of the Palestinian condition and the founding principle of Israel and its legal system. The fact that "The Israelis make sure that they remain the only victims" remains a significant component of drafting laws that ostracize Palestinians outside Israel's jurisdiction.[29] In *Golda Slept Here*, houses are indexical of loss and retrieval, forgetfulness and remembering, and the presence of the absence as a haunting ubiquity that unsettles the colonial settler's official discourse on nationalism and redemption. Andoni Baramki devoted his life to pleading his case in Israeli courts and lost his mind in this process. His son, Gabi, embraces his father's legacy through the painful act of remembering and signaling the prolonged suffering and loss across past, present, and future Palestinian generations.

The story of Baramki's houses is a telling instance for inheriting loss and pain as a family's legacy. Gabi goes to Jerusalem and patiently queues in front of his family's house, which was lost in 1967. The scene dramatizes his despair and helplessness, for his own house has been turned into "The Tourjeman Post Museum." He waits outside with a queue of Israeli youth who are not even born when the house came under attack and was later used as a Jewish military post before it fell under Israeli occupation in 1967. The house "was once the last Israeli outpost overlooking the convoys" of Palestinians leaving their homes after the annexation of the West Bank and Gaza.[30] The author juxtaposes in the same chapter two stories of the same house that cannot be reconciled: the museum-transformed house

[27] Amiry, *Golda Slept Here*, 50.
[28] Amiry, *Golda Slept Here*, 76.
[29] Amiry, *Golda Slept Here*, 10.
[30] Amiry, *Golda Slept Here*, 62.

to celebrate Israel's national unity and Gabi's family home. In Gabi's mind, the converted space is a narrative of loss and colonial brutality, epitomizing his family's uprooted existence. There is an unbridgeable difference between the Palestinian and Israeli conceptions of the land and its history. In Said's words, "There is no way I know to reconcile the messianic-driven and Holocaust-driven impulse of the Zionist with the Palestinian," ending his thoughts on a gloomy note: "the essence of the conflict is its irreconcilability."[31] The divide triggered by the annexation of East Jerusalem in 1967 had an enduring effect on the lives of the Palestinians and resulted in the loss of all Palestine and other Arab territories: "East Jerusalem, the West Bank and Gaza strip, as well as Syria's Golan heights and Egypt's Sinai desert."[32] Amiry's "illegal" trip to Jerusalem comes after the two intifadas, which resulted in the tightening control over Palestinian movement in the colonized territories and the revocation of their work permits in Israel. The narrative gestures toward consolidating the irreconcilability of the Palestinian and Israeli positions by focusing on the impact of Israel's colonial wars, land-loss, property theft, and colonial aggression.

In his forward to *The Wretched of the Earth*, Homi Bhabha argues that colonial law does not only subjugate the colonized subject in an attempt to make them inferior, but enacts injustice as fairness as long as it helps in the process of land appropriation or settlement: "dominated but not domesticated. He is made to feel inferior, but by no means convinced of his inferiority," and thus "the colonized knows no authority."[33] By implication, Palestinians who lost their homes have not lost sight, despite the passage of time, their memories are lived and relived every time they encounter Israeli soldiers, stop at checkpoints, or visit their own properties. For the author and the protagonists, there is no sign of memories receding or waning with time and dislocation, making resistance to occupation and hope for future delivery a staple Palestinian trait. Literature and life narratives postulate the possibilities of return and the imperative to weave the personal into the political in art to resist.

---

[31] Edward Said, "My Right of Return," in *Power, Politics, and Culture: Interviews with Edward W. Said*, ed. Gauri Viswanathan (New York: Vintage, 2001), 447–8.

[32] Amiry, *Golda Slept Here*, 40.

[33] Homi Bhabha, forward to Franz Fanon, *The Wretched of the Earth*, trans. Richard Philcox (New York: Grove Press, 1963), xxxviii.

Golda Slept Here is a self-reflective cross-generic text that incorporates Palestinian conditions inside the occupied land—that grounds the experiences of its protagonists in the everyday life of colonialism—and authenticates the history of lost houses that are still standing and able to tell their stories against continued attempts of erasure. The text, a composition set at the intersection of a myriad of genres, defies standard generic boundaries, while at the same time defining new ones by witnessing the author and the protagonists challenge the rigid Israeli constraints on their movements—notwithstanding the travel permits that are almost impossible to get to visit Jerusalem.[34] Despite strict security checks, the separation wall, checkpoints, other forms of abuse, and intimidation, Amiry and her female protagonists jump all the hurdles and get to the houses of their childhood memories. The focus on space and its cultural and historical significance defines *Golda Slept Here*, a text tied to its space; that is, the Palestine they used to know before 1948 and their colonized land that they try to grapple with and understand now. The text explicates the ubiquity of mobility as synonymous with freedom and thus defiance. Moving within the colonized space of pre-1948 by evoking past memories is an overriding theme and a key structuring device that unifies *Golda Slept Here* with many of Palestinian literary works. The urgency to lay claim to the land Israel occupied in 1948 and 1967 and the ongoing land confiscation is evocative of the past/present dichotomy of the Palestinian plight.

In the text as in life, the Palestinian-Israeli struggle is most articulate when it comes to remembering and recording the past and present of the land. Palestinian land rhetoric is intertwined with their defeat in 1948 and 1967 and the bitter experiences of refugee status and scattering to new areas within their own land or to far-flung countries. The dismembering of the land is compounded by a visceral fear of their own disrupted memories. Personal memories, argues Lila Abu-Lughod in "Return to Half-Ruins," are a legacy bound with present lives, never abating, always floating, because the loss of Palestine and the destruction of lives have never been recognized or redressed.[35] Unlike the Holocaust, the Nakba

---

[34] The only one who managed to get a Jerusalem ID is the author's dog Nura. As crazy as it seems, the soldier at the checkpoint is convinced that Nura has the right to be driven to Jerusalem by her owner since "she" has the right paper. See Suad Amiry, *Sharon and my Mother-in-Law* (Norwell, MA: Anchor Press, 2005), 108.

[35] See Lila Abu-Lughod, "Return to Half-Ruins: Memory, Postmemory, and Living History in Palestine," in *Nakba: Palestine, 1948, and the Claims of Memory*, eds. Lila Abu-Lughod and Ahmad H. Sa'di (New York: Columbia University Press. 2007), 77–104.

has never been "denounced" and its horror is still unfolding: "memory and post memory have a special valence because the past has not yet passed."[36] Abu-Lughod's writing on her father's life and his legacy as a Palestinian scholar and activist exemplifies how the personal in the colonized context becomes history: memoirs become a political tool to inscribe the personal into the wider context of the political and historical struggle of the subaltern to be heard and for the silenced to break through the cracks of the thundering Zionist discourse despite its hegemony and military might. The Arab houses therefore bear witness to the fragility not only of the dispossessed but also to the occupiers who are frightened and unsettled by the visits of the legitimate owners despite their relatively cushioned position in modern day Israel. Fanon's contribution with regard to the colonizer's relation to the past of the colonized helps to understand how the past is more challenging than the present they control through violence and military force.[37] The past of Palestine before 1948 and 1967 is still felt, lived, and passed to future generations despite colonial attempts of falsification and legal manipulation in order to transform legitimacy into an irrelevant anachronistic discourse. *Golda Slept Here* articulates the urgent need to remember by continually mapping the history of land in order to negotiate its present and resist its loss.

The sub-title of the diary, *Palestine: The Presence of the Absent*, creates what Fanon calls "the perverted logic" of Israeli attempts to erase Palestine from the map of memory/history.[38] The past carried out by people's collective memory resides in people's everyday lives, the literature they write, and the songs they recite. In this text, Palestinians trying to go to Israel in an attempt to see their houses and towns and seek cosmic harmony with a bond that cannot be broken, even in the face of forced exile and extreme colonial measures of wiping the past of the land. Palestinians within Palestine and Israel are a bloc of resistance and the ultimate bastion against which colonial hope of effacement is shattered. In her lecture "Shadows of the Absent Body," Judith Butler evokes mourning in its materiality through living objects that stand as testimonies to the loss of the

---

[36] Abu-Lughod, "Return to Half-Ruins," 79. For the continuity of Nakba and the prolongation of pain see Rosemary Sayigh, "On the Exclusion of the Palestinian Nakba from the "Trauma Genre," *Journal of Palestine Studies* 43, no. 1 (2013): 51–60.

[37] Franz Fanon, *The Wretched of the Earth*, trans. Richard Philcox (New York: Grove Press, 1963), 210–11.

[38] Fanon, *The Wretched of the Earth*, 210.

inhabitable world.[39] In commenting on the Harvard art gallery about art and mourning loss, she argues the significance of mourning against the overwhelming power of oblivion and how art objects; art's production becomes the representative of both vulnerability and resistance.[40] The loss of the inhabitable space and the practice of mourning are dominant traits in Palestinian art and literature. In *Gold Slept Here* the protagonists, who are real people inhabiting real space, transformed the colonial presence into a surreal world of illogic and ridicule.

The testimonial in Palestinian art, namely life narratives, is instrumental in mapping and conjugating colonial subjugation and resistance in real-life contexts. This genre is carefully devised to resist cultural and physical effacement; the testimonial in Palestinian art is a process of mourning that engages a people's loss under dire colonial presence. The narrative discourse exposes the colonized vulnerability in the face of colonial violence and international silence. Israel, portrayed by many Western democracies as the only democracy in the Middle East, enacts a form of legality to justify the confiscation of houses in 1948 and 1967. The asymmetry between justice as a continuous struggle and a human strife and colonial legality exposes the lack of accountability for the powerful and their impunity. Colonial laws segregating nature acknowledge only Jews as legal entities and reject Palestinians' cases on racial and religious ground as simply absent despite their presence.

Boundaries and the Colonized Space in *Out of It* (2011): Gaza and the Outside World

Border negotiations are a way of life for the occupied when the occupier continually shifts boundaries. The 369 checkpoints and the numerous road-blocks characterize the relationship between two people living in one land. Selma Dabbagh's text resists borders while representing them as realities amid the open prison of Gaza and the numerous checkpoints and other barricades to stop people from moving. *Out of It*, the debut novel of Selma Dabbagh, a British Palestinian writer, is set in Gaza during a series of Israeli air raids. The Mujahed family—Sabri, Rashid, and his twin sister

---

[39] See Judith Butler, "Shadows of the Absent Body," YouTube, March 2, 2017, Menschel Hall, Harvard Art Museums, Cambridge, MA, 1:40:48, https://www.youtube.com/watch?v=9o9_ZP2Z7aI

[40] See Judith Butler, "Shadows of the Absent Body."

Iman, along with their mother—lives on the first floor of a two-story house, the only standing building on a demolished block. The father, Jibril, lives in Kuwait with his girlfriend and sends the family money. Like Jibril, every character wants to flee Gaza in one way or another. Gaza is compared to a concentration camp in a Holocaust-like setting. The room where Iman meets the Women's Committee is "the type of room you would find in a holocaust museum."[41] Sabri, who lost his wife and child and is crippled as a result of an Israeli air strike, spends his time reading and writing about the history of the Palestinian/Israeli conflict. In his search to historicize the conflict objectively, he realizes the difficulties of such an endeavor. As a militant who had an active role in Palestinian youth and student organizations before and during the Intifada, Sabri's studying is bound to call the past into the present. Yet Sabri treats this as an experience of exploring the self rather than the enemy, as a means to judge one's failure rather than to lay the blame on the enemy: "He, Sabri Mujahed knew the truth. Our neighbours collaborated with them when they took our country in 1948. Our stinking feudal system allowed for that."[42] Nevertheless, Sabri's ideas and scholarly search inspire Rashid, who wins a scholarship and goes to London for a Master's degree.

The events of the novel draw heavily on the phantasmagoria, the delirium-based world Rashid inhabits thanks to his much loved Gloria, the hashish tree he nurtures and cultivates in his room in Gaza: "Her soil was moist, her leaves were green. Everything about her was captivating, luscious, plentiful. She was divine."[43] He cares a lot about his Gloria, depicted as sensuous, beautiful, and tempting, and hates his mother for not caring for "her" while he was in London studying. Gloria helps him survive the raids by providing pure, well-tended Hashish. Gaza's bombing nightmares are consistently endured by "royally" smoking Hashish at night, watching the rockets light the skies in a pitch black night: "His perception was cushioned and brightened by Gloria's leaves."[44] When he moves to London, Rashid continues to secure hash for himself and his English roommate, Ian, from a Moroccan snooker bar. Always stoned and drunk while walking the streets of London, as if the world he moves in physically was not real, Rashid does not focus on his studies and ends up in prison in a case

---

[41] Selma Dabbagh, *Out of It*, (Doha: Bloomsbury Qatar Foundation, 2011), 7.
[42] Dabbagh, *Out of It*, 103.
[43] Dabbagh, *Out of It*, 27.
[44] Dabbagh, *Out of It*, 3.

5 MOBILITY, INCARCERATION, AND THE POLITICS OF RESISTANCE...   105

of mixed identity, charged for supplying illegal substances. He is detained and later released with an order of deportation. Hash plays a crucial role in the dramatic structure of the novel and the portrayal of Rashid. Rashid's use of hash becomes a device for imaginary border crossings between various places and times in the narrative. His altered perception of events, namely Israeli raids, affords a new vision to life outside the catastrophes of war, poverty, and corrupt Palestinian leaders who fight for power and money. The world he sees creates a new reality that lays outside real time and space.

Unlike Rashid, Iman is more involved in the politics and humanitarian work in her community. After the devastating air raids and the death of two people, Iman starts looking for ways to fight back, which makes her vulnerable to being recruited and radicalized by religious militant groups. These groups perpetrate terrorist attacks of no significance, but with grave consequences for the people in Gaza. Before getting entangled in such schemes, her father's PLO friends arrange for her departure to Kuwait.[45] After a short stay in the Gulf, she moves to London to study. While in London she briefly dates an English man and has her first sexual experience. The novel breaks away from the rhetoric of blame and addresses issues such as Palestinian failure, escape, and betrayal, collaboration with the enemy, and corruption, a common denominator of the National Authority leaders: "*The corruption! The corruption! The corruption.*"[46] The novel is a pentalogy and is divided according to the spatial movement of its characters: Gaza Skies, London Views, Gulf Interiors, London Crowds, and the Gazan Sea.

The geographical space where Iman and Rashid move is contrasted with the world of their wheelchair-bound brother, Sabri, and all Gazans who are defined as "amputees": "the siege have made amputees of all of us, crawling around the mud, legless in Gaza."[47] The narrative space's important scenes occur in Gaza where Gazans populate the bombed and sieged town along with the burnt bodies, the destroyed camps, and wailing mothers. "Gazan Skies" is followed by "London Views" where Rashid goes to study and meets his girlfriend's family in their nestling village house at the heart of the English countryside. Unlike Rashid's physical

---

[45] Palestinian Liberation Organization, referred to after the Oslo Agreement as the National Authority and the return of some of its leaders.

[46] Dabbagh, *Out of It*, 79.

[47] Dabbagh, *Out of It*, 107.

escape, Sabri's escape is solely intellectual in nature and is arguably more significant because his voice affords a serious commitment to a better understanding of the conflict. His research into the history of the present, the events that are happening now, as well as the past that informs the present, is paralleled with the research of Rashid on a similar topic at an unnamed university in London. As we learn from Rashid's narrative the study of colonialism in a colonial country is flawed and remains limited, for knowledge is always shaped by power and money. The brief "Gulf Interiors" where Iman is forced to go in order to escape the Islamic terrorist group that recruited her offers insights into the affluent life of her father. Jibril enjoys his whiskey, designer clothes, and gilded cigarette box, removed from Gaza and his family, and exposes the materiality, shallowness, and superficiality of life in Kuwait. All characters are dwarfed by their mother, whose affinities with the land are symbolically linked to her small garden and her disabled son. Her love for the land extends toward all the neighbors who lost their homes and whose pain she tries to alleviate by offering them a place to sleep, wash, and eat after the execution of their neighbor, who, it is revealed, is a spy working for Israel. Her role in the novel highlights the role of mothers in Palestinian resistance. Sabri and his mother spend a lot of time together gossiping and discussing his mother's role in the armed resistance. She turns to be the famous plane hijacker Leila Khaled of the Palestinian Popular Front.

The conflation of imagination with reality and the fictionalization of a real person's life, namely Leila Khaled, solidify the real dimension within the surreal space of Gaza. This space is a sea of pain that holds people together and keeps them afloat despite the apocalyptic scenes of utter devastation that surround them. The physical reality of the novel is the macabre that shrouds Gaza and its inhabitants, which the narrator finds difficult to convey in language; yet, the narrative technique incorporates the atrocities in Gaza by deploying cinematographic sequences that paint the tableaux-vivant of raids and falling bombs. The pictorial rendering of characters' movements and actions, even when they are somewhere else, conjures Gaza. Theodor Adorno states in his "Cultural Criticism and Society" that "To write poetry after Auschwitz is barbaric. And this corrodes even the knowledge of why it has become impossible to write poetry today."[48] This suggests the unrepresentability of extreme horror and unwarranted

---

[48] Theodor Adorno, *Prisms*, trans. Samuel and Shierry Weber (Cambridge: MIT Press, 1983), 34.

5 MOBILITY, INCARCERATION, AND THE POLITICS OF RESISTANCE... 107

cruelty, such as the concentration camps and gas chambers. Dabbagh's *Out of It* coalesces a conglomerate of images and emotions, including those happening in Rashid's stoned mind, into realities that resist reification. The barbarity of what is happening in Gaza evades representability. In his article, "Gaza: Poetry after Auschwitz," Hamid Dabachi suggests that what happened in Gaza in 2014 offers significant insights into Adorno's "uncanny sentence," which reads as a "metaphor that points decades forward to Gaza."[49] The importance of Adorno's claim in relation to Gaza, according to Dabachi, exposes the bloody history of Zionism in Palestine and its cruelty amid the silence of the world.[50]

The novel's setting draws heavily on apocalyptic scenes that frame its sinister surrounding. Gazan Mediterranean Sea, depicted as both a refuge and a threat, is juxtaposed to the consuming sea of violence and devastation. Forming a barrier that further isolates Gaza, the sea and the sky seem to intensify the suffering of Gazans. The sea, in particular, is personified and her anger is translated through the threatening waves that gain momentum every time Israeli raids and military incursion hit the land. The creation of such fantastic surroundings conjures up the maddening realities on the ground: bombing, killing, and charred and decomposed bodies under the sizzling heat of a Gazan summer day. Gaza in the text becomes synonymous with and a symbol of Auschwitz. The novel itself is bearing witness to excesses of violence: the slaughter of Gazans and their imprisonment in an open-air prison wherein their suffering is met with more killing and raids. The moral failure of the world with regard to such catastrophes is made more acute by the "debilitating factor in the ability to tell their stories and make public their memories," which "the powerful

[49] Hamid Dabachi, "Gaza: Poetry after Auschwitz," *Aljazeera*, August 8, 2014, https://www.aljazeera.com/opinions/2014/8/8/gaza-poetry-after-auschwitz. The 2014 Gaza invasion is also known as Operation Protective Edge, launched on July 8, 2014, and resulted in the killing of 2200 Palestinian, the majority of them civilian. See "World Report 2015: Israel/Palestine," Human Right Watch, 2015, https://www.hrw.org/world-report/2015/country-chapters/israel/palestine

[50] See for example, Robert Mackey, "Israelis Watch Bombs Drop on Gaza from Front-Rows Seats," *The New York Times*, July 14, 2014, https://www.nytimes.com/2014/07/15/world/middleeast/israelis-watch-bombs-drop-on-gaza-from-front-row-seats.html?_r=1. Lizzie Dearden, "Israel-Gaza Conflict: 50-day war by Numbers," *The Independent*, August 27, 2014, https://www.independent.co.uk/news/world/middle-east/israel-gaza-conflict-50-day-war-by-numbers-9693310.html. Kate, "Tomorrow there's no school in Gaza, they don't have any children left'—Israeli chant," *Mondoweiss*, July 28, 2014, https://mondoweiss.net/2014/07/tomorrow-children-israeli/

108   L. AOUADI

nations have not wanted to listen."[51] The seminal event that changed Palestinian lives in 1948, Nakba, is still unfolding in the present, blurring the lines between the present and the past.[52] Rashid's character is of particular significance insofar as his presence enhances the novelistic modes by creating an imaginary space, a new narrative channel to express what the conventional temporal and spatial demarcation of language cannot convert into plausible meaning. Always high and constantly paranoid, Rashid's heavy hash consumption blurs the borders between what happens in his mind and what occurs in Gaza. Moving across the ruins of Gaza, flying the skies of the bombed and ablaze landscape, riding the waves of the Mediterranean Sea, running through the minefields, and bleeding to death are sequences from the mind of a character who has wanted to flee Gaza and failed. In other words, the heavy home-made hash he consumes daily is of no help in attenuating his pain.[53] However, and, in transcending borders and barbed wires, the narrative end relies heavily on magical realism to dramatize the composition's struggle with the incapacitating power of Gaza, blocking the conveyance of the intricacies and quasi-impossibility of representing through language Gaza, the relentless raids, and the traumatized human mind.

The novel relies on contrasting spaces and dramatizing geographical distances; in so doing, it foregrounds the destruction of Gaza as a haunting presence, a curse that torments the characters who think they can get on with their lives and forget by living "out of it." A juxtaposition of London with Gaza happens inside Rashid's mind, who doesn't know what it means to have a normal life, a house, a permanent home. London is cruel in its indifference, its complicity, and British imperialism is an ever-present specter, only sometimes seen, but always present. Furthermore, Iman notes that Kuwait is another space that lacks the heritage and culture, as well as the freedom and multiculturalism of London. The Gulf is rich and opulent, but empty and superficial with its big malls, suffocating heat, and Asian workers who seem to be the only visible human presence that Iman sees. As she experiences it, Kuwait is a big air-conditioned cave where people live, earn money, and forget themselves in the materiality of life. The novel therefore articulates the characters' awareness of their

[51] Abu-Lughod, "Return to Half-Ruins," 11.

[52] Joe Sacco, *Footnotes in Gaza: A Graphic Novel* (London: Palgrave, 2000), xi.

[53] Note that Gaza is on the Mediterranean coast and like many Mediterranean towns its land is good for planting Hash.

belonging to Gaza as a destiny that they have to embrace within and without the Gazan space. Furthermore, these experiences underscore Gaza as an all-encompassing sky and sea of pain and expose London, Kuwait, and the whole world for failing Gazans.

Places such as cities and countries carry a profound symbolic dimension in the novel; they are maneuvered dramatically to highlight thematic concerns and the psychological dislocations of characters in Gaza and elsewhere. Siege and deprivation of basic human needs (i.e., running water, sanitation, food, and medication) are Gazan in essence—though there is acknowledgment of other people's suffering, namely the Asian workers in Kuwait who toil under the searing heat of the desert and build more and more flats to house money-seekers and the locals. But, while the depiction of Gaza in *Out of It* can be easily traced to the horror of the Holocaust and concentration camps, it is also a space inhabited by characters with aspirations, focus, and determination to carry on living and fighting. Rashid, the only character who combines the real and the fantastic, the natural and the supernatural, and his twin sister Iman are able to move outside Gaza and align the plight of Palestinians in Gaza with other human catastrophes, namely the situation of "construction workers" in Kuwait whose "newness and foreignness" is sickening for Iman.[54] Construction workers are piled in a "lopsided bus" wearing "blue boiler suits with stenciled numbers sprayed in their backs" they were jumping out of "the bus and swinging multi-layered tin canisters, T-shirts wrapped around their heads, ragged checked scarves tied to their necks."[55] These images are contrasted with Jibril, Iman's father, who talks about the suffering of Palestinians in his air-conditioned car and his designer clothes while his daughter is glancing at "his horse embossed" T-Shirt he is wearing.[56] Kuwait is a fantastic world of unpreceded growth where people are caught inside an air-conditioned goldfish bowl, with the exception of construction workers whose situation is akin to modern day slavery. The cultural production of space foregrounds human concerns such as individual or collective pain, encapsulating the unfair division of the world into zones within zones of suffering and dependency. Iman and her brother are bridges between Gaza and the outside world.

---

[54] Dabbagh, *Out of It*, 166.
[55] Dabbagh, *Out of It*, 170.
[56] Dabbagh, *Out of It*, 170.

Gaza in the novel is a byword for hell, and the narrative wrestles to register the pain of Gazans through the characters' confusion, desperation, and helplessness in the face of "the forces of destruction."[57] The oppressiveness of the place and vulnerability of people are channeled through religiosity and the prevalence of religious parties. Iman seems to be the only unveiled woman in Gaza, and is the only one who moves freely in the public space, smokes, and is, of course, conspicuously at odds with her milieu. She thus becomes a source of gossip in her community. The novel relates suicide bomb attacks on Israeli civilians that are carried out in public spaces by radicalized young women. Iman is recruited to carry an attack on Israeli targets, but is stopped by an official from the National Authority. People do not condone suicide bombers, but Islamists see them as resistance and an integral part of their political agenda to confront Israeli state terror. Importantly, these suicide bombers are referred to as dupes and puppets at the hands of various religious political players. The novel denounces the use of violence while showing the position of people who, when faced with the atrocities of war and poverty, become radicalized and carry out desperate attacks.

The novel engages religious radicalization in Gaza and political Islam's ability to persuade people to their views, especially young men and women. Though not uniquely a Palestinian phenomenon, radicalization is a worldwide concern and also resonates among Muslims who are born in the West. Youth vulnerability to terrorist organizations looms large in the narrative, alongside political corruption and colonialism—two important variables for radicalization. Israel's terrorist attacks are more frequent, holding the whole city hostage. The condition of Sabri, who lost legs, his wife, and baby in an Israeli attack, exemplifies the destructive effect of Israeli bombs on people's life and minds. Sabri, whose life stands as a symbol for the predicament of his people, is a source of hope and endurance for all the characters. Other characters, such as the mother and Rashid, are umbrageous sketches of inchoate personas who take their cues from memories and, in the case of Rashid, from the delirium of a stoned mind. Rashid's substance abuse not only makes it difficult to disentangle facts from fiction, but also, unsurprisingly, affects his decision-making. Unlike Sabri who compensates for his loss by fully immersing himself in his study and research, Rashid copies from his brother's emails and notes in order to write his thesis in London. Both brothers' research into the history of

[57] Dabbagh, *Out of It*, 96.

5 MOBILITY, INCARCERATION, AND THE POLITICS OF RESISTANCE...

Palestine exposes the failure of political fractions, namely the left and the National Authority, to help relieve the pain of Palestinians. The Islamists, on the other hand, are gaining momentum by capitalizing on the corruption and incompetence of outside leadership.[58] *Out of It* pairs education and knowledge to fight Israel and Islamism. The internet is an important tool to reach the outside world and social media is a weapon that the characters resort to as a means to break the Israeli siege. Crimes can no longer be hidden from the eyes of the world and Gaza has acquired such an unpreceded fame that it has become a symbol, a cause, and the epitome of Israeli racial cleansing in the occupied land. As a result, border crossing has become virtual as well as physical in this global age.

Both *Out of It* and *Golda Slept Here* are sites of negotiation, resistance, and hope despite the bleak conditions caused by the economic and social policies of the colonizers. Borders are terrains for staging resistance by dramatizing characters' movements in *Golda Slept Here* and *Out of It*. Notwithstanding their focus on the mundane, these texts are consciously crafted in order to politicize Palestinians' everyday life under siege and imprisonment whereby the intimate becomes political and a platform for resistance. Interwoven with momentous political events such as the two Intifadas, the invasion and the siege of Ramallah, the bombing of Gaza, or the revocation of work permits for Palestinian workers, private lives become the embodiment of suffering under colonial violence. In both works, humor is part of the dramatic fabric of the narratives because even in the face of despair and helplessness, humor creates solidarity and constitutes important relationships. The absurdity of living under arbitrary colonial laws manifest in all sectors of Palestinian public and private lives is endured largely by the need to move and cross boundaries. The intended aim of colonial policies, namely subjugation, humiliation,

---

[58] Modern terrorism, nonetheless, is based on a literal reading of the Koran that transcends current contexts and Daesh (ISIS) or Taliban are instances of how Wahhabism can easily go wrong. Wahhabism is an ideology first initiated by Najd scholar Muhammad Ibn Abd el Wahhab (1703–91), who formed an alliance with Muhammad Ibn Saud in 1747 and resulted in the establishment of Saudi Arabia, fusing religion and politics to secure its continuity and legitimacy. Dominant more in Saudi Arabia and Qatar, and less appealing in other parts of the Islamic world, Wahhabism values the study of Islam and Sharia over all studies. Its puritanical, rigid interpretation of Islam still forms the basis of extreme reformists and terrorists' views on the Islamic nation or the concept of Umma. See for example, Karen Armstrong, "Wahhabism to Isis: how Saudi Arabia Exported the Main Source of Global Terrorism," *The New Statesman*, November 27, 2020, https://www.newstatesman.com/world-affairs/2014/11/wahhabism-isis-how-saudi-arabia-exported-main-source-global-terrorism

impoverishment, and all forms of control, is hallowed out by the Palestinian spirit of survival through patience. In the deeply spatial works of Suad Amiry and Selma Dabbagh, characters resist incarceration by always being on the move. Much like the characters' mobility, these texts move between fiction and reality, the biographical and the historical, and the comic and the tragic, and in so doing the two compositions resist Western generic classification.

Works Cited

"Absentees' Property Law." *The Knesset*. Accessed September 15, 2020. https://www.knesset.gov.il/review/data/eng/law/kns1_property_eng.pdf

Abu-Lughod, Lila. "Return to Half-Ruins: Memory, Postmemory, and Living History in Palestine." In *Nakba: Palestine, 1948, and the Claims of Memory*, edited by Lila Abu-Lughod and Ahmad H. Sa'di, 77–104. New York: Columbia University Press, 2007.

Adorno, Theodor W. *Prisms*. Translated by Samuel and Shierry Weber. Cambridge: MIT Press. 1983.

Agamben, Georgio. *Remnants of Auschwitz*. Translated by Daniel Heller-Roazen. New York: Zone Books, 1999.

Amiry, Suad. *Golda Slept Here: Palestine: the Presence of the Absent*. Doha: Bloomsbury Qatar Foundation Publishing, 2014.

———. *Sharon and my Mother-in-Law*. Norwell, MA: Anchor Press, 2005.

Bhabha, Homi. K. Foreword to *The Wretched of the Earth*, xii–xli. Text by Frantz Fanon. New York: Grove Press 2004.

Bornstein, Avram. *Crossing the Line between the West Bank and Israel*. Philadelphia: Pennsylvania State University Press, 2002.

Bransky, Robert. *Wall and Piece*. London: Century, 2005.

Butler, Judith. "Shadows of the Absent Body," YouTube, March 2, 2017. Menschel Hall, Harvard Art Museums, Cambridge, MA. 1:40:48. https://www.youtube.com/watch?v=9o9_ZP2Z7aI

Dabachi, Hamid, "Poetry after Auschwitz." *Aljazeera*, August 8, 2014. https://www.aljazeera.com/indepth/opinion/2014/08/gaza-poetry-after-auschwitz-20148715341896737 1.html

Dabbagh, Selma. *Out of It*. Doha: Bloomsbury Qatar Foundation, 2011.

Dearden, Lizzie. "Israel-Gaza Conflict: 50-day war by Numbers." *The Independent*, August 27, 2014. https://www.independent.co.uk/news/world/middle-east/israel-gaza-conflict-50-day-war-by-numbers-9693310.html

Deleuze, Gilles. "*What is the Creative Act?*" In *Two Regimes of Madness: Texts and Interviews 1975–1995*, edited by David Lapoujade. Translated by Ames Hodges and Mike Taormina, 312–324. New York: Semiotext(e), 2007.

Fanon, Franz. *The Wretched of the Earth*. Translated by Richard Philcox. New York: Grove Press, 1963.

Harlow, Barbara. *Resistance Literature*. New York: Routledge, 1987.

Hogan, Rebecca. "Engendered Autobiographies: The Diary as a Feminine Form." In *Autobiography and the Question of Gender*, edited by Shirley Neuman, 77–106. London: Frank Cass, 1991.

Kanafani, Ghassan, *Adab Al Mouqawama fi Falstin al Mohtala: 1948–1966*. Cyprus: Rimal Books, 2015.

Kate. "Tomorrow there's no school in Gaza, they don't have any children left'— Israeli chant." *Mondoweiss*, July 28 2014. https://mondoweiss.net/2014/07/tomorrow-children-israeli/

Mackey, Robert. "Israelis Watch Bombs Drop on Gaza from Front-Rows Seats." *The New York Times*, July 14, 2014. https://www.nytimes.com/2014/07/15/world/middleeast/israelis-watch-bombs-drop-on-gaza-from-front-row-seats.html?_r=1

Compan, Magali and Katarzyna Pieprzak. Introduction to *Land and Landscape in Francographic Literature: Remapping Uncertain Territories*, 1–10. Edited by Magali Compan and Katarzyna Pieprzak. New Castle upon Tyne: Cambridge Scholar Press, 2007.

Sacco, Joe. *Footnotes in Gaza: A Graphic Novel*. London: Palgrave, 2000.

Said, Edward. "My Right of Return." In *Power, Politics, and Culture: Interviews with Edward W. Said*, edited by Gauri Viswanathan, 443–58. New York: Vintage, 2001.

Sayigh, Rosemary. "On the Exclusion of the Palestinian Nakba from the 'Trauma Genre.'" *Journal of Palestine Studies* 43, no. 1 (2013): 51–60.

"World Report 2015: Israel/Palestine." Human Right Watch. 2015. https://www.hrw.org/world-report/2015/country-chapters/israel/palestine

Zalloua, Zahi. *Continental Philosophy and the Palestinian Question: Beyond the Jew and the Greek*. London: Bloomsbury, 2017.

CHAPTER 6

Matriarchal Mobility: Generational Displacement and Gendered Place in Marilynne Robinson's *Housekeeping*

Marisa Stickel Higgins

In Marilynne Robinson's *Housekeeping*, the conceptualization of home is complex and heady, constantly shaped by patriarchal ideologies. For the women in the novel, their understanding of the home-place is contrived by their respective interpretations of gender roles, entrapment, loyalty, and femininity. Historically, within a heteronormative culture, a woman's "proper" place has been confined to the private sphere, relegating her to tasks that coincide with domesticity in the home, which suggests that a life separate from child-rearing and housekeeping is an immoral form of social decorum. By confining women to a home-place in order to perform domestic tasks, their mobility is discouraged, prohibited, and/or regulated. Gender-restricted mobility reinforces the notion that a woman's separation or absence from the home is improper or detrimental; thus, how the women in *Housekeeping* engage in mobility reflects their perception of place and gender roles with the subtle undercurrents of Protestanism serving as the backdrop to the text.

M. Stickel Higgins (✉)
University of Tennessee, Knoxville, TN, USA

© The Author(s), under exclusive license to Springer Nature Switzerland AG 2021
C. Beck (ed.), *Mobility, Spatiality, and Resistance in Literary and Political Discourse*, Geocriticism and Spatial Literary Studies,
https://doi.org/10.1007/978-3-030-83477-7_6

115

Housekeeping is a story about (white) womanhood, home, and transience, narrated by Ruth—a young girl whose mother commits suicide. The novel encapsulates the experiences of three generations of women who live within one particular home-space, and the text focuses specifically on Sylvie, a transient who is asked to care for her two nieces after their mother and grandmother pass away. The idea of transience prompts a cry of alarm from the women within the text who view "unrootedness" as a form of impropriety. What is most noticeable about the contention between housekeeping and transience within the text—and how both of these terms characterize a perception of womanhood—is the fact that the Fingerbone home is never able to contain any of the women within the text. All of the women that call the house their "home" in some semblance of the word end up vacating the place. Sylvia is the only woman who remains there to her death, implying that she is the only woman to uphold heteronormative expectations, and that with her death, social decorum also dies as Sylvie's return to the home eradicates all forms of patriarchal oppression. Sylvia's inability to leave the home is in contrast to the women who pass through imperceptibly, staying only briefly after encountering the weight of domesticity. The women who are unable to be contained within the home reject its confinement, displaying how a woman's mobility shapes her perception of womanhood and her identity more generally. Furthermore, the idea of mobility cannot be separated from the concept of displacement, because the terms operate in conjunction together; how bodies move and interact with space is based on a sense of connection, belonging, and security. In other words, displacement has the capacity to shape or hinder mobility.

Women's mobility and (dis)placement are focal points of my argument, which reaffirms how gender identity is central to *Housekeeping,* considering that the novel concentrates on the roles of women and domestic tasks. As I will further elucidate in my argument, the women within the text each have a distinct interaction with the Fingerbone home—and how they move, whether statically or dynamically, is indicative of their identity and femininity. For example, the great aunts who briefly care for Ruth and Lily reject the ideologies of Sylvia's home, overwhelmed by the confinement it imposes. More explicitly, if women cannot move freely, if their intentional movement is restricted, they encounter displacement, a feeling of constraint or expulsion that prohibits their full mobility. Similarly, I use Cameron Duff's methodologies in "On the Role of Affect and the Production of Place" to approach *Housekeeping*. Using Duff's discussion

6 MATRIARCHAL MOBILITY: GENERATIONAL DISPLACEMENT... 117

of affective investment and place production to foreground my own claims, I extend his methodologies to describe how gender intersects with issues of place and affect. In the context of *Housekeeping*, the female characters are positioned within the house uniquely, which contributes to the women's mobility inside and outside of the home-place. Each woman's mobility reflects her understanding of home, as well as the lifestyles that are attached to the affective investment in her particular view of the domiciliary environment.

Moreover, this essay seeks to explore the three generations of women in *Housekeeping*, and their position and/or displacement in the home. I will delineate the different understandings of womanhood, and how these varying definitions and expectations of womanhood significantly influence a woman's mobility and perception of the home-place. This exploration of womanhood will evaluate the influence of matriarchal mobility in the domestic sphere and how it yields displacement by producing women who are either resistant to entering or adamant about matriculating into the heteronormative social constructions of gender identity. More specifically, this essay explores women's movement, how they perceive the limitations and restrictions of movement, how they reject, subvert, or abide by those limitations, and what it suggests about home, gender, and the regulation of women's bodies.

Indubitably, and not surprisingly, there is extensive scholarship on the role of the house in Robinson's *Housekeeping*, because it is impossible to extract the home-space from the connotations of housekeeping, domesticity, and gender. As Elizabeth Klaver emphasizes in "Hobo Time and Marilynne Robinson's *Housekeeping*," the house, lake, and train have received critical attention, as these facets are integral to the novel, nearly functioning as characters in their own rights.[1] *Housekeeping* is a novel about the home, which means that the house takes precedence—it is unavoidable. In "Home-Space in Marilynne Robinson's *Housekeeping*," Fatima Zahra Bessedik illustrates how *Housekeeping* is "a narrative about spatial-crisis."[2] Bessedik does not focus on the detriment of gendered spaces within the text, but rather positions her argument to adopt Christian Norberg Schulz's *Genius Loci* and his theory on "Spirit of Place." Schulz

---

[1] Elizabeth Klaver, "Hobo Time and Marilynne Robinson's Housekeeping," *The Journal of the Midwest Modern Language Association* 43, no. 1(2010): 28.
[2] Fatima Zahra Bessedik, "Home-Space in Marilynne Robinson's *Housekeeping*," *Interdisciplinary Literary Studies* 17, no. 4(2015): 560.

insists that "genius loci," or "spirit of place," is what gives space/place "character" or "identity."[3] Bessedik argues that the home in which the three generation of women inhabit is a maternal space. While this is true, she dismisses the fact that this "maternal sensation" is a ramification of a heteronormative culture that favors proper womanhood and motherhood.[4] The space is imbricated with "maternal sensations," but at the cost of oppressing the women into perpetuating the proper roles of womanhood based on patriarchal culture and ideology. Thus, while Bessedik asserts that Sylvie disrespects the home-space, making it a meaningless space, I claim that it is through Sylvie's "disrespect" that she is able to move freely both inside and outside the home, intermingling the natural world with the constructed home-space. I appreciate Bessedik's recognition of the home-space and her discussion of the "spirit of place," but I contest her anti-feminist approach as she tries to consider the home-space as a male and female "integrated whole."[5] In Bessedik's conclusion, she insists that Robinson interweaves Sylvie's homelessness to highlight that Sylvie "has infected the house like a parasite and plagued it with meaninglessness,"[6] which I refute, positing that it is through Sylvie's homelessness we see her and Ruth embrace transience as a means of self-discovery and identity-forming insurrection.

Continuing this discussion of insurrection, it is pertinent to identify how Sylvie and Ruth's dismissal of the home-space acts as a rejection of heteronormative culture. In "Burning Down the House? Domestic Space and Feminine Subjectivity in Marilynne Robinson's *Housekeeping*," Paula E. Geyh evaluates the role of the home in *Housekeeping* and discusses both female subjectivity and transient subjectivity.[7] Recognizing that the gendered architecture of the Fingerbone home has the capacity to entrap women in the institution of patriarchy, Geyh expounds on Mieke Bal's theories of the "father-house,"[8] insisting that "women can maintain their places within patriarchal systems even in his [the father's] absence."[9] As Geyh explores the task of "housekeeping" and how it contributes to a

[3] Christian Norberg Schulz qtd. in Bessedik, 561.

[4] Bessedik, 561

[5] Bessedik, 571.

[6] Bessedik, 571.

[7] Paula E. Geyh's, "Burning Down the House? Domestic Space and Feminine Subjectivity in Marilynne Robinson's *Housekeeping*," *Contemporary Literature* 34, no. 1(1993).

[8] Mieke Bal qtd. in Paula E. Geyh's, 107.

[9] Geyh, 108.

reification of the father-home and its patriarchal ideologies, she discusses how a woman becomes interpellated within a home-space and "recognizes and constitutes herself as a subject within that place."[10]

Though this is a brief scope of scholarship, it evidences how attention to the house has been privileged and centralized; even more, this overview accentuates the inextricable connection between home and gender. In my own exploration of the house, I choose to extend these conversations about the role of house to consider how this *unlikely place* operates by either holding women hostage and indoctrinating them into a system or forcing them out. While the presence and function of the home is a necessary point of focus in this essay, it serves primarily as a means to discuss women's movement and mobility. In *Queer Phenomenology*, Sara Ahmed postulates, "Bodies do not dwell in spaces that are exterior but rather are shaped by their dwellings and take shape by dwelling."[11] She continues, "Phenomenology reminds us that spaces are not exterior to bodies; instead, spaces are like a second skin that unfolds in the folds of the body."[12] As Ahmed states, spaces and bodies are intimately connected, each influencing the other; but even more, Ahmed inadvertently expresses the significance of affective environments, which connects with Duff's description of affective investments as a place with deep emotional resonance, experiential connections, and habitual routine.[13] As Ahmed writes about queer phenomenology, she describes how the human body and space become interwoven, inextricable; as I will discuss in this essay, it is this second-skin that constrains or influences mobility—it has the capacity to become an ill-fitting article of clothing that restricts many of the women's movements. Some women are able to fully remove themselves from the Fingerbone home, while others physically die within the confinement, suffocated by the home-place and its affective qualities.

In the opening scene of the novel, Ruth's narration conveys an ambiguous sense of displacement as she describes the generation of women who had preceded her in occupying the house in Fingerbone, Idaho: "I grew up with my younger sister, Lucille, under the care of my grandmother, Mrs. Sylvia Foster, and when she died, of her sisters-in-law, Misses Lily and

---

[10] Geyh, 109.

[11] Sara Ahmed, *Queer Phenomenology* (Durham: Duke University Press, 2006), 9.

[12] Ahmed, 9.

[13] Cameron Duff, "On the Role of Affect and Practice in the Production of Place," *Environment and Planning: Society and Space* (2010), 888.

Nona Foster, and when they fled, of her daughter, Mrs. Sylvie Fisher. Through all these generations of elders we lived in one house ... in this *unlikely place.*"[14] Though the text suggests that Fingerbone itself is an "unlikely place" for the family patriarch to settle, the phrase functions dualistically, referencing both the town Fingerbone and the Foster home. Fingerbone, as an unlikely place, is depicted as a mausoleum, holding the literal dead within the lake and the figurative dead, those who are static and unchanging. The Foster home, constructed by the family patriarch Edmund Foster, reflects the sentiment of Fingerbone as it models a similar dynamic, holding its inhabitants captive and bound to continue in a similar pattern of orthodoxy unless they break free.

Thus, the house as an "unlikely place" is immediately characterized as an anchor, a stationary monument that either operates as a place of confinement, a point of return, or a house of destruction; and through all of this, the house tends to displace those who inhabit it. The home remains immobile and static, yet each generation who lives or passes through the home are surrounded by its constant presence: an affectual presence that binds, displaces, or immobilizes its inhabitants. By conceiving of the house as an entity capable of affecting its inhabitants, Robinson positions the house as a place of significance, a mausoleum that chokes out the fresh growth of new ideologies with decaying ones that uphold patriarchal oppression. Similar to the "father-house" theories adapted by Paula E. Geyh's article, the Fingerbone home continues to perpetuate patriarchal ideologies long after Edmund's death. The relationship between the house and the generation of women that passes through the home illustrates how gendered places cause displacement and hinder mobility, which I will further discuss shortly.

In examining each woman positioned in the Fingerbone home, the stigma of gender expectations lingers throughout each generation situated in the house. The first generation of inhabitants are Edmund Foster, the home's builder, and his wife, Sylvia Foster, and their three daughters, Helen, Sylvie, and Molly. The concept of place is a creation rooted in an individual's, or a group of people's, identity, belonging, and emotional resonance.[15] Edmund's agency and investment in patriarchal ideolo-

---

[14] Marilynne Robinson's, *Housekeeping* (New York: Picador, 1980), 3. Emphasis added. Future citations of Robinson's work will be from this edition and will be noted parenthetically by page numbers.

[15] Duff, 881.

gies permeate the home, engendering it to represent a system of power dynamics, which consequently causes generational displacement for the women who occupy the home. As Geyh writes, "The father-house does not require the actual presence of a father; the women can maintain their places within patriarchal systems even in his absence."[16] As proof of this "father-house" theory, Sylvia supports her husband's gendered foundation of the home and executes the lifestyle of matriarch long after his death. Subsequently, she is the only woman within the home who engages in a form of *nonmovement* mobility; she moves according to a sense of domestic obligation, whereas her daughters and sisters move at their own pace, rejecting domesticity. Sylvia maintains the rote movements of someone accustomed to submitting to her husband, the dominant male figure of the household, a distant figure who financially contributes to his family, yet is distant and removed from the innerworkings of their life (10). As Robinson writes, "if immortality was to be this life held in poise and arrest, and if this world urged and this life unconsuming could be thought of as world and life restored to their proper natures" (13). After Edmund's death, Sylvia is frozen in time, static in "poise and arrest"; her actions habitual, familiar, and indicative of the patriarchal culture she continues to uphold, despite their dead, obsolete connotations.

According to Edward S. Casey, the phenomenology of place is understood by how humans experience it; he states the human body "is what links [the] self to lived places in its sensible and perceptible features."[17] Casey also insists that "places come to be embedded in us; they become part of our very self, our enduring character, what we enact and carry forward."[18] Using Casey's theories of place and how place is constructed in the context of *Housekeeping*, it becomes evident that because the Fingerbone home is built by a man, the home endorses heteronormativity and requires gender roles to be upheld. However, Edmund's character is nearly absent from the text, and it is Sylvia's actions that indicate her behavior is a continuation of the life she lived as a wife. The text describes these actions in a number of instances as "performing the rituals of the ordinary" or "the dear ordinary" (15,16). In "Gender, Space," Jane Rendell suggests that power relations are inscribed in built places, and that

---

[16] Geyh, 108.

[17] Edward S. Casey, "Between Geography and Philosophy: What Does It Mean to Be in the Place-World?" *Annals of the Association of American Geographers* 91, no. 4(2001): 683.

[18] Casey, 688.

122   M. STICKEL HIGGINS

there is a relationship between gender and space that defines power relations.[19] Through its very construction and habitation by the same man, the place necessarily becomes imbued with social expectations for women to keep the home maintained, which reiterates the gendered notion of power dynamics cultivated in the creation of place.

After Edmund's tragic passing, Sylvia endures a life of widowhood, and becomes as "good a widow as she had been a wife" (9–10). Sylvia decides to remain at her home and does not consider leaving Fingerbone, as it had been her home for her entire life. This decision designates her house in Fingerbone as a "thick place," which Cameron Duff describes as being "contrived in the imbrications of affect, habit, and meaning … presenting opportunities for 'personal enrichment' and a deepening of affective experience."[20] Her desire to remain in the home expresses a sense of attachment to that place, emphasizing how places "root us—to the earth, to our own history and memories, to our families and larger community."[21] Sylvia's home is a place of affective investment, and due to this, she refuses to leave her home. As Brian Massumi writes, affect is a "dimension of life (vii),"[22] and it has the power to "affect and be affected."[23] Massumi later states, "Bodies can be inducted into, or attuned to, certain regions of tendency, futurity, and potential, they can be induced into inhabiting the same affective environment."[24] Though Sylvia might have an emotional connection, an intensity or affinity to the Fingerbone home, Massumi's discussion of affect suggests that Sylvia has little desire to leave because the home is codified as a patriarchal environment that she has been indoctrinated into. The house encompasses her as a second-skin, so deeply embedded within her that she never questions a form of movement contradictory to domesticity.

Sylvia's movements as a widow are stale and static, appearing ghostlike, reflective of her wifely duties, insisting that the affect that binds her to Fingerbone and her home is a deadly form of patriarchal oppression. Her

---

[19] Jane Rendell, "Gender, Space," in *Gender Space Architecture: An Interdisciplinary Introduction*, eds. Jane Rendell, Barbara Penner, and Iain Borden (New York: Routledge, 2000), 102.

[20] Duff, 882.

[21] Clare Cooper-Marcus and Carolyn Francis., *People Places: Design Guidelines for Urban Open Space* (New York: Wiley & Sons, 1998), xi.

[22] Brian Massumi, *Politics of Affect* (Cambridge: Polity Press, 2015), ix.

[23] Spinoza qtd. in Massumi, ix.

[24] Massumi, 57.

actions cultivate her children's perceptions of this archaic form of womanhood and they respond in a variety of ways: Helen attempts to set up housekeeping and falls into a routine similar to her mother's, but ultimately ends up taking her own life (which speaks volumes about the confinement of womanhood); Molly escapes the realm of domesticity and becomes a missionary in China; Sylvie marries but chooses to act single and live as a transient, embracing her mobility and continual movement through unconfined spaces. Grounded in heteronormativity, which, as I show, shares links to generational displacement, the home functions as a mausoleum, the "proper natures" of patriarchy forcing Sylvia into a familiar groove that she habitually continues to function within. Both Fingerbone and the Foster home represent a grave—a place for the dead, the unmoving—and Sylvia's daughters and her sisters struggle to be contained by the home. Similar to Ahmed's discussion of how bodies are shaped by space and also shape the space, the gendered nature of the Fingerbone home instigates generational displacement; it is this displacement, this constricting second-skin, that initiates how the women within the house move, align, gesture. Prior to Sylvie's unorthodox housekeeping tactics, the women who encounter the residual effects of Sylvia's housekeeping feel displaced, unwelcomed by the Fingerbone home.

Sylvia's actions embody a traditional form of womanhood through her unwavering dedication to her late husband and her three young daughters. Her mobility is located in her role as mother, as "she [has] always known a thousand ways to circle them all around with what must have seemed like grace" (11). Her children revolve around her, interacting with her in a way that exalts her matriarchal mobility—actions that uphold the social constructions of womanhood and the gender ideals of a heteronormative culture. She upholds the sanctity of proper womanhood and motherhood in her tasks, making sure her children are provided for and taken care of within the privacy of their domiciliary:

> She knew a thousand songs. Her bread was tender and her jelly was tart, and on rainy days she made cookies and applesauce. In the summer she kept roses in a vase on the piano, huge, pungent roses, and when the blooms ripened and the petals fell, she put them in a tall Chinese jar, with cloves and thyme and sticks of cinnamon. Her children slept on starched sheets under layers of quilts, and in the morning her curtains filled with light the way sails fill the wind. (12)

124   M. STICKEL HIGGINS

These tasks and actions, while mundane and gendered, magnify her strengths as a codified proper woman within the context of the novel. She performs motherly responsibilities in the domestic realm that exemplify her attachment to her home and children. Furthermore, her dedication to her role as mother represents a commitment to maintaining the proper actions of the socially constructed ideals of womanhood, which are embedded within the structure of the home. Sylvia moves within a choreographed performance of motherhood, her gestures rote, consistent, distinctly feminine. However, as Edmund's passing forces her back into her previous life, her actions depict a form of domestic confinement where her habitual movements are actually *nonmovements*; her daughters move around her as though she is static, unchanged by the passage of time and mobile only as she engages in domestic tasks.

Through this choreographed performance of rote and gendered non-movement, Sylvia's relationship with her children demonstrates a sense of moral obligation above anything else. While there is a palpable bond permeating the mother and daughter relationships, the passage of time and its expression explicates Sylvia's conscious effort to maintain her socially determined role in the home. As the years pass, "their lives [spin] off the tilting world like thread off a spindle, breakfast time, supper time, lilac time, apple time" (13); likewise, the progression of time signifies the feeling of displacement and detachment. In "Hobo Time and Marilynne Robinson's *Housekeeping*," Elizabeth Klaver discusses the differentiations of "railway time," "natural time," and "hobo time." Klaver writes, "given the decision that Sylvie and Ruth make at the end of the novel, the question arises as to what extent hobo time has offered an alternative to social time in the dominant culture, and whether hobo time is capable of suggesting for women an escape from patriarchy through transience."[25] Though Sylvie's "hobo time" could easily be deemed displacing, her transience provides her fluidity and unrestrained movement through spaces. The regimented nature of Sylvia's schedule imposes limitations on how her daughters long to move; she and her daughters begin to discover a rift between their respective roles and their relationships with each other. "[Sylvia's] girls were quiet, she must have thought, because the customs and habits of their lives had almost relieved them of the need for speech" (15). Instead, they continuously engage in tasks that are extensions of their mother's domestic duties, until they fully unravel from her orbit,

[25] Klaver, 28.

leaving Sylvia to realize, "she had never taught them to be kind to her" (19). The kindness Sylvia is referring to is not a form of genuine altruism and magnanimity, but rather a type of womanly decorum and meekness that would reflect her own character. As her daughters grow into their own identities, breaking from Sylvia's repetitive trajectory, she perceives their behavior and personalities as immoral, unjust, and hateful toward her.

Although Sylvia is a stable and consistent figure, the duties associated with her maternal role and the commitment to raising her children are a result of the burden of gender. Helen, Sylvie, and Molly are cultivated by social norms, which necessitate Sylvia to continually dedicate herself to being a pillar that her children move around; they "hover around her, watch everything she [does], follow her through the house, [get] in her way" (10). Until they discover their identities and their desire to break from her orbit, their mobility is subject to her position, which is grounded in the construction of patriarchal social ideals. As Sylvia supports social constructions of womanhood, she also situates herself as to ensure all of her daughters "take on all the postures and vestments of matron[hood]" (19). Consequently, because of Sylvia's consistent support of gender expectations, her daughters unravel from their orbit around her and intentionally remove themselves from the environment they have been taught to call "home."

When Sylvia takes in Ruth and Lucille after Helen's suicide, the routine of a past life emerges and she cares for her granddaughters "like someone reliving a long day in a dream" (24). Almost instantly, she falls back into her maternal tendencies and goes about polishing shoes, braiding hair, making dinner, and cleaning house—all characteristics of a woman stationed specifically in the domestic sphere who has been taught to move in a distinctly feminine and maternal manner (25). Upon Sylvia's death, her sisters Lily and Nona move into the Fingerbone home to take care of Ruth and Lucille and become aware of their displacement in the home immediately: Lily and Nona "enjoyed nothing except habit and familiarity, the precise replication of one day in the next. This was not to be achieved in Fingerbone, where any acquaintance was perforce new and therefore more objectionable than solitude" (32). Lily and Nona's displacement, or their lack of attachment or investment, designates the home as a "thin place." A thin place lacks the substance of a thickly lived place; thin places "offer nothing to hold the self in place, and no memorable or resonant command

126   M. STICKEL HIGGINS

of placial experience,"[26] which suggests that Sylvia is the only one who has a strong attachment to the Fingerbone home. More specifically, Lily and Nona's experience with the Fingerbone home as a thin place displays how though these women look like "buxomly maternal" figures, they are instead elderly maiden women who have secluded themselves in a gated lifestyle that resists heteronormative and gendered expectations (29).

Lily and Nona's home, the Hartwick Hotel, is a gated community in the sense that its "bubbled" state allows them to live in solitude, keeping themselves distanced and divided from the outside world. The idea of Lily and Nona being "bubbled" comes from David Hill, which he describes as "a sense of remove and safety from the heterogeneous, unpredictable"[27] In the context of *Housekeeping*, Lily and Nona's "bubbled mobility" is a result of gating themselves in a lifestyle that rejects traditional views of womanhood. For example, they are unaccustomed to cooking meals for themselves (or subsequently, children). The hotel does not accept children, indicating that Lily and Nona's preference to live in the Hartwick shows an aversion to motherhood, and by consequence, traditional womanhood. In a protected community that does not force them to participate in the hegemonic infrastructures, they are able to place affective investment in their home as it discards the restrictions of a gendered place, thus allowing them to forego the ideals of motherhood. Their movement inversely mirrors Sylvia's, as their restricted mobility is a form of self-imposed removal, not obligating them to engage with cultural expectations. Their "bubbled mobility," or restricted mobility, is a form of nonmovement that serves as a form of resistance to heteronormativity.

Upon relocating to Sylvia's house, Lily and Nona are overwhelmed by the haunting presence of Sylvia's conceptualization of matriarchal mobility—Sylvia's instinctual habitudes of making dinner, braiding hair, washing clothes. As Lily and Nona enter Sylvia's home and being accustomed to the "impermeability ... [of] an increasingly private lifestyle"—a place tinged with the requirements and responsibility of social restraints and implications—they become conscious of the consequences of their relocation.[28] Recognizing their unpreparedness in taking on two pre-teenage girls as Sylvia had done, Lily and Nona's fear and insecurity arise from the

---

[26] Duff, 882.

[27] David W. Hill, "'Total Gating': Sociality and the Fortification of Networked Spaces," *Mobilities,* 7, no. 1(2012): 121.

[28] Hill, 119.

responsibility that comes with parenting. They realize that being unmarried, childless older women who have intentionally removed themselves from being the social order, they are ill equipped to perform associated with parenting. In their discomfort and displacement in the Fingerbone home, "they long to return to their basement room in the red-brick and upright Hartwick Hotel, with its stiff linens and its bright silver, where the arthritic bellhop and the two old chambermaids deferred so pleasantly to their age and their solitude and their poverty" (43). Lily and Nona are attached to the Hartwick Hotel as a place, and their displacement in Fingerbone not only emphasizes their inability to conform to traditional female social standards, but their loyalty to the affective investment they have placed into the cultivation of their lifestyles.

Hoping to return to Hartwick Hotel, Lily and Nona plan for Sylvie to return to Fingerbone so that she can raise Ruth and Lucille. Their desire to return to their home is rooted in their incapacity to take care of and provide for Ruth and Lucille appropriately; even more, they also recognize their inability to remain in the Fingerbone home, as it reveals its affective alignment with Sylvia's performance of traditional womanhood. As Duff says, an affective atmosphere "[shapes] the experience of place" and "[captures] the emotional feel of place, as well as the store of action-potential, the dispositions and agencies potentially enactable in that place."[29] He goes on to discuss how "affective force" contributes to the production of thick places, which suggests that Lily and Nona feel an "intensification of the affective pull" to return to their home.[30] In this continual pull to return their home at the Hartwick Hotel, the potency of displacement is a continual reminder of the life they do not have, or necessarily want. The intensity of affective pull, in conjunction with a force of displacement, drives Lily and Nona to extricate themselves from the home, and secure as Sylvie as a prospect to raise Ruth and Lucille.

Lily and Nona pinpoint Sylvie as a maiden unlike themselves (only because she had been omitted and excluded from Sylvia's conversation and will), yet they see Sylvie as the only option to raise Ruth and Lucille (43). Likewise, Sylvie's exclusion from her mother's will is not entirely concerning to Lily and Nona:

[29] Duff, 882.
[30] Duff, 882.

128   M. STICKEL HIGGINS

> All that could be said against Sylvie was that her mother omitted her name from virtually all conversation, and from her will. And while this was damaging, it gave neither us nor our great-aunts anything in particular to fear. Her itinerancy might be simple banishment. Her drifting, properly considered, might be no more than a preference for the single life, made awkward in her case by lack of money. (42)

Lily and Nona recognize Sylvia had little patience for those who chose not to marry (including themselves), and they dismiss the fact that Sylvia had not provided monetarily for Sylvie in her estate. Instead, they willingly accept Sylvie's preference for a single lifestyle, since they share a similar lifestyle. Sylvie is Lily and Nona's only hope to return to their thick place and relinquish the foreign maternal responsibilities Sylvia bequeathed to them.

Lily and Nona's immersion into a foreign environment tinged with the associations of womanhood and domesticity makes Sylvie's presence in the Fingerbone home very welcome. Sylvie's arrival frees Lily and Nona from obligations associated with womanhood, but at the same time, it introduces Ruth and Lucille to a transient lifestyle. Upon Lily and Nona's departure, Ruth, Lucille, and the house become Sylvie's. "That evening Lily and Nona were taken by a friend of my grandmother's back to Spokane and we and the house were Sylvie's" (59). The continued transferal of ownership of the house after Sylvia's passing subverts the social construction of home, especially in regard to the tasks specifically designated to women. The immorality of Sylvie's transience is palpable in the discussion of her exclusion from Sylvia's will. "'It's only the truth,' one said, 'that her mother had very little patience with people who chose not to marry'" (42). Sylvia perceives being unmarried as a form of immortality because it allows women a form of unrestrained movement—very dissimilar to her own nonmovement. Ruth narrates, "We knew enough about Sylvie to know that she had simply chosen to not act married, though she had a marriage of sufficient legal standing to have changed her name" (43). Though Sylvie does marry, it might be an attempt to offer solace to her mother, yet Sylvia is not fooled by the act, and still leaves her out of the will, reaffirming her strong aversion to unmarried women and what it represents about womanhood and matriarchal obligation. Moreover, as the house's ownership passes to Sylvie and her transient lifestyle, what the house represents in regard to womanhood shifts. Returning to her childhood home restricts her ability to pass through spaces, yet she participates in duties that oppose typical domestic tasks, which then reframes the home's foundational hegemonic structure. Sylvie overwrites what the place represents as she gains ownership of the home, dismantling the patriarchal gender ideals built into the home and upending ideas of domesticity.

Sylvie challenges the implications of domesticity with her transiency, disrupting the idea that "domestic ideology is embodied in domestic practices ... in the daily work of caring for the home and its occupants."[31] While the home is never gender neutral, Amos Rapoport, in his research about the home environment and identity, suggests women "tend to be more intimately linked to the dwelling in terms of their self-identity."[32] Considering this view of the home in conjunction with Sara Ahmed's *Queer Phenomenology*, it becomes evident that Sylvie is "disorientated" within the Fingerbone home. "The question of orientation becomes, then, a question not only about how we 'find our way' but how we come to 'feel at home.'"[33] Because Sylvie defies the gender expectations associated with the home-place, she is initially disorientated within the space until she begins inhabiting the home with her unusual domestic traits. Sylvie's habits are "clearly the habits of a transient:"

> For example, Sylvie's room was just as my grandmother had left it, but the closet and the drawers were mostly empty, since Sylvie kept her clothes and even her hairbrush and toothpowder in a cardboard box under the bed. She slept on top of the covers, with a quilt over her, which during the daytime she pushed under the bed also ... she always slept clothed, at first with her shoes on, and then, after a month or two, with her shoes under her pillow. (103)

Sylvie's transience becomes an antidote to her disorientation. As Ahmed writes, "Orientation involves aligning body and space: we only know which way to turn *once we know which way we are facing.* If we are in a strange room, one whose contours are not part of our memory map, then the situation is not so easy."[34] Recognizing her disorientation, feeling the

---

[31] Peter Somerville, "The Social Construction of Home," *Journal of Architectural Planning and Research* 14, no. 3(1996): 228.

[32] Amos Rapoport, "Identity and Environment: A Cross-Cultural Perspective," in *Housing and Identity: Cross-Cultural Perspective,* ed. JS Duncan (London: Croom Helm, 1981), 23.

[33] Ahmed, 7.

[34] Ahmed, 7.

weight of awkwardly inhabiting a space and feeling how the home "impresses" upon her body with its gendered nature, Sylvie rebels against this feeling, orientating herself by dismantling the home-space with the actions and movements of someone who is eager to exist fluidly, unconstrained.

As Ruth and Lucille observe Sylvie and her actions, their reactions are comparatively different. Lucille "[hates] everything that [has] to do with transience," which is why she withdrawals from Sylvie's lifestyle (103). For as often as Sylvie talks a "great deal about housekeeping," her approaches are contradictory to the perceived ideals of domesticity: "She believed in stern solvent, and most of all in air. It was for the sake of air that she opened the doors and windows. … It was for the sake of air that on one early splendid day she wrestled my grandmother's plum-colored daven-port into the front yard, where it remained until it weathered pink" (85–86). Sylvie suggests an antithetical conception of housekeeping, one that is not agreeable to other "proper" domestic practices. By opening the windows and allowing for fresh air, she is closing the divide between pub-lic and private and blurring the lines between proper and improper, moral and immoral. By placing furniture in the front yard, not only does Sylvie transgress the boundaries between public and private, destroying the impermeable point of access into the domestic sphere, she also openly (and publicly) defies the standards of proper womanhood. Placing the furniture on the front lawn signifies a distaste for proper housekeeping ideals, which coincides greatly with the displacement she encounters upon returning to the Fingerbone home. Sylvie publicly embraces her tran-sience, and in essence, this non-conformity caused by generational dis-placement triggers Lucille to fight desperately to uphold the morality of a socially constructed womanhood. As Sylvie forges a new orientation for herself, she disorientates Lucille in the process, forcing her to reach for the familiar—anywhere that she can find it.

Ruth conceptualizes Lucille's resistance to transience as a "loyalty to the other world," in turn displaying Ruth's separation from domesticity and matriarchal mobility (95). This partition of worlds indicates a divide between the morality of traditionally defined womanhood and the immo-rality of transience. Ruth's act of separating the worlds offers a divide between public and private, and the disconnection and revolt against strictly gendered places. As Sylvie gains possession of the Fingerbone home, she dislodges the concept of domesticity and the gendered ideol-ogy her father had incorporated in his creation of the place. This shift in the home's representation pushes Lucille from the home, muddling her identity as a woman and emphasizing her displacement; in turn, Ruth's acceptance of belonging in the home is accentuated. Ruth is aware that her entrance into a world of idealistic representations and expectations of womanhood would displace her, and she recognizes her need to push against socially constructed gender expectations:

> It seemed to me then that Lucille would busy herself forever, nudging, pushing, coaxing, as if she could supply the will I lacked, to pull myself into some seemly shape and slip across the wide frontiers into that other world, where it seemed to me then I could *never wish to go.* For it seemed to me that nothing I had lost, or might lose, could be found there, or, to put it another way, it seemed that something I had lost might be found in Sylvie's house. (123–124, emphasis added)

Ruth's acceptance of Sylvie's transience and lifestyle situates her as (re) conceptualizing the ideals of place, home, and womanhood.

Lucille's abrupt relocation to live with the Home Economics teacher accentuates her desire for the socially constructed version of white, religious womanhood, a longing for a familiar orientation, demonstrating the affective investment involved with creating a place premised on "personal enrichment." As she recognizes that the Fingerbone home will hinder her enhancement as a proper woman, her only option is to extricate herself from the place that is impacting her perceived ideals of womanhood. In returning to Edward S. Casey's discussion of how place can become embedded in its occupants, it is also evident how place can become embedded in a destructive way—as a pollutant to an individual. "The relationship between self and place is not just one of reciprocal influence (that much any ecologically sensitive account would maintain) but also, more radically, of constitutive coingredience: each is essential to the being of the other. In effect, there is *no place without self and no self without place.*"[35] This suggests that there is a dual formation of place: while there are many positive sensations and emotions that are correlated to a place, negative impressions can exist as well. Furthermore, the dual production of place speaks to the generational displacement that infiltrates into the Fingerbone home and its occupants. Sylvie's entrance into the home immediately deviates from the original formation of the home, shifting the perception of

[35] Casey, 684.

gender ideals and womanhood. As Sylvie claims ownership of the home, her displacement morphs into activating her transience into the domestic sphere; her unwillingness to conform forces her to (re)gender the home. In doing this, Lucille is displaced from an environment encapsulated with the affective investment of a young woman pursuing the proper forms of domesticity.

The three generations of women in *Housekeeping* each represents a specific position and identity that correlate to, or detract from, gender ideals and expectations. The displacement that each woman faces is a unique cultivation based on her own experiences and perceptions in the home, as well as her different understandings of womanhood. Although the idea of displacement can easily be recognized as lingering ramifications of generational trauma, that fact neglects to recognize how place is as constructed as gender, and with that, patriarchal religiosity even further complicates what it means to live as a woman. Womanhood and the matriarchal mobility of the women in the text emphasize displacement in identity, not the home. The idea of place and home is as fluid as transience itself, as it is created and linked to humans and their identities, elucidating how the dynamic emotional resonance is in continual flux. Each woman's unhappiness or discontentment with the Fingerbone home lies within the affect of their identity, rather than how their affective investment shapes place.

Works Cited

Ahmed, Sara. *Queer Phenomenology*. Durham: Duke University Press, 2006.

Bessedik, Fatima Zahra. "Home-Space in Marilynne Robinson's *Housekeeping*." *Interdisciplinary Literary Studies* 17, no. 4 (2015): 556–576.

Casey, Edward S. "Between Geography and Philosophy: What Does It Mean to Be in the Place-World?" *Annals of the Association of American Geographers* 91, no. 4 (2001): 683–93.

Cooper-Marcus, Clare and CarolynFrancis.*People Places: Design Guidelines for Urban Open Space*. 2nd ed. New York: Wiley & Sons, 1998.

Duff, Cameron. "On the Role of Affect and Practice in the Production of Place." *Environment and Planning D: Society and Space* 28 (2010): 881–95.

Geyh, Paula E. "Burning Down the House? Domestic Space and Feminine Subjectivity in Marilynne Robinson's *Housekeeping*." *Contemporary Literature* 34, no. 1 (1993): 103–122.

Hill, David W. "'Total Gating': Sociality and the Fortification of Networked Spaces." *Mobilities* 7, no. 1 (2012): 115–29.

6 MATRIARCHAL MOBILITY: GENERATIONAL DISPLACEMENT...   133

Klaver, Elizabeth. "Hobo Time and Marilynne Robinson's *Housekeeping.*" *The Journal of the Midwest Modern Language Association* 43, no. 1 (2010): 27–43.

Massumi, Brian. *Politics of Affect.* Cambridge: Polity Press, 2015.

Rapoport, Amos. "Identity and Environment: A Cross-Cultural Perspective." In *Housing and Identity: Cross-Cultural Perspectives,* edited by JSDuncan, 255–286. London: Croom Helm, 1981.

Rendell, Jane. "Gender, Space." In *Gender Space Architecture: An Interdisciplinary Introduction,* edited by JaneRendell, BarbaraPenner, and IainBorden, 101–111. New York: Routledge, 2000.

Robinson, Marilynne. *Housekeeping.* New York: Picador, 1980.

Sheller, Mimi. "Sociology After the Mobilities Turn." In *The Routledge Handbook of Mobilities,* edited by Peter Adey, David Bissell, Kevin Hannam, Peter Merriman, Mimi Sheller, 45–54. New York: Routledge, 2013.

Somerville, Peter. "The Social Construction of Home." *Journal of Architectural Planning and Research* 14, no. 3 (1996): 226–45.

PART II

Spatiality

CHAPTER 7

Interiorized Imperialism in Native American and Japanese American World War II Narratives

Olivia Hulsey

Throughout our wars of the twentieth century, African Americans' service in the U.S. military was "a definitive argument for black citizenship rights," Jennifer James argues in *A Freedom Bought with Blood*.[1] I suggest that a similar bid for inclusion was put forth by Native Americans and Japanese Americans after World War II, particularly in light of the tremendous successes of the Navajo Code-Talkers and the all-Nisei 442nd Combat Regiment. Histories of the oppression of Native Americans and Japanese Americans are often peripheralized due to what Sabine Sielke calls "processes of forgetting and denial," whereby black and white racial tensions in America have "overshadowed and overdetermined the history of Indigenous cultures," as well as, I argue, that of Japanese American

---

[1] Jennifer James, *A Freedom Bought with Blood: African American War Literature from the Civil War to World War II* (Chapel Hill: University of North Carolina Press, 2007), 2.

O. Hulsey (✉)
University of Memphis, Memphis, TN, USA

© The Author(s), under exclusive license to Springer Nature
Switzerland AG 2021
C. Beck (ed.), *Mobility, Spatiality, and Resistance in Literary and Political Discourse*, Geocriticism and Spatial Literary Studies,
https://doi.org/10.1007/978-3-030-83477-7_7

137

citizens.[2] Native Americans and Japanese Americans share a historic struggle for civic inclusion in American society, despite an exclusion manifest in specific places such as internment camps and reservations.[3] As the American government and non-Native society confined Indigenous cultures to the reservations, similarly the late twentieth-century stereotyping of Asian Americans as the "model minority" has diminished national memory of the Japanese American internment camps. Narratives of life in these places expose a national past marked by the tensions between assimilation and resistance, the marginalization of perceived Others by the white hegemony, and an imperialism of the interior—the conquering and colonizing of American people on American soil.

In addition to the collective impact of American imperialism upon Indigenous and Japanese cultures within the reservations and camps, the narratives reveal the impact of place upon individual identities. Yi-Fu Tuan argues that place, in its defining of the individual, can actually "limit the self" and therefore can be "a form of subjugation."[4] For many young men residing in the aforementioned places, military service was perceived as a route to self-definition—to belonging or being perceived as truly American. Their expectations were more often disappointed than fulfilled, and their return to a home space where they were more or less colonized, subjugated to the pressures and exclusionary discourse of empire, wrought a particular trauma. Featuring young male protagonists who have recently returned to the reservation after serving in the U.S. military during World War II, N. Scott Momaday's *House Made of Dawn* (1966) and Leslie

[2] Sabine Sielke, "Multiculturalism in the United States and Canada," in *The Palgrave Handbook of Comparative North American Literature,* ed. Reingard Nischik (London: Palgrave, 2014), 51.

[3] In *Space and Place* (1977), Yu-Fi Tuan distinguishes between the two concepts by asserting that "'space' is more abstract than 'place.' What begins as undifferentiated space becomes place as we get to know it better and endow it with value." Yi-Fu Tuan, *Space and Place: The Perspective of Experience* (Minneapolis: University of Minnesota Press, 1977), 6. Later, he insists that "enclosed and humanized space is place." Tuan, *Space and Place*, 54. I interpret the internment camps and reservations as Tuanian "places" because they are indeed endowed with value—with the value of community by the Japanese Americans and Native Americans who lived there, and with the value of a subordinate colony by the American government who used the space as an outpost of interiorized imperialism. Furthermore, these places are "enclosed" both literally and metaphorically, as I discuss later in my analysis of their confined nature.

[4] Tony Lack, "An Interview with Yu Fi Tuan, Professor Emeritus, University of Wisconsin-Madison," *Interdisciplinary Humanities* 32, no. 3(2015): 8.

Marmon Silko's *Ceremony* (1977) exemplify this individual crisis as a microcosm of the broader cultural phenomena of Native American marginalization and colonization. These two novels bear striking parallels to Jeanne Wakatsuki Houston's internment memoir *Farewell to Manzanar* (1973), and John Okada's *No-No Boy* (1957), considered the first Japanese American novel. This chapter explores the Native American reservation and the Japanese American internment camp as places of interiorized imperialism and interrogates their effects upon the postwar identities of Japanese Americans and Native Americans as narrativized by Momaday, Silko, Okada, and Wakatsuki Houston. The analytical juxtaposition of these four works invites a consideration of multicultural American literature as a genre that can transcend constructed and divisive boundaries to bring about a deeper understanding of frequently overlooked episodes of imperialism in American history.

In *Reflections on Exile* (2000), Edward Said argues that, although historical rhetoric associates the term "imperialism" with older regimes such as the Ottoman and British Empires, America is the post-World War II empire *par excellence*; it "has replaced the great earlier empires as *the* dominant outside force."[5] Confiscation of Native land and attempted control of or assimilationist pressure exerted upon Natives by the U.S. government during the nineteenth and twentieth centuries is comparable to extra-continental imperialism like the British Empire's colonization of India or the Dutch colonies in South Africa. In this case, the Natives became an oppressed and ostensibly inferior darker-skinned Other, like the Asian Indians and the South Africans. I qualify this imperialism as "interiorized" because it occurred within the North American continent, much like the problematic subsuming of native Mexicans when California claimed statehood. Moreover, I extend the term "interiorized" to mean confined within a specific space—the reservation. This hardscrabble, drought-stricken land was not necessarily chosen by the Natives who came to inhabit it; they were often relegated to it because whites didn't want it or had already ravaged it with uranium mining and other environmental abuses.

Silko employs a trope of fences to represent this interiorized imperialism. The fences in *Ceremony* separate white ranchers' land from

---

[5] Edward Said, *Reflections on Exile and Other Essays* (Cambridge: Harvard University Press, 2000), 305.

reservation land, though the former was once part of the latter. These physical boundaries also represent the tensions between the preservation of Natives' nature-oriented culture versus the cultural illogic of late capitalism. Silko points out that "the people knew what the fence was for: a thousand dollars a mile, to keep Indians and Mexicans out; a thousand dollars a mile to lock the mountain in steel wire, to make the land his [the white rancher's]."[6] Natives had been cut off from most of the arable land that they'd been able to use for self-sustenance (farming and raising livestock), thus many became reliant upon their "conquerors" (the U.S. government) for assistance. Therefore, seizure of land led to the colonized Other's dependence upon their empire, the white American hegemony.

Throughout *Ceremony*, repeated images of barbed-wire fences recall the Nazi concentration camps operating during that time in Germany and Poland, as well as the Japanese internment camps operating then in North America. In all three uses of the fence for the confinement of human beings (Native Americans, Jews, and Japanese Americans), those restricted to a specific space while their land and homes are taken over are themselves residents of that country, rather than geographical outsiders. Their fellow countrymen are perpetrating the persecution. What emerges during World War II, then, is a triangle of cultural groups, each pushed to the outer corners by the dominant white patriarchy. Not surprisingly, resistance arises. Phrases repeated throughout *Ceremony*—"crossing the fence," "riding along the fence line," "breaks in the fences"—illustrate tensions between colonizer and colonized. Silko's protagonist Tayo, the colonized, strikes back. His cutting of a boundary fence, the pivotal plot event, is an act of subversion both literally and symbolically. In addition to defying the boundaries set by the colonizer, it allows him to recover his grandfather Josiah's cattle from white men, a reclaiming that facilitates Tayo's own recovery from trauma—his individual combat trauma, as well as the collective cultural trauma of Natives' loss of land, of livelihood, and of self-sufficiency.

Josiah's cattle symbolize the Native Americans—particularly a New Native who can adapt to twentieth-century capitalist culture the way the cattle adapt to survive the droughts and stark terrain. Their connection to the land is crucial, for what Josiah says about the cattle is also demonstrated by the Natives: "If you separate them from the land for too long ...

---

[6] Leslie Marmon Silko, *Ceremony* (New York: Penguin Books, 1986), 188.

7 INTERIORIZED IMPERIALISM IN NATIVE AMERICAN AND JAPANESE... 141

they lose something ... they are lost."[7] Particularly tenacious, they continuously strive to maintain their tie to the land, even as it is threatened by agents of imperialism—the U.S. government and white society. Just as Tayo breaches the fence, "fences had never stopped the speckled cattle either."[8] The adaptability of the cattle parallels the adaptability of the New Native, for "You never knew when you might be traveling some place and a fence might get in your way;" that is, the barriers presented by white culture are ubiquitous, so Natives must learn to navigate them in order to survive outside the reservation.[9] Thus, Tayo's reclaiming of Josiah's cattle not only symbolizes a subversion of the white man's interiorized imperialism of the reservation as explained above, it also implies a sense of hope via adaptation. This interpretation is further supported by the medicine doctor Betonie's insistence that the ceremonies themselves must continue to change and adapt. He says it is "necessary to create new ceremonies," because "things which don't shift and grow are dead things."[10] The danger, though, is that this adaptability, this willingness to change, could lead to assimilation into white culture, which could further diminish the already endangered Native culture. Assimilation into the world outside the interiorized space comes with a set of difficulties of its own, as Silko's veteran characters come to realize.

The interiorized imperialism of the reservation wrought particular injury upon those who came of age there, especially those like the veterans who left, experienced the world outside, and returned. The historic archetype of the traumatized and neglected war veteran as fictionalized in *Ceremony* and other World War II-era reservation narratives is Ira Hayes, a Pima Native American who became a U.S. Marine during the war and was later transformed into legend via film and song. One of the six flag-raisers on Mount Suribachi at Iwo Jima (later memorialized in the famous statue), Hayes returned to America a celebrated war hero but was soon forgotten when he resumed life on the reservation. He died a destitute alcoholic. Like Hayes, Silko's protagonist Tayo faces reintegration difficulties when he returns to the reservation after serving in World War II. He is not greeted with fanfare, and his homecoming is delayed because he had first been a prisoner of war during the Bataan Death March and then spent

[7] Silko, *Ceremony*, 74.
[8] Silko, *Ceremony*, 187.
[9] Silko, *Ceremony*, 188–189.
[10] Silko, *Ceremony*, 126.

time recovering in a VA hospital. The novel's sensory descriptions of these places—the Philippine jungles, the sterile white hospital, and, ultimately, the reservation—create an array of spatial connections to Tayo's psychological trauma.

Several critics have analyzed the connections between combat trauma and the specific space of the reservation in terms of the land. Sharon Holm, for example, attributes Tayo's psychological distress to "his sense of betrayal by the army and by the U.S. government over the illegal appropriation of land,"[11] while Michelle Satterlee explores the myriad ways that "Silko's novel demonstrates that individual trauma is rooted within a cultural context [on/of the reservation] and tied to specific landscapes."[12] What these and other scholars have overlooked, however, is the aspect of *confinement* characteristic of the interiorized imperialism I defined earlier. In addition to the loss of much of their land and the memories of injustice and slaughter thereupon, the separation and confinement of Native Americans under the U.S. government's reservation policies are central to their collective cultural trauma. The aforementioned fence trope represents the boundaries of this confinement, as do certain characters' emphasis upon the white-versus-Native boundary, by which reservation life and the "white outside world" constitute an interior/exterior dichotomy. For example, before he was killed in the war, Tayo's cousin Rocky had planned to leave the reservation. His teachers had told him, "Nothing can stop you now except one thing: don't let the people at home hold you back."[13] Here, the reservation is deemed a hindrance; Rocky's future success is predicted because he "understood what he had to do to win in the white outside world."[14] He was willing to cast aside his Native American culture (of life *within* the reservation) and assimilate into the white mainstream (of life *outside* the reservation). Tayo reflects upon his own relation to this interior/exterior spatiality, feeling that the white world was "distant from him,"[15] and that life on the reservation was "so pitiful and small compared to the world he knew the white people had—a world of comfort in the

---

[11] Sharon Holm, "The 'Lie' of the Land: Native Sovereignty, Indian Literary Nationalism, and Early Indigenism in Silko's *Ceremony*," *American Indian Quarterly* 32, no. 3(2008): 258.

[12] Michelle Satterlee, "Landscape Imagery and Memory in the Narrative of Trauma: A Closer Look at Leslie Marmon Silko's *Ceremony*," *Interdisciplinary Studies in Literature and Environment* 13, no. 2(2006): 74.

[13] Silko, *Ceremony*, 51.

[14] Silko, *Ceremony*, 51.

[15] Silko, *Ceremony*, 102.

7 INTERIORIZED IMPERIALISM IN NATIVE AMERICAN AND JAPANESE... 143

sprawling houses ... a world of plenty."[16] However, the hierarchical opposition of the white world over the reservation begins to disintegrate as he realizes that the white world is not one to aspire toward, because it had been built out of what was once the Natives' own:

> He wanted to scream at Indians like Harley and Helen Jean and Emo that the white things they admired and desired so much—the bright city lights and loud music, the soft sweet food and the cars—all these things had been stolen, torn out of Indian land: raw living materials ... The people had been taught to despise themselves because they were left with barren land and dry rivers. But they were wrong. It was the white people who had nothing; it was the white people who were suffering as thieves do, never able to forget that their pride was wrapped in something stolen, something that had never been, and could never be, theirs.[17]

Here, Tayo transcends the other characters' desire to belong to the white world by recognizing what Holm calls "the lie of the land."[18] However, he too had once believed in the promise of civic inclusion, for he too had enlisted to fight in the white man's war. Early in the novel, as Tayo drinks at the reservation bar with Emo, Harley, and Leroy (all veterans recently returned home), he realizes that they were "trying to bring back that old feeling, that feeling they belonged to America the way they felt during the war. ... They never saw that it was the white people who gave them that feeling and it was white people who took it away again when the war was over."[19] As the narrative continues, it becomes increasingly apparent that their alcoholism and violence stem from this sense of betrayal and bitterness. Even non-veteran Natives notice this failure of the promise of belonging. An observer laments, "they had been treated first class once, with their uniforms. As long as there had been a war and the white people were afraid of the Japs and Hitler. But these Indians got fooled when they thought it would last."[20] The outside world these veterans had expected to join is ultimately a space that remains inaccessible to them, and the confines of the reservation become a place permeated with their trauma. Tayo can recover from this and learn to live peacefully on the land again only

---

[16] Silko, *Ceremony*, 127.
[17] Silko, *Ceremony*, 204.
[18] Holm, "The 'Lie' of the Land," 243.
[19] Silko, *Ceremony*, 43.
[20] Silko, *Ceremony*, 165.

after he realizes the lie of ownership and symbolically collapses that interior/exterior boundary by breaching the fence and reclaiming Josiah's cattle.

Like Tayo, Momaday's protagonist Abel in *House Made of Dawn* leaves the reservation to serve in World War II and, upon his return, suffers traumatic stress that is linked both to his combat experience and to the land. Their homecomings bear striking resemblance: both are associated with sickness and shame upon re-entering the reservation. When Tayo got off the train, "his legs were shaky and the sleeves of his coat smelled like puke. ... He didn't want them to know how sick he had been."[21] Similarly, when Abel stepped off the bus, "he was drunk, and he fell against his grandfather and did not know him. His wet lips hung loose and his eyes were half closed and rolling."[22] Their sickness and shame are physiological and psychological symptoms of what I will call an *internalized* imperialism, a state in which Natives begin to believe the white colonizer's perception of them, which leads to a diminished sense of self that perpetuates the cycle of poverty and alcoholism. In *Ceremony,* the Native vets "blamed themselves for losing the new feeling" of belonging they'd had during the war; "they never talked about it, but they blamed themselves just like they blamed themselves for losing the land the white people took. They never thought to blame white people for any of it; they wanted white people for their friends."[23] Later, Tayo realizes that "the blame on the whites would never match the vehemence the people [Natives] would keep in their own bellies, reserving the greatest bitterness and blame for themselves."[24] Silko's repeated use of the word "blame" in these passages highlights their perceived self-culpability and reflects the beleaguered consciousness of a people conquered both geographically and psychologically.

While Silko employs tropes of fence and cattle in *Ceremony* to emphasize the U.S. empire's confinement of Natives and their culture to the reservation, Momaday draws attention to this same imperial act with a trope of hands in *House Made of Dawn*. Two distinct events stage the significance of hands and associate them with the characteristics of interiorized imperialism: Abel's murder of the Albino on the reservation, and the

---

[21] Silko, *Ceremony*, 29.

[22] M. Scott Momaday, *House Made of Dawn* (New York: Harper Perennial Modern Classics, 2010), 8.

[23] Silko, *Ceremony*, 43.

[24] Silko, *Ceremony*, 253.

breaking and mangling of Abel's hands by a police officer in L.A. Of the first event, Christopher Douglas explains that the Jemez Albino's "alien dominance and monstrous and hairless whiteness return us to the image of the imperial,"[25] while Guillermo Bartelt argues that the Albino's paleness represents "the White Man, the White Man in the Indian, and the White Man in Abel himself."[26] This trifold whiteness-of-being equates the visible whiteness of the Albino to the often-invisible impact of white culture and imperialism upon Natives, positioning the Albino as an allegorical figure, while the "White Man in Abel himself" refers to the deleterious effects wrought upon Abel by fighting in the "white man's war." This simultaneous in-between-ness and both-ness complicates Abel's assimilation back into reservation life right after the war and into the white world after prison, exacerbating his individual trauma and representing Native cultural trauma.

Momaday emphasizes hand imagery via repetition of the phrase "white hands" no less than fifteen times in the two-page murder scene. Germanic origins of the word "hand" define it as "an instrument of agency," of "possession," or of "power,"[27] so its emphatic presence at the scene of the Albino's murder implies that Abel is taking back the power and agency that he (and, arguably by allegorical extension, Native Americans in general) has lost at the hands of white colonizers. This scene occurs when Abel seeks revenge a few days after the Albino had beaten and humiliated him in the presence of the entire village during the Feast of Santiago. After a mysterious conversation in the reservation bar, a space persistently violent in its atmosphere, Abel and the Albino exit into the darkness and rain. As the scene intensifies and Abel fatally stabs the Albino in the chest, his "white hands" rose into the air, grasped Abel's shoulders, attempted to overcome him, and eventually "jerked and trembled helplessly."[28] As he struggled, the Albino "closed his hands upon Abel and drew him close," which made Abel "sick with terror and revulsion," for "the white immensity of flesh lay over and smothered him."[29] In their final throes of

---

[25] Christopher Douglas, "The Flawed Design: American Imperialism in N. Scott Momaday's *House Made of Dawn* and Cormac McCarthy's *Blood Meridian*," *Critique* 45, no. 1(2003): 4.

[26] Guillermo Bartelt, "Hegemonic Registers in Momaday's *House Made of Dawn*," *Style* 39, no. 4(Winter 2005): 473.

[27] "hand, n," OED Online, accessed November 12, 2020, https://www.oed.com

[28] Momaday, *House Made of Dawn*, 73.

[29] Momaday, *House Made of Dawn*, 73.

146   O. HULSEY

resistance, "the terrible strength of the hands" is ultimately overcome by Abel's knife, and the last image is of "the white hairless arm [with] the open palm of the hand exposed."[30] This frequency of hand imagery signifies Abel's revolt against white imperialism as symbolized by the Albino.

The weight of the murder scene's plot significance in the novel's first half is mirrored by Abel's own beatings in L.A. in the second half, which leave his hands broken and mangled. These two attacks are executed by the crooked cop Martinez, who identifies as a white man because of his position of power, and whose violence toward the Natives stems from his racial hatred and the conviction that they are taking area jobs. In the first attack, he corners Abel in an alley and demands his money. When Abel responds that his pockets are empty, Martinez asks him to hold out his hands, then brings his night-stick "down hard and fast," to make it "crack on the bones of [Abel's] hands."[31] The next day, Abel, who works with his hands for a living, "could barely move his fingers and there were big ugly marks above his knuckles, all yellow and purple."[32] Thereafter, Abel's alcoholism and depression intensify, and he becomes obsessed with exacting revenge upon Martinez for putting him out of work and humiliating him.

The second time Martinez attacks, it nearly kills Abel. When his roommate finds him the next day, Abel was "all broken and torn and covered with blood. ... He had lost an awful lot of blood, and his skin was pale and yellow in the light. His eyes were swollen shut and his nose was broken and his mouth was raw and bleeding. And his hands were broken; they were broken all over."[33] Often associated with labor and self-defense, as tools and as weapons, hands occupy a symbolic position of power comparable to the phallus. By breaking Abel's hands, Martinez has taken away his ability to make a living (thereby rendering him further dependent upon white-powered institutions like federal welfare), as well as his ability to fight back or retaliate. This hand-castration nullifies Abel's murder of the Albino as a symbolic act wherein he had taken back power by slaying whiteness, because now Martinez as a second representation of whiteness has reclaimed it. Significantly, Abel's power grab as represented by hand imagery in the passage of the Albino's murder occurs *within* the reservation, while Abel's power loss as represented by his broken, now-defunct

---

[30] Momaday, *House Made of Dawn*, 74.
[31] Momaday, *House Made of Dawn*, 153.
[32] Momaday, *House Made of Dawn*, 153.
[33] Momaday, *House Made of Dawn*, 161.

hands (his *hand*icap) occurs *outside* the reservation. This binary reaffirms the concept of interiorized imperialism by insinuating that he can only exert power within the space allowed to him by the white hegemony, because that is where they are able to confine and control him, and he is only able to exert power over those of his own ethnicity, since the Albino is, despite his pallor's evocation of whiteness, a Jemez Indian.

The colonizing confinement and control of Natives—as demonstrated by Indian Removal and other practices of Congress's Department of the Interior throughout the nineteenth century and forced assimilation and tribal reorganization into the twentieth century—culminated in Termination during and after World War II. Despite the efforts of Lyndon B. Johnson's War on Poverty to improve conditions throughout the country, including Native communities, the Bureau of Indian Affairs thwarted the sovereignty and self-determination many tribes attempted to achieve through taking control of their own welfare programs. The imposition of the federal welfare system upon Natives perpetuated the "colonized" Natives' dependence upon their "colonizers" and obstructed much of the work toward self-determination put forth by groups like the American Indian Movement.

In addition to imperialism by way of paternalism and assimilation, *House Made of Dawn* also recalls past generations of this imperialism in a militaristic sense. One of the characters reflects,

> Warfare for the Kiowas was pre-eminently a matter of disposition rather than survival, and they never understood the grim, unrelenting advance of the U.S. Cavalry. When at last, divided and ill-provisioned, they were driven onto the Staked Plain in the cold of autumn, they fell into panic ... they abandoned their crucial stores to pillage and had nothing then but their lives. In order to save themselves, they surrendered to the soldiers at Fort Sill and were imprisoned in the old stone corral that now stands as a military museum.[34]

The Natives' imprisonment at the hands of the U.S. military (who were taking the land to annex it into the great American empire) provides a physical image of interiorized imperialism. The concrete imagery of the uniformed cavalry on horseback and the confinement of Natives in the enclosed corral is a more tangible counterpart to the abstract or symbolic

---

[34] Momaday, *House Made of Dawn*, 113.

148   O. HULSEY

nature of imperialism represented elsewhere in the novel. Similar tangibility is manifest in the recurrence of "walls" in Momaday's descriptions of the reservation, like Silko's fence trope. One of Abel's earliest childhood memories features the "narrow box canyon" on the reservation: its "bright red walls were deep, deeper than he could have imagined, and they seemed to close over him."[35] From a young age, he'd felt boxed in by the landscape of his home, lacking a sense of freedom and the open spaces in which pre-colonized Natives thrived. Wall-oriented spatial imagery appears in other interiorized locations of conquest or control, both on and off the reservation. For instance, Abel's flashback to his time spent in prison illustrates how a physical confinement becomes psychological via a process of abstract symbolization: "The walls of his cell were white. ... After a while he could not imagine anything beyond the walls except the yard outside. ... [The walls] were abstractions beyond the reach of his understanding, not in themselves confinement but symbols of confinement."[36] In this way, the walls of his incarceration align with the identity-forming symbolic aspects of the other walls that have closed him in or contained him, or that have enclosed the site of his being conquered or dominated. The prevalence of walls in these descriptions, particularly the "white" walls, further corroborates the interpretation of enclosed interiors as spaces used by whites in power to confine and control those perceived as cultural outsiders.

While Silko and Momaday emphasize the continued colonization of Native Americans on reservations, Wakatsuki Houston and Okada emphasize the confinement and control of Japanese Americans into internment camps, also on American soil, a colonizing authorized by President Roosevelt's Executive Order 9066 in 1942. Despite their similar settings (the western U.S. during and right after World War II) and characters (all four feature World War II veterans recently returned home), neither *Ceremony* nor *House Made of Dawn* has been critically compared to *Farewell to Manzanar, No-No Boy*, or an other Japanese American-authored literature. Peter Beidler, however, observes the sympathetic depictions of Japanese individuals in scenes of Silko's novel, wherein Tayo had been taken as prisoner of war by Japanese soldiers and forced along the Bataan Death March. He interprets Silko's positive portrayal of the Japanese as a deliberate departure from the brutality described in

---

[35] Momaday, *House Made of Dawn*, 11.
[36] Momaday, *House Made of Dawn*, 92.

non-fiction accounts written by or about survivors of the march and POW camps.[37] Silko looks beyond the violence found in POW memoirs and interviews to narrativize a common humanity between these soldiers of opposing nations. Instead of vilifying the Japanese, Tayo's encounters foster empathy for them. In battle, there had been times when he could not bring himself to kill enemy Japanese soldiers because "they looked too familiar."[38] At one point, delirious with fever, he "could not pull the trigger" when ordered to kill some Japanese POWs because he imagined he saw the face of Josiah, his late grandfather and guardian, in one of them.[39] Later in the war, Tayo observes that "They looked tired, too, those Japanese soldiers. Like they wanted this march to be over too."[40] And when Tayo confesses his inability to kill the Japanese soldiers due to seeing Josiah's face among them, Betonie responds, "It isn't surprising you saw him with them. You saw who they were. Thirty thousand years ago they were not strangers."[41] Betonie is referring to the anthropological Bering Strait theory which suggests that the ancestors of Native Americans migrated to North America from what is now Asia. Yet archival research reveals a more recent relationship between Native Americans and Japanese Americans, which socio-geographically links reservations to internment camps during World War II via an *interconnected* imperialism wrought upon the groups by the U.S. government. One of the places where the two cultures meet is the town of Gallup, also featured in *Ceremony*.

Tayo goes to meet Betonie in Gallup, which is right outside of the Laguna Pueblo Reservation. Silko portrays Gallup as a run-down town where Natives go to try to get jobs when they want to escape the poverty of the reservation. However, they are ultimately disappointed, for "they were educated only enough to know they wanted to leave the reservation; when they got to Gallup there weren't many jobs they can get. ... Gallup was a dangerous place, and by the time they realized what had happened to them, they must have believed it was too late to go home."[42] A town inhabited by whites, Hispanics, and Natives, it functions in the novel as a

---

[37] Peter Beidler, "Bloody Mud, Rifle Butts, and Barbed Wire: Transforming the Bataan Death March in Silko's *Ceremony*," *American Indian Culture and Research Journal* 28, no. 1(2004): 23–33.

[38] Silko, *Ceremony*, 7.

[39] Silko, *Ceremony*, 7.

[40] Silko, *Ceremony*, 43.

[41] Silko, *Ceremony*, 124.

[42] Silko, *Ceremony*, 115.

threshold between the reservation and the white world. The role of the real city of Gallup, New Mexico during World War II reiterates the link between the two cultural groups studied in this chapter. Gallup archives reveal that in 1942, the City Council fought successfully to prevent its Japanese American citizens from being placed in internment camps, insisting that they were "upstanding members of the Gallup community."[43] In a local newspaper interview, Gallup-born Japanese American Hiroshi Miyamura, veteran of World War II and the Korean War, claims that over 800 townspeople were kept out of the internment camps because "Gallup was the only town in New Mexico not to detain its Japanese-American residents during World War II."[44] Beyond her choice to weave the town of Gallup into the fictional fabric of *Ceremony*, Silko also draws attention to the Japanese American internment through character dialogue. After Tayo is startled by a Japanese woman and child in the train station, he comments to a bystander, "Those people ... I thought they locked them up."[45] The response he receives indicates that by the time he had been discharged from the hospital, the internment camps had closed: "Oh, that was some years back. Right after Pearl Harbor. But now they've turned them all loose again. Sent them home."[46] Thus, Tayo's homecoming parallels that of the interned Japanese Americans. However, as both *Ceremony* and internment narratives illustrate, neither homecoming is untroubled.

The colonization of Native Americans is further interconnected with the interned Japanese Americans through the U.S. government's construction of internment camps on reservations, namely the Gila and Colorado River Reservations in Arizona. Archives disclose that tribal leaders opposed the project but acquiesced in fear of losing their land if they refused. After the war ended and the internees were released, the government used the camps as housing for displaced Hopi and Navajo as part of a relocation program. Worse yet, the Poston Internment Camp on the Colorado River Reservation was erected with the express intent of providing free labor for the federal government. Its 17,000 Japanese American internees were forced to build an infrastructure that could sustain several thousand Natives relocated from smaller reservations after the war.

[43] Joe Kolb, "Gallup Stood Firm Against US Government in 1942," *Gallup Independent,* February 1, 2003.

[44] Ron Warnick, "Gallup bucked the system during World War II," *Route 66 News,* May 9, 2014.

[45] Silko, *Ceremony*, 18.

[46] Silko, *Ceremony*, 18.

Therefore, this consolidation was facilitated by the forced labor of one confined and marginalized group for the purpose of confining and controlling another. In a scheme of disingenuous ingenuity, a feat of interiorized imperialism, the American empire employed its own colonized subjects to advance the work of colonizing more subjects.

In addition to the historical and spatial interconnectivity of the reservation and the internment camp, literary narratives of the time period reveal thematic commonalities. The previously discussed tropes of empire in *Ceremony* and *House Made of Dawn* are similar to those presented in Jeanne Wakatsuki Houston's internment memoir *Farewell to Manzanar* and John Okada's novel *No-No Boy*. All four texts emphasize the interiorized nature of this American imperialism, as particularly highlighted in Jeanne's description of the internment camps: "Most of those interned in the United States were native-born American citizens; they were all civilians, imprisoned inside the borders of their own country, without a trial, and their captors were other Americans."[47] Notably, later investigations revealed that the internment was completely unnecessary. In 1947, after all the camps had been shut down, Harper's Magazine published the following statement: "It is sobering to recall that though the Japanese relocation program, carried through at such incalculable cost in misery and tragedy, was justified on the grounds that the Japanese were potentially disloyal, the record does not disclose a single case of Japanese disloyalty or sabotage during the whole war."[48] Although the camps operated for only three years, a short time when compared to the lifetime most Natives spend on the reservation, the "misery and tragedy" did not end when the camps closed. Wakatsuki Houston's memoir chronicles their lasting effects.

Farewell to Manzanar details Jeanne's experience as a child in the camps, from the evacuation shortly after the bombing of Pearl Harbor to her difficulties readjusting to American society after the camps closed. Her first glimpse of Camp Manzanar, with its "barbed-wire fence" and "rows of black barracks that seemed to spread for miles," illustrates how the space of an internment camp was similar to an Indian reservation.[49] Its image of enclosed confinement parallels the fence trope in *Ceremony* and

---

[47] Jeanne Wakatsuki Houston, *Farewell to Manzanar* (New York: Random House, 2007), 206.

[48] Wakatsuki Houston, *Farewell to Manzanar*, xvii.

[49] Wakatsuki Houston, *Farewell to Manzanar*, 19.

152   O. HULSEY

the canyon walls surrounding Abel's reservation in *House Made of Dawn*. All three sets of imagery represent the interiorized imperialism imposed upon Native Americans and Japanese Americans by the U.S. government, with white mainstream society backing it. The cycle of poverty perpetuated by the colonized space of the reservations is mirrored by the evacuation and internment of Japanese Americans. Forced to leave their lifelong homes and communities on the Pacific coast and to sell or discard any belongings they couldn't carry (just as Natives were forced off of their arable acres and onto untenable reservation land), they were crowded into the camps, living in shacks "built of one thickness of pine planking covered with tarpaper."[50] They had "bare floors, blanket partitions, one bulb in each compartment dangling from a roof beam, and open ceilings overhead,"[51] and their light and heat were sourced by "one bare bulb hanging from the ceiling and an oil stove for heat" that did little to protect them from the "bitter cold" and "wind [that] did not abate."[52] Large families were crammed into close quarters with no privacy, outhouses were over-run, and shallow graves dug for the deceased were precariously near the barracks and water supply. The camp was constantly surveilled by searchlights that scanned every square inch of Manzanar from guard towers set up along the perimeter, as if its inhabitants were dangerous criminals rather than bewildered women and children.

Moreover, just as the attitudes of some of the Natives in *Ceremony* and *House Made of Dawn* demonstrate an internalized imperialism in that they began to believe the "white lies," blamed themselves for their plight, and in some cases *became* the stereotypes imposed upon them by white society, so too did the interned Japanese Americans begin to internalize the assumptions and accept the fate they'd been dealt. They became accustomed to internment life and were afraid to leave it when the camps began to close. Jeanne recalls that, "in time, staying there seemed far simpler than moving once again to another, unknown place."[53] Their day-to-day living together among other Japanese Americans created a sense of home that at times seemed to transcend the wrong done to them: "The fact that America had accused us, or excluded us, or imprisoned us, or whatever it might be called, did not change the kind of world we wanted," which

---

[50] Wakatsuki Houston, *Farewell to Manzanar*, 20.
[51] Wakatsuki Houston, *Farewell to Manzanar*, 28.
[52] Wakatsuki Houston, *Farewell to Manzanar*, 21–22.
[53] Wakatsuki Houston, *Farewell to Manzanar*, 100.

included a sense of community among other Japanese Americans that the camps provided.[54] Ultimately, however, they were cast out of the camp as abruptly as they had been forced in. Jeanne reflects upon their desire to stay and remembers the day they realized the life they'd made for themselves was over: "The last hope that something might postpone our returning to the outside world was extinguished on August 6 when the atomic bomb fell on Hiroshima. That ended the Second World War. America had won. Internment camps were undeniably a thing of the past."[55] Instead of rejoicing at the prospect of freedom, many were distraught at the prospect of the unknown, of an American society outside of the camps that had made clear it didn't want people of Japanese lineage in their midst. Consequently, the physical fact of their interiorized colonization became a psychological state of internalized oppression that persisted long after the camps were closed and the internees were released.

Like Momaday's protagonist Abel, who in a sense remains a colonized Other even after he leaves the confines of the reservation and goes to L.A. (evident in his interactions with whites, social workers, and paternalist government institutions like the BIA and the welfare system), Jeanne retains a similar identity after leaving the camp. Her adolescence and young adulthood are marked by what she calls "intangible barriers" by which she is "excluded" to the point of feeling as if she wears a "form of invisibility."[56] Throughout the rest of the memoir, she narrativizes her struggle "to overcome the war-distorted limitations of [her] race."[57] In her Afterword, looking back thirty years later, she recognizes her own internalization of the American attitude toward Japanese Americans: "As I came to understand what Manzanar had meant, it gradually filled me with shame for being a person guilty of something enormous enough to deserve that kind of treatment. In order to please my accusers, I tried, for the first few years after our release, to become someone acceptable."[58] But this grasping toward a sense of belonging and acceptable American-ness distanced her from her conservative Japanese parents, who clung desperately to the old ways of their mother country. The post-internment chapters of *Farewell to Manzanar* thus stage the colonized Other's tension

---

[54] Wakatsuki Houston, *Farewell to Manzanar*, 100.
[55] Wakatsuki Houston, *Farewell to Manzanar*, 139.
[56] Wakatsuki Houston, *Farewell to Manzanar*, 163.
[57] Wakatsuki Houston, *Farewell to Manzanar*, 164.
[58] Wakatsuki Houston, *Farewell to Manzanar*, 185.

between assimilation into mainstream American culture versus preservation of traditional cultural heritage, as previously demonstrated in *Ceremony* and *House Made of Dawn*.

Upon attending a mostly white school after the internment, Jeanne quickly realized the perceived inferiority of her visual difference. She "yearned to be invisible" because she knew the other students "wouldn't see me, they would see the slant-eyed face, the Oriental."[59] She wants to hide her Japanese-ness, to transform herself into a "real" American, exhibiting a longing to assimilate rather than maintain ties to her Japanese heritage. As she progresses on to high school, it becomes easier for her "to adopt white American values."[60] Her desire to belong to American society—to "become" American—mirrors the yearning for civic inclusion felt by Silko's Tayo and Momaday's Abel.

Jeanne's Papa, on the other hand, emerges as the memoir's voice of the preservation of Japanese culture, challenging the U.S. government's attempt to colonize and assimilate him into American culture. Papa was taken prisoner as a suspected enemy alien before the rest of the family was sent to the camp, despite there being no evidence that he was in collusion with the Japanese government. When he is finally able to join them at Manzanar several months later, Jeanne recalls that "he was not the same man," and she later "understand[s] how Papa's life could end at a place like Manzanar.[61] He didn't die there, but things finished for him there, whereas for me it was like a birthplace. The camp was where our life lines intersected."[62] This cycle of death and rebirth recalls a similar cycle enacted on the reservation: Abel's recovery occurs as his grandfather Francisco dies, and Silko implies that Tayo's recovery is a symbolic rebirth. The Native characters also exhibit Papa and Jeanne's feelings of displacement and dislocation. Jeanne writes that Papa "had become a man without a country. The land of his birth was at war with America; yet after thirty-five years here he was still prevented by law from becoming an American citizen. He was suddenly a man with no rights who looked exactly like the enemy."[63] This disintegration causes him to turn to alcoholism, also taken up by Abel in *House Made of Dawn* and several of the veteran characters in

---

[59] Wakatsuki Houston, *Farewell to Manzanar*, 158.
[60] Wakatsuki Houston, *Farewell to Manzanar*, 171.
[61] Wakatsuki Houston, *Farewell to Manzanar*, 45.
[62] Wakatsuki Houston, *Farewell to Manzanar*, 47.
[63] Wakatsuki Houston, *Farewell to Manzanar*, 8.

7 INTERIORIZED IMPERIALISM IN NATIVE AMERICAN AND JAPANESE... 155

Ceremony. Like these Natives, Papa "kept pursuing oblivion through drink,"[64] because the humiliation of being rounded up like animals and penned in a POW camp, then in an internment camp, "brought him face to face with his own vulnerability, his own powerlessness. He had no rights, no home, no control over his own life. This kind of emasculation was suffered, in one form or another, by all the men interned at Manzanar."[65] Abel and Tayo suffer similar blows to their identity: they are men without countries within the country of their citizenship.

More strikingly than Papa's, Jeanne's brother's experience bears resemblance to that of Tayo and Abel. Woody enlists in the U.S. military to prove his allegiance to America in a hopeful bid for civic inclusion. As they depart for war from the reservation's space of interiorized imperialism to seek the opportunities promised by the military, Woody leaves his family at the internment camp to do the same. When Papa tried to dissuade Woody from enlisting, the young man responds, "I am an American citizen. America is at war."[66] His paradoxical patriotism is recognized by young Jeanne, who later realizes that "the most effective way Japanese Americans could combat the attitudes that put them in places like Manzanar was to shed their blood on the battlefield."[67] Fortunately, like Tayo and Abel, Woody survives the war and rejoins his family once they have left the camp. But also like the Native veterans, the expectation of having earned a place in American mainstream society was ultimately disappointed. When Woody returns to America, he still looks Japanese at a time when Japanese were an enemy of the U.S., so his re-entry into American society is met with suspicion and distrust.

Woody's decision to enlist was precipitated by the U.S. government's issuing of a "loyalty questionnaire" in 1943, formally known as Selective Service Form 304A, "Statement of United States Citizen of Japanese Ancestry," which all interned men over the age of 17 were required to complete and submit. The two most controversial questions on this form created a Catch-22 situation because if they were answered with "No," it was documented as proof of treason to the U.S. and allegiance to enemy Japan (which led to arrest and separation from family in the internment camp), but if they were answered with "Yes," the internee was essentially

---

[64] Wakatsuki Houston, *Farewell to Manzanar*, 71.
[65] Wakatsuki Houston, *Farewell to Manzanar*, 72.
[66] Wakatsuki Houston, *Farewell to Manzanar*, 83.
[67] Wakatsuki Houston, *Farewell to Manzanar*, 85.

156 O. HULSEY

rejecting his Japanese heritage and agreeing to be sent off to fight in a war that had already caused unprecedented rates of mortality. The questions were as follows:

27. Are you willing to serve in the Armed Forces of the United States on combat duty, wherever ordered?
28. Will you swear unqualified allegiance to the United States of America and faithfully defend the United States from any or all attack by foreign or domestic forces, and forswear any form of allegiance or obedience to the Japanese emperor, or any other foreign government, power, or organization?[68]

Having answered "Yes" to both questions, Jeanne's brother Woody became one of the "Yes-Yes Boys." John Okada's protagonist Ichiro Yamada, however, became one of the "No-No Boys." He did so to please his conservative Issei mother, who still thinks her family will return to her beloved Japan as soon as they make a little more money as grocers in America. But the price Ichiro must pay for answering "No" to questions 27 and 28 is two years in prison—after the two years in the internment camp with his family.

Okada's novel *No-No Boy* begins on the day Ichiro comes home from prison, which recalls Tayo's and Abel's homecomings in *Ceremony* and *House Made of Dawn*. Throughout the narrative, Ichiro reflects back on his confinement in both the internment camp and prison, while presently feeling trapped in a psychological prison symptomatic of a colonized identity. Ichiro suffers under a metaphorical interiorized imperialism that outlasts his bodily confinement of the four previous years, yet he also exhibits the internalized imperialism of one who blames himself for his condemnation. Even after he is free from the camp and the prison cell, he feels that "The prison which he had carved out of his own stupidity granted no paroles or pardons. It was a prison of forever."[69] He blames his dilemma on himself just as Tayo, Abel, and Jeanne blamed themselves and began to believe the negative traits attributed to them by white mainstream society. Thus, Okada represents a double trauma in *No-No Boy*: the colonizing and confinement of Japanese Americans in the internment camps (and additional imprisonment for "no-no boys") during the war, and the

---

[68] Wakatsuki Houston, *Farewell to Manzanar*, 81.
[69] John Okada, *No-No Boy* (Seattle: University of Washington Press, 1998), 40.

psychological continuation of this interiorized imperialism after the camps closed and the prison sentences were carried out.

This duality of concrete and abstract space persists. The oppression of living as a colonized entity within the country of his own birth is demonstrated with both psychological and physical tropes of prisons and walls throughout the novel. Ichiro's suffocation is symbolic of his being a subject of American empire, and his psychological imprisonment is actualized by his physical surroundings when he comes home. Outside the railroad depot, when he's returned to Seattle after being released from prison, "he felt as if he were in a small room whose walls were slowly closing in on him. ... The walls had closed in and were crushing all the unspoken words back down into his stomach."[70] He goes to live at his parents' residence behind their quick-stop grocery store, which is described as "a hole in the wall with groceries crammed in orderly confusion on not enough shelving, into not enough space."[71] Here they "lived in cramped quarters above the shop because, like most of the other Japanese, they planned some day to return to Japan and still felt like transients even after thirty or forty years in America."[72] In addition to the cramped physical space, Ichiro feels smothered by his father, who has become an alcoholic; his mother, who has gone crazy and believes that Japan has really won the war and that American newspapers have all conspired in concealing it; and his naïve younger brother Taro, who despises what he perceives as Ichiro's weakness in not having gone to war and plans to enlist himself in the military as soon as he is of age to do so. Between family tensions, his instability and embarrassment among the Japanese American community (since many of his acquaintances are "yes-yes boys" who *had* fought in the war and view "no-no boys" as "big, black marks on their new laundry"[73]) and his inner struggle, Ichiro is overwhelmed with existential despair.

Despite being legally free for the first time in four years, his sense of belonging neither to the Japanese cultural community nor to American society prevents Ichiro from feeling free anywhere he goes. His personal identity crisis as a no-no boy transcends his individual struggle and signifies a collective Japanese American cultural crisis during the World War II era. Like Jeanne in high school after internment, "he felt like an intruder

---

[70] Okada, *No-No Boy*, 3.
[71] Okada, *No-No Boy*, 6.
[72] Okada, *No-No Boy*, 25.
[73] Okada, *No-No Boy*, 228.

in a world to which he had no claim."[74] He wants to belong to American society and stop being labeled a foreign Other, but he doubts that possibility, for though "his heart mercifully stacked the blocks of hope into the pattern of an America which would someday hold an unquestioned place for him, his mind said no, it is not to be, and the castle tumbled and was swallowed up by the darkness of his soul."[75] Though he feels ashamed in the presence of those Japanese Americans who did serve in the war, it turns out that their anticipated reward was out of reach. Participating in the war as a means to prove their American-ness didn't pan out the way they thought it would either.

The yes-yes boys and no-no boys viewed themselves as opposites, as "two extremes, the Japanese who was more American than most Americans because he had crept to the brink of death for America, and the other who was neither Japanese nor American because he had failed to recognize the gift of his birthright when recognition meant everything."[76] Though the novel is mostly narrated through Ichiro's consciousness, brief passages of extradiegetic monologue reveal the mentality of an unknown yes-yes boy and allow the reader to empathize with both equally difficult stances. The rationale of a young man who answered "Yes," who went from internment camp as a person of possible disloyalty to the U.S. to the battlefield as a soldier for the U.S., is as follows:

> It was because he was Japanese and, at the same time, had to prove to the world that he was not Japanese that the turmoil was in his soul and urged him to enlist. There was confusion, but, underneath it, a conviction that he loved America and would fight and die for it because he did not wish to live anyplace else. ... It was not a time for clear thinking because the sense of loyalty had become dispersed and the shaken faith of an American interned in an American concentration camp was indeed a flimsy thing. So, on this steadfast bit of conviction that remained, and knowing not what the future held, this son had gone to war to prove that he deserved to enjoy those rights which should rightfully have been his.[77]

Here we see the colonized Other's devotion and service to his empire. Instead of striking a revolution, as Ichiro does in his own small way by

---

[74] Okada, *No-No Boy*, 1.
[75] Okada, *No-No Boy*, 52.
[76] Okada, *No-No Boy*, 73.
[77] Okada, *No-No Boy*, 121.

twice saying No, the imperial subject can be seen as joining the ranks of the colonizers in hopes that he will earn his rightful place as one of them and will thus be able to assimilate into the dominant group. However, Ichiro observes that these yes-yes boys "were being deluded," because they "believed and fought and even gave their lives to protect this country where they could still not rate as first-class citizens because of the unseen walls."[78] Like the metaphorical walls closing in around Ichiro, those who answered "Yes" when questioned about their loyalty to the same America that had interned them had their own walls that obstructed their endeavors. For both the no-no and the yes-yes boys, service was a lose-lose situation.

In addition to portraying the crises of Japanese Americans throughout the novel itself, Okada preempts it with a polyvocal preface that emphasizes the concept of interiorized imperialism by comparing the internment camps to Nazi concentration camps through four distinct voices. This preface is composed as a series of vignettes set on the evening of the Pearl Harbor bombing. First, Okada gives voice to a Jewish American businessman who sympathizes with the Japanese, who he recognizes "had taken their place beside the Jew. ... The Jap-Jew would look in the mirror this Sunday night and see a Jap-Jew."[79] Here, the Japanese-as-victim and Jew-as-victim are transposed one upon the other, literally in a mirror image, equating the internment and atomic bombing to the Holocaust genocide. A second narrator in this preface stresses the geographical distancing of the internment camps, which recalls the placement of Nazi concentration camps in out-of-the-way locations away from civilians' view. The Japanese Americans likewise were "transported to the hinterlands and put in a camp," with an eerie similarity of foreboding in the "whisking and transporting of Japanese and the construction of camps with barbed wire and ominous towers supporting fully armed soldiers in places like Idaho and Wyoming and Arizona,"[80] notably located in regions also occupied by Native reservations. The concentration-camp analogy is voiced a third time in Okada's preface by a pair of American soldiers on duty in Europe, with attention drawn to the government's rhetoric that was intended to distance the concept of internment from the Nazi death-camps: "And then the Japanese-American [soldier] whose folks were still

---

[78] Okada, *No-No Boy*, 104.
[79] Okada, *No-No Boy*, viii.
[80] Okada, *No-No Boy*, ix.

160   O. HULSEY

Japanese-Japanese, or else they would not be in a camp with barbed wire and watchtowers with soldiers holding rifles, told the blond giant from Nebraska about the removal of the Japanese from the Coast, which was called the evacuation, and about the concentration camps, which were called relocation centers."[81] The fourth and final voice in Okada's revelatory preface is that of a no-no boy who wished he'd had the courage at his trial to confront a condemning judge about the bitter irony of internment and military service: "You can't make me go in the army because I'm not an American or you wouldn't have plucked me and mine from a life that was good and real and meaningful and fenced me in the desert like they do the Jews in Germany."[82] Delivered powerfully before the central narrative of no-no boy Ichiro begins, these four diversely voiced comparisons of American internment camps to Nazi concentration camps expose the harsh reality of interiorized imperialism and the hypocrisy of American exceptionalism.

Ultimately, the interior/exterior separation attempted by interiorized imperialism is deconstructed. Seongho Yoon articulates this best with her assertion that "the nation's interiority is actually established by its interaction with the outside that is therefore itself a part of what constitutes national interior, and that interior is apt to be turned *out* insofar as it depends on an outside that provides its conditions of possibility."[83] In other words, the interior is mutually dependent upon the exterior; the "insiders" have reciprocal relation to the "outsiders" in regard to the formation of national identity. Marginalized undesirables like the Native Americans and Japanese Americans discussed in this chapter become people who actually *matter* to the national consciousness, who "remap" the nation that has tried to exclude them, and who create the nation's history through the production of cultural memory via literature like the works studied here. The Holocaust is *the* most remembered event in Germany's history, but it would not be so without the stories told by those who chose to bear witness. The plight of Native Americans and the internment of Japanese Americans—constitutive of an imperialism that is simultaneously interiorized, internalized, and interconnected—*should* be more central to

[81] Okada, *No-No Boy*, x–xi.
[82] Okada, *No-No Boy*, 31.
[83] Seongho Yoon, "'No Place in Particular': Inhabiting Postinternment America, Articulating Postinternment Anxieties in John Okada's *No-No Boy*," *Ariel: A Review of International English Literature* 43, no. 1(2012): 60.

the annals of American history and our collective cultural memory, and will be so as more writers like Silko, Momaday, Wakatsuki Houston, and Okada emerge to help us to remember.

Work Cited

Bartelt, Guillermo. "Hegemonic Registers in Momaday's *House Made of Dawn*."*Style* 39, no. 4 (Winter 2005): 469–78.

Beidler, Peter G. "Bloody Mud, Rifle Butts, and Barbed Wire: Transforming the Bataan Death March in Silko's *Ceremony*."*American Indian Culture and Research Journal* 28, no. 1 (2004): 23–33.

Douglas, Christopher. "The Flawed Design: American Imperialism in N. Scott Momaday's *House Made of Dawn* and Cormac McCarthy's *Blood Meridian*."*Critique* 45, no. 1 (2003): 3–24.

"hand, n."*OED Online*. Accessed November 12, 2020. http://www.oed.com

Holm, Sharon. "The 'Lie' of the Land: Native Sovereignty, Indian Literary Nationalism, and Early Indigenism in Silko's *Ceremony*." *American Indian Quarterly* 32, no. 3 (2008): 243–75.

James, Jennifer. *A Freedom Bought With Blood: African American War Literature from the Civil War to World War II*. Chapel Hill: University of North Carolina Press, 2007.

Kolb, Joe. "Gallup Stood Firm Against US Government in 1942." *Gallup Independent*, February 1, 2003.

Lack, Tony. "An Interview with Yu Fi Tuan, Professor Emeritus, University of Wisconsin-Madison." *Interdisciplinary Humanities* 32, no. 3 (2015): 7–12.

Momaday, N. Scott. *House Made of Dawn*. New York: Harper & Row, 1968. Reprint, New York: Harper Perennial, 2010.

Okada, John. *No-No Boy*. Rutherford, Vermont: Charles E. Tuttle, 1957. Reprint, Seattle: University of Washington Press, 1998.

Said, Edward. *Reflections on Exile and Other Essays*. Cambridge: Harvard University Press, 2000.

Satterlee, Michelle. "Landscape Imagery and Memory in the Narrative of Trauma: A Closer Look at Leslie Marmon Silko's *Ceremony*." *Interdisciplinary Studies in Literature and Environment* 13, no. 2 (2006): 73–93.

Sielke, Sabine. "Multiculturalism in the United States and Canada." In *The Palgrave Handbook of Comparative North American Literature*, ed. ReingardNischik, 49–64. London: Palgrave, 2014.

Silko, Leslie Marmon. *Ceremony*. New York: The Viking Press, 1977. Reprint, New York: Penguin Books, 1986.

Tuan, Yi-Fu. *Space and Place: The Perspective of Experience*.Minneapolis: University of Minnesota Press, 1977.

WakatsukiHouston, Jeanne. *Farewell to Manzanar.* Boston: Houghton Mifflin,1973. Reprint, New York: Random House, 2007.

Warnick, Ron. "Gallup bucked the system during World War II." *Route 66 News,* May 9, 2014.

Yoon, Seongho. "'No Place in Particular': Inhabiting Postinternment America, Articulating Postinternment Anxieties in John Okada's *No-No Boy.*" *Ariel: A Review of International English Literature* 43, no. 1 (2012): 45–65.

CHAPTER 8

Turning the Earth, Changing the Narrative: Spatial Transformation in Frances E. W. Harper's *Iola Leroy; or, Shadows Uplifted* (1892)

Mike Lemon

Published in 1892, Frances Ellen Watkins Harper's *Iola Leroy; or, Shadows Uplifted* proves a coda to Watkins Harper's lifelong advocacy for African American and women's rights.[1] The novel presents to readers the story of African American characters who transition from surviving enslavement to thriving in the Reconstructed American South. In the recent Broadview Press edition of the novel, editor Koritha Mitchell notes the novel's presentations of "community conversations" within formal and informal settings, including the market, parlor, hotel, and "secret gatherings of the

---

[1] Koritha Mitchell, introduction to *Iola Leroy; Or, Shadows Uplifted*, ed. Koritha Mitchell (Peterborough: Broadview Press, 2019), 13. Like Mitchell and other literary critics, I will use Watkins Harper to note the author's professional life before and after her marriage to Fenton Harper.

M. Lemon (✉)
Texas Tech University, Lubbock, TX, USA
e-mail: Mike.Lemon@ttu.edu

© The Author(s), under exclusive license to Springer Nature Switzerland AG 2021
C. Beck (ed.), *Mobility, Spatiality, and Resistance in Literary and Political Discourse*, Geocriticism and Spatial Literary Studies,
https://doi.org/10.1007/978-3-030-83477-7_8

164   M. LEMON

enslaved, risking life and limb, in the woods."[2] While Mitchell focuses on self-determination, freedom, and identity as embodied practices within the novel, Watkins Harper's varied—at times de-emphasized—depictions of physical and social settings signal her African American characters' nuanced encoding of dominant and subversive locations.

An investigation of Watkins Harper's *Iola Leroy* reveals the novel's characters' patterns of spatial negotiation. In the novel, the author divides these spatial negotiations into recognizable chronological events: antebellum and Reconstruction Southern United States. During the antebellum through the Civil War, Watkin Harper's black Southern characters understand the interrelationship of dominant social spaces and their physical manifestations; this awareness of spaces like the plantation and the boarding house can be framed with Lefebvrean representations of space. As a result, the enslaved African American community uses peripheral locations—the market, kitchen, woods, and slave cabins—to hold meetings; these physical locations become representational, or "lived in," spaces that challenge dominant representations of space. Such representational spaces are often difficult to geolocate, although cultural geographers have sought to situate black geographies.

Watkins Harper's challenging of dominant social spaces continues into the Reconstruction Period, as the Southern black community actively transforms the landscape. By emphasizing landownership and community involvement, Watkins Harper explicitly recalls earlier determiners for political enfranchisement; effectively, she argues through spatial transformation that the African American community belongs within the U.S.'s national citizenry. Even as she exposes lynching culture and its impact on the black Southern community, Watkins Harper emphasizes through the novel's conclusion that Iola, her family members, and the larger black Southern community are actively transforming the physical and social landscapes of the United States.

MAKING ROOM IN THE MARKET AND WOODS: CHALLENGING THE NARRATIVE

Late nineteenth-century regionalized American literatures, like Watkins Harper's *Iola Leroy*, invite readers to recognize intersections between physical spaces and socially constructed spaces. These literary productions

[2] Mitchell, introduction, 30–31.

argue for the social production of space. Regional literature emerges during the middle nineteenth century, simultaneously with legislation like the Homestead Act of 1862 that encouraged Western expansion. Such land policies invited naturalized citizens and recently arrived European immigrants to attempt small-scale farming. They are physical manifestations of early nineteenth-century Jeffersonian democracy, implicitly linking land-ownership and agrarian economic production to acceptance into an imagined national identity. The homestead and limitless frontier become what Henri Lefebvre identifies as *"representations of space"* where physical space becomes ideologically conditioned.[3] While the French theorist notes government buildings, historical monuments, patriotic public art, and even national parks as representations of space, rural settlements like the homestead and Southern plantation also become marked through ideological conceptions. Such representations of social space, Lefebvre argues, transparently produce dominant social, political, or economic institutions. In the United States, race becomes another ideological marker through which these "frontal (and hence brutal) expressions of these relations" manifest.[4]

Dominant American culture's brutal manifestations within representations of space often reinforced racialized policies, and the plantation is no exception. The Southern plantation's physical, political, and economic construction is predicated on the removal of indigenous peoples and the enslavement of African peoples. Clifton Ellis and Rebecca Ginsburg note the overlap between environments and buildings constructed by and for enslaved African people as perpetuating racializing ideologies.[5] Physical disparities between the opulent "big house" and slave quarters all serve to argue racial differences. Katherine McKittrick puts it more bluntly: "The plantation evidences an uneven colonial-racial economy that, while differently articulated across time and place, legalized black servitude while simultaneously sanctioning black placelessness and constraint. [...] [T]his system forcibly secured black peoples to the geographic mechanics of the

---

[3] Henri Lefebvre, *The Production of Space*, trans. Donald Nicholson-Smith (Malden: Blackwell Publishing, 1991), 33.

[4] Lefebvre, *Production*, 33.

[5] Clifton Ellis and Rebecca Ginsburg, introduction to *Cabin, Quarter, Plantation: Architecture and Landscapes of North American Slavery*, ed. Clifton Ellis and Rebecca Ginsburg (New Haven: Yale University Press, 2010), 6.

166   M. LEMON

plantation economy."[6] McKittrick's language emphasizes the paradox that enslaved and free Southern black communities encountered; confined to a geographical location, they simultaneously recognized placelessness. Brutal practices such as the separation of families, physical and sexual violence, and removal of culture further reinforced their dislocation on physical and social geographies.

Yet in spite of these representations of brutal social spaces, enslaved peoples found ways to exercise control of marginalized representational spaces. Representational spaces, according to Lefebvre, "embraces the loci of passion, of action, and of lived situations, [...] because it is essentially qualitative, fluid, and dynamic."[7] Representational spaces exist concurrently to representations of dominant space, and their often "underground side of social life" necessitates critical mediations to identify the competing narratives. Physically, slave quarters existed on the periphery of plantations; kitchens were often detached from the "big house." Socially, these locations remain far removed from many historical preservations of plantations, just as they physically did during the antebellum period. Carolyn Finney argues that Magnolia Plantation in Natchitoches, Louisiana, and the fight over developing programs about the lives of slaves become an example for "how certain experiences and memories of the past are often rendered invisible in the present, both in institutions and on the landscape, and how African Americans experience the reverberations of this 'forgetting' as well as the stories themselves."[8] McKittrick similarly observes that "a black sense of place is not a steady, focused, and homogenous way of seeing and being in place, but rather a set of changing and differential perspectives" that signal continuing efforts to dismiss African American's location in physical and historical settings.[9] Furthermore, McKittrick observes in an analysis on the Underground Railroad that "Geographic ignorance"—and for that matter, enslaved people's ignorance of social spaces—"is an impossibility in the underground because this strategy of subversively claiming and living unmapped routes demands

[6] Katherine McKittrick, "On Plantations, Prisons, and a Black Sense of Place," *Social & Cultural Geography* 12, no. 8 (2011): 948.

[7] Lefebvre, *Production*, 42.

[8] Carolyn Finney, *Reimagining the Relationship of African Americans to the Great Outdoors*, (Chapel Hill: University of North Carolina Press, 2014), 52.

[9] McKittrick, "On Plantations," 950.

that black subjects are, in fact, intimately aware of their surroundings[.]"[10] In order to locate black experiences onto physical and cultural maps, critics and readers alike must look for ways in which authors point toward representational spaces. In doing so, they might recognize how African American characters exercise agency by learning to "read" physical and social environments. From the opening chapters of *Iola Leroy*, Watkins Harper locates enslaved African American characters into representational spaces, where they can discuss their forced servitude and negotiate plans to escape. In the market, kitchen, woods, and slave cabins, Watkins Harper's character demonstrate what Rebecca Ginsburg has defined as black landscape, or the "ways that enslaved people knew the land, to the modes by which they made sense of and imagined their surroundings."[11]

The novel opens in the market and kitchen, which becomes encoded representational spaces for enslaved people to share information. Two "bondsmen"—Robert Johnson and Tom Anderson—seemingly share a conversation about the market's wares, although the narrator is quick to note that "every now and then, after looking furtively around, one would drop into the ear of the other some news of the battle then raging between the North and South."[12] In this brief explanation for contemporary readers, Watkins Harper explores verbal signifyin(g), or how enslaved men and women used indirect language to convey information about the war while simultaneously passing misinformation to their white owners. Signifyin(g) also extends to Robert and Tom's understanding of the market's spatiality. The act of looking around signals the men's understanding of their placement within the market. The market itself becomes representative of dominant culture; it is a site dominated by commerce, including the sale of chattel slaves. However, these men create representational space, as they discuss the war through coded language. In this, they overlap verbal, visual, and spatial signifyin(g) to indicate their knowledge of a black encoded landscape, where Robert and Tom "[become] aware of what many white people never did—namely, the extent of the sphere of black

[10] Katherine McKittrick, "'Freedom is a Secret': The Future Usability of the Underground," in *Black Geographies and the Politics of Place*, eds. Katherine McKittrick and Clyde Woods (Cambridge: South End Press, 2007), 102–103.

[11] Rebecca Ginsburg, "Escaping Through a Black Landscape" in *Cabin, Quarter, Plantation: Architecture and Landscapes of North American Slavery*, ed. Clifton Ellis and Rebecca Ginsburg (New Haven: Yale University Press, 2010), 56.

[12] Frances E. Watkins Harper, *Iola Leroy; Or, Shadows Uplifted*, ed. Koritha Mitchell (Peterborough: Broadview Press, 2019), 67.

activity that coexisted with but was out of the control of planter-enslavers and their allies."[13] This tension of representational black spaces, which permitted symbolic acts of resistance, and representations of white space allows Watkins Harper to depict her characters' understanding of encoded conversation; moreover, she argues these characters recognized spaces that would permit these discussions. In a separate conversation, held within the boarding home where Robert lives, the cook Aunt Linda offers this spatial analysis: "'Anyhow, Bobby, things goes mighty contrary in dis house. Ole Miss is in de parlor prayin' for de Secesh to gain de day, and we's prayin' in de cabins and kitchens for de Yankees to get de bes' ob it."[14] In this concise observation, Aunt Linda offers a summation of Watkins Harper's initial presentation of enslaved black landscapes and their tension with representations of dominant white space. While their mistress offers prayers in the parlor—a nineteenth-century space coded for middle-class, white women—Robert, Aunt Linda, and their enslaved peers operate in unseen black spaces to find freedom.

The use of unseen black landscapes is further emphasized through unsanctioned meetings in the woods. These meetings reinforce Watkins Harper's black characters' understanding of landscape. The narrator notes that while patrollers surveilled the land to curtail movement, enslaved people would hold "these meetings miles apart, extending into several States."[15] At these meetings, participants would share news of Union victory; additionally, the gatherings served as a spiritual experience. In this presentation of the woods, Watkins Harper seemingly downplays threats of violence; while she does mentions patrollers and home guards—military units tasked with preserving the Confederate home front—the author emphasizes the positive collective memory. Such a portrayal counteracts readers' perception of the woods as a representation of violent social space, in which white Americans perpetrated violence onto African Americans. Finney argues that most twenty-first-century African Americans remember "the act of terror perpetrated on a black person in the woods," to the detriment of recalling the woods as a site of "spiritual rejuvenation," physical sustenance, and cultural transmission.[16]

[13] Ginsburg, "Escaping," 63.
[14] Watkins Harper, *Iola Leroy*, 69.
[15] Watkins Harper, *Iola Leroy*, 72.
[16] Finney, *Reimagining*, 55, 64.

8 TURNING THE EARTH, CHANGING THE NARRATIVE: SPATIAL... 169

Robert Johnson's later recollections of these woods demonstrate layered representational spaces. As he, Iola, Aunt Linda, and others journey to a church meeting to search for lost loved ones, the narrative reveals his thoughts "of his boyish days, when he gathered nuts and wild plums in those woods; he also indulged pleasant reminiscences of later years, when, with Uncle Daniel and Tom Anderson, he attended the secret prayer-meetings."[17] This description supports Finney's argument that the woods were a source of physical and spiritual nourishment; moreover, Robert situates these memories onto a changing landscape. However, Robert's recollections take a dark turn later in the same chapter. When he chances upon a woman that may be his mother, Robert begins to speak. Curiously, Watkins Harper does not reveal much of Robert's speech, instead relying on the narrative "to tell his experiences [...] in the lonely woods and gloomy swamps."[18] Here, Robert's reminiscences take on sinister notes; they seemingly position the woods as a site of loss. The woods here become a representation of dominant space; because Robert's mother had been sold from him, the woods and the prayer meetings held there became a reminder of Robert's lost mother. In these moments, the woods become coded differently. At certain points, they become a site of comfort; at other times, it reverts to the dangerous representation of space that threatens black bodies and families.

Perhaps no character better demonstrates an understanding of black representational spaces than Tom Anderson. As a character who dies relatively early in the novel, Tom seemingly serves as a plot device; he facilitates the freeing of Iola Leroy from captivity. However, a reading of representational spaces reveals that Tom's knowledge of the land is a central characterization. Like, Robert, he recognizes the market as a space to relay coded messages. When he escapes to Union lines, Tom's knowledge of the land proves invaluable to the army. Even though he cannot fight due to "physical defects," Tom serves the Union. Watkins Harper writes, "He was well versed in the lay of the country, having often driven his master's cotton to market when he was a field hand. After he became a coachman, he had become acquainted with the different roads and localities of the country. Besides, he had often accompanied his young masters on their hunting and fishing expeditions."[19] Tom possesses an intimate

[17] Watkins Harper, *Iola Leroy*, 180.
[18] Watkins Harper, *Iola Leroy*, 184.
[19] Watkins Harper, *Iola Leroy*, 89.

knowledge of the land; moreover, Watkins Harper links Tom's knowledge to his forced servitude. In doing this, she implicitly links Tom again to Robert Johnson. Robert's mistress had taught him to read, not realizing that "the time would come when he would use the machinery she had put into his hands to help overthrow the institution which she was so ardently attached."[20] Whereas Robert's literacy becomes the tool that metaphorically tears down the master's house, Tom's knowledge of the land follows a similar practice. By entrusting him to take the cotton to market and guide hunting trips, Tom's masters did not realize that he would use his understanding of the land to help the Union army.

Unfortunately, Watkins Harper links Tom's death to the land, which further demonstrates competing social spaces. Union soldiers request that Tom row them around a nearby sound, even though Confederate snipers are still in the area. Even though Robert reminds readers that Tom "knows the lay of the land better than any of us," the freedman's and soldiers' boat runs aground, and they come under enemy fire.[21] Tom chooses to save the solders and sacrifices his life to free the boat. On its surface level, Tom's death works within Watkins Harper's sentimentalist lens, providing another opportunity to emphasize black bravery at a time when cultural forces promoted stereotypes of cowardice. Conducting a spatial analysis, though, reveals that Union soldiers needlessly placed Tom in harm's way. Notwithstanding Tom's understanding of representational spaces, the Union soldiers place him within a representation of space—the sound. They effectively ask him to perform a task within this space that replicates his servitude. The soldiers ask him to row, in a similar fashion to his former master asking him to guide a fishing trip. In doing so, they position Tom into a representation of space that limits his agency and endangers his physical body. For all his knowledge of the land, Tom cannot overcome the brutal representation of space that ultimately leads to his death.

In her opening chapters, Watkins Harper portrays enslaved people with complex understandings of representational spaces. Notwithstanding dominant social spaces shaping representations of space that limit black movement and agency, Watkins Harper depicts the market, kitchens, cabins, and woods as representational spaces where Robert, Tom, Aunt Linda, and many others create space to exercise agency. These moments in the early chapters are inspiring, although Watkins Harper is mindful of the

---

[20] Watkins Harper, *Iola Leroy*, 73.
[21] Watkins Harper, *Iola Leroy*, 89.

8 TURNING THE EARTH, CHANGING THE NARRATIVE: SPATIAL... 171

dangers that exist outside these shifting representational spaces. Patrollers might discover their prayer meetings in the woods, and Tom loses his life because Union soldiers underestimate the hazards of rowing during a war. Still, these early conceptions of black landscapes indicate the transformative potential of physical spaces; this becomes a point of discussion within the later chapters, as Watkins Harper moves into the early Reconstruction period.

Turning the Earth: From Plantation (Slaves) to Homeowners (Citizens)

Iola Leroy might seem a curious choice for a spatial analysis, because Watkins Harper often obscures georeferenced locations. The early descriptions of the market, boarding house, and woods are very sparse. Even the North Carolina town is elided. Watkins Harper simply refers to it as C—. Rather than provide accurate locations for her characters, Watkins Harper opts to obscure locations for two reasons. One, she demonstrates the transformation of social and physical spaces in C—, North Carolina after the Civil War. The novel's sole indication of C—'s georeferenced location comes through its connection to the enslaved community. As mentioned earlier, the slaves hold secretive meetings that occur across several different states.[22] This minor geographic reference positions the city's location perhaps in the state's northwestern corner, which would allow meetings to occur in Virginia, Tennessee, and North Carolina. This would also facilitate the army's movement toward the Battle of Five Forks in Dunwiddie County, Virginia. This speculation further implies Watkins Harper's reason to obscure physical geographies. The author destabilizes the region's physical, as well as social spaces that threaten growing lynching concerns. Beginning and ending the novel in C—, North Carolina offers a powerful example for how the black Southern community actively transforms the Southern landscape through economic and intellectual achievements.

Furthermore, the elision of actual location permits Harper to argue the destabilization of social spaces, even at a time when social and political movements sought to overturn the Civil War's tenuous victories for civil rights. Fears of marginalization by America's dominant social demographic—broadly conceived as racially white, religiously Protestant, and economically middle class—caused the physical and ideological

[22] Watkins Harper, *Iola Leroy*, 69.

172   M. LEMON

marginalization of actual minority communities during the mid to late nineteenth century. Communities of color—including Mexican Americans, indigenous Americans, and African Americans who recently received citizenship—were precluded from the imagined American community, because of their ethnicity and subsequent racialization. These preclusions impacted land legislation that explicitly curtailed nonwhite people's physical movement, as well as access to civic rights and privileges.[23] Finding an overlap between the two, Finney notes that in addition to the Homestead Act, the Freedmen's Bureau managed the parceling of confiscated Confederate land to formerly enslaved people. This promise of access to land and the possibility of economic wealth, however, were challenged by recently pardoned white Southerner landowners. Finney summarizes, "The freedmen were forced off their newly acquired land, and it was returned to the former white plantation owners."[24] The seizure of former plantation land—surrendered back to white landowners—recalls the old plantation economy that "sanctioned," as Katherine McKittrick observes, "black placelessness and constraint."[25]

The loss of acquired property also signals the entrenchment of ideological conceptions of land use that calls into question the freedmen's newly secured freedoms. That questions of citizenship coincide with restrictions on landownership only reaffirms Jeffersonian democracy's continued acceptance as markers of an individual's political rights. Promoted by Thomas Jefferson, this political framework imagined American citizenship through landownership and small-scale economic production. The Homestead Act, the Freedmen's Bureau's original land management policy, and other land legislations encouraged immigrants and naturalized citizens to explicitly participate in Jefferson's sociopolitical experiment. However, Finney, McKittrick, and others have noted the exclusion of African Americans, Chinese immigrants, Latinos, and other minority groups from accessing lands offered by the federal government. The late nineteenth century saw the United States undergo radical demographic shifts that caused what Rebecca Edwards summarizes as "struggles over the United States' new identity as a multiracial society and over whether people of color (including not only African Americans, but also

[23] Finney, *Reimagining*, 37.
[24] Finney, *Reimagining*, 37.
[25] McKittrick, "On Plantations," 948.

Asians and Latinos) had equal citizenship rights."[26] The exclusion of these minorities from owning property explicitly argues their removal from the nation's imagined national identity, thus precluding them from representations of dominant social space. Indeed, Nina Silber has argued, "Southern blacks, like various immigrant groups, stood outside this more exclusive view of the nation and thus become invisible in the overall picture of the South."[27] It is within these brutal representations of space that Watkins Harper presents a community that literally transforms the landscape, as they argue for their position in the United States' citizenry.

Watkins Harper centers landownership and industry as markers of the black Southern community's argument for their citizenship. When Robert returns to C—, he encounters a transformed location and community, because black industry has entered the market. After meeting with his former mistress, he ventures to the woods where he and his fellow slaves had held their last prayer meeting. This initiates a comparative moment, as Robert contemplates the current location with its past. The narrative explains, "Now the gloomy silence of those woods was broken by the hum of industry, the murmur of cheerful voices, and the merry laughter of happy children. Where they had trodden with fear and misgiving, freedmen walked with light and bounding hearts. The school-house had taken the place of the slave-pen and auction-block."[28] The final statement describes actual and metaphoric transformation, yet the opening comparisons speak to the transformation of communal attitude. Whereas the enslaved population moved through the representations of space—the woods—in fear or through representational black landscapes, the newly freed community conceives the physical space differently. It is now a social space filled with optimism and industry. Instead of being a cowered populace, Robert contemplates the community's optimistic outlook on freedom. Furthermore, the narrative explicitly situates children within this scene, suggesting that future generations are optimistic concerning the uplift of the black Southern community. Their presence returns readers to the school-house's physical and metaphoric importance. Having replaced the "slave-pen and auction-block" as physical referents to slavery's oppres-

---

[26] Rebecca Edwards, "Politics, Social Movements, and the Periodization of U.S. History," *The Journal of the Gilded Age and Progressive Era* 8, no. 4 (2009): 472.

[27] Nina Silber, *The Romance of Reunion: Northerners and the South, 1865–1900* (Chapel Hill: University of North Carolina Press, 1993), 140.

[28] Watkins Harper, *Iola Leroy*, 165.

sive institution, the school-house offers stability and mental growth. Moreover, the school-house and children transform the location into a place that maintains family structures. The sentiment and building form domestic structures that speak to the black community's future. The school-house, however, does not indicate the only avenue for social and communal growth.

Notwithstanding the novel's emphasis on education as one means for the black Southern community to redefine their location into a black-coded place, Aunt Linda and other illiterate characters also transform C— into a vastly different representation of social space. Recognizing Robert as he admires her "garden filled with beautiful flowers, clambering vines, and rustic adornments," Aunt Linda invites him into her home.[29] Situating the freedwoman within a domestic setting suggests her industry; by extension, emphasizing her flower garden implicitly positions Aunt Linda within the cult of domesticity. Notwithstanding the presence of farm animals and vegetable gardens, the initial description of flowers suggests that like expectations for white middle-class women, the newly freed woman has found time to beautify her home with non-essential plants. This description seemingly becomes an extension of the swept yards of slave quarters; whereas enslaved women would sweep the yard around their houses to carve out a representational understanding of their space, Aunt Linda plants flowers to argue her position within a genteel American citizenry. The fact that she cannot read, however, seemingly excludes Linda from the American middle class. She claims to Robert, "'I'se been scracthin' my head too hard to get a libin' to put my head down to de book.'"[30] This statement functions within a pattern for Linda's refusal to gain literacy, which for some readers may place her and other illiterate black characters as outside of the novel's theme for improvement. For Elizabeth Young, Linda "remains a beloved and venerated figure, [but] this refusal [to learn to read] inevitably diminishes her as a model for racial uplift in comparison with the novel's literate middle-class characters."[31] Young's argument seems accurate, if critics and readers deem education as the novel's only avenue for black community improvement. Linda and her husband's

---

[29] Watkins Harper, *Iola Leroy*, 165.

[30] Watkins Harper, *Iola Leroy*, 167.

[31] Elizabeth Young, *Disarming the Nation: Women's Writing and the American Civil War* (Chicago: University of Chicago Press, 1999), 229.

8 TURNING THE EARTH, CHANGING THE NARRATIVE: SPATIAL... 175

post-war activities, however, signal ways in which illiterate former slaves transformed their position and location.

Despite her illiteracy, Linda gains some financial freedom through her domestic skills. Like earlier depictions of Tom, Watkins Harper wants to demonstrate how newly freed African Americans use skills learned during slavery to demand respectability; for Aunt Linda, her knowledge of cooking enables her to earn income. She reports, "'I made pies an' cakes, sole em to de sogers, an' jist made money han' ober fist. An' I kep' on a workin' an' a savin' till my ole man got back from de war wid his wages and his bounty money. I felt right set up an' mighty big wen we counted all dat money.'"[32] Applying her knowledge of cooking, Linda finds a market for her baked goods. Combined with her husband's wartime savings, she and Salters/John Andrews purchase a home.[33] The act of purchasing the home is significant for the spatial analysis for two primary reasons.

First, purchasing land permits Watkins Harper to address the duplicitous history of land sales to freedmen. As mentioned earlier, the Freedmen's Bureau initially reallocated seized Confederate plantations to freed slaves; however, "President [Andrew] Johnson ordered all land titles rescinded" and "vetoed every proposal that provided land to former slaves."[34] Mitchell confirms this; in a footnote in her edition of *Iola Leroy*, she contends, "White civilians could always easily take land from African Americans because all laws and cultural practices viewed white people as legitimate owners and black people as natural servants."[35] This history of given and rescinded land becomes a nodal point within the novel itself. Speaking with Robert and Uncle Daniel, Salters admits "'I'se 'fraid arter I'se done buyed it an' put all de marrer ob dese bones in it, dat somebody's far-off cousin will come an' say de title ain't good, an' I'll lost it all."[36] Salter's comment corroborates Finney and Mitchell's twenty-first-century criticism, meaning that Watkins Harper was aware of and was actively criticizing the federal government's heavy-handed policies. She demonstrates her

---

[32] Watkins Harper, *Iola Leroy*, 166.

[33] Watkins Harper, *Iola Leroy*, 167–167. Salters/John Andrews has two names within the text. The former is his preferred, "home" name. The latter is his slave name that he used when he enlisted and continues to use in his economic dealings. In this chapter, I will refer to him as Salters.

[34] Finney, *Reimagining*, 37.

[35] Koritha Mitchell, footnote to *Iola Leroy; Or, Shadows Uplifted*, ed. Koritha Mitchell (Peterborough: Broadview Press, 2019), 178–179.

[36] Watkins Harper, *Iola Leroy*, 178.

176 M. LEMON

criticism by having Linda persuade her husband to purchase land rather than rent. That they have successfully maintained—and improved—the land signals to Watkins Harper's readership that newly freed Southern African Americans deserved equal access to land.

Second, their purchased home proves to be a transformative location, for they have bought the land of Salters' former master. The narrative explains that while most plantation owners swore they would not sell their land to former slaves, the Civil War had crippled the white Southern economy; coupled with the emancipation of their "property," many white families in C—lost their lands. Linda reports that even though Salter's former master said "dat he would let de lan' grow up in trees 'fore he'd sell it to us," an outside group of Jewish land speculators bought and sold the land.[37] Her seemingly throwaway comment speaks to the history of Jewish people in North Carolina; in a footnote, Mitchell claims "No doubt some Northerners who relocated South were Jewish."[38] Harry L. Golden has also noted that emigrating Jewish merchants after the war and during the first decades of the twentieth century were helpful to black Southerners, because they would allow their customers to try on merchandise before purchasing.[39] This suggests that minority communities in the South helped each other establish themselves within a hostile physical and social space. Moreover, this land plot also has a significant edifice: Salter's former overseer's house.

Now established in his former overseer's home, Salters and Linda have transformed the place and its social messaging. They have worked in the local economy and have saved their money to mediate their social space, sense of place, and community. In addition to the gardens, Watkins Harper offers a little description of their home. Salters and Linda entertain Robert, his niece Iola, and Uncle Daniel in their kitchen; even though the physical description is scant, Watkins Harper defines this space through Linda's domestic industry. After their dinner, the narrator remarks, "Salters and his guests returned to the front room, which Aunt Linda regarded with so much pride, and on which she bestowed so much care."[40] Again, Watkins Harper does not provide much physical description; however, the

[37] Watkins Harper, *Iola Leroy*, 166–167.
[38] Mitchell, footnote to *Iola Leroy*, 167.
[39] Harry L. Golden, "The Jewish People of North Carolina," *The North Carolina Historical Review* 32, no. 2 (1955): 204.
[40] Watkins Harper, *Iola Leroy*, 176.

narrative positions this material space within the social expectations of these rooms. Whether called sitting rooms, parlors, or front rooms, these spaces often reflected the family's public-facing tastes. That Aunt Linda pays special attention to this room signals a similar social space as the garden; Linda sees herself as a participant within the nation's conception of domesticity and femininity. Reviewing his and Linda's improvement to the house, Salters remarks, "I'se fixed it up sence I'se got it. Now I'se better off dan he is."[41] In this comparative moment, Salters uses rhetoric often identified with homesteading; he effectively argues that he has improved the land and its edifices more than its former owner. That the former owner was Salters' overseer calls into question the suppose racial superiority narrative. While continuing to recognize the history of that place, Aunt Linda has a more defiant remark: "My! but ain't dem tables turned."[42] Improvement through economics and land ownership becomes another powerful message with Watkins Harper's novel for how to uplift the black Southern community.

Whereas Iola, Harry, and their respective spouses work through education, religion, and medicine to uplift the black community, Robert works through economic and land development in ways that align him with Linda and Salters. In the concluding chapter, the narrative relates that Robert sells his Northern hardware store. With this money, "[h]e bought a large plantation near C—, which he divided into small homesteads, and sold to poor but thrifty laborers, and his heart was gladdened by their increased prosperity and progress."[43] Robert's parceling of land to industrious black families permits them to avoid sharecropping and become landowners. Purchasing the plantation and redistributing property to black landowners also alters the location's social space. Robert's generosity and the black homesteaders' prosperity shift the land's previous ideological conception. Formerly operating a large-scale agricultural production through the forced labor of enslaved black Southerners, freed black Southerners now own and demonstrate their industry on that land. Through Robert's philanthropy, these homesteaders participate in a dominant American economic ideology; through their land ownership and industry, they argue their rights to citizenship and equal protection under the law. Implicitly, Robert's decision aligns him with Linda, Salters, and

[41] Watkins Harper, *Iola Leroy*, 179.
[42] Watkins Harper, *Iola Leroy*, 167.
[43] Watkins Harper, *Iola Leroy*, 250–251.

178 M. LEMON

the "folk" community rather than his blood relations. Despite his literacy serving as an important tool during the Civil War, Robert does not actively participate in educating his peers. Rather, he advocates economic progress as another avenue for building the black Southern community. Doing so does not diminish the novel's racial uplift message; instead, Watkins Harper desires to introduce multiple progressive means by which her characters—regardless of education and racial makeup—can aid in the community's development.

Something to See Here: Unearthing Racial Violence and Survival in the Reconstructed South

Notwithstanding the novel's optimistic tone, Harper does not ignore the lynch culture that impacts black Southern bodies and communities. Through explicit and veiled events, her black characters experience resistance to the formation of developed free black Southern communities. In *Iola Leroy*, Watkins Harper openly challenges social and literary texts that obscure physical, sexual, and psychological violence against Southern black people. Increasingly entrenched "Lost Cause" rhetoric informed a new form of Southern American writing, Plantation fiction, that "sought to convince northern readers that southern life was harmonious, and thus, they need not worry about 'reconstructing' it anymore."[44] This New South writing created an aestheticized history that ignored the depravations of slavery, arguing that like those white Southern men and women who acted as benevolent owners, the post-Reconstruction white Southern population would continue to serve as honorable patrons to the black community. Moreover, these popular late nineteenth-century texts invert gendered regional metaphors, which effectively reassign masculine dominance onto the South's representations of white space. Young contends these texts—through their content and metaphors—transfer sexually coded regional language regarding the North's "rape of the South" "to authorize accusations of interracial rape against black men and subsequent lynchings."[45] These metaphors and popular literature function alongside

[44] Leslie Petty, *Romancing the Vote: Feminist Activism in American Fiction, 1870–1920* (Athens: University of Georgia Press, 2006), 66. See also Silber, *Romance of Reunion,* 181, 185–186; and Young, *Disarming,* 217.
[45] Elizabeth Young, "Warring Fictions: *Iola Leroy* and the Color of Gender," *American Literature,* 64, no. 2 (1992): 287.

8 TURNING THE EARTH, CHANGING THE NARRATIVE: SPATIAL... 179

other systems to obscure racist violence and confirm dominant social productions of space.

In challenging those dominant social narratives, Watkins Harper reveals the varying degrees of violence that impair black Southerners' physical, political, psychological, and mental well-being. Iola's first school-room—housed in a church—is burned. The school-room and its hosting church are important physical markers, because they confirm black Southern civil liberties. The physical edifice becomes a representational space that asserts the freed people's entrance into the nation's political body. Watkins Harper does not reveal the culprits of the arson; instead, she writes, "the elements of evil burst upon [Iola's] loved and cherished work."[46] Rather than implicate the responsible individuals, the author decides to indict the dominant culture. Linking white Southern violence to evil rejects popular depictions of plantation owners as benevolent. Rather, they participate in the burning of schools and churches.

Watkins Harper further discusses violence against the exercising of political enfranchisement; in doing so, she links Linda and Salters' family history to the Leroys. Linda and Salters are raising their grandson. Linda tells Robert and Iola, "his fadder war killed by the Secesh, one night, comin' home from a politic meetin', an' his pore mudder died a few weeks arter."[47] Her evocation of Secessionists connects antebellum white Southern mentality and the Lost Cause to lynch culture. Watkins Harper further explores how politic violence impacts women. In the years before women suffrage, she notes that the father's death directly connects to the mother's death. The threat of physical violence also troubles Marie Leroy because her son, Harry, has become politically and socially active. With his Northern education and experience during the war, he teaches, and has established himself as a leader for the black community in Georgia. But becoming a leader makes him a target for racist reprisals. Marie particularly fears election seasons, telling her son, "I am afraid that you will get into trouble and be murdered, as many others have been."[48] She fears for her son's life; moreover, Marie's argument implies lynch culture's effects on other black people. Although these individuals remain nameless, Marie's fears are actualized in Linda and Salters' experience. Through its physical and rhetorical violence against black Southern people and their communi-

[46] Watkins Harper, *Iola Leroy*, 161.
[47] Watkins Harper, *Iola Leroy*, 177
[48] Watkins Harper, *Iola Leroy*, 197.

180   M. LEMON

ties, lynch culture becomes a critical undercurrent within the narrative. Yet notwithstanding the very real possibility of physical and psychological violence, Iola and her family choose to return to North Carolina.

Iola's decision to return South centers on the main character's desire to improve the community through activism, as well as the Southern region's potential to transform socially and spatially. Iola aligns herself with late nineteenth-century domestic social issues and frames her discussions in gender appropriate (i.e., sentimental, religious, and domestic) language. For Marilyn Elkins, this means that Iola and other women like Lucille Delany and Linda "emerge as essential to the goals and aims of Reconstruction within the black community. No longer the objects of patriarchal exchange, the women have become participants in a system that stresses relationships of equality."[49] This equality extends across gender and education levels; in her analysis, Elkins validates Linda's position as one of the novel's most vocal community leaders and advocates.[50] Yet, Iola becomes the central activist, in addition to being the novel's protagonist. She articulates the need for domestic and employable skills. For example, she advocates that "every woman should have some skill or art which would insure her at least a comfortable support. I believe there would be less unhappy marriages if labor were more honored among women."[51] This statement contextualizes Iola's desire for suitable employment, extending to how she conceives a woman's role within domestic and social circles. Women ought to develop their talents, so they can actively participate in domestic and community economies. Iola's desire to apply her knowledge and art influences her decision to journey back to C—, because she will be of greater service to her community there. She recognizes her kinship to these freed Southern blacks and longs to help them improve.

The potential for community building through spatial transformation also informs Iola's decision to return south. Unlike the novel's black Northern communities, black populations in C—and other elided Southern locations actively build their communities. Material and educational achievements become symbolic of racial achievement in the South

---

[49] Marilyn Elkins, "'Reading Beyond the Conventions: A Look at Frances E. W. Harper's *Iola Leroy, or Shadows Uplifted*," *American Literary Realism, 1870–1910* 22, no. 2 (1990): 50–51.

[50] Elkins, "Reading Beyond," 47.

[51] Watkins Harper, *Iola Leroy*, 201.

8 TURNING THE EARTH, CHANGING THE NARRATIVE: SPATIAL... 181

and become doubly impressive considering lynching culture. For one commentator within the novel, the black Southern community's material presence becomes a powerful counter narrative to the plantation school's lazy shiftless black stereotype, because, "[t]he men who are acquiring property and building up homes in the South show us what energy and determination may do even in that part of the country. I believe such men can do more to conquer prejudice than if they spent all their lives in shouting for their rights and ignoring their duties."[52] Given the novel's emphasis on Linda and Salters' post-war experiences in C—, this statement reaffirms that economic improvement and land ownership challenge racial prejudices. Freed men and women effectively revise the national imagined identity, as they take ownership of the nation's narrative on citizenship.

As they revise the narrative through agroeconomic pursuits, these black Southern communities alter the landscape and by extension the social spaces that grant meaning to the land. Another commentator within the novel, Reverend Carmicle, who recently toured the Southern states, explicitly links spatial transformation to the community's progress. Embedded within a report on improvements in education and literacy, he declares, "Comfortable homes have succeeded old cabins of slavery. Vast crops have been raised by free labor."[53] The position of the reverend's comment becomes important, for while his report primarily focuses on educational improvement, he still includes a discussion on physical labor. This suggests that while Watkins Harper emphasizes growth through her character's educational and spiritual developments, she does not exclude material alterations to the landscape. Specifically, the replacement of slave quarters with 'comfortable homes' conflates economic gains and the novel's emphasis on domestic circles. It also implies that black Southern woman have entered the cult of domesticity, establishing domestic spaces in locations where they previously could not raise a family. Coupled with the statement on agricultural pursuits, Rev. Carmicle presents a fully formed black Southern community, with both genders' labor represented.

The Reverend's inclusion of active female community members and their comfortable homes shapes Iola's domestic and community activism in C—. The concluding chapter reports that she "quietly" becomes "a strong and powerful ally" to the local church as a Sunday school teacher;

---

[52] Watkins Harper, *Iola Leroy*, 228.
[53] Watkins Harper, *Iola Leroy*, 236.

furthermore, Iola opens her home "for the instruction of the children before their feet have wandered and gone far astray."[54] Working alongside her husband, Iola seeks to improve the community through domestic circles; she strengthens her kinship in the church and home. While this may seem to reify limiting conceptions of female activism, the narrative's description of Iola as "a strong and powerful ally" suggests that Watkins Harper reconceives the black cult of domesticity as socially, religiously, and politically active. Considering Iola's experiences within the novel, she becomes representative of Watkins Harper's ideal black woman. Rather than becoming a submissive actor after marriage, she engages in activities that build her community. Thus, Iola too works to transform the black Southern community.

CONCLUSION

By investigating how characters interact with physical settings within the novel, Frances Ellen Watkins Harper's *Iola Leroy; Or, Shadows Uplifted* provides complex understandings of physical and social spaces. During the novel's antebellum period, characters negotiate brutal representations of space like the market and Mrs. Johnson's boarding house to pass encoded news about the war. Furthermore, Watkins Harper situates the black Southern community within representational spaces that provide them more freedom. By analyzing the novel's complex presentation of social spaces, readers can reevaluate the importance and role of Tom Anderson's characterization. Tom's understanding of the land makes him more than a plot device; rather, he becomes a precursor to Watkin Harper's Reconstruction characters who actively transform that land and its symbolic meaning.

As the narrative shifts to the early Reconstruction period, Watkins Harper emphasizes economic and spatial transformation as other vital avenues for the black Southern community's development. Admittedly, education and religion are the novel's primary emphases for communal improvement, because these are the avenues that Iola, Harry, and their spouses advocate through their personal and professional lives. However, Watkins Harper uses Linda, Salters, and Robert as examples of characters who transform the land or enable landownership to others; through these characters, she argues for the entire black Southern community's

[54] Watkins Harper, *Iola Leroy*, 249.

acceptance into the American national imagery, regardless of educational or religious standing. In doing so, Watkins Harper provides various avenues to political and community activism that seems prescient for twenty-first-century readers. The novel's characters wrestle with questions on voter suppression, participation in American society, access to education, wrongful incarceration, and housing discrimination that are still relevant today.

Moreover, Watkins Harper connects these avenues for communal development to violent efforts to suppress black agency. Again, twenty-first-century readers will find relevant themes. Increased scrutiny of racial violence at the hands of dominant social institutions, efforts by lawmakers to invalidate votes, and the rise of transparent white supremacy in American society are chief concerns shared between Watkins Harpers' characters and her readership. But rather than have her characters run from lynch culture, Watkins Harper has Iola and her family ultimately choose to return to C—, North Carolina. There, they actively participate to turn the land—and its social spaces—into a vibrant, loving black Southern community. She provides, then, a historic blueprint for solidarity and resistance that offers space for the entire black community to thrive in the face of violent dominant social spaces.

Works Cited

Edwards, Rebecca. "Politics, Social Movements, and the Periodization of U.S. History." *The Journal of the Gilded Age and Progressive Era* 8, no. 4 (2009): 463–473.

Elkins, Marilyn. "'Reading Beyond the Conversations: A Look at Frances E. W. Harper's *Iola Leroy, or Shadows Uplifted*." *American Literary Realism, 1870–1910* 22, no. 2 (1990): 44–53.

Ellis, Clifton, and Rebecca Ginsburg. Introduction to *Cabin, Quarter, Plantation: Architecture and Landscapes of North American Slavery*, edited by Clifton Ellis and Rebecca Ginsburg, 1–15. New Haven: Yale University Press, 2010.

Finney, Carolyn. *Reimagining the Relationship of African-Americans to the Great Outdoors*. Chapel Hill: University of North Carolina Press, 2014.

Ginsburg, Rebecca. "Escaping Through a Black Landscape." In *Cabin, Quarter, Plantation: Architecture and Landscapes of North American Slavery*, edited by Clifton Ellis and Rebecca Ginsburg, 51–65. New Haven: Yale University Press, 2010.

Golden, Harry L. "The Jewish People of North Carolina." *The North Carolina Historical Review* 32, no. 2 (1955): 194–216.

Harper, Frances E. W. *Iola Leroy; Or, Shadows Uplifted*. Edited by Koritha Mitchell. Peterborough: Broadview Press, 2019.

Lefebvre, Henri. *The Production of Space*. Translated by Donald Nicholson-Smith. Malden: Blackwell Publishing, 1991.

McKittrick, Katherine. "'Freedom is a Secret': The Future Usability of the Underground." In *Black Geographies and the Politics of Place*, edited by Katherine McKittrick and Clyde Woods, 97–114. Cambridge: South End Press, 2007.

McKittrick, Katherine. "On Plantations, Prisons, and a Black Sense of Place." *Social & Cultural Geography* 12, no. 8 (2011): 947–963.

Mitchell, Koritha. Introduction to *Iola Leroy; Or, Shadows Uplifted*. Edited by Koritha Mitchell, 13–50. Peterborough: Broadview Press, 2019.

Petty, Leslie. *Romancing the Vote: Feminist Activism in American Fiction, 1870–1920*. Athens: University of Georgia Press, 2006.

Silber, Nina. *The Romance of Reunion: Northerners and the South, 1865–1900*. Chapel Hill: University of North Carolina Press, 1993.

Young, Elizabeth. *Disarming the Nation: Women's Writing and the American Civil War*. Chicago: University of Chicago Press, 1999.

Young, Elizabeth. "Warring Fictions: *Iola Leroy* and the Color of Gender." *American Literature* 64, no. 2 (1992): 273–297.

CHAPTER 9

Woolf in the Background: Distance as Visual Philosophy, Then and Now

Amy A. Foley

Throughout her writings, Virginia Woolf presents a spatial dichotomy according to background and foreground, often privileging background while simultaneously and subversively conjoining the far and the near. In her memoir "A Sketch of the Past," Woolf highlights the centrality of background as a philosophical force according to which the "figure" cannot operate or live:

> If I were painting myself I should have to find some—rod, shall I say—
> something that would stand for the conception. It proves that one's life is
> not confined to one's body and what one says and does; one is living all the
> time in relation to certain background rods or conceptions. Mine is that
> there is a pattern hid behind the cotton wool ... these moments of being of

---

A. A. Foley (✉)
Providence College, Providence, RI, USA

© The Author(s), under exclusive license to Springer Nature
Switzerland AG 2021
C. Beck (ed.), *Mobility, Spatiality, and Resistance in Literary and
Political Discourse*, Geocriticism and Spatial Literary Studies,
https://doi.org/10.1007/978-3-030-83477-7_9

185

186 A. A. FOLEY

mine were scaffolding in the background; were the invisible and silent part of my life as a child. But in the foreground there were of course people.[1]

Woolf's dialectic is not a classical one; rather, it conveys a new relationality because of its spatial nature. Hers is a phenomenon that can only occur according to a positionality by which two things are in tension with one another. Woolf's articulation of background as central to a philosophy of space and experience well before twentieth-century phenomenologists illustrates our experience with depth and also gives greater meaning to the aesthetic and cultural value of space inherited from the nineteenth century.

Woolf's 1928 novel, *Orlando*, attends to distances while conjoining the near and the far. She writes that Orlando "loved … vast views,"[2] that "sights disturbed him"[3] and that as a poet, and therefore inclined to perpetually describe, he "looked (and here he showed more audacity than most) at the thing itself."[4] Orlando stands on high ground, observing between nineteen and forty English counties as well as his family's estate in the distance: "Rivers could be seen and pleasure boats gliding on them; and galleons setting out to sea; and armadas with puffs of smoke from which came the dull thud of cannon firing; and forts on the coast; and castles among the meadows; and here a watch tower; and there a fortress; and again some vast mansion like that of Orlando's father."[5] Orlando postures in this scene as he does in so many others, "counting, gazing, recognising."[6] Woolf's authorial attention to the striations of space and their relative distance from the focalizing character describe an acute phenomenon, that of the vacillating look. Her narration of vacillating perception is best described as a toggle or an attentive and focused switch between one space and another: background, foreground, and often a middle ground. The following scene is one of many where Orlando becomes entranced with what lies in the distance, noting relative distance of objects from his own body:

---

[1] Virginia Woolf, "A Sketch of the Past," in *Moments of Being*, ed. Jeanne Schulkind, (London: Harcourt, Inc., 1985), 72–3.

[2] Virginia Woolf, *Orlando* (London: Harcourt, Inc., 2006), 14.

[3] Woolf, *Orlando*, 13.

[4] Woolf, *Orlando*, 13–4.

[5] Woolf, *Orlando*, 15.

[6] Woolf, *Orlando*, 15.

9 WOOLF IN THE BACKGROUND: DISTANCE AS VISUAL PHILOSOPHY, THEN... 187

> As the sun sank, all the domes, spires, turrets, and pinnacles of London rose in inky blackness against the furious red sunset clouds. Here was the fretted cross at Charing; there the dome of St. Paul's; there the massy square of the Tower buildings; there like a grove of trees stripped of all leaves save a knob at the end were the heads on the pikes at Temple Bar. Now the Abbey windows were lit up and burnt like a heavenly many-coloured shield (in Orlando's fancy); now all the west seemed a golden window with troops of angels (in Orlando's fancy again) passing up and down the heavenly stairs perpetually.[7]

"Here" and "there" are part of a spatial-temporal correlation in Woolf's perceptual mode. We understand in this passage how the author mimics the experience of perceiving objects as they appear to us from a specific and relative position in time and space. The "here" corresponds with the "now," just as what is "there" corresponds with what was "then."[8] Woolf's way of presenting space as time is cohesive with the design of the entire novel, as a satirical dramatization, and therefore theatrical staging of history itself.

It is fair to say that Woolf's direct reference to background and foreground spaces in her memoir especially is informed by her experience with the space of the stage. She repeatedly makes use of theatrical space and the dramatic perception that its space makes possible throughout her entire body of work. The events of her final novel, *Between the Acts* (1941), revolve around a village performance in an outdoor space of a country manor. With Shakespeare as a guiding spirit, Woolf shows a repeated relationship between the theater of life and the theatrical stage. The connection between theater and dramatized events are both thematic and spatial. Both events on stage and events imagined in Woolf's work invite and evoke an entrance and absorption that occurs between poles. Orlando sees a play that seems to dramatize his own feelings, a device by which Woolf recreates a toggling between the external and the internal world:

> The main press of people, it appeared, stood opposite a booth or stage something like our Punch and Judy show upon which some kind of theatrical performance was going forward. A black man was waving his arms and

---

[7] Woolf, *Orlando*, 39.

[8] For a related consideration of the intersections of temporality and spatiality, see Doreen Massey, "Some Times of Space," in *Olafur Eliasson: The Weather Project,* ed. Susan May (London, UK: Tate Modern, 2003), 111.

188 A. A. FOLEY

vociferating. There was a woman in white laid upon a bed. ... The frenzy of the Moor seemed to him his own frenzy, and when the Moor suffocated the woman in her bed it was Sasha he killed with his own hands.[9]

Similarly in *Between the Acts*, Isa reads about a violent event in a newspaper and imagines the action playing out in front of her, almost as on a stage.[10] In both novels, the space of the stage is interchangeable with the space of consciousness. The depth of stage and consciousness itself are simultaneously entered upon, which is made possible by the structures or rods of the background, in Woolf's terminology, and the figures themselves in the foreground. The space of the theater, whether or not directly evoked in Woolf, ties together background and foreground as well as thought and thing, idea and object.

Woolf's own participation in theater, dance, and ballet is integral to her spatial dialectics. Her connection with Sergei Diaghilev and the Ballet Russes was concurrent with her writing of *Orlando*. After 1930 the Camargo Society, London's premiere ballet company, included ballets composed by Erik Satie, Maurice Ravel, and Frédéric Chopin. In "Virginia Woolf and the Dance," Susan Jones thoroughly reviews Woolf's engagement with her contemporary ballet scene, including references to Vanessa Bell's own aesthetic work on stage. Bell painted the background for Gavin Gordon's *High Yellow*, performed in 1932 at the Savoy Theater in London, and for Thomas McGreevy's *Pomona* in 1930. Also noteworthy is Woolf's connection with painter Duncan Grant, Vanessa's partner and a member of the Bloomsbury Group who designed theater stages. Woolf showed an intense interest in the dancers themselves and befriended Lydia Lopokova, spouse of John Maynard Keynes and a member of the Ballet Russes. She notes in her diary her obsservervation of Lydia as a type for *Mrs. Dalloway*'s Lucrezia Smith.[11] In addition to her many references to performances as well as time spent with Lydia, Woolf refers to the "Russian dancers,"[12] and specifically to Vaslav Nijinsky[13] in *The Years*. The author's ongoing reading and writing about Greek and Shakespearean drama also inform Woolf's

---

[9] Woolf, *Orlando*, 42–3.

[10] Virginia Woolf, *Between the Acts* (London: Harcourt Inc., 1969), 20.

[11] Virginia Woolf, *The Diary of Virginia Woolf: Volume Two, 1920–1924*, ed. Anne Olivier Bell (London: Harcourt Inc., 1978), 265.

[12] Woolf, *The Years* (London: Harcourt Inc., 1939), 254.

[13] Woolf, *The Years*, 255, 393.

concept of the background and its changing importance in twentieth-century thought.

Woolf's spatial philosophy implies a theatrical relation between foreground and background. Though Woolf studied Greek drama intensely, the aesthetic importance placed on visualizing distant views in juxtaposition with nearby objects comes out of an especially Renaissance-era emphasis on the vanishing point in painting. As Rush Rehm points out, backgrounds in ancient Greek theater did not emphasize perspective but rather a metaphorical relationship between objects in the play and their meaning. Philosopher James Gibson contrasts the importance placed on depth-perception through the use of landscape painting in Renaissance theater with Greek theater. In Renaissance aesthetics a "framed optic array comes from a fixed, flat picture to the (properly placed) eye" versus the ancient Greek perspective in theatrical staging with the more "natural" view of objects and staging in the open air.[14] Interestingly, Woolf employs both spatial theatrical styles in her work. It is important that she uses the Renaissance visualization, resembling landscape painting throughout *Orlando*, and especially when Orlando occupies the Renaissance era. In *Between the Acts*, however, the village stage production resembles the natural space of Greek theater, with cows in fields surrounding the stage and without a narrative interest in distances beyond the flying of planes overhead. Woolf's repeated attention to distances is part of her critique of idealism in relation vision and the fantasizing of distant views. The reader witnesses the disintegration of fantasy distances as Orlando moves into the nineteenth century.[15]

The act of toggling permeates her thought as an overall pattern of movement, transcending the creation of space in her fiction. This motion between two things, poles, or ideas dominates her aesthetic as well as her philosophy of consciousness and ethics. It is useful to think of toggling in the context of its typical meaning, as both a movement and also as an object, such as a toggle in nautical terms or as it functions on clothing. The toggling of perception between the near and the far, background and foreground in Woolf is both a switch-like change in perception as well as a means of fastening two pieces together. I suggest that toggling is a necessary and everyday phenomenological mode of perception, as is the related

---

[14] Rush Rehm, *The Play of Space: Spatial Transformation in Greek Tragedy* (Princeton: Princeton University Press, 2002), 18.

[15] Woolf, *Orlando*, 166–7.

glance. This action is necessary and immanent since we cannot focus on two spatial zones simultaneously. Toggling is also essential to immanent experience since it makes the experience of depth possible. The process by which consciousness unites disparate spaces of the near and far is the fastening of depth and consciousness itself. While much sensory description in Woolf is visual, which is fitting given her milieu in the visual arts with Vanessa Bell and Roger Fry, perception is not only visual. In fact, the toggling of vision in her work is aligned with the toggling of other senses. Orlando enters into distant views at times by hearing sounds coming from a distance. Observe: "The distant stir of that soft plumage roused in him a thousand memories of rushing waters, of loveliness in the snow and faithlessness in the flood; and the sound came nearer."[16] The synesthesia and toggling of perception in *Orlando* is consistent with perception in "A Sketch of the Past," in which Woolf refers to "color-and-sound-memories,"[17] commenting that "sight was always then so much mixed with sound."[18]

We should first establish how the toggling between the near and the far, foreground and background occurs and its broader significance for Woolf. The movement between objects, both small and large, near and far away, is part of Woolf's toggling. Orlando sees Sasha in his ecstasy "like a fox or an olive tree; like the waves of the sea when you look down upon them from a height; like an emerald; like the sun on a green hill which is yet clouded."[19] Even in metaphors, Woolf vacillates: "One cupboard is much like another, and one molehill not much different from a million."[20] Toggling also characterizes the reader's perception of the text, since the move between one thing and another suggests contrast and a type of narrative closure that surrounds each object so that the reader attends to each one at a time. Woolf juxtaposes items in an abstract space; indeed, the reader may picture the fox in front of the olive tree or the emerald in the hands of one standing on the height while looking at the sea, but each one is given its equal space.

Perceptual toggling is an essential expression of Woolf's philosophy which extends to the everyday. Woolf often toggles between states of

---

[16] Woolf, *Orlando*, 86.
[17] Woolf, "A Sketch of the Past," 66.
[18] Woolf, "A Sketch of the Past," 67.
[19] Woolf, *Orlando*, 34.
[20] Woolf, *Orlando*, 80.

9 WOOLF IN THE BACKGROUND: DISTANCE AS VISUAL PHILOSOPHY, THEN...   191

natural or cultural contraries. In *Orlando* and *Between the Acts*, the quotidian question of the weather being either "wet or fine" colors and converses with all other experience. In her last novel, she explores the space between the two poles of love and hate, which occupies theatrical, dramatic, and visual space. This gestural and attitudinal toggling creates joy, contemplation, recognition, and ultimately depth of thought. In *Orlando*, she overtly expresses the jouissance of moving between "yielding" and "resisting."[21] The toggling of spatial orientation is coextensive with the toggling of memory, which she describes as a back-and-forth movement: "Memory runs her needle in and out, up and down, hither and thither."[22]

Woolf's whole body of work proposes a toggling move between ideas and things, which creates a feedback loop of consciousness between thought and environment. The relationship between the internal and external is truly not a blending of the two, since Woolf frequently narrates either the studying of the scene in front or the shutting out of environment. Orlando "opened his eyes, which had been wide open all the time, but had seen only thoughts, and saw, lying in the hollow beneath him, his house."[23] As Orlando observes each aspect of the scene before him in isolation, each part speaks to the other. Orlando's back and forth between figure and background results in a toggle between the scene and his thoughts. He begins with the house as his perception moves around it:

> There it lay in the early sunshine of spring. It looked a town rather than a house, but a town built, not hither and thither, as this man wished or that, but circumspectly, by a single architect with one idea in his head. Courts and buildings, grey, red, plum colour, lay orderly and symmetrical; the courts were some of them oblong and some square; in this was a fountain; in that a statue; the buildings were some of them low, some pointed; here was a chapel, there a belfry; spaces of the greenest grass lay in between and clumps of cedar trees and beds of bright flowers; all were clasped—yet so well set out was it that it seemed that every part had room to spread itself fittingly— by the roll of a massive wall; while smoke from innumerable chimneys curled perpetually into the air. This vast, yet ordered building, which could house a thousand men and perhaps two thousand horses was built, Orlando

[21] Woolf, *Orlando*, 115.
[22] Woolf, *Orlando*, 58.
[23] Woolf, *Orlando*, 77.

thought, by workmen whose names are unknown. Here, have lived for more centuries than I can count, the obscure generations of my own obscure family.[24]

This toggling between thoughts and things correlates with the toggling between what is "here," "there," and "in between." What is remarkable about this ostensibly concrete description of the natural and material world is how close it is in structure and intention to Woolf's metaphor for consciousness in her memoir. In the same way the author imagines her own past as being supported and held together by a background structure, this scene is spatially assembled and supported by the wall. The background makes possible the mutual relation between distance and nearness while also hosting relations between items in the foreground. The centrality, ironically, of the background makes possible both spatial phenomenon and consciousness. Orlando's opening his eyes to the distant scene, and not the shutting out, is the only activity which leads him to his deepest thought, his final revelation about time and permanence.

Woolf's toggling ultimately suggests that the movement of our perception correlates with the movement of thought. Orlando's vision of background and foreground in distinction aligns with her inhabitance and examination of gendered existence. In the tradition of Tiresias, manhood and womanhood are states of being taken one at a time by Woolf and Orlando. Man and woman are presented as concretized embodiments in Orlando's history, each with a definite tenure. Orlando's biographer insists, "It is enough for us to state the simple fact; Orlando was a man till the age of thirty; when he became a woman and has remained so ever since."[25] The biographer identifies where Orlando "vacillate[s]," being a man one moment and woman the next.[26] This complete and divisible movement between the two allows for their eventual fastening together. In the end, the vacillation or toggle is fastened by the interchange between womanhood and manhood. Yet the biographer attests that Orlando's identity is preserved as she considers herself "combined in one the strength of a man and a woman's grace."[27] Eventually the two states serve one another to "quicken and deepen those feelings" she has as a man or as a

[24] Woolf, *Orlando*, 77–78.
[25] Woolf, *Orlando*, 103.
[26] Woolf, *Orlando*, 117.
[27] Woolf, *Orlando*, 102.

woman.[28] Looking and being are parallel. As Woolf toggles, she seeks out along with her created figure a pattern, a way of fastening the two states together. Just as Woolf does in her memoir, so Orlando "does not do the thing for the sake of doing; nor looks for looking's sake; but sees … something else."[29] This fastening together of thing and self is necessary for what Woolf calls being.

But the author upsets the fixedness of background and foreground in her writing. She dismantles Orlando's fantasy of a fixed and stable background by having him learn in the concrete world how positions are changeable and unstable. It is the very exchange between thought and thing, idea and material, which guides Orlando to think of his own contribution in terms of background and foreground. After equating the wall and those who built it with the distant past and background, Orlando concludes that he might contribute something to the foreground. After all, the wall is established and holds everything together in Orlando's view, which is still a fantasized imagining of both distance and history: "Better it was to go unknown and leave behind you an arch, a potting shed, a wall where peaches ripen, than to burn like a meteor and leave no dust."[30] In his decision that his greatest contribution would be to provide the foreground in the form of furniture, Orlando fills the mansion with blankets, chairs, fabrics, and cabinets. He only discovers after fully furnishing the mansion with the intention of providing foreground, that he has, in fact, contributed a "scaffolding in the background" of his own, just as Woolf writes in her memoir. She points to the relativity of space, perception, and of the moving narrator for which space is ever-changing positionally:

He had matter now, he thought, to fill out his peroration. … Yet, as he paraded the galleries he felt that still something was lacking. Chairs and tables, however richly gilt and carved, sofas, resting on lions' paws with swans' necks curving under them, beds even of the softest swansdown are not by themselves enough. People sitting in them, people lying in them improve them amazingly.[31]

The furniture becomes background and not any less valued in the process, since this furniture is the "pattern" behind the figures. Toggling indicates

[28] Woolf, *Orlando*, 119.
[29] Woolf, *Orlando*, 108.
[30] Woolf, *Orlando*, 78.
[31] Woolf, *Orlando*, 81–2.

the relativity of distanced perception and the reciprocity of figure and background. Orlando has this realization again when she climbs mountains and looks out from them, realizing that "often she had looked at those mountains from her balcony at the Embassy; often had longed to be there; and to find oneself where one has longed to be always, to a reflective mind, gives food for thought."[32]

In a similar process, we see how particular people are perceived as part of the background, or even furniture themselves. Woolf marks the ethnographic style of the time in describing the working class, servants, non-Europeans, and non-white people as part of the background. Her fictional and historical character writes of a party that it is "wondrous ... utterly beyond description ... gold plate ... candelabras ... negroes in plush breeches ... pyramids of ice ... swans made to represent water lilies ... birds in golden cages ... gentlemen in slashed crimson velvet."[33] Woolf sets the stage, quite literally, for the reader to perceive the Janissaries as part of the background, which creates a way for the reader to experience depth between themselves and the rulers she specifically calls "figures": "On reaching the courtyard, the Janissaries struck with their fans upon the main portal, which immediately flew open revealing a large chamber, splendidly furnished. Here were seated two figures, generally of opposite sexes."[34] This scene too shows space as hierarchically in flux and relative since the rulers who would be considered figures in a theatrical schema are described as being "there" in the distance, framed by guards. It is important to note that Woolf calls the scene a "wild panorama,"[35] which indicates her own situatedness in a culture of panoramic vision. The scene described is akin to the nineteenth-century theatrical moving panorama, in which players were elements of the background.

A Philosophy of Depth

In her philosophy of perception, Woolf anticipates the specific phenomenological arguments and discoveries of Maurice Merleau-Ponty in his 1952 course notes, entitled *The Sensible World and the World of Expression*. His larger goals of conjoining nature and history, expression and

[32] Woolf, *Orlando*, 104.
[33] Woolf, *Orlando*, 94–6.
[34] Woolf, *Orlando*, 90.
[35] Woolf, *Orlando*, 89.

perception, as well as our general understanding of perception are all founded on the theory of figure and background as expressed in Gestalt psychology. Merleau-Ponty asserts the reciprocal relationship between figure and background throughout his lectures with special attention to the vitality of the background, since it is a space we often ignore or overlook, both culturally and perceptively.[36] Woolfian scholarship has seen a wave of phenomenological analysis, including Mark Hussey's *The Singing of the Real World: The Philosophy of Virginia Woolf's Fiction* (1986); Carole Bourne-Taylor and Ariane Mildenberg's *Phenomenology, Modernism, and Beyond* (2010); Mildenberg's *Modernism and Phenomenology: Literature, Philosophy, Art* (2010); Claudia Olk's *Virginia Woolf and the Aesthetics of Vision* (2014); Yuko Rojas' *Space and Female Consciousness in Virginia Woolf's Fiction: Idealist and Phenomenological Perspectives* (2017); and Emma Simone's *Virginia Woolf and Being-in-the World: A Heideggerian Study* (2017). Though her phenomenology of vision is central to much scholarly writing, her perception of distances and backgrounds have not been the subject of substantial study.

Merleau-Ponty is useful here since he attempts to capture in theory the phenomenon by which we switch back and forth between foreground and background. When we try to perceive and grasp each one or both together, the other is lost. The philosopher's very language conveys the feeling of incompletion, how we think about a space and believe we have it, when in fact, we never possess it. He expresses the illusory nature of our perceiving that which is near and far: "The simplest consciousness ([according to] *Gestalttheorie* [Gestalt theory]) is consciousness of a figure on a background: inasmuch as there is figure, there is also inarticulate background, inasmuch as we <u>have</u> being (figure), we don't have it, and inasmuch as we don't have it (background), [inasmuch as] we let it be without thinking about it, that's when we have it."[37] Merleau-Ponty expresses the problem of grasping and possessing spatial positions. We can only truly "have" background if we ignore it. He seems to also suggest that the idea of possessing being in the figure is impossible since figure relies on background. Since the background is ignored, then figure also eludes our grasp.

---

[36] Maurice Merleau-Ponty, *The Sensible World and the World of Expression: Course Notes from the College de France, 1953*, trans. Bryan Smith (Evanston: Northwestern University Press, 2020), 14–5.

[37] Merleau-Ponty, *The Sensible World*, 22.

Woolf's realization that being lies in her grasping what goes on in the background or the "hidden pattern" is also Merleau-Ponty's thought many years later. He confronts the belief that the important position is the figure or, that which is near, not in the form of memoir, but in his confrontation with the patterns of western philosophy and, therefore popular thought as well. We believe that existence can be found in the player on the stage, whereas Woolf and Merleau-Ponty locate being in the background, in that which we ignore or that which is in the distance: "The background or horizon forms part of the definition of the being."[38] Depth as a phenomenon cannot be experienced without the mutual relations of the two.

The philosophical concept of depth at this point is like toggling in Woolf's thought, where two opposites are given attention in isolation with a rapid switching back and forth. Merleau-Ponty expresses a similar relationality between foreground and background as Woolf in establishing that the two positions must be attended to in isolation, creating depth, which he calls an "awakening." Depth is made possible by the experiencing body which creates space as a "relation [between] my here (incarnate self) [and] another here (over there). Depth shows that [the] relation [between] self [and] thing supports [the] relation [between] things."[39] Merleau-Ponty's description here is similar to Orlando's feedback loop of consciousness between the world external to his body and his thoughts as well as the exchange between the things themselves within the view, both far and near. Merleau-Ponty even goes as far as to call this process, resulting in depth, the "teleological organization of a <u>feedback</u>" (43). He quotes Paul Valéry, who wrote on the phenomenon of attention and the fact that we cannot perceive two items at once. "Exchange between the end and the means, chance and choice, substance and accident, prediction and opportunity, matter and form, power and resistance, which, like the burning, strange, intimate battle of the sexes, involves all the energies of human life, grinds them against each other, [and] creates."[40] We are reminded of Orlando's pleasure in toggling between yielding and resisting.

Orlando's elation at occupying a high mountainous place that he had only seen from a distance illustrates the constant reorientation of the viewer in Woolf's narrative. Similar to Woolf, Merleau-Ponty's notion of

---

[38] Merleau-Ponty, *The Sensible World*, 22.
[39] Merleau-Ponty, *The Sensible World*, 31.
[40] Merleau-Ponty, *The Sensible World*, 43.

consciousness is grounded in the relativity and interchanging of positions and even specifically extends to the experiences of sex and gender. In describing what he calls "ambiguous consciousness," and therefore an ambiguous spatiality, he writes, "There is another view of what we see, which places in the figure what we see in the background, relation of liberating dialectic. ... The fact that we perceive others and not simply fantasies of ourselves, that we are open to other perspectives through the background that we know could become figure ... suffices to prove that we are not cut off from the true."[41] He describes how the reciprocity and interchangeability of positions correlate with our ability to understand the perspectives of others. Notice how Merleau-Ponty likens figure to reality and background to fantasy too, which is rooted in nineteenth-century aesthetic thought about fantasy, escapism, and the past. The constant movement, shifting and toggling between these positions, makes truth possible according to both Merleau-Ponty and Woolf.

Depth is a visual and ontological experience for both thinkers. The reciprocity, ambiguity, mediation, and tension of sexuality and gender produce an ontological depth that mirrors the perceptive tension and depth of foreground and background. Merleau-Ponty's critique of structuralism, specifically the Freudian duality between homosexuality and heterosexuality, also echoes Woolf's proposal of ambiguity and relationality between both sexes and orientation. Orlando's experiences with visual depth as well as the ever-shifting positions of the far and the near parallel her feeling that being a woman deepens the feelings she had as a man. Merleau-Ponty expresses the toggling of consciousness itself and the production of depth in his discovery that the movement between foreground and background is like the movement between heterosexuality and homosexuality. He asserts that "to be heterosexual is to be homosexual in a mediated way" and vice versa.[42] This "reciprocal implication" means that "we see in ourselves what we're not."[43] Therefore, there is no fixity in being a man or a woman, nor in loving men or women. This ongoing shift in positionality and reciprocal relationality creates a depth of being for Woolf as well. Her work anticipates later philosophies of experience, yet it is still unclear how Woolf's philosophy of distances springs from, overlaps with, and also stands starkly against the visual cultures of her age.

[41] Merleau-Ponty, *The Sensible World*, 26
[42] Merleau-Ponty, *The Sensible World*, 24.
[43] Merleau-Ponty, *The Sensible World*, 25.

WOOLF IN THE PANORAMA

While Woolf's philosophy of space and a related gendered ontology is subversive, the question remains as to how her thinking about background as an experience, but also in relation to ontology, engages with contemporaneous aesthetics and cultural attitudes. Woolf was situated in one of the most avant-garde artistic circles of her time; at the same time, she emerged from a background herself which popularly valued the visual phenomenon of depth, heightened and manipulated by technologies and media of the nineteenth century. Attending to mass media, even Merleau-Ponty repeatedly evokes the visual impact of depth as experienced in the stereoscope and in cinema. He refers to the "panoramic views" and "stroboscopic movement" of cinema.[44] Significantly, he anchors his comments about the pleasure and desire we feel when we encounter depth in the stereoscope, kaleidoscope, and in the specific effect of depth created in film, which he refers to with the word "ciné-relief."[45] Subtly harkening back to the nineteenth century, the philosopher questions the "pleasure that we take in these spectacles."[46] This pleasure is essential to Orlando's toggling, as she seeks relationality between spaces and between herself and the world.

Aesthetic trends in theater, dance, visual art, and cinema during Woolf's time point to concurrent desires for distances to be brought into relation with the body and our compulsion for seeing depth in all things, a desire that remains true for us today. At the same time, the values of distant views during the nineteenth century were forms of entertainment that enabled fantasy, idealism, and escapism. The association of distant views with the past and history allowed the viewer to bring the past closer in the form of panorama but also solidified the place of the past as nostalgic and therefore to some extent, escapist. The complete absorption in landscapes allows the dissociation of the distant past from the near present. The panorama and all its manifestations such as the cyclorama, georama, and diorama, beginning with Robert Barker's 1793 panoramic painting of London, vitally inform Woolf's vision. In his thorough excavation of panoramic history, *Illusions in Motion*, Erkki Huhtamo urges us to think of the entrance of the panorama in its many forms, as a discursive practice that forever changed our way of seeing and manipulating distances.

---

[44] Merleau-Ponty, *The Sensible World*, 30.
[45] Merleau-Ponty, *The Sensible World*, 49.
[46] Merleau-Ponty, *The Sensible World*, 42.

9 WOOLF IN THE BACKGROUND: DISTANCE AS VISUAL PHILOSOPHY, THEN... 199

Woolf's contemporary, Walter Benjamin, delineates in his montage of ideas, *The Arcades Project*, the draw of distances and backgrounds during the nineteenth century and their continuing meaning into the 1920s and 1930s. In his konvolute on "Panorama" Benjamin identifies our collective desire for "deep relief" and "deep perspective,"[47] exemplified in the fact that the diorama quickly replaced the magic lantern.[48] He even locates our ongoing pursuit of depth in popular literature of the time. Serialized crime fiction found in newspapers mimicked the aesthetic of deep perspective with its close attention to main characters and landscape like that in a diorama.[49] Benjamin famously calls attention to the "desire of contemporary masses to bring things 'closer' spatially and humanly,"[50] which he illustrates best in his analysis of film and the many cinematic techniques of mechanical reproduction. He reminds us in *The Arcades Project* that the panorama's aim, in its "perfect imitation of nature,"[51] is that the "city opens out, becoming landscape."[52] In our obsession with media in its variations during the nineteenth century and enhanced in the twentieth century, Benjamin identifies the common factor of desiring both nature and closeness. He also highlights our obsession with landscapes and panoramas as a way of idealizing the past, pointing to the role of distant spaces as the fantasy of the interior.[53] Significantly though, one of Benjamin's closing quotes on panorama is one by Charles Baudelaire, in which the poet expresses his preference for the "scenery" and "illusion" of the dioramas and theater, finding ultimate truth in its falseness. It is Benjamin's argumentative style in *Das Passagen-Werk* to insert those quotes which reflect his argument toward the end of the konvolute. In this closing quotation, we realize Benjamin's agreement with Woolf in making the background a space not of fantasized idealism but one of truth.

Woolf recognizes the mixed bag of values in representing spaces and especially distances. Orlando's Elizabethan dreams disappear as she gazes into the nineteenth-century landscape, which is no longer idyllic but

---

[47] Walter Benjamin, *The Arcades Project*, trans. Howard Eiland and Kevin McLaughlin (Cambridge, MA: Harvard University Press, 1999), 530.

[48] Walter Benjamin, *The Arcades Project*, 531.

[49] Walter Benjamin, *The Arcades Project*, 531.

[50] Walter Benjamin, "The Work of Art in the Age of Mechanical Reproduction," *Illuminations*, trans. Harry Zohn (New York: Schocken Books, 2007): 223.

[51] Walter Benjamin, *The Arcades Project*, 5.

[52] Walter Benjamin, *The Arcades Project*, 6.

[53] Walter Benjamin, *The Arcades Project*, 533.

industrial and grimy. Perhaps one explanation for the desire for travel landscapes reproduced in as many forms as possible during the nineteenth century is not only the increased ability to travel, and therefore tourism marketing, but also what Woolf recognizes as an unsavory view of England's urban places. She critiques our manipulation of fantasized distances in her essay on "The Cinema," in which she describes the "dream architecture of arches and battlements": "No fantasy could be too far-fetched or insubstantial. The past could be unrolled, distances annihilated." In the same passage about the fantasizing potential of destroying distance and bringing it closer, she notes that using the same background for characters in disparate spaces can also obliterate the gaps which inherently "dislocate" novels and therefore create a useful continuity.[54] Woolf sees the potential for the very technology which has enhanced our ability to escape and fantasize to allow us a form of inspection that is impossible in our unmediated looking.

While the panorama was allowed a certain fantasy of escapism into distant spaces and the transporting visual experience of depth itself, it also augmented viewers' ability to access background spaces differently. More than sheer fantasy, panoramas allowed viewers to bring the distance into relation through inspection. Huhtamo cautions us away from conceptualizing the panorama as simply romantic entertainment, but as the "spectator's scopic-ambulatory mastery over the surrounding scenery."[55] Like any technology, the panoramic mode introduced ways of seeing that were both limiting and augmenting, educational and reductive. On one hand, Huhtamo calls it a "vehicle for homogenization,"[56] encouraging a view of all people and places as subject to the imperial view, especially from the perspective of American and European artists. On the other hand, panoramic practices invited a reciprocity of spatial focus and attention, which encouraged the viewer to be a mobile and participatory agent. This newfound concern for visual attention during the nineteenth century is the cultural shift Jonathan Crary argues for in *Suspensions of Perception*.[57] Huhtamo writes on how the moving panorama shifted our attention to backgrounds when they became central to theater and the players became

---

[54] Virginia Woolf, "The Cinema," *The Nation and Athenaeum*, July 3, 1926: 383.

[55] Erkki Huhtamo, *Illusions in Motion: Media Archaeology of the Moving Panorama and Related Spectacles* (Cambridge, MA: The MIT Press, 2013), 5.

[56] Huhtamo, *Illusions in Motion*, 8.

[57] See also: Jonathan Crary, *Suspensions of Perception: Attention, Spectacle, and Modern Culture*, (Cambridge, MA: The MIT Press, 2001).

"elements of the scenic view."[58] This form of spatial reciprocity is conveyed in Orlando's view of furniture, related to a new way of understanding interiors as exteriors and vice versa which Benjamin identifies in nineteenth-century thought as the "dialectical reversal."[59] Though Woolf's fictive vision is a product of a relatively new attention to backgrounds, her focus on background as a philosophy of living is emergent and resistant to the values of mediated perception.

Woolf's narration in *Orlando* calls attention to an imperialized use of distances while subverting our valuing of backgrounds. What may seem like a disparagement of an aerial view of America refers to a broader perceptive context in which views of countries captured in photos and films from overhead were objects of fascination among her contemporaries. In the act of "peering over Mr. Sherwood Anderson's shoulder" in her 1925 essay "American Fiction," Woolf writes "America appears a very strange place. What is it that we see here? A vast continent, scattered here and there with brand new villages which nature has not absorbed into herself with ivy and moss, summer and winter, as in England, but man has built recently, hastily, economically, so that the village is like the suburb of a town."[60] She contrasts the disjointed American landscape with its lack of structure or background to the English inability to escape the historically burdened rooms of the interior. In seeing English spaces, history is close up and figural, not in the background: "Its centre is an old house with many rooms each crammed with objects and crowded with people who know each other intimately, whose manners, thoughts, and speech are ruled all the time, if unconsciously, by the spirit of the past."[61] Woolf takes a surprisingly honorific turn in then characterizing American distances as spaces to shape and occupy rather than fantasize. It's "prairies, its cornfields flung disorderly about like a mosaic of incongruous pieces waiting order at the artist's hands."[62] She departs from many dominants of visual culture in upsetting spatial dualities and separatism between those spaces. Most importantly, background does not forever emblematize fantasy; instead, Woolf suggests that the background is a space that we occupy and co-create for ourselves.

[58] Huhtamo, *Illusions in Motion*, 94.
[59] Walter Benjamin, *The Arcades Project*, 833.
[60] Woolf, "American Fiction," in *Collected Essays* (London: Harcourt Inc., 1967), 112.
[61] Woolf, "American Fiction," 120.
[62] Woolf, "American Fiction," 120.

Some of Woolf's contemporaries also represented backgrounds in originative ways. Picasso and Jean Cocteau's *Parade* assembled artists inclined to rethink the theater's latitude for space and movement, particularly with the aim of overturning the public's expectations. Woolf did not attend this ballet, but it was in her circle of influence. Performed in London at the Empire Theatre in 1919 with the Ballet Russes, *Parade* had originally featured Lopokova as a performing acrobat in the Paris debut. I put forth Jones' assertion that there is substantial evidence of Woolf being influenced by dance and performance beginning in 1912.[63] Woolf's connection with modern dance and ballet is especially important for considering how contemporaneous artists conceived of background and foreground. Picasso's surrealist aesthetics alone in *Parade* were significant in reimagining relations between foreground and background. Instead of the background as either an aspect of distant fantasy which interplays with the sometimes equally fantastical figures in the foreground, Picasso's background consisted of jarring angles and shapes in an expressionist mode, which are more like figures themselves. The choreography of the dancers was stiff and angular, limited by the geometric and cubist cardboard forms. Rather than a strong divergence between the still background and foreground in motion, the stiff forms of the figure were balanced with and in conversation with the background.

Satie continued to compose experimental music after *Parade* and is well-known for his "furniture music," which is credited as the progenitor of elevator music, also known as Muzak. Though his critics persist, Satie approached his own work always with a sense of irony, as Robert Orledge has remarked.[64] Satie's other compositions are an attempt to capture and illustrate bodily experiences. For example, his 1914 short composition *Choses vues à droite et à gauche (sans lunettes)* or *Things Seen Right to Left (Without Glasses)* tries to reproduce in the form of music the sensations and rhythms of eye movement, peripheral vision, and the wandering of the eyes, including the "Groping Fugue" and the "Muscular Fantasy." This work lead to his Musique d'ameublement, or literally "Furnishing Music," a phrase he used for his compositions in 1917. While the various pieces seem to be obviously entitled according to the location of the performance, such as "Curtain for a Prefectural Office," "Acoustic Tiling," and

---

[63] Susan Jones, "Virginia Woolf and the Dance," *Dance Chronicle* 28, no. 2 (2002): 170.

[64] Robert Orledge, *Satie the Composer* (Cambridge: Cambridge University Press, 1990), 100.

"A Drawing Room," they also bring attention to the space and indeed, movement, of those spaces themselves.

Location and position within the room and upon the stage itself accrues meaning in these works. At the same time, those who should be figures in a performative scheme are made part of the background as live performers in Satie's thinking. These pieces have a spatial reversibility in the world of performance, since Satie's intention was for the music played live at a show to be considered as distant and disconnected from the center; at the same time, their intended peripherality is centralized, as if furniture itself were the actor. Herve Vanel argues in *Triple Entendre* that when Satie's furniture music was performed as part of Max Jacob's play in 1920, it was made central to the performance itself as an object of consumption and ambiguous placial occupation. An announcement about it before the play encouraged audience members not to notice it, going on to describe that the music "claims to make a contribution to life in the same way as a private conversation, a painting of the gallery, or the chair in which you may or may not be seated. You will be trying it out."[65] He also notes that the first audience members disobeyed the announcement, fleeing back to their seats to listen when the music played, as was called for by decorum. The composer demonstrates a similar spatial relativity as Woolf in making the furniture at one point the foregrounding figure and then the background in another.

Maurice Ravel, also a collaborator for *Parade* and with Satie, performs along with librettist Colette a similar and related attention to the background as having a vitally shifting and relational value, both aesthetically and thematically. French author Colette is perhaps more responsible for the conceptual manipulation of the story itself. Their one-act opera written between 1917 and 1925, *L'enfant et les sortilèges: Fantaisie lyrique en deux parties* or *The Child and the Spells: A Lyric Fantasy in Two Parts*, tells a tale in which décor become active dramatic players in conversation with people. The furniture, such as a clock and an armchair, come to life to reprimand a child who mistreats objects and animals. It was originally performed in Paris in 1926. Later, it was readapted and made part of an arrangement of Parisian Avant-Garde operas in *La Parade*, performed at the Metropolitan Opera in New York City in 1981, 1986 and again in New York in 2002. It is a whimsical fantasy, yet it overturns in an imposing

---

[65] Herve Vanel, *Triple Entendre: Furniture Music, Muzak, Muzak-Plus* (Urbana: Illinois University Press, 2013), 16.

204   A. A. FOLEY

manner the notion that there is an inanimate and fixed world of objects apart from the subjective world. Though still playful, Colette and Ravel remove background from a space of fantasy and, in their case, foreground fantasy.

DISTANCES AND DEPTH IN VIRTUAL MEDIA

Digital space continues to idealize distances, not as spaces we may visually escape to and set up for us by some creators alone, but as fantasy spaces that we can inhabit immediately and manipulate ourselves as individuals. Derived from what used to be only the jurisdiction of the director or cameraperson, the zoom is now the power to control distances and bring them closer to us as only the individual desires. It is apparent how panoramic vision endures in virtual and digital spatial perception today. Programs such as Google's Augmented Reality (AR) and Virtual Reality (VR) allow a "Street view" as well as a 360 view, which are direct offspring of the nineteenth-century moving panorama. It is arguable that our current mode of mobile manipulation is not as influenced by cinematic techniques in zooming because of its limitation in requiring the immobility and passive observation of the viewer. Huhtamo especially asserts that the circular panorama was a predecessor of our use of mobile devices since it allowed the free motion of the observer.[66] Our devices also require a kinesthetic related to the crank panorama, exemplified in the act of scrolling. Huhtamo observes the ways in which we create, host, and watch as a form of panoramic engagement,[67] though much digital manipulation of screens is also related to Woolf's understanding of the toggling of natural perception. For example, our movement back and forth between screens and tabs are related to our perception of foreground and background, by which two items must be viewed in isolation.

Digital distances are not experienced in the same way as in panoramic or cinematic vision since the observer is the participant and also the creator; however, distances today are still idealized as objects of infinite and limitless manipulation and mastery. Nanna Verhoeff also asserts the more democratic values of visual media in *Mobile Screens: The Visual Regime of*

---

[66] Huhtamo, *Illusions in Motion*, 337.
[67] Huhtamo, *Illusions in Motion*, 368.

Navigation. She identifies our "spatio-visual or navigational turn"[68] as key to our "mobilized spectator[ship]."[69] Our "dialogical" vision, as Verhoeff calls it, in our mobility and ability to be looked back at,[70] is unlike the purely aerial view which Woolf looked upon with suspicion in her time.

A significant and related trend in our current visual culture is mapping. Graham and Elizabeth Coulter-Smith argue for an essential shift from the "disembodied gaze" in traditional fine art to "embodied interactivity."[71] They identify a new mode of vision in digital art, which is "locative," prioritizing both position and collaboration.[72] They site examples of drawings made by artists using GPS maps, created using gathered data from the general public, which illustrate a relationship between near spaces and the individual's belief in affecting a view of distances. This approach to vision and information is concurrent with the digital humanities. Websites dedicated to the writings of both Virginia Woolf and William Faulkner illustrate maps according to geographies and walking routes narrated in their novels. The user can zoom in and manipulate the bird's eye view to get closer to the route itself. This fact alone demonstrates the essential contribution of Woolf's embodied seeing represented in fiction, in which the natural perception of the eyes from within and looking out from the body acquire the unique and inimitable experience of depth in unmediated perception. She shows depth as only attainable in the toggle between here and there, near and far, man and woman, choice and chance. This may be one more way in which words do not fail.

Works Cited

Benjamin, Walter. *The Arcades Project.* Translated by Howard Eiland and Kevin McLaughlin. Cambridge, MA: Harvard University Press, 1999.

———. "The Work of Art in the Age of Mechanical Reproduction." In *Illuminations,* translated by Harry Zohn, 217–51. New York: Schocken Books, 2007.

---

[68] Nanna Verhoeff, *Mobile Screens: The Visual Regime of Navigation* (Amsterdam: Amsterdam University Press, 2012), 13.

[69] Verhoeff, *Mobile Screens*, 38.

[70] Verhoeff, *Mobile Screens*, 43.

[71] Graham and Elizabeth Coulter-Smith, "Mapping Outside the Frame: Interactive and Locative Art Environments," in *Digital Visual Culture: Theory and Practice*, ed. Anna Bentkowska-Kafel and Hazel Gardiner (Chicago: Intellect Books Ltd., 2009): 50.

[72] Coulter-Smith, "Mapping Outside the Frame," 57.

Coulter-Smith, Graham and Elizabeth. "Mapping Outside the Frame: Interactive and Locative Art Environments." In *Digital Visual Culture: Theory and Practice*, ed. Anna Bentkowska-Kafel and Hazel Gardiner 49–66. Chicago: Intellect Books Ltd., 2009.

Crary, Jonathan. *Suspensions of Perception: Attention, Spectacle, and Modern Culture*. Cambridge, MA: The MIT Press, 2001.

Huhtamo, Erkki. *Illusions in Motion: Media Archaeology of the Moving Panorama and Related Spectacles*. Cambridge, MA: The MIT Press, 2013.

Jones, Susan. "Virginia Woolf and the Dance." *Dance Chronicle* 28, no. 2 (2002): 169–200.

Orledge, Robert. *Satie the Composer*. Cambridge: Cambridge University Press, 1990.

Massey, Doreen. "Some Times of Space." In *Olafur Eliasson: The Weather Project*, edited by Susan May, 107–118. London: Tate Modern, 2003.

Merleau-Ponty, Maurice. *The Sensible World and the World of Expression: Course Notes from the College de France, 1953*. Translated by Bryan Smith. Evanston: Northwestern University Press, 2020.

Rehm, Rush. *The Play of Space: Spatial Transformation in Greek Tragedy*. Princeton: Princeton University Press, 2002.

Vanel, Herve. *Triple Entendre: Furniture Music, Muzak, Muzak-Plus*. Urbana: Illinois University Press, 2013.

Verhoeff, Nanna. *Mobile Screens: The Visual Regime of Navigation*. Amsterdam: Amsterdam University Press, 2012.

Woolf, Virginia. "The Cinema." *The Nation and Athenaeum*. July 3, 1926.

———. *The Years*. London: Harcourt, Inc., 1939.

———. "American Fiction," *Collected Essays*. London: Harcourt, Inc., 1967.

———. *Between the* Acts. London: Harcourt, Inc., 1969.

———. *The Diary of Virginia Woolf: Volume Two, 1920–1924*. Edited by Anne Olivier Bell. London: Harcourt, Inc., 1978.

———. "A Sketch of the Past," in *Moments of Being*, edited by Jeanne Schulkind, 64–161. London: Harcourt, Inc., 1985.

———. *Orlando*. London: Harcourt, Inc., 2006.

PART III

Radical Positions

CHAPTER 10

A New Cartographer: Rabih Alameddine and *An Unnecessary Woman*

François-Xavier Gleyzon

Mobility, for Gilles Deleuze, is tantamount to mapping: "I used to like to walk then. Now I can walk less well it can no longer even be thought of. I was quite fond of walking, yes, I personally remember going through Beirut on foot, from morning till night, without knowing where I was going there. I quite liked to go through that city on foot."[1] Movement and mapping; movement and understanding. Only through motion, through mapping, can one *know* a city or any place. A city has veins, arteries that are full of life and maintain the memory of those that once walked its streets. "And yet those beings, who are long gone, are within us, as predisposition, they lay upon our destiny, as blood that pulsates, and as

---

[1] Gilles Deleuze with Claire Parnet, "V comme voyage," in *L'Abécédaire de Gilles Deleuze* (Paris: Ed. Montparnasse, 1989).

F.-X. Gleyzon (✉)
University of Central Florida, Orlando, FL, USA
e-mail: Francois-Xavier.Gleyzon@ucf.edu

© The Author(s), under exclusive license to Springer Nature Switzerland AG 2021
C. Beck (ed.), *Mobility, Spatiality, and Resistance in Literary and Political Discourse*, Geocriticism and Spatial Literary Studies,
https://doi.org/10.1007/978-3-030-83477-7_10

210 F.-X. GLEYZON

gesture that rises up out of the depths of time."[2] This navigating, this cartography with the living and dead is a becoming felt in the deepest, most profound ways: "She felt the intimate loss of who she was meant *to become*."[3]

* * *

How do we enter Rabih Alameddine's text of *An Unnecessary Woman*? How do we navigate and, above all, how do we survey the body of this text? Interspersed with quotes, flux, and reflux of memories and reminiscences, within which are engrafted afflictions, *pathos*, and survivals from the past, Rabih Alameddine's novel could be summed up, if not translated, with the help of the expression coined by Aby Warburg in *Mnemosyne* as a vast "treasury of sufferings" [*Leidschatz*].[4] If the life of Aaliya Saleh appears insignificant, *unnecessary*, even impersonal, she is none the less singular and proud, precisely inasmuch as the intrinsic specificity of her life—the *vital* character of her life, that is to say her energy, or her *virtus*—is presented as a veritable *stake,* a *challenge* to pain or even an *act of resistance*. A Lebanese septuagenarian, alone and solitary, a blue-haired translator, Aaliya Saleh's life, with all its vicissitudes, trials, and tribulations, is privileged enough to see itself confined to the active memory of her books: "books into boxes—boxes of paper, loose translated sheets. That's [*her*] life."[5] In other words, all these books and all these pages to translate, the accumulation of quotations that do not cease to split/fragment Alameddine's text do not only touch on and echo the objects and the circumstances of Aaliya's sufferings but also punctuate the deepest rhythms of her life:

> I long ago abandoned myself to a blind lust for the written word. Literature is my sandbox. In it I play, build my forts and castles, spend glorious time. It is the world outside that box that gives me trouble. I have adapted tamely, though not conventionally, to this visible world so I can retreat without

[2] Rainer Maria Rilke, *Letters to a Young Poet*, trans. M. D. Herter Norton (New York: Norton, 1962), 50.

[3] Rabih Alameddine, *An Unnecessary Woman* (New York: Grove Press, 2014), 154–155.

[4] Martin Warnke, "Der Leidschatz der Menschheit wird humaner Besitz," in *Die Menschenrechte des Auges. Über Aby Warburg* (Frankfurt-on-Main: Europäische Verlagsanstalt, 1980), 113–86.

[5] Alameddine, *An Unnecessary Woman,* 4.

much inconvenience into my inner world of books. Transmuting this sandy metaphor, if literature is my sandbox, then the real world is my hourglass—an hourglass that drains grain by grain. Literature gives me life, and life kills me.[6]

Escaping, emptying oneself, evading, fleeing are perhaps the first words that come to mind. This is to say that Aaliya's existential trajectory comes within the remit of an almost kenotic movement in which the very act of emptying oneself consists in *dépeupler* [depopulating] to use Beckett's expression, or in other words escaping from external realities ("the world outside") so as to transmute oneself and engage in quite a different possibility of life, a potent life or even a potent nonorganic life ("my inner world of books").[7] One would be wrong to think, however, that *fleeing* necessarily denotes a kind of cowardice as in to flee the world or even to flee one's responsibilities or commitments. There is at work here, as Gilles Deleuze has pointed out, quite a different reasoning, quite a different conception. There is nothing more honest, nothing more sincere, concrete, and courageous than *to flee* through a line of flight. To leave, to escape, to "flee," writes Deleuze, "is to trace a line. [...] The great mistake and only error lies in thinking that a line of flight consists in fleeing from life, fleeing into the imaginary [...]. On the contrary, to flee is to produce the real, to create life, to find a weapon."[8] Henceforth, a line of flight may be understood both as action and creative vital impulse [*élan créateur*], the very purpose of which would be to "force [oneself] out of the customary furrows" and, at last, "to penetrate into *another* life."[9] Access to this *other* possibility for life is given, according to the processes developed by Gilles Deleuze and Félix Guattari, to the extent of a dynamic of *deterritorialization*—"a movement by which 'one' leaves the territory"—and reterritorialization.[10] But this dynamic of passage does not imply *a fortiori*,

---

[6] Alameddine, *An Unnecessary Woman*, 4.

[7] Samuel Beckett, *Le Dépeupleur* [The Depopulator] (Paris: Minuit, 1970). Translated by Beckett into English as *The Lost Ones* (London: Calder & Boyars, 1972), 7. The English text is included in *Samuel Beckett: The Complete Short Prose, 1929–1989,* ed. S. E. Gontarski (New York: Grove Press, 1995), 202–23.

[8] Gilles Deleuze and Claire Parnet, *Dialogues*, trans. Hugh Tomlison and Barbara Habberjam (New York: Cornell University Press, 1977), 60.

[9] Ibid., 36.

[10] Gilles Deleuze and Félix Guattari, *A Thousand Plateaus: Capitalism and Schizophrenia*, trans. Brian Massumi (London: University of Minneapolis, 1987), 508.

212   F.-X. GLEYZON

a displacement, and therefore a far destination. Alameddine shows through Aaliya that mobility is entirely relative, nearly imperceptible, and even almost *unnecessary*. The most effective and probing deterritorializations, according to Deleuze and Guattari, are perhaps those engaged in "a stationary process" and which are therefore effected "on a *fixed* plane of life upon which [however] everything stirs, everything rushes forward."[11] "Motionless with great steps," "intense motionless voyage": Aaliya is *almost*, so to speak, *always* seated while moving and reaches, in situ, at the heart of her apartment, "the windowless maid's room," in other words: the absolute space/territory, the *absolute* deterritorialization—the very place in which are found "overflowing" all those translated pages, those books that "open cells [...], open your eyes and quicken your soul."[12] Sensations of vertigo, of delirium, tremors, spasms, almost hysterical crises, it is with this "irrational heart [...] reach[ing] the point of seizing [...] thump[ing] to the point of bursting [or] slow[ing] to the beat of torpor, [her] veins throb[bing] with a big, blooming, buzzing confusion" that Aaliya's body exerts an effort upon itself, it exerts itself or, more precisely, *waits to escape, to flee*, in short *to deterritorialize itself*.[13] "Indeed it is inside the body that something is happening."[14] The implication is tantamount to saying that, as Deleuze writes, in this instance "the line of flight is a deterritorialization," and brings about, in this sense, "terror but also a great joy."[15] But what, *after all*, is this joy? This joy designates nothing less than the *afterward* of a deterritorialization—in other words, *joy* in the lived experience of a reterritorialization—through which a pure event is both incarnated and actualized, allowing a *becoming of possibilities* or, as

[11] Deleuze and Guattari, *A Thousand Plateaus*, 290, 403. For the relations and distinctions between *displacement/movement* and *speed* we refer again to *A Thousand Plateaus*: "We must try to conceive of this world in which a single fixed plane—which we shall call a plane of absolute immobility *or* absolute movement—is traversed by informal elements of relative speed that enter this or that individuated assemblage depending on their degrees of speed and slowness" (255); See also: "Here, fixed does not mean immobile: it is the absolute state of movement as well as of rest, from which all relative speeds and slownesses spring, and nothing but them," 267.

[12] Deleuze borrows the first expression "immobile à grands pas" from Paul Valéry in *Le Cimetière Marin* and will use it again subsequently in "The smooth and the striated," in *A Thousand Plateaus*, 592; Alameddine, *An Unnecessary Woman*, 35, 60–61.

[13] Alameddine, *An Unnecessary Woman*, 61.

[14] Gilles Deleuze, *Francis Bacon: The Logic of Sensation*, trans. Daniel W. Smith (London and New York: Continuum, 2003), 15.

[15] Deleuze and Parnet, *Dialogues*, 36, 66.

the posthumous work of Félix Guattari posits, another life in another "World of Possibles," to dawn.[16] It is by "let[ting] the wall crumble, the barricade that separates [her] from books," from that "stockroom of books, [...] Only books [...] stacks and stacks, shelves and bookcases, stacks atop each shelf" that Aaliya "*is involved*" and gains access for just a moment to another world, invents herself and conquers another life: "During these moments, I am no longer my usual self, yet I am whole-heartedly myself, body and spirit. During these moments, I am healed of all wounds."[17] What Aaliya describes singularly here through the concat-enation and processes of a deterritorialization, a reterritorialization, and finally a pure event is the sudden emergence of a vital, joyful, and pregnant experience; one that transforms life, one that "leads into *a life*,"[18] and through which wounds and affects, on a plane of immanence, are less a matter of *pensée,* of thoughts per se than, in a homophonic interplay inher-ent to the terminology of Bernard Stiegler, a curative matter of *pansée,* of healing over, of "*care-ful* thinking."[19]

Wholeheartedly myself and healed: it is at this juncture that Alameddine's mode of writing assigns itself very closely with perhaps the most intimate and most essential motifs in the philosophy of Gilles Deleuze on *Literature and Life,* in other words "literature as an enterprise of health" or "health as literature."[20] For Deleuze, the problematic takes on a quite special ontological and ethical dimension. It begins initially by deploying a series of pragmatic questions: "What uses are there for literature?"[21] What is its function? What is its necessity? Deleuze's answer is unambiguous: Literature's essential power [*puissance*] resides in its ability to connect to a certain "vitalist and joyful conception of life."[22] Literature, just like art,

[16] Gilles Deleuze, *The Logic of Sense*, trans. Mark Lester (New York: Columbia University Press, 1990), 63: "The event is always that which has just happened and that which is about to happen, but never that which is happening"; Félix Guattari, *Lignes de fuite. Pour un Autre Monde de Possibles* (Paris: Éd. de l'Aube, coll. Monde en cours, 2011), 12.

[17] Alameddine, *An Unnecessary Woman*, 82–84, 100, 109.

[18] Gilles Deleuze, *Pure Immanence: Essays on A Life,* (New York: Zone Books, 2005), 25, 31.

[19] Bernard Stiegler, *The Neganthropocene,* ed. and trans. Daniel Ross (London: Open Humanities Press, 2018), 203. See also Bernard Stiegler, *Qu'appelle-t-on panser? Au-delà de l'Entropocène* (Paris: Editions Les liens qui libèrent, 2018).

[20] Gilles Deleuze, *Critical and Clinical*, trans. Daniel W. Smith and Michael A. Greco (London & New York: Verso, 1998), 3, 4.

[21] Gilles Deleuze, *Coldness and Cruelty* (New York: Zone Books, 1991), 15.

[22] Gilles Deleuze, "Letter by way of preface," in Mireille Buydens, *Sahara: L'Esthétique de Gilles Deleuze* (Paris: Vrin, 1990), 5.

does not have and never *is* an end in itself. Literature does not have as its aim to reflect or to close in on itself.[23] Neither intransitive nor closure, literature subscribes to the very production of the *transitive.* If "literature is a health," writes Deleuze, it is precisely because it acts *ex*trinsically, and gives forth to that vital flux, that vitality or, according to Nietzsche's expression, that "great health" that offers the subject/the individual the ability to develop an act of resistance toward life's vicissitudes, toward the wounds and the sufferings of the lived.[24] It is on this basis that Aaliya can say: "life kills me" but "literature gives me life," "I am healed."[25] Through literature, Aaliya reveals herself to be, no longer in a *critical* sense but henceforth in a *clinical* one, her own physician, or, as Deleuze would postulate, "a fairly special doctor" or "a great symptomatologist."[26] Aaliya, however, does not stop at just diagnosing the conditions that apply to her own life. Moving beyond diagnosis, Aaliya both exhibits a major resistance and deploys a veritable will to power [*puissance*]. *Diagnosis, Power [puissance], Invention*: inversely to Kafka's *Metamorphosis,* in which the character of Gregor Samsa "resigns himself to be a cockroach and accepts being the blade of grass upon which the stormtrooper's boot stomps," Aaliya resists and envisages/invents in counterpoint her own *becoming,* her own *metamorphosis,* by affirming herself through the following question: "[…] is it immoral for someone like me to want to be more?"[27] This question is certainly not one as such. The question mark exclaims and declaims as much as it claims. It obviously punctuates the force of a reasoning stance for resisting but it also denotes the jump and the emergence of *a vital challenge*, which transmutes itself and opens out onto an existential will— the very one "to be more," to *become more.*[28]

If Aaliya's life is marked by a certain *pathos* coupled with an *ethos* inherent to the social and political conditions in Lebanon, *never* forasmuch will

[23] See Gilles Deleuze, "What is the creative act?" in *Two Regimes of Madness: Texts and Interviews 1975–1995,* ed. David Lapoujade, trans. Ames Hodges and Mike Taormina (New York: Semiotext(e), 2007), 327–328.

[24] Deleuze, *Critical and Clinical,* iv. See also in regards to the act of writing, and literature as a whole: "a passage of Life that traverses both the liveable and the lived," Ibid., 1. In regard to Nietzsche's concept of "great health," see Friedrich Nietzsche, *The Gay Science,* trans. Walter Kaufmann (New York: Vintage, 1974), 346–347.

[25] Alameddine, *An Unnecessary Woman,* 4, 109.

[26] Gilles Deleuze, *Negotiations 1972–1990,* trans. Marin Joughin (London & New York: Columbia University Press, 1995), 142.

[27] Alameddine, *An Unnecessary Woman,* 116.

[28] Ibid.

she utter the slightest expression of self-pity, the slightest complaint about her mode of existence or even her solitude: "Please, no pity or insincere compassion. I'm not suggesting I feel sorry for myself [...]. Still, I made my bed—a simple, comfortable, and adequate bed."[29] The character of Aaliya is dignified and singular—it conforms very closely to the Deleuzian conception of literary characters to the extent that "all [her] individual traits elevate [her] to a vision that carries [her] off to these becomings or powers [*puissance*]."[30] Besides *pathos,* beyond *tragedy,* Alameddine's novel is not only "a river-book," but also a "subterranean book of fire," operating in fragments and proceeding by flashes.[31] Traversed by a single and singular act of seeking, the novel raises questions both *ethical* and *practical,* whose tonality refers to a mode of thinking akin to Spinoza (*Ethics*) and Deleuze (*Spinoza, Practical Philosophy*). How can one, as an individuated subject, augment joy and diminish sadness? Deleuze uncovers the question with precision: "How does one arrive at a maximum of joyful passions?, proceeding from there to free active feelings (although our place in Nature seems to condemn us to bad encounters and sadness)?"[32] Far more than a rhetorical response, Deleuze and Guattari, in *A Thousand Plateaus,* provide a concrete method:

> *This is how it should be done*: Lodge yourself [*s'installer*] on a stratum, experiment with the opportunities [*les chances*] it offers, find an advantageous place on it, find potential movements of deterritorialization, possible lines of flight, experience them, produce flow conjunctions here and there, try out continuums of intensities segment by segment, have a small plot of land at all times.[33]

First and foremost, this method is an initiatory journey, a long experimentation that begins initially with the identification of a *stratum* so as to lodge oneself, to install oneself *within*.[34] It is then from this platform

---

[29] Ibid., 7.

[30] Deleuze, *Critical and Clinical*, 3.

[31] Ibid., 151. The expressions "river-book" and "subterranean book of fire" are used by Deleuze in relation to Spinoza's *Ethics*.

[32] Gilles Deleuze, *Spinoza, Practical Philosophy,* trans. Robert Hurley (San Francisco: City Light Books, 1998), 28.

[33] Deleuze and Guattari, *A Thousand Plateaus*, 161.

[34] Among the proteiform meanings of the concept of the stratum in Deleuze and Guattari, the word 'stratum' is here being used in the first place in the sense of "liveable zone." Quoting this same extract from *A Thousand Plateaus,* Nicholas Tampio argues that "Deleuze

216   F.-X. GLEYZON

through which are captured and experienced *outside* the lines of flight and movements of deterritorialization, and ultimately "having a place;" said differently: "establishing an endurable zone [*zone vivable*] in which to install ourselves, confront things, take hold, breathe [...] and manage to live [...]."[35] In this operation-experimentation, there is simultaneously a certain *dynamic of captation* (the lines of flight and movements of deterritorialization) and a *topological structure and organization* (from a stratum to a place) implying here a dialogic in which, as Deleuze describes, "the space inside is in contact with the space outside."[36] But if the subject positions and exerts itself toward this outside-space, toward "this passion of the outside" according to Maurice Blanchot's expression, it is only to the extent that the distant outside is converted into the near interior where the immensity of the outside unfolds into the depth of the inside-space, transmuted as "intimacy."[37]

Here lies, according to Deleuze, "an art of living" or, more pragmatically, how "to manage to live: a matter of life or death."[38] *A Novel on the Method, A Practical Novel*: it is also with diligence that Aaliya observes that method and manages to live. In the midst of her own tumult, Aaliya walks "back to the stack of books" and *installs herself* "in her reading chair," withdrawn into her tiny room.[39] It is from this place, from this stratum, that Aaliya counteracts and fills herself with this necessity-will to *live*—"no longer to think about [*her*] life, but to *lose* [*herself*] in someone else's"—and ultimately to depart for "a long voluptuous ride"—in brief, to reach a vast outside world that deposits unsounded and infinite spaces into the very depth of her being: "In order to live, I have to blind myself to my infinitesimal dimensions in this infinite universe. [And, quoting Fernando Pessoa:] *I can't even wish to be anything. Aside from that, within*

---

invites us to imagine ourselves inhabiting this landscape. The lodge is from the Frankish *laubja* 'shelter'; stratum is a 'horizontal layer.' To lodge yourself on a stratum means to inhabit a slice of the world: [...] a family, country, religious group, profession, school of thought or any other customary practice." Nicholas Tampio, "Entering Deleuze's Political Vision," in *Deleuze Studies*. Vol. 8. (Edinburgh: Edinburgh University Press, 2014), 14.

[35] Deleuze, *Negotiations*, 111.

[36] Gilles Deleuze, *Foucault*, trans. Sean Hand (Minneapolis: University of Minnesota Press, 2006), 118–119.

[37] Ibid., 123.

[38] Deleuze, *Negotiations*, 111.

[39] Alameddine, *An Unnecessary Woman*, 115, 116. My italics.

me I have all the dreams of the world."[40] Here then is the macrocosm of the outside effectuating/converting itself into the microcosm of the inside—to paraphrase Edgar Morin, "the open resting on the closed."[41]

Ah, splendid Microcosms, the deliciousness of *discovering* a masterwork. The beauty of the first sentences, the "what is this?," the "how can this be?," the first crush all over again, *the smile of the soul. My heart begins to lift.* I can see myself [...] *immersed in lives,* [...] and sentences, intoxicated by words and chimeras, paralyzed by satisfaction and contentment, reading until the deepening twilight, until I can no longer make out the words, until my mind begins to *wander,* until my aching muscles are no longer able to keep the book aloft. *Joy* is the anticipation of *joy.* Reading a fine book for the first time is as sumptuous as the first sip of orange juice that breaks the fast in Ramadan. [...]. I flip delicate pages with an unhurried and measured beat, a lazy metronome timing. I lose myself in the book's languorous *territories.* I'm *transported* [...] I *travel* along the book's meandering *paths*—breakfast with a young man in one village, lunch with a crone in another—[...] salivate over beautiful sentences, celebrate holidays I'd never heard of. I read and read [...].[42]

The vast outside is enveloped in the depths of the inside, in this "splendid microcosm."[43] The immensity of the inside traces here a whole "interstitching" of itineraries, of networks in which each step covered actualizes and opens multivalent spaces, "continuous regions of intensity": *exaltation of the heart and spirit, joy, journey, transportation and immersion in other lives, ceaseless walking and surveying, discovery of other peoples, unknown territories, lands, and landscapes.*[44] Is it not here, at the heart of this dynamic concatenation of deterritorialization and reterritorialization, of the outside toward the inside, that the very aim of literature is inscribed,

---

[40] Ibid., 277. See the seminal studies of Gaston Bachelard, *The Poetics of Space,* trans. Maria Jolas (Boston: Beacon Press, 1994), and in particular Chapter 8: "Intimate immensity," 183–210, and Chapter 9: "The Dialectics of the Outside and the Inside," 211–232. There is also a significant parallel between Aaliya's room and the room described by Maurice Blanchot in *L'Arrêt de Mort:* "About this room, which was plunged in utter darkness, I knew everything. I had entered into it, I bore it within me. I made it live, with a life that is not life, but which is stronger than life, and which no force in the world can vanquish." Blanchot quoted in Gaston Bachelard, Ibid., 229.

[41] Edgar Morin, *La Méthode, tome II* (Paris: Seuil, 1986), 203.

[42] Alameddine, *An Unnecessary Woman,* 116, 117.

[43] Ibid.

[44] Deleuze, *Critical and Clinical,* 63; Deleuze and Guattari, *A Thousand Plateaus,* 158.

218   F.-X. GLEYZON

its "ultimate aim," as Gilles Deleuze proposes, "to set free, in the delirium, this creation of a health or this invention of a people, that is, a possibility of life."[45] There is always within Aaliya that vital resistance, that capacity for invention, to re-invent and to recreate oneself. *Even if* Aaliya seems to exhaust herself in struggling against her own sufferings and asks her readers only "to retain from reading these paltry pages" the acoustic image "of [her] mother's screaming, the frail body, the position of her hands, the skirl of terror [...] her skirl of terror to be [her] last memory of her"—and even cites the daughter, Sin, of Milton's *Paradise Lost*, retorting to her father, Satan: "Hast thou forgot me then, and do I seem/Now in thine eye so foul?"—*one will not be mistaken*: Aaliya *persists* and *fights* within herself and against herself.[46] In terms befitting Hamlet, Aaliya possesses this "*within*," she "hath that *within* which passeth the show" (I, ii, 85), and faced with the *Paradise Lost* of her life; with this *missed* paradise, she still remains capable of reaching a *Paradise Regained* and harnessing/ capturing a power of life [*puissance de vie*] amongst an *areopagus* of books in which she immerses herself unconditionally.[47] John Milton's *Areopagitica*

[45] Deleuze, *Critical and Clinical*, 4.
[46] Alameddine, *An Unnecessary Woman*, 202.
[47] William Shakespeare, "Hamlet," in ed. Stephen Greenblatt, *Norton Shakespeare* (New York: WW Norton, 2015); Alameddine, *An Unnecessary Woman*, 253: "I plunged into my books." On the subject of books' powers, I refer to Sergei M. Eisenstein, "Encounters with Books," in *Beyond The Stars: The Memoirs of Sergei Eisenstein, Selected Works, Volume IV*, ed. Richard Taylor, trans. William Powell (London: The British Film Institute, 1995) whose room and mode of existence come very close to those of Aaliya. I quote the passage in its entirety without interruption by reason of its dynamic continuity:

> Books cluster around me. They fly to me, run to me, cling to me. So long have I loved them: large and small, fat and slender, rare editions and cheap paperbacks, they cry out through their dustcovers, or are perhaps sunk in contemplation in a solid, leather skin, as if wearing soft slippers. They need not be too neat, like suits fresh from the tailor; nor cold, like starched cuffs. But neither must they shine like greasy rags. [...] I love them so much that they finally begin to reciprocate my love. Books burst open like ripe fruit in my hands and, like magical flowers, open up their petals, carrying a fertilizing line of thought, an inspiring word, an affirming quotation, an illustration to prove a point. I am whimsical in my selection.

And they readily drop into my hands.
Fatefully they surround me.
Once only one room was designated for books.
But insidiously, room by room, my flat has filled up with books which loop themselves around things like hoops on a barrel. So, after the 'library,' the study was taken over; after

provides the full measure of this vitalist paradigm: "For books are not absolutely dead things, but do contain a potency of life in them to be as active as that soul was whose progeny they are, [...] they do preserve as in a vial the purest efficacy and extraction of that living intellect that bred them. I know they are [...] lively, and [...] vigorously productive. A [...] book, a precious life-blood [...] on purpose to a life beyond life."[48]

It is precisely in this sense that Alameddine's novel does not manifest despair, annihilation, or self-destructiveness per se, but tends toward that respiration through which literature is thought through as a *potency of life*. Despite the "inexplicable and impenetrable" aberrations of the world, literature still instills this breath of life: "Literature is the air I breathe," says Aaliya.[49] It is this coextensive condition, which enables the subject/the individual to live and therefore to think as a living-self by reason of its direct connection/relation to a vital source of life: *Literature*. As Deleuze prescribes, one must, therefore, "cease to think in terms of self, so as to live as flux, beyond and in oneself," and finally find joy, even if this joy comes, under certain circumstances, from what is horrible, terrifying, or even lethal: "there is always an indescribable joy which bursts out of great books, even when they are treating ugly, heart-breaking or terrifying matters. The transmutation already takes effect with every great book and every great book constitutes a health of tomorrow."[50] Aaliya's mode of existence reveals not only the transmutation of a suffering by the implementation of a form of healthy resistance, but also the capacity of knowing

the study, the walls of my bedroom. [...] That is how I sometimes perceive my rooms. Currents flow from the small cells of grey matter of the brain, through the cranium and the sides of bookcases, through the walls of bookcases and into the hearts of the books. Not true! None of the bookcases has sides—I keep them on open shelves, and in response to the flow of thoughts they hurl themselves at my head. Sometimes the greed radiating towards them is the stronger. Sometimes the infectious force emanating through their covers is the stronger. I feel like a latter-day St Sebastian, pierced by arrows flying from the shelves. And the small sphere of bone, containing splinters of reflections like Leibniz' reflecting monad, seems no longer a cranium but the outer walls of the room, and the layer of books covering the surfaces of its walls are like stratifications extending inside my own head. (350–2)

[48] John Milton, *Areopagitica* (Cambridge: Cambridge University Press, 1918), 618–619.

[49] Alameddine, *An Unnecessary Woman*, 253.

[50] Fanny Deleuze and Gilles Deleuze, "Preface to D. H. Lawrence," in *Apocalypse*, trans. Fanny Deleuze (Paris: Editions Balland, 1978), 35; Gilles Deleuze, "Pensée nomade," in ed. David Lapoujade, *L'Ile Déserte et Autres Textes de Gilles Deleuze* (Paris: Editions de Minuit, 2002), 359.

220   F.-X. GLEYZON

how to remain worthy, how to "become worthy of what happens to us and thus to will and release the event, to become the offspring of one's own event, and thereby to be reborn [*renaître*], to have one more birth [renaissance] and to break with one's *carnal* birth [*sa chair de naissance*]."[51]

To live as flux, beyond and in oneself and to break with one's carnal birth, with one's flesh. Everything starts with a name. All is said, all says itself, and all signs itself with the name عالية, Aaliya. The name Aaliya originates from its Arabic root *ain l a*, and emerges in its adjectival form in the Qur'an to signify both a quality and a movement of exaltation, of grandeur, of *sublime elevation*. Mentioned twice directly in the suras Al-Ghashiyah (The Overwhelming) and Al-Haqqah (The Reality/The Inevitable Truth) عالية, Aaliya always directs and pushes the gaze to contemplate a space, a suspended territory: "Fee jannatin 'aaliya" (*Qur'an* 69: 22), "jannat 'aaliya" (*Qur'an* 88: 10). As if, lurking in the interiority of her name, a movement of exit and an Icarian perspective of flight or even a certain "ascensional psyche" were operating simultaneously.[52] Aaliya weathers gravity and the fixity of letters, the static written trace, the *graphein*, assigned to her name and opens the sign and the signature of a transgression, of a dematerialization to come. The name of Aaliya does not thus *in*scribe an identity or a circumscribed laden destiny but is *ex*scribed in the very sense that it tends entirely toward its own limit or toward its own outside.[53] "Proper names," Deleuze recalls, "designate primarily forces, events, movements, moving objects, winds, typhoons, [...] places and moments before they designate persons."[54] *In itself* the proper name Aaliya liberates and projects *something outside itself* in order, writes Nietzsche, "to stand above

---

[51] Deleuze, *Logic of sense*, 149–150.

[52] Gaston Bachelard, "Nietzsche and the Ascensional Psyche," in *Air and Dreams: An Essay On the Imagination of Movement,* trans. Edith R. Farrell and C. Frederick Farrell (Dallas: The Dallas Institute Publications, 1988), 127–60.

[53] The richness of the classical Arabic language, *fushá,* has in certain well-defined and specific cases the characteristic of furthering zones of semantic indiscernibility or, in other words, of tracing a primary meaning in order to release its opposite, and vice versa: a deterritorialization of verbal syntax culminating into another semantic possibility or becoming. It is a question here of auto-antonyms, the *addád. Lamaqa* can signify both "to write" and "to erase." *Assara* "to divulge" and "to conceal" a secret. *Tala'a* "to appear" and "to disappear." Christine Buci-Glucksmann mentions the polysemic property of these cases, cf. Christine Buci-Glucksmann, *The Madness of Vision: On Baroque Aesthetics,* trans. Dorothy Z. Baker (Athens: Ohio University Press, 2013), xviii.

[54] Deleuze, *Negotiations,* 34.

everything as its own sky."[55] *Exit* Aaliya: perhaps one of the most pregnant characteristics of Alameddine's mode of writing is that of conceiving of and *conceptualizing* the subject—Aaliya—as a veritable vector-operator of flux and flights, thus giving rise to both a deterritorialization and a phenomenon characteristic of autoscopia in which the subject's own body discovers itself, (*re*)produces, (*re*)presents itself in another body. In other words, and according to Deleuze's own definition of autoscopia: "it is no longer my head, but I feel myself inside a head, I see and I see myself inside a head; or else I do not see myself in the mirror, but I feel myself in the body that I see, and I see myself in this naked body ... and so forth."[56] We find in Alameddine's novel a passage in which Aaliya recalls to mind the memory of Ahmad—a transient encounter through which the body rejoices while the soul wanes. But it is precisely through these sharp and carnal reminiscences of the past that Aaliya frees her voice and engages herself in an upward aerial and celestial impulse so as to lean over her own body. This process-movement is not without recalling the reasoning pertaining to the question *What is the creative act?* to which Deleuze tracks the following answer: "A voice rises into the air. [...] A voice is talking about something. Something is being talked about. At the same time we are shown something else. And [...], what is being talked about lies *under* what we are being shown."[57] Rabih Alameddine carries out this *creative act* or rather, he takes it up again. Alameddine initiates and triggers this creative process/movement by making the passage begin with the proper name—Aaliya—providing immediately afterward its signification as well as the whole of its etymological span:

Aaliya, the high one—Aaliya with the bird's-eye view, above the muck and mud and life's swamps. What seeped through the mortar of my walls was not his technique (adequate) or his ardor (more than). I was on my knees facing away, he behind me still smelling of licorice and anise, engaged in an age-old rhythm. He slowed and his fingers explored the topography of my lower back. I could feel his face descending, examining a *tiny city on a map.* His fingers squeezed gently before he removed them. At first, I tried to dismiss this interruption, considered it a possible sexual quirk, but his fin-

---

[55] Friedrich Nietzsche, "Before Sunrise," in *Thus Spake Zarathustra*, trans. Thomas Wayne (New York: Algora, 2003), 126.

[56] Gilles Deleuze, *Francis Bacon: The Logic of Sensation*, trans. Daniel W. Smith (London and New York: Continuum, 2003), 49.

[57] Deleuze, "What is the creative act?," 326.

222 F.-X. GLEYZON

gers resumed the exploration of the *region*, lower back and upper derrière. His fingers squeezed once more, and this time I realized what he was doing, I recognized the feel of a blackhead being extruded. When he removed a third, I looked back, and it was more likely that I'd have turned to butter than to salt. He apologized, begged my forgiveness. It had been unconscious. He couldn't see a blackhead on his own skin without removing it and didn't realize he was doing the same with me. I asked him not to stop. I loved it. His fingers happily reconnoitered my entire back, delicately, gently, and ever so slowly turned my skin into a smorgasbord of delicious feelings. I was touched. I buried my face in the pillow to hide my ecstasy and my tears. My heart had momentarily found its pestle.[58]

How to proceed with an analysis of this passage without qualifying it first as pure event? This passage is an event to the very extent to which Alameddine traces a whole trajectory, a line of intensity in which *height, depth, and surface* are linked to one another, all three constitutive of life.[59] *Height,* first of all, or even *verticality* and *speed:* "very high," "with bird's-eye view" the body, "floating high in the air," overhangs, leans forward and sees itself as in a dream outside itself to then coalesce in "the mud," the "muck" of its own corporality.[60] If the vision opens with the intimacy of a sex act, none of this is relevant, let alone significant. Alameddine is not concerned with the sex act per se. It is not his point, and even all its details will be discarded, relegated to the bare minimum, and *à la lettre* placed in brackets: "his technique (adequate)" or "his ardor (more than)."[61] Henceforth it is no longer a question of *verticality* or *speed* but of their diametric opposite: the plane undergoes a change of direction, overturns, and is now coordinated by the *horizontality of a flat surface,* namely the body of Aaliya. It is this singular reversal that animates all of Alameddine's genius and transforms the scene into pure event. The sex act is slowly interrupted to give way to a vision of a bodily surface, *a cutaneous vision,* in which the body of the beloved is deployed and unfolded as so many regions to be surveyed, to be discovered. It belongs to Alameddine to sublimate the carnal act by operating such a shift/displacement insofar as the jouissance of pleasure finds itself transmuted into a libidinal potency

[58] Alameddine, *An Unnecessary Woman,* 43–44. My Italics.
[59] In relation to the complex relationships between height, depth, and surface along with "the surface-depth problem," see Deleuze, *Logic of sense,* 10–23.
[60] Alameddine, 43.
[61] Ibid.

[*puissance*] prior to its ultimate prolongation as the jouissance of desire. What Alameddine gives to see behind the mortar of these walls is perhaps the answer to what the act of love(-making) means, or, formulated otherwise: "How can one describe [...] beyond the probing, poking, and panting, beyond words, the infinite mystery of the sex act?"[62] If Aaliya is penetrated to the deepest part of her being, "touched" by "ecstasy," the sex act and its lubricious "technical aspects" are, however, categorically, inconsequential.[63] "The age-old" practice, the *sexual habitus* which implies and marks depth and penetration into the flesh, makes way for display, for deployment of surface, and, finally, for the intimate exploration of skin. And it is indeed at the very moment that her body is comprehended no longer in terms of *depth* but in terms of cutaneous surface that Aaliya encounters jouissance. *Copernican revolution of jouissance*: no longer to penetrate (in-)depth, but to slide sideways over the body's surface and survey the surface of the skin so as to follow each membrane. Deleuze in his *Logic of Sense* picks up with relevance on Paul Valéry's discovery: "what is most deep is the skin."[64] There is nothing superficial about surface— and, it is equally through the very same epistemological scheme that the principle of love and sexuality must be grasped. Deleuze makes explicit the implications of "the discovery of surface and the critique of depth" through Lewis Carroll's *Alice in Wonderland* and *Through the Looking Glass,* and Michel Tournier's *Friday*: "It is a strange prejudice which sets a higher value on depth than on breadth, and which accepts 'superficial' as meaning not 'of wide extent' but of 'little depth,' whereas 'deep,' on the other hand, signifies 'of great depth,' and not 'of small surface.' Yet it seems to me that a feeling such as love is better measured, if it can be measured at all, by the extent of its surface than by its degree of depth."[65] It is therefore by the dismissal of depth that the art of surfaces comes into being through which skin is touched, is *looked at by contact* with the finger that follows each of its membranes and traces out a course over its loops, its wandering lines, its ridges, its growths, its backward movements and returns, even its deviations: "[...] His fingers [Ahmad's] explored the topography of my lower back [...] his face descending, examining a *tiny*

---

[62] Alameddine, *An Unnecessary Woman*, 43.

[63] Ibid.

[64] Deleuze *Logic of Sense*, 10.

[65] Deleuze *Logic of Sense*, 336 n7.

224   F.-X. GLEYZON

city on a map [...] his fingers resumed the exploration of the *region* [...]."[66] In other words, the body-flesh is invested with a geography in motion and becoming.

What Alameddine achieves through this passage corresponds precisely to the construction of desire—*a geography of desire*—which, according to Deleuze, does not relate to the "Law of the Lack," namely: an internal lack impossible to fill or a sort of deprivation which defers or rejects the endpoint of coitus-pleasure.[67] "Desire does not have pleasure as its norm [and] desire lacks for nothing."[68] It is "by virtue of its own positivity" that desire is conceived.[69] For desire are connection, assemblage, and combination. It is the function of a creative process that aims to construct an assemblage by coordinating heterogeneous elements emanating from a subject or an object. It would therefore be erroneous to say: I desire someone or something *solely* and *exclusively.* "One always desires *within the context of* a whole."[70] In other words, according to Deleuze: "I do not desire a woman, I also desire a landscape that is enveloped in that woman and as long as I have not enfolded the landscape she envelops, my desire will not have been fulfilled, it will remain unsatisfied" or "What beloved being does not envelope landscapes, continents, and populations."[71] How does this relate to that intimate scene that Alameddine invites us to read in which the interruption of pleasure is converted into a potency [*puissance*] of desire and a continuum of intensity? First, man and woman must not be construed here "as sexual entities" and reified as such in a binary apparatus with each other. Beyond a heteronormative law-authority, "a man and a woman are fluxes" as Deleuze writes, which is to say: the subjects are fluxes.[72] And it is to the extent that subjects are fluxes that the sexuality Alameddine proposes here manifests "a pure and simple, inventive and amazed sexuality [...] in comparison with the laborious, punctilious and controlled trash [*cochonnerie*] [of some] writers."[73] Here the sexuality of the two subjects is otherwise conceived of—and is *otherwise* more fertile,

---

[66] Alameddine, 43. *My italics.*

[67] Deleuze and Parnet, *Dialogues,* 100.

[68] Deleuze and Parnet, *Dialogues,* 100.

[69] Ibid.

[70] Deleuze with Parnet, "D comme Désir," in *L'Abécédaire de Gilles Deleuze*; Deleuze, *Critical and Clinical,* 62.

[71] Ibid.

[72] Deleuze and Parnet, *Dialogues,* 47.

[73] Ibid.

more creative for Alameddine. It is assembled, fabricated, and invented—one to/by the other—through the combination of the fluxes of each of the two subjects in order to enter into a rapport with or close vicinity to other desiring elements, and form and discover the whole of a becoming. "All the becomings which there are in making love," Deleuze says, and adds: "every line in which someone gets carried away is a line of modesty [*pudeur*]."[74] It is by discovering each trait, by exploring and following each line through their intertwining and concatenation on the "body-flesh" of Aaliya that the latter is transmuted into a becoming: body-landscape, body-"region," body-"topography," body-"map," body-"city," a body-world in short, a whole geography, or even: a whole *geo-corporality*. Hence the words of Deleuze that partake of Alameddine's very own process of writing: "I am trying to explain that things, that people, are made up of very varied lines and that they do not necessarily know what line of themselves they are on, nor where they should make the line that they are tracing pass: in short, there is a whole geography in people with rigid lines, supple lines, lines of flight, etc."[75]

But how to read now the meaning of that incongruous act, performed on the very surface of Aaliya's skin? Why this repugnant, repulsive, and almost hysterical act? Why pierce and extract these blackheads on the lineaments of the skin? The work by Manola Antonioli, *Géophilosophie de Deleuze et Guattari*, seems to find an answer to this series of questions by emphasizing that "reading individuals like landscapes, maps or intertwinings of lines means forcing thought to think what repels it, the possibility of a radical multiplicity and a radical unforeseeableness which trigger horror."[76] However, in the tegumentary context of the scene Alameddine presents, and if indeed comedones can be repugnant and instill horror, the act of extrusion or *expression*, in medical terminology, signifies also a new motility, and henceforth a modality for thinking the skin surface anew. Dermatology teaches us that blackheads or "comedones" obstruct the lines and the most superficial layer of the epidermis. It is on this clinical basis that Ahmad's act is pure *expression* and endorses a signifying dimension in the very expression of desire itself. On the outermost layer of the skin, one must examine, unblock obstructions, and liberate lines from points of resistance so that, according to Deleuze's expression, "the fluxes

---

[74] Ibid., 47 & 48.

[75] Deleuze and Parnet, *Dialogues*, 10.

[76] Maniola Antonioli, *Géophilosophie de Deleuze et Guattari* (Paris: L'Harmattan, 2003), 29.

226   F.-X. GLEYZON

may *literally* escape and flow," and ultimately find ecstasy, jouissance.[77] The abject nature of the scene becomes then splendor. For these lines on the tegumentary surface of the body, as Félix Guattari would write, are "active, positive lines of flight [since] these lines open up desire, desire's machines, and the organization [...] of desire: it is not a matter of escaping 'personally' from oneself, but of allowing something to escape, like bursting a pipe or an abscess."[78] Faced with a literature that is all too often *spermatographic*, Alameddine therefore becomes a creator, an inventor-innovator of an alternative libidinal economy—he discovers, instates, and releases marginal and anormative liquid-fluxes (sebum-flux or even pus-flux) on the surface of the skin. Never, *nevertheless, in* depth, for it is, on the contrary, the depths of the being which, by extrusion, rise and are snapped up on the surface, to then concatenate in unlimited becomings: becoming-"topos," becoming-"map," becoming-"city." As Deleuze would write: "[an] event of this type [is] the more profound since it occurs at the surface, the more it skirts bodies [...]," adding subsequently, "[The] history [of surveying] teaches us that sound roads have no foundation, and geography that only a thin layer of earth is fertile."[79]

As a writer, Rabih Alameddine would never perhaps have written a single sentence. Rabih Alameddine does not *write*, he *traces* and *forges* lines. He weaves a dynamic map onto which all is arrayed as an extensive series of bodies: organic-body, corpus-body, city-body. "Not a writer, no, but a new cartographer, yes."[80] "Arpenteur de lieux," surveying the various faces of the outside, Alameddine's narrator, Aaliya, walks through the streets of Beirut as much as she walks through the texts she reads, writes, and translates: "Walking shoes—I am *walking, walking, walking*."[81] Her body follows the lines, the twists and turns, the points of resistance in the very space she walks through. Beirut's geographical space, in its incessant *becoming,* is transformed, actualizes itself in an immanent movement just as if the place, the territory took shape at the very moment of the body's approach and traversal. The map or Aaliya's cartographic activity must not only be understood by rapport to a space simply constituted by specific

---

[77] Deleuze with Parnet, "D comme Désir," in *L'Abécédaire de Gilles Deleuze.*

[78] Deleuze, *Negotiations,* 19.

[79] Deleuze, *Logic of Sense,* 10.

[80] Gilles Deleuze, "Ecrivain non: Un nouveau cartographe," in *Critique* 343 (Paris: Editions de Minuit, 1975), 1207.

[81] "Arpenteur de lieux," expression borrowed from George Didi-Huberman, *L'homme qui marchait dans la couleur* (Paris: Editions de Minuit, 2001), 9; Alameddine, 174.

trajectories, such as from point A to point B, but in its qualitative dimension of *intensity* or, as Deleuze writes, "as an evaluation of *displacements.* [...] Each map is a redistribution of cul-de-sacs and breakthroughs, of thresholds and enclosures [...]."[82] Hence Aaliya's cartographic activity:

> Hear me on this for a moment. [...] Rarely can I walk the same path from point A to point B [...] for more than a month. I constantly have to adjust my walking maps [...]. Life in Beirut is much too random. I can't force myself to believe I'm in charge of much of my life.[83]

The map made by Alameddine cannot be grasped however through the traditional conception assigned to this practice. It in no way imitates a map and cannot be conceived of as an arbitrary process of codes, projection, and graphic description of a space or a territory.[84] Alameddine's cartography, according to Deleuze and Guattari, turns "entirely towards an experimentation in contact with the real" and moves "in a creative mode of exploration and discovery of new realities."[85] Even if these new realities participate in the imaginary and coalesce into virtual images—according to Deleuze, "The real and the imaginary do [not] form a relevant distinction."—there is certainly with Alameddine *intensity* and *density*. Both are produced through the dynamic proliferation of paths and trajectories that redesign the cartography of the real on an imaginary plane. For the streets and the alleys of Beirut move: "they undergo a transformation at night [...], and multiply like rats—like rats I tell you!"[86] "It is as if," Deleuze would say, "the real paths were intertwined with virtual paths that give it new courses or trajectories. A map of virtualities, drawn up by art, is superimposed on the real map, whose distances [*parcours*] it transforms."[87]

But Alameddine will not stop there. This dynamic proliferation of streets, of cartographic lines, boils to acquire intensity and fullness, spilling over in space and exceeding their geographic frame, so as to transform in the extreme. All these streets, all these alleys that Alameddine sets in

---

[82] Deleuze, *Critical and Clinical,* 84.

[83] Alameddine, 53.

[84] On Gilles Deleuze and Félix Guattari's concept of cartography, see Gleyzon, François-Xavier, "Deleuze and the Grandeur of Palestine: Song of Earth and Resistance," in *Journal for Cultural Research* 20, no. 4 (2016): 398–416.

[85] Deleuze and Guattari, *A Thousand Plateaus,* 5 & 12.

[86] Deleuze, *Critical and Clinical,* 84; Alameddine, *An Unnecessary Woman,* 31.

[87] Deleuze, *Critical and Clinical,* 62.

228   F.-X. GLEYZON

motion in the Beirut space, are active and creative lines of flight. It is not a textual digression, or even a detail, as its author can claim, but these are precisely all the details of the lines and streets, previously invoked, which are going to converge and assemble themselves so as to engender a work of art. Everything happens during an encounter:

> After the war, in the mid-nineties, a local artist asked me to help him sell prints of a map of Beirut and its suburbs that he had lovingly painted by hand. He was obviously smitten with our city. He'd painted Beirut as if it were the whole world, complete within itself, each neighborhood a different country with its own color, streets as borders, the tiniest road documented, every alley, every corner. He'd even drawn in little hydrographic symbols (fleurs-de-lis) where all the water wells are supposed to be—Beirut, whose name is derived from the word well in most Semitic languages because of the abundance of its belowground water. A complete sphere, Beirut as the total globe, the entire world. The painter even created a Greenland effect, stretching the longitude lines at the top and bottom, with increasing distortion of size as one moved north or south of the city. In the map, Beirut existed outside of Lebanon, apart, not part of the Middle East. It was whole.[88]

A prodigious and vertiginous will to power: "this little block of Lebanon," as Deleuze used to describe it, dreams itself in becoming-world: Beirut-World.[89] Such a delirious expansion suggests a phenomenon of extremum of matter in which a minimum of geographic surface entails not only a maximum of matter but also a spatial becoming, *unlimited* and *global*. Each corner, each street, each road, even the tiniest, is a "power to enlarge and distend the world."[90] And it is not by accident that Alameddine marks on this map all the points of water that flow abundantly underground level, for it is these flows of liquid-flux which ensure as much for the exponential growth as for the production/realization of a desire, namely: Beirut-*Earth,* "Beirut as the total globe, the entire world."[91]

Is it by chance if, at the end of the novel, Alameddine creates an accident through which Aaliya's world falls apart, *submerged under water?* All her writings are drowned, damaged by water: "Everything has gone [...].

---

[88] Alameddine, *An Unnecessary Woman,* 30–31.

[89] Gilles Deleuze, *Lettres et autres textes* (Paris: Les Editions de Minuit, 2015), 47. In this context, Deleuze is referring to the Lebanese origins of Jacques Nassif.

[90] Gilles Deleuze, *The Fold,* trans. Tom Conley (Minneapolis: University of Minnesota Press, 1999), 124.

[91] Alameddine, *An Unnecessary Woman,* 31.

I see water damage everywhere [...]. The water chose to do so among my papers. Every crate is wet."[92] The incident is significant as it points toward a question which does not cease to haunt and spread insidiously from one end of Alameddine's textual landscape to the other. While Fadia and Joumana try to salvage all these sheets of paper by meticulously hanging them out, one by one, on a washing line—a method which is not unreminiscent of the montage and manipulation of maps advocated and described by Deleuze and Guattari—the question, as personal as it is secret, is finally asked: "Don't you want people to read your writing? Don't you want your work to be read?"[93] In other words, and fundamentally: *Why write? What is writing?* The answer, though "honest," is at first brief and seems to be tentative: "I'm not sure [...] I don't know, [...] I want her to understand, I want to understand."[94] But the real answer lies elsewhere. It is initiated when, through Aaliya, Alameddine questions the relevance of literature and envisages the necessity of writing in a new form, from another perspective, from a different angle on life: "There should be a new literary resolution [...]. Dear contemporary writers, you make me feel inadequate because my life isn't as clear and concise as your stories. I should send out letters to writers, writing programs, and publishers. You're strangling the life out of literature, sentence by well-constructed sentence, book by bland book."[95] Contemplating after the incident all her writings hung out on a line, Aaliya then notices: "the water damage makes the pages look like a stranger wrote them. Everything is written in a foreign language [...]. Letters are thickened randomly; some word endings are extended. In a few instances, the tip of the Arabic letter r runs like a river tributary until it either dries up or pours itself into the lake of the letter that follows."[96] Alameddine, creator-inventor, resists typographic and syntactic conventions. The language becomes agitated, turns into performance, a calligraphy in motion, and enters into a state of delirium to become other. It is for

---

[92] Ibid., 276 & 264–5.

[93] See Deleuze & Guattari, *A Thousand Plateaus*, 1: "The map is open and connectable in all of its dimensions; it is detachable, reversible, susceptible to constant modification. It can be torn, reversed, adapted to any kind of mounting [*montage*], reworked by an individual [or] group [...]. It can be drawn on a wall, conceived of as a work of art [...]."; Alameddine, *An Unnecessary Woman*, 284.

[94] Alameddine, *An Unnecessary Woman*, 284.

[95] Ibid., 148.

[96] Ibid., 277–278.

230   F.-X. GLEYZON

this reason that all the lines that constitute the work of Alameddine align with Deleuze's conception of writing:

> In order to write, it may perhaps be necessary for [...] language to be odious, but only so that a syntactic creation can open up a kind of foreign language in it, and language as a whole can reveal its outside, beyond all syntax. We sometimes congratulate writers, but they know that they are far from having achieved their becoming, far from having attained the limit they set for themselves, which ceaselessly slips away from them. To write is also to become something other than a writer.
>
> To those who ask what literature is, Virginia Woolf responds: To whom are you speaking of writing? The writer does not speak about it but is concerned with something else. If we consider these criteria, we can see that, among all those who make books with a literary intent, even among the mad, there are very few who can call themselves writers.[97]

One day perhaps, the century to come, *in becoming,* will be Alameddian.[98]

WORKS CITED

Alameddine, Rabih. *An Unnecessary Woman*. New York: Grove Press, 2014.
Antonioli, Maniola. *Géophilosophie de Deleuze et Guattari*. Paris: L'Harmattan, 2003.
Bachelard, Gaston. "Nietzsche and the Ascensional Psyche." In *Air and Dreams: An Essay On the Imagination of Movement*. Translated by Edith R. Farrell and C. Frederick Farrell. Dallas: The Dallas Institute Publications, 1988.
————. *The Poetics of Space*. Translated by Maria Jolas. Boston: Beacon Press, 1994.
Beckett, Samuel. *The Dépeupleur*. Paris: Les Editions de Minuit, 1970.

---

[97] Deleuze, *Critical and Clinical,* 5–6. On the necessity and the reason for writing, I also refer to the following, powerful and poignant, a passage from Deleuze: "One only writes through love, all writing is a love-letter, the literature—Real. One should only die through love, and not a tragic death. One should only write through this death, or stop writing through this love, or continue to write, both at once. [...] 'What is writing?' [It is] the impossibility of another choice which indeed makes writing [...] another becoming or comes from another becoming. Writing, the means to a more than personal life, instead of life being a poor secret for a writing which has no end other than itself. Oh the poverty of the imaginary and the symbolic, the real always being put off until tomorrow." Deleuze, *Dialogues,* 50–51.

[98] I modify and reassign the famous and often quoted phrase of Michel Foucault with regard to the philosophy of Gilles Deleuze: "Perhaps one day this century will be known as Deleuzian." to Rabih Alameddine. Cf. Michel Foucault, "Theatrum Philosophicum," in *Language, Counter-Memory, Practice,* ed. and trans. Donald F. Bouchard (Oxford, Blackwell and Ithaca: Cornell University Press, 1977), 165–96.

————. *The Lost Ones.* London: Calder & Boyars, 1972.

————. *Samuel Beckett: The Complete Short Prose, 1929–1989.* Edited by S. E. Gontarski. New York: Grove Press, 1995.

Buci-Glucksmann, Christine. *The Madness of Vision: On Baroque Aesthetics.* Translated by Dorothy Z. Baker. Athens: Ohio University Press, 2013.

Deleuze, Fanny and Deleuze, Gilles, "Preface to D. H. Lawrence." In *Apocalypse.* Translated by Fanny Deleuze. Paris: Editions Balland, 1978.

Deleuze, Gilles. *Francis Bacon The Logic of Sensation.* Translated by Daniel W. Smith. London and New York: Continuum, 2003.

————. "Ecrivain non: Un Nouveau Cartographe." In *Critique* 343. Paris: Les Editions de Minuit, 1975.

————. "Letter by way of preface." In *Sahara: L'Esthétique de Gilles Deleuze.* Edited by Mireille Buydens. Paris: Vrin, 1990.

————. *The Logic of Sense.* Translated by Mark Lester. New York: Columbia University Press, 1990.

————. *Coldness and Cruelty.* Translated by Jean McNeil. New York: Zone Books, 1991.

————. *Negotiations 1972–1990.* Translated by Marin Joughin. London & New York: Columbia University Press, 1995.

————. *Critical and Clinical.* Translated by Daniel W. Smith and Michael A. Greco. London & New York: Verso, 1998.

————. *Spinoza, Practical Philosophy.* Translated by Robert Hurley. San Francisco: City Light Books, 1998.

————. *The Fold.* Translated by Tom Conley. Minneapolis: University of Minnesota Press, 1999.

————. "Pensée nomade." In *L'île Déserte et Autres Textes de Gilles Deleuze.* Edited by David Lapoujade. Paris: Les Editions de Minuit, 2002.

————. *Francis Bacon: The Logic of Sensation.* Translated by Daniel W. Smith. London and New York: Continuum, 2003.

————. *Pure Immanence: Essays on A Life.* New York: Zone Books, 2005.

————. *Foucault.* Translated and edited by Sean Hand. Minneapolis: University of Minnesota Press, 2006.

————. "What is the creative act?" In *Two Regimes of Madness: Texts and Interviews 1975–1995.* Edited by David Lapoujade & translated by Ames Hodges and Mike Taormina. New York: Semiotext(e), 2007.

————. *Lettres et autres textes.* Edited by David Lapoujade. Paris: Les Editions de Minuit, 2015.

Deleuze, Gilles and Guattari Félix. *A Thousand Plateaus: Capitalism and Schizophrenia.* Translated by Brian Massumi. London: University of Minneapolis, 1987.

Deleuze, Gilles with Parnet, Claire. "D comme Désir." & "V comme Voyage." In *L'Abécédaire de Gilles Deleuze.* Paris: Editions Montparnasse, 1997.

—————. *Dialogues*. Translated by Hugh Tomlison and Barbara Habberjam. New York: Cornell University Press, 1977.

Didi-Huberman, Georges. *L'homme qui marchait dans la couleur*. Paris: Les Editions de Minuit, 2001.

Eisenstein, Sergei M. "Encounters with Books." In *Beyond The Stars: The Memoirs of Sergei Eisenstein, Selected Works, Volume IV*. Edited by Richard Taylor, translated by William Powell. London: The British Film Institute, 1995.

Foucault, Michel. "Theatrum Philosophicum." In *Language, Counter-Memory, Practice*. Edited and translated by Donald F. Bouchard. Oxford, Blackwell and Ithaca: Cornell University Press, 1977.

Gleyzon, François-Xavier. "Deleuze and the Grandeur of Palestine: Song of Earth and Resistance." *Journal for Cultural Research* 20, no. 4 (2016): 398–416.

Guattari, Félix, *Lignes de fuite. Pour un Autre Monde de Possibles*. Paris: Éditions de l'Aube, coll. Monde en cours, 2011.

Milton, John. *Areopagitica*. Cambridge: Cambridge University Press, 1918.

Morin, Edgar. *La Méthode, tome II*. Paris: Seuil, 1986.

Nietzsche, Friedrich. *The Gay Science*. Translated by Walter Kaufmann. New York: Vintage, 1974.

—————. *Thus Spake Zarathustra*. Translated by Thomas Wayne. New York: Algora, 2003.

Rilke, Rainer Maria. *Letters to a Young Poet*. Translated by M. D Herter Norton. New York, NY: Norton 1962.

Shakespeare, William. "Hamlet." *Norton Shakespeare*. Edited by Stephen Greenblatt. New York: WW Norton, 2015.

Stiegler, Bernard. *The Neganthropocene*. Edited and translated by Daniel Ross. London: Open Humanities Press, 2018.

—————. *Qu'appelle-t-on panser? Au-delà de l'Entropocène*. Paris: Editions Les liens qui libèrent, 2018.

Tampio, Nicholas. "Entering Deleuze's Political Vision." *Deleuze Studies* 8, no. 1 (2014): 1–22.

Warnke, Martin, "Der Leidschatz der Menschheit wird humaner Besitz." In *Die Menschenrechte des Auges. Über Aby Warburg*, 113–86. Frankfurt-on-Main: Europäische Verlagsanstalt, 1980.

CHAPTER 11

Vulnerable Erotic Encounters: A Chronotopic Reading of the Bus-Space in Chicu's *Soliloquy*

Prerna Subramanian

As of 2020, LGBT rights in India have seen the decriminalization of sexual relations deemed homosexual under Section 377 of the Constitution. However, with the passing of the Transgender Persons (Protection of Rights) Act 2019, there has been an incremental erosion of transgender rights. The act, going against the NALSA Supreme Court Judgement of 2014 that affirmed right to self-determination of gender, proposes humiliating screening processes for issuing a valid gender certificate. Not only does this remove a previously established right but produces transgender communities as untrustworthy subjects in the eyes of law. Additionally, the act carries no provisions for reservations[1] of seats for transgender persons

[1] Positive discrimination in terms of allocating a definitive number of admission seats in colleges and offices.

P. Subramanian (✉)
Queen's University, Kingston, ON, Canada
e-mail: 17ps23@queensu.ca

© The Author(s), under exclusive license to Springer Nature Switzerland AG 2021
C. Beck (ed.), *Mobility, Spatiality, and Resistance in Literary and Political Discourse*, Geocriticism and Spatial Literary Studies,
https://doi.org/10.1007/978-3-030-83477-7_11

233

234 P. SUBRAMANIAN

in either employment or educational sectors and designates sexual crimes committed against trans communities as petty crimes. Furthermore, criminalizing their occupations of sex work and begging exacerbates the community's vulnerability precisely because their presence in the streets, in transit spaces, or in a local neighborhood becomes subject to harsher policing and surveillance. Marginalization then is not a metaphor, but a real, everyday, spatial occurrence with grave consequences for trans communities in India. This essay, with this context in mind, addresses a narrative of a transgender protagonist's intimate experience on a bus in India, and calls for reading the textually rendered sexual and spatial encounter as simultaneously material, discursive, and affective. I argue that taking our real and storied spaces and spatial experiences seriously help us understand the contradictorily limiting and liberating processes that cathect a community's navigation of the everyday.

"Soliloquy," authored by Chicu, is one of the fourteen stories of a queer[2] erotic anthology called *Close Too Close*, published in India in 2012.

---

[2] Use of queer and trans in India: Ani Dutta has shown us how even if "transgender" as a term can be a political terminology that is life-saving and important for accessing rights and resources, it has to be read through the dominant structures it is imbricated in and the silences it comes with (see Aniruddha Dutta, "Claiming citizenship, contesting civility: The institutional LGBT movement and the regulation of gender/sexual dissidence in West Bengal, India," *Jindal Global Law Review* 4, no. 1(2012): 320–336.). Jennifer Ung Loh on the other hand has shown us how identifying a "queer" subject in India is to acknowledge the gaps between the normative queer subject (gay, upper-class, upper-caste male) and the non-normative, deviant queer subject that discomfits the heteropatriarchal structure of the Indian society via non-normative sexual practices and gender nonconformity (who Dutta sees as rendered vernacular, regional, and thus less-than). Thus, these are terms which cannot be applied without acknowledging these contestations that they are embedded in. In the context of India, gender identity and sexual orientation have often been deliberately seen as unrelated categories which have led to privileging of some forms of gender variance over others (as seen in NALSA judgment's considering Kaushal judgment of criminalising same-sex relations "a different matter altogether"). In order to avoid repeating this violence, I do not disassociate gender identity with sexual orientation and see gender identity as always-already inflected with issues of sexuality, while also noting how both may inform each other but do not necessarily precondition each other. With regard to the erotica, the self-identification of the editors as being a "queer" erotica, encompassing all that is not cis-heterosexual, is used in this essay. Throughout the essay, my notes will provide the reader with important caveats to reckon with when reading invocation of and contestations around "trans" in India. Their position in the footnote by no means undermines their importance but indeed works as important checkpoints lest the essay's main body invites homogenizing conclusions. J. Ung Loh, "Representation, Visibility, Legibility: The "Queer" Subject in Contemporary India," *Scholar and Feminist Online* 14, no. 2(2017): np.

The collection is written by persons who identify as queer in its multiple resonances: queer suggests self-identification in some stories, or as defining a particular sexual act or is used as an umbrella term to describe the entirety of an intimate relation. For purposes of this essay, I want to direct attention to how the editors, in their introduction to the collection, repeatedly refer to the spatial pervasiveness and everydayness of these queer erotic stories. By calling attention to how "[s]ex is taken into the public arena," they ensure that the readers are attuned to the geographical situatedness of the stories.[3] Grappling with the notions of the private and public, the familiar and the unfamiliar becomes an integral part of reading the stories in this collection. "Soliloquy," the focus of this essay, narrates an erotic encounter of a transwoman with a stranger on an Indian metropolitan city bus. The story explores the uneven organization of vulnerability and the linked intimacy of the bodies by narrating the specifics of the journey on a bus. I argue the story reveals that encounters do not simply "happen" in space where space is just a container, but happen through the process of spatialization, through our practices and discourses which co-evolve to produce space, senses of place, and our spatial experiences. I highlight how the spatio-temporal configuration of the bus conditions the intimate encounters and lays bare vulnerabilities particular to the protagonist.

Erotica, as a genre, attends to specific kinds of encounters: sexual, provocative, intimate, and transgressive are a few ways in which erotica is characterized. For this reason, erotica has been approached through a geographical lens in academic works by authors interested in questions of gender and spatiality. Marcia England, in her work on mediated geographies of gender, states that erotica should be seen as a matter of "geographical concern," because "there is a collision of public and private in the world of erotica. There is a move from the private space of the bedroom to the public/private space of the mediated space."[4] Citing Michael Bronski, she states: "the explosion of private sexual fantasy into public view is a powerful political statement."[5] England refers to the very public nature of the *consumption* of private fantasies in the act of reading erotica.

---

[3] Meenu and Shruti, introduction to *Close, Too Close: The Tranquebar Book of Queer Erotica*, ed. Meenu and Shruti (New Delhi: Tranquebar, 2012), xiv.

[4] Marcia R. England, *Public Privates: Feminist Geographies of Mediated Spaces* (Lincoln: University of Nebraska Press, 2018), 144.

[5] England, *Public Privates*, 144.

My focus, however, will be on what I call the "storied spaces" of erotica—spaces that are produced in our stories. In the next section, I will first develop "encounter" as an analytic vantage point to read literary spaces like that of the bus by showing how it allows us to be sensitive to the multidimensional, imaginative, material, and affective processes that produce space. I will further connect the literary concepts of chronotope and genre to frame the importance of the encounter and thus, the spatiality, as simultaneously real and storied.

ENCOUNTERS AND SPACE

The concept of the encounter is seen as the meeting of contraries and is usually "historically coded as contacts that are marked by dynamics of power."[6] We often hear of terms like colonial encounters, encountering the other, or in India, extrajudicial killings by the police are often referred to as "encounters."[7] Encounters are either marked by some kind of intimidating tension or unpredictability/surprise upon meeting other individuals, with simultaneous possibilities of unexpectedness and normative practices that envelope the relational event. In the academic context, Helen Wilson notes, texts have dealt with ethnographic and cultural accounts of representation of newness, of a different "culture" or "people." More often than not, scholars of post-colonial studies engage with the politics of encounter. This scholarship often focuses on the processes of colonialism, conquest, and authors deal with ideas of representation, imagining, and producing knowledges about people, places, and social orders. In sum, an encounter entails a particular kind of meeting that produces realities and attendant knowledges often due to confronting something previously unknown or unthought of: the encounter is both process and product of struggle of contraries and contradictions.

Unsurprisingly, discussions around encounters are about the posited contradictions between the self and other. Such an approach to the encounter helps us view how "otherness" itself is interpreted or understood. For our purposes, let us consider this approach through the issues

---

[6] Helen F. Wilson, "On Geography and Encounter: Bodies, Borders, and Difference," *Progress in Human Geography* 41, no. 4(2016): 451. https://doi.org/10.1177/0309132516645958

[7] For more information on this, See N. Prabha Unnithan, *Crime and Justice in India* (New Delhi: SAGE, 2013).

of transgender representation and representability. Questions of how transgender persons are represented in media and discussions around the implications, modes, codes, and norms that produce such representations have often centered on issues of *encountering* previously un-, mis-, or underrepresented stories of people, communities, and attendant worldviews. Scholars like Reina Gossett and Emmanuel David have argued that encountering transgender persons in visual or textual narratives does not always translate to an improvement in material conditions of trans lives. That is, proliferation of representation in stories does not lead to less vulnerable encounters in daily life for transgender persons precisely because these practices are adjusted within the "trap doors" of dominant views of gender[8] or incorporated in dominant logics to further "bolster the status quo."[9] Critical analyses of such representations discuss multiple contradictory valences of visibility. "Visibility" in images and texts can implicate and complicate the regimes of hypervisibility: surveillance, disproportionate regulation of bodies, and hyperinvisibility in processes that entail material access to subsistence, care, and education. Gossett summarizes these seemingly "visible" contradictions succinctly:

> We are living in a time of trans visibility. Yet we are also living in a time of anti-trans violence. [...] This is the trap of the visual: it offers—or, more accurately, it is frequently offered to us as—the primary path through which trans people might have access to livable lives. Representation is said to remedy broader acute social crises ranging from poverty to murder to police violence, particularly when representation is taken up as a 'teaching tool' that allows those outside our immediate social worlds and identities to glimpse some notion of a shared humanity.[10]

I want to avoid the trap of the visual that comes with broaching questions of encounters in terms of seeing, being seen, and being heard. Rather, I want us to see the encounter for what it actually entails on an everyday basis: as a geographical process. That is, we ought to see encounters as real, embodied, affective, material, discursive spatio-temporal events of meeting, of coming-togetherness of social relations that entail intertwined

---

[8] See Reina Gossett, Eric A. Stanley, and Johanna Burton, *Trap Door: Trans Cultural Production and the Politics of Visibility* (Cambridge, MA: The MIT Press, 2017).

[9] Emmanuel David, "Capital T: Trans Visibility, Corporate Capitalism, and Commodity Culture," *Transgender Studies Quarterly* 4, no. 1(2017):30.

[10] Gossett, Stanely, and Burton, *Trap Door*, xv–xvi.

questions of power and vulnerability. Helen Wilson writes how encounters can be seen "as a specific genre of contact with key issues ... as a distinctive event of relation ... a remit of difference, rupture and surprise."[11] To see encounters as geographical, where geography entails grappling with the multidimensionality of space—as imagined, real, material, and metaphorical—has multiple, important, and fruitful implications for analyzing the processes through which stories of marginalized communities are circulated in cultural productions. The concept of the encounter brings together the simultaneity of the lived world and representations and helps us escape the binary of reality and representation, real and imagined space. This approach entails looking at space not as container or background of encounters, but as emerging, as animating through encounters that are produced via our social relations. Doreen Massey's definition of space, inextricable from time, refers to space as encounters:

> Space has its times. To open up space to this kind of imagination means thinking about time and space together. You can't hold places and things still. What you can do is meet up with them, catch up with where another's history has got to 'now', and acknowledge that 'now' is itself constituted by that meeting up. 'Here', in that sense, is not a place on a map. It is that intersection of trajectories, the meeting-up of stories; *an encounter*. Every 'here' is a here-and-now.[12]

The encounter for Massey is not between people but between social relations which produce people and in turn, produce our spatialities. Social relations are not static but produced through what Massey terms "power-geometries": the power-differentials that locate people hierarchically in a social order.[13]An encounter thus is not something that "happens in space," a viewpoint that puts us in the trap of seeing space as a product, but rather it is the very *becoming* of space.

Encounters, it follows, can thus be understood through the theories of social space. Following Lefebvre, the dialectic unity of what are seen as seeming contradictions form space as we know it: everyday spatial

[11] Wilson, "On Geography and Encounter," 452.

[12] Doreen Massey, "Some Times of Space" in *Olafur Eliasson: The Weather Project*, ed. Susan May (London: Tate Modern, 2003), 108.

[13] Doreen Massey, "Power-Geometry and a Progressive Sense of Place," in *Mapping the Futures: Local Cultures, Global Change*, ed. John Bird, Tim Putnam, Lisa Tickner, and Barry Curtis (London: Routledge, 1996), 63.

practices (encountering people on a daily basis in conventional, routine trajectories), representations of space (encounters ordered through the designs, the infrastructure, and dominant architectural development of spaces), and representational/lived spaces produced through the spatial practices and representations of space.[14] It is in the lived space where materiality and imagination co-evolve and mutually condition each other. Thus, space and encounters that produce it are materially and discursively constituted. An analytical differentiation between how space is produced through material conditions and constructed through practices and imaginative processes can help us be sensitive to their simultaneity. As geographer and ethnographer Setha M. Low posits:

> the social production of space includes all those factors—social, economic, ideological, and technological—that result, or seek to result, in the physical creation of the material setting. Social construction, on the other hand, refers to spatial transformations through peoples' social interactions, conversations, memories, feelings, imaginings and use—or absences—into places, scenes and actions that convey particular meanings. Both processes are social in the sense that both the production and the construction of space are mediated by social processes, especially being contested and fought over for economic and ideological reasons.[15]

While warning us that this differentiation is purely analytical, Low states that this binary distinction has to be enriched with the inclusion of bodies and affect in order to fully grasp the multivalence of spatiality. The encounter, interestingly, brings the embodied, the affective, the material, and the discursive together precisely because encounters are geographical events that are not merely materially and ideologically conditioned, but constitute the meeting of bodies, exchange of emotions, and affective attachments. Thus, by seeing the encounter as shaping and shaped by spatiality in all its dimensions, I want to read encounters as lived (as embodied, spatial practices), but also as instances that carry storied encounters (in our images, texts). To read the storied encounters then is to not eschew materiality of space, but grapple with it through the meaning-making, the imaginative processes people deploy in their renditions of spatiality and

---

[14] Henri Lefebvre, *The Production of Space*, trans. Donald Nicholson-Smith (Malden: Blackwell Publishers Ltd., 1991), 188.

[15] Setha M. Low, "Spatializing Culture," in *The People, Place, and Space Reader*, ed. Jen Jack Gieseking and William Mangold (New York, NY: Routledge, 2014), 35.

240   P. SUBRAMANIAN

spatial experiences. Here, I turn to the Bakhtinian concept of chronotope to help us locate the construction of spatiality within narratives that shape textual encounters.

CHRONOTOPES AND GENRE

If Massey says space-times are inextricable in our real, material worlds, Mikhail Bakhtin, in his discussion of the chronotope, believes the same holds true for the worlds we construct in our literary texts. For Bakhtin, a chronotope is the "intrinsic connectedness of temporal and spatial relationships that are artistically expressed in literature."[16] Bakhtin also notes how the "motif" of encounters is a feature of not only literature, but also daily life and both can be understood, analyzed, written, read, or interpreted through chronotopes: specific spatio-temporal processes, limits, and constraints produce particular encounters and make specific relations possible. In turn, these specific encounters are artistically expressed through particular space-time configurations that become conventionalized in our artistic works. Chronotopes, simply seen as space-time configurations produced out of our social relations, produce genres of encounters we read about. Bakhtin calls for identifying genres by looking at the "values" chronotopes generate and naturalize, the characters they produce through the convergence of space and time in texts, and what kind of work they do for the storied world.

If storied encounters have genres and are produced in a real world, it will be useful to turn to scholars who see genre as a shorthand for dominating, naturalized social orders that shape our spatialities and make them seem as they have always-already existed, as ontological givens and not processual, power-laden realities. This is done famously by Lauren Berlant, who stretches the concept of genre to include both the modes of stories we read and the modes of our everyday life: "Genre also figures the nameable aspiration of discursive order through which particular life narratives and modes of being become normalized as the real, the taken for granted. Genre thus is a particular normative, conventionalized mode, taken for granted of being and narrating marked by particular expectations, social

---

[16] M. Bakhtin and Michael Holquist, *The Dialogic Imagination: Four Essays* (Austin, TX: University of Texas Press, 1983), 84.

relations, practices."[17] Genre is formed out of spatio-temporal organization of relations and thus expectations and possibilities in our life. This view of genre as defining both conventions of stories and the world has been also held by Marxist semiotician and a contemporary of Bakhtin: Valentin Voloshinov. David McNally states that for Voloshinov, life-genre was the "unique social context of life and labor which produce their own shared values and accents," through which certain "speech-genres" emerge.[18] McNally uses Bakhtinian chronotopes in conjunction with life-genres to posit that literary works are "unique refractions of specific life genres, as entailing conceptions of life, labour, space, time, and the body formed through the everyday socio-material practices in which people engage."[19] That is, institutions in our lived world organize our space-times and provide for the conditions and constitute the genres of our storied worlds.

This discussion of story-genres and genres of the world helps us see the co-constitution of the storied world and the lived world: they are tied to and inform each other in deep and complex ways. In the genre of erotica, the discourses and materially conditioned practices that codify and create life-genres of sexual relations and intimate acts become specifically important to consider. This is because questions of sexual intimacy are also questions of gender and sexuality, which frame normative institutions of the family that further codify the ideals of a nation-state. In India, for example, one need only look at how the story *Lihaaf* (1942), written by Ismat Chughtai, was interpreted and received. The story narrates a homoerotic encounter between two women in a harem and gestures toward male homosexual relations. Chughtai was subsequently charged for obscenity not only for the sexual provocation in her stories about women in and around Muslim households, but also because these household stories located the erotic in the corners of an all-female setting of a harem (*zenana*) in a familiar neighborhood of an Indian city.[20] The anxiety was

[17] Lauren Gail Berlant, "The Compulsion to Repeat Femininity: Landscape for a Good Woman and The Life and Loves of a She-Devil," in *The Female Complaint the Unfinished Business of Sentimentality in American Culture* (Durham: Duke University Press, 2008), 259.

[18] David McNally, *Bodies of Meaning: Studies on Language, Labor, and Liberation* (Albany, NY: State University of New York Press, 2001), 115.

[19] McNally, *Bodies of Meaning*, 115.

[20] For more information, see Nandi Bhatia, "Censorship, 'Obscenity' and Courtroom Drama: Reading Ismat Chughtai's 'Lihaaf' and 'The 'Lihaaf' Trial,'" *Law & Literature* 32, no. 3(2020): 1–19, https://doi.org/10.1080/1535685x.2020.1721197

not about the storied *zenana* anymore, but real women who lived in *zenanas* were seen as subjects whose fantasies were to be regulated and bodies to be disciplined: the story mattered because it was produced in a world whose material conditions and discourses were called into question. In other words, the jump from the storied to the real encounters of the world happens precisely because the chronotopes of the encounters in the story call for a reacknowledgment or reassessment of our daily socio-spatial configurations. Although this is a story before the post-colonial Indian state was formed, the charges of obscenity to erotic encounters have only marginally shifted and have acquired vocabularies of progress, tradition, and national interests and dignity. The recent agitation against the film *Lipstick Under my Burkha* (2017) for its depiction of a woman reading erotica and orgasming on screen in a small town in India serves to show that the state's deep anxieties around gender and gendered relations that form communities.[21] Thus, with this discussion in mind, my analysis of the construction of encounter through the chronotope of the bus in Chicu's *Soliloquy* will entail simultaneously reading the discourses, affects, and material conditions that animate these storied encounters by taking "space and place seriously as dynamic features of a text, which constantly interact with and affect each other."[22]

---

[21] One must note that this film, released in 2017, itself carries particular bourgeois, urban, and upper-caste notions of the Muslim woman and man that have been heavily and rightfully criticized. That the two examples I quote both carry "Muslim" characters is also an example of how the dominant public discourse on obscenity, oppression, and civility is not only gendered but has other axes of regulations: namely caste and religion. That non-Muslim writers of the film choose to portray Muslim women as signifiers of ultimate and multiple oppressions and to essentialize symbols patriarchy in general, while flattening patriarchy for upper-caste women as mere matter of gender inequality and nothing to do with caste, is a marker of how such depictions of intimate relations and sexual relationships often carry allegories of deep-seated cartographic anxieties. A very trenchant criticism of the film can be found here: Rahmath EP, "Why Not Janeu Under My Kurta?," Round Table India, August 10, 2017, https://roundtableindia.co.in/index.php?option=com_content&view=article&id=9150:lipstick-under-my-burkha&catid=120&Itemid=133

[22] Robert T. Tally, Jr., *Topophrenia: Place, Narrative, and the Spatial Imagination* (Indiana University Press, 2018), 39.

11 VULNERABLE EROTIC ENCOUNTERS: A CHRONOTOPIC READING... 243

ENCOUNTERING VULNERABILITY: ANALYSIS OF *SOLILOQUY*

Bakhtin states that storied encounters are often narrated through the chronotope of a threshold space and used to detail a crisis or a decisive moment in life:

> It can be combined with the motif of encounter, but its most fundamental instance is as the chronotope of crisis and break in a life. The word "threshold" itself already has a metaphorical meaning in everyday usage (together with its literal meaning), and is connected with the breaking point of a life, the moment of crisis, the decision that changes a life (or the indecisiveness that fails to change a life, the fear to step over the threshold).[23]

In "Soliloquy," the bus is the threshold chronotope through which the story's erotic encounters unravel and where the transgender protagonist's fear, indecisiveness, and crisis are narrated. Our unnamed protagonist is in a crowded Indian metropolitan city bus where there is not much space to breathe comfortably. While fighting and then consequently adapting to the constricted and suffocating space available to her, she explores the small, insignificant features of people on the bus. In this process, she realizes that a man has chosen to step backward and she quickly notes that this intimate movement toward her was a "matter of his choice."[24] This unprecedented and unexpected move is risky but also exciting for the protagonist. She feels "overwhelmed" by her "intimate gaze"[25] enabled by the enforced proximity of the crowd. There is also a woman behind her, forcing her to be even closer to the man, and preventing her from "shutting him out" from both her thoughts and the literal space.[26] In such close proximity, she says it is riveting how "breasts are groped, and buttocks pressed against genitals; anything is permissible as long as it is done without a nod to the other's humanity."[27] People in such an intimate crowd can hear each other's breath, smell each other's perfumes and even as it is "claustrophobic," the protagonist finds the experience erotogenic, intimate, stimulating. She describes this "unexpected and anonymous

---

[23] Bakhtin and Holquist, *The Dialogic Imagination*, 248.

[24] Chicu, "Soliloquy," in *Close, Too Close*, ed. Meenu and Shruti (New Delhi: Tranquebar, 2012), 92.

[25] Chicu, "Soliloquy," 92.

[26] Chicu, "Soliloquy," 92.

[27] Chicu, "Soliloquy," 92.

grouping" as pleasurable, as something which fulfills her needs of momentary intimacy, closeness. She construes the bus-space as a "place without judgement" or "shame" given no one has control over the space they take up and thus there is no control over what one can or cannot do.[28]

However, she realizes, the unpredictability of this encounter comes with its countless challenges—this place is not without its constraints and contradictions. She grows uncomfortable with the momentary intimacy as she comprehends that there could be a gap between her interpretations of the encounter and how others may view it. She tries to move away while the man continues to touch her where she feels the most vulnerable: the erogenous, genital zones of her body. He stiffens when he finds something unexpected. At this point, our protagonist's fear overwhelms her as she feels "disrobed" in public, "exposed, dirty, ashamed" when her "truth" becomes known to the man.[29] She feels her "secret" has been uncovered and that the man now knows she is hiding something others can't see.[30] She decides to leave the bus immediately: "I step off the bus determined to walk off, but then hesitate. I look up at the bus. There is one passenger standing where I was, staring at me."[31] She fears that there may be disgust on his face, but instead she finds pity. The fact that there "is no revulsion in his eyes" comes as a welcome emotion for the protagonist, who sees the "pain and bewilderment" as a form of "shared knowledge and shared desire"; her truth seems to be accepted, even if it is through pity.[32] She decides to come back to the bus the next day. This is where the protagonist leaves us and ends her soliloquy.

In order to fully understand the implications of the protagonist's fears and the narrated spatial encounter, I would like to attend to the historical and contemporary processes, practices, and conditions that transgender people in India navigate. Although there could be multiple vantage points to explicate such a complex reality, I will limit myself to the regulation of spatiality in relation to the disciplining of sexually dissident and gender-variant bodies in India. Historically speaking, The Criminal Tribes Act of 1871 in India sought to regulate public space and in turn, the itinerant communities and bodies that the British Administration couldn't tie down

[28] Chicu, "Soliloquy," 92.
[29] Chicu, "Soliloquy," 93.
[30] Chicu, "Soliloquy," 92.
[31] Chicu, "Soliloquy," 96.
[32] Chicu, "Soliloquy," 96.

to a definitive place. This included non-normatively gendered and sexed persons being criminalized by categorizing them as suspicious individuals known for castrating and kidnapping children: "the Act provided for the imprisonment for up to two years with fine of [a]ny eunuch ... who appears, dressed or ornamented like a woman, in a public street or place, or in any other place, with the intention of being seen from a public street or place, or who dances or plays music, or takes part in any public exhibition."[33] Although this act was itself amended and was replaced by the Habitual Offenders Act in 1952, the present legal narrative of the Trafficking Bill 2019 also continues proffering this criminalizing lens onto the historically "suspicious" bodies—specifically the *hijra* community, by refusing to distinguish between consensual and forced sex work and criminalizing organized begging. The process of defining bodies through suspicion and regulating their presence in the public via criminalization of their occupations actively contributes to the marginalization of trans and gender-variant persons in India today.[34]

To further understand the production of spatiality and regulation of gender and sexuality as co-constitutive processes, one can look at how the organization of a social order is deeply imbricated in the organization of spatial order that entails the disciplining of bodies deemed deviant. This is exemplified through how Dhrubo Jyoti poignantly pens the story of the colonizer's encounter with Khairati. Jyoti tells us how in 1884, "an unusual case came up in the then colonial Allahabad high court. ... For months, the police had been tailing a person named Khairati on the suspicion that he was a "eunuch" after being tipped off that on a visit to his

---

[33] Jessica Hinchy, *Governing Gender and Sexuality in Colonial India: The Hijra, C.1850–1900* (Cambridge: Cambridge University Press, 2019), 274.

[34] Here, a caveat is necessary: although popular imaginary of *hijra* community may obfuscate the lifeworlds of multiple gender-variant, gender non-conforming, and trans communities and identities that exist, reading the mechanisms of creating state-effects show that residues of the colonial imaginary find new ways of replicating themselves in how gender-variant people are governed, categorized, and recognized. It is in this dominant, homogenizing conflation of hijra as all-encompassing of sexual and gender "deviance" and the emergent, contested categories of trans* formed through the processes of transnational LGBT and feminist activism, one must locate the survival vulnerabilities of gender-variant communities in India. Indeed, it is in these moments of legible categorization we see the dominant imaginary of the middle-class sexual and gender norms unsubtly at work. For a deeper analysis of these interstitial contestations, see: Shraddha Chatterjee, "Transgender Shifts: Notes on Resignification of Gender and Sexuality in India," *Transgender Studies Quarterly* 5, no. 3(2018): 311–320.

ancestral village, he was found dancing and singing dressed as a woman."[35] Khairati was eventually arrested "on the suspicion that he was a habitual sodomite and subjected him to a medical examination." He was prosecuted under Section 377 of the Indian Penal Code, the first in the recorded history of convictions under the code that criminalizes homosexual acts. Movement of some bodies is enabled at the expense of regulation of dissident others, or as Jyoti puts it, these reforms help a privileged few enter the "regimen of privacy" and define the rules of respectability and dignified spatialities.[36] These privileged few are those who fit into a dominant socio-spatial imaginary that disciplines deviant bodies in order to maintain the exclusionary, heteronormative, patriarchal configuration of social relations. In India, this is often referred to as the "middle class" respectability, but is just another term for naming the hegemony of caste relations that hierarchize the society into a vertical structure of stratification.[37] The cultural politics of such a social stratification requires that gendered bodies be disciplined in order to maintain the sanctity of the institution of the heteropatriarchal family that is the centralizing unit of this hierarchical order, which also becomes the microcosm of the ideal nation itself. In this scenario, sexually deviant and gender-variant bodies are an anomaly that has to be either fixed, adjusted, or outright criminalized in order to conserve the dominant social order. This includes discourses and practices which elevate certain norms as aspirational while rendering others as a danger to respectability and morality of those who claim supremacy. Jessica Hinchy notes:

> Middle-class gender and sexual norms—which combined Victorian morality and ambiguous notions of women' uplift with redefined notions of 'tradition'—were central to the self-fashioning of the middle class. ... A number of middle-class men *denounced the Hijra community*, as a part of their

---

[35] Dhrubo Jyoti, "Section 377: The Fight for LGBT Rights Has Just Begun," *Hindustan Times*, September 7, 2018, https://www.hindustantimes.com/india-news/section-377-the-fight-for-lgbt-rights-has-just-begun/story-odLFyR0eOctAuIJELMMOxL.html

[36] Jyoti, "Section 377."

[37] More on the hegemonic work of the middle class: Satish Deshpande, "The Centrality of the Middle Class," in *Contemporary India: A Sociological View* (New Delhi: Penguin Books, 2003), 125–150. I also take my understandings of dominant, residual, and emergent from Raymond William's conceptualization of the same: Raymond Williams, "Dominant, Residual, and Emergent," in *Marxism and Literature* (Oxford: Oxford University Press, 1977), 121–127.

broader efforts to establish their respectability through calls for the elimination of 'immoral' social practices.[38]

These gender and sexual norms are important for a certain class of individuals in India. Dominant caste-classes in particular claim supremacy through colonial to post-colonial times precisely because they entailed certain forms of kinship; this type of community is not only ideal and "better" than others but serves as foundational to the social imaginary of the nation. Further discussion on this is beyond the scope of the essay; however, I want to summarize few points here that directly relate to Chicu's story. First, one may notice how trans and gender-variant communities are not a monolith and are marked by the variegated processes of caste-class nexus which contribute to the regulations of their bodies and attendant rights. This excludes them from the ideal social imaginary of the nation and entails regulation of their bodies and sexual practices.[39] Intimate lives

---

[38] Hinchy, *Governing Gender*, 85.

[39] It is important to note that these norms of respectability aren't merely rooted in their colonial construction, but were replicated in the induction of HIV/AIDs mediated transnational LGBT rights activism. Ani Dutta's work shows that this transnational process led to contingent development of new "legible" identities that were gender-variant, sexually variant, and coordinated under the HIV/AIDS NGO efforts to enumerate and govern. This has also led to a repetition of the respectability politics within LGBT Civil rights movement in India albeit now in the registers of globalization. Certain practices and identities are subordinated over others precisely because there are new modes of identification which are rendered as terrains of legibility and as pathways to civil rights. In this process, Ani Dutta has noted, Indian LGBT organizational efforts have a history of trying to "contain" transfeminine, "traditional" ways of being gender-variant so as to not reinforce the dangerous stereotypes of them as disorderly, suspicious, and dangerous, lest they trouble the pathway to rightful citizenship. They write:

> a range of practices and subject positions at the intersections of class/caste and gender marginality—particularly manifested in gestures of public assertion and gendered flamboyance by lower class subjects—are sought to be *excluded or disciplined* by emergent modes of sexual/political subjecthood. Such practices may be condemned both as flouting cultural norms of *respectability* through their *indecency or disreputability* and as interrupting the process of gaining formal equality within civil society through their unruliness or incivility. Dutta, "Claiming Citizenship, Contesting Civility," 112.

This confirms how we noted that the colonized conflation and homogenization, surveillance has taken a new form at the juncture of globalization: rather than preoccupying itself with who is a hijra, now the preoccupation is with identifying legible trans subjects. The dominant imaginary then rests in the selective tradition that is routinely sedimented in order

of trans and gender-variant persons then are matters of encountering insti-
tutionally conditioned hyper-surveillant others. The risks and fears of violence in spaces, like that of a bus, are something that shapes the geography
of their everyday lives. Relatedly, one could say that it is in the regulation
of their bodies that we also see the regulation of the spaces they navigate,
wherein norms of sexuality, decency, and respectability are disproportion-
ately signified through the bodies of transgender and gender-variant communities and thus rendered more vulnerable to violence and violation.

However, to see the bus-space only through the practices that regulate
gender and sexuality is to oversimplify the social organization of space. In
relation to Lefebvre, one may note how the bus is not only produced
through spatial practices but also infrastructural designs and conditions
which constitute a social space. The bus of the story serves as the conduit,
context, and also the simultaneous enabling and disabling space of the
intimate encounter of the protagonist, precisely because of structures of
bureaucracy, lack of public funding, and transit disparities of class-caste
differences produce the infrastructure[40] of a bus. Helen Wilson has
inquired into the bus-space as a site of negotiating multi-culture and sees
the bus-space as a site of mobile-dwellings:

> In a space of such extraordinary intimacy with others and intense materiality,
> where bodies are pressed up against each other, seats are shared, and per-
> sonal boundaries are constantly negotiated, we find an important and often
> overlooked site of ordinary multiculture, where differences are negotiated
> on the smallest of scales. The bus can therefore make important contributions

to legitimize the rights to citizenship: a tradition that is invariably authored by the hegemonic middle-class, upper-caste formation. It is in these drives to define who deviates from
the heteropatriarchal norm and how, we see the work of hegemony of not only what is a
legible trans subject but what is India's legibility as an imagined community of people. My
understanding of selective tradition here is derived from Raymond Williams, where selective
tradition is the process through which we select legacy of the past to explain the present: "an
intentionally selective version of a shaping past and a pre-shaped present, which is then powerfully operative in the process of social and cultural definition and identification." Raymond
Williams, "Hegemony and the Selective Tradition," in *Language, Authority and Criticism*,
eds. Suzanne de Castell, Allan Luke, and Carmen Luke (London: The Falmer Press,
1989), 56–60.

[40] Infrastructure here does not merely mean the buildings we see around, but also, as Ara
Wilson contends, "includes a sense of systems, management, and energy, as well as planning
and design—hence, discourse, symbols, and, arguably even affect." Ara Wilson, "The
Infrastructure of Intimacy," *Signs: Journal of Women in Culture and Society* 41, no. 2(2016):
247, https://doi.org/10.1086/682919

to studies of everyday multiculture and the daily negotiation of difference and intercultural relations.[41]

To add to Wilson's conceptualization of the bus-space as a place constructed out of negotiations of difference, *Soliloquy's* bus-space helps us see how gender and sexuality get negotiated, enabling us to see the bus as an affective, material, and discursive site of enforced intimacy. With the context of India, overcrowding becomes a routine phenomenon through which the bus becomes a site of bodily encounters and corporeal intensities. Urban geographers and analysts like Ananya Roy and Judy Baker have shown us that overcrowding of transport facilities like the bus have to be read with the realities of rising urban poverty, gentrification, evictions of urban poor that result in a spatial mismatch between geographies of opportunity, mobility, and residence.[42] This leads to overcrowding, congestion, and also variegated approaches to public transport based on affordability, available livelihood choices, and access to shelter. Thus, the overcrowded bus of the story is enabled by this specific infrastructure of public transport in Indian cities, which, in turn condition the encounters. Moreover, bus-spaces in India are often associated with and reported on in media for their rampant cases of sexual harassment: incidences of frottage and exhibitionism have become common in the city-buses of Delhi.[43]

In the story then, the enforced proximity described in the bus is also an all-too common occurrence in a restricted system of public transport that always falls short for the population it is supposed to serve. The crowding of the bus, a signifier of the constrained material conditions in which the public transportation of the city operates, allows, or provides for the

---

[41] Helen F. Wilson, "Passing Propinquities in the Multicultural City: The Everyday Encounters of Bus Passengering," *Environment and Planning A* 43, no. 3(2011): 635.

[42] See Judy Baker, Rakhi Basu, Maureen Cropper, Somik Lall, and Akie Takeuchi, "Urban Poverty And Transport: The Case Of Mumbai" *Policy Research Working Paper No. 3693*, 2005; Ananya Roy, *City Requiem, Calcutta: Gender and the Politics of Poverty* (Minneapolis: University of Minnesota Press, 2003).

[43] For instance, in the Nirbhaya Rape case which took place inside a private bus, a lot of narratives blamed the couple's choice to ride a private bus in a city like Delhi which was seen as an invitation to harassment. This is also a social meaning attached to private ownership of buses leading to less people in a bus (based on its high price), while at the same time the operations of private buses are still managed by the urban poor (in terms of driving and ticketing occupations). For more on transit spaces and gendered violations, see Shilpa Phadke. "Unfriendly Bodies, Hostile Cities: Reflections on Loitering and Gendered Public Space," *Economic and Political Weekly* 48, no. 39(2013): 50–59.

250   P. SUBRAMANIAN

circumstances of an erotic encounter between the protagonist and the man. The erotic encounter is thus built into the social and physical design of the bus, but also facilitated by a series of material conditions that produce the bus as such—the infrequency of buses catering to a burgeoning population, limited seating provisions, and even the uneven roads on which the buses ply ensuring that the crowds of people are not only close, but touch each other in spaces considered erogenous. However, as I have noted, these infrastructurally rendered possibilities are all but constrained by the unequal, gendered terrains through which the bodies that constitute the crowd encounter each other.

Encounters are also affective. Chicu's story lays bare the affective exchanges and emotional investments of the protagonist on the bus. The excitement of encountering a stranger and being attracted to the very strangeness of their encounter soon paves way for the shame that emanates from feeling exposed or anticipating exposure, and the recognition of pain leaves the protagonist with hope—these affective exchanges shape the erotic experience in the story. Not only is the protagonist positioned between a man and a woman, but the only interaction is through touch. In this process, the "intimate gaze" that the protagonist feels is not of literal eye-contact, but of bodily contact, of tactile reading of the body as a way of knowing.[44] Sara Ahmed, in her work on touch and encounter, helps us better frame bus-space vis-à-vis touch:

> to be touched in a certain way, or to be moved in a certain way by an encounter with another, may involve a reading not only of the encounter, but of the other that is encountered as having certain characteristics. ... Such responses are clearly mediated: materialization takes place through the 'mediation' of affect, which may function in this way as readings of the bodies of others.[45]

The protagonist's body is not read by the man through seeing her, but through known scripts of understanding a body of a woman, the risky implications of which overwhelm the protagonist and push her to leave the bus altogether. The protagonist, upon the man's exploration of her erogenous zones, feels "disrobed" and "naked" in front of others and is filled with shame. It is in this moment that the intimacy of the protagonist

[44] Chicu "Soliloquy," 92.
[45] Sara Ahmed, *The Cultural Politics of Emotion* (Edinburgh: Edinburgh University Press, 2014), 28.

reveals itself to be what Talia Mae Bettcher calls "interpretive."[46] Intimate encounters, especially those involving sexual relations, become a site of both contestation and possibility for transgender persons who negotiate normative interpretation of their body via alignment of specific gender presentation with genital status. Bettcher states that interpretation could be validating or invalidating from both the trans person's perspective and the sexual partner who, in our example, is a cis-male. The "trans vulnerability" that defines the intimate encounter is incumbent upon the kind of interpretations at work from both perspectives and if they are in sync with each other.[47] This vulnerability is thus relational: it is not inherent to the body of the protagonist but how it is produced through the conditions in which the body itself materializes. The man, for example, does not show signs of disgust, if only excited exploration, but that does not stop the protagonist from feeling fear and shame. Here, it does not matter for the protagonist if this sexual partner has a validating interpretation of her body because, as Bettcher explains, a positive recoding could help the trans person reinterpret certain body parts often centralized in sexual acts (i.e., genitalia). Bettcher's examples are indeed about trusting, consensual sexual relations. This particular encounter in the story however involves a crowd of people even as they are not involved in the sexual act itself. The bus, previously a space without judgment and pleasure for the protagonist, turns out to be a limited and limiting space for such intimacy—a space where the crowd turns into a witness, which enables her feelings of shame. As Ahmed states, it is in the "imagined view of the other that is taken on by subject in relation to itself" that shame is produced.[48] By anticipating what the crowd's dominant mode of relating with her body would be, the protagonist acts on her instincts and saves herself from possible harm.

Stories, however, do not always entail ideological fixture, but also what Steven Best calls "utopian longings": textually realized desires that seek to resolve real complications of the world by mediating what is and what could be.[49] When the narrator exits the bus, she looks at the man for the first time from the outside in order to confirm her fears as valid and her

[46] See Talia Mae Bettcher, "Trans Women and 'Interpretive Intimacy': Some Initial Reflections," in *The Essential Handbook of Women's Sexuality*, edited by Castañeda Donna (Santa Barbara, CA: Praeger, 2013), 51–68.

[47] See Bettcher, "Trans Women and 'Interpretive Intimacy,'" 51–68.

[48] Ahmed, *The Cultural Politics of Emotion*, 105.

[49] Steven Best, "After the Catastrophe: Postmodernism and Hermeneutics," *Canadian Journal of Political and Social Theory* 12, no. 3(1988):100.

flight as expedient to the situation. Instead she finds pity and a faint acknowledgment of her need to leave. Being outside of the bus temporarily avoids the possibility of unfriendly others but also helps the protagonist see the man's eyes for the first time—the pain in the man's eyes gives way to the possibility for the bus to become a meeting place in the future. Perhaps the proximity and intimacy would not be forced and fearsome but acted upon mutually with pleasure. Perhaps, next time, they would leave together.

Chicu's story of a crowded bus, its enforced proximity, its movement in an Indian city narrated by a transgender protagonist lays bare the complex discursive, affective, and material processes that animate our socially organized world. Especially by explicating sexual and intimate encounters, this erotic story opens up matters concerning the naturalized discourses of gender and sexuality that are prevalent in contemporary India. It should also be noted that the English speaking, city-based context of the story cannot account for the fears and violence of those who do not relate to such a positionality and may have more to add to our understanding of affective and material-discursive socio-spatial processes. With that limitation in mind, my analysis of the story has been twofold: first, I strive to see the real and storied world as animated through encounters which are mutually constitutive, spatially realized, and thus produced out of prevailing social conditions, practices, and power relations. Thus, reading the storied encounters confronts the social conditions which produce our lived world. Second, I identify quotidian (and in my example, queer and trans) erotica as a genre which can help us broach questions of spatially experienced intimacy and vulnerability via an analysis of its chronotopes, like that of the bus, to focus on the particular trajectories of gender, sexuality, and sex. In the end, this approach aids in identifying the containments and conventions, possibilities, and workings of the social order through which encounters are produced both in our storied and lived worlds. Future work can build on how chronotopes help us study storied worlds in films and other mediated worlds like public art, which are constructed and produced in and through social organization of space-times: chronotopes of encounters. As Chicu's *Soliloquy* shows us, encounters carry the possibilities of violence, they can be imposing and intimidating, but they can also be shaped by openness and unpredictability imbued with surprise and unimagined possibilities. Both geographies and geographical knowledges like the ones produced through our social relations in our daily life, in our essays, and in our stories should always strive to find the latter.

WORK CITED

Ahmed, Sara. *The Cultural Politics of Emotion*. Edinburgh: Edinburgh University Press, 2014.

Baker, Judy, Rakhi Basu, Maureen Cropper, Somik Lall, and Akie Takeuchi. "Urban Poverty And Transport: The Case Of Mumbai." *Policy Research Working Paper No.3693*, 2005. https://doi.org/10.1596/1813-9450-3693

Bakhtin, Mikhail and Michael Holquist. *The Dialogic Imagination: Four Essays*. Austin, TX: University of Texas Press, 1983.

Berlant, Lauren Gail. "The Compulsion to Repeat Femininity: Landscape for a Good Woman and The Life and Loves of a She-Devil." In *The Female Complaint: The Unfinished Business of Sentimentality in American Culture*, 248–63. Durham: Duke University Press, 2008.

Best, Steven. "After the Catastrophe: Postmodernism and Hermeneutics." *Canadian Journal of Political and Social Theory* 12, no. 3 (1988): 87–100.

Bettcher, Talia Mae. "Trans Women and 'Interpretive Intimacy': Some Initial Reflections." In *The Essential Handbook of Women's Sexuality*, edited by Donna Castañeda, 51–68. Santa Barbara, CA: Praeger, 2013.

Bhatia, Nandi. "Censorship, 'Obscenity' and Courtroom Drama: Reading Ismat Chughtai's 'Lihaaf' and "The 'Lihaaf' Trial."" *Law & Literature* 32, no. 3 (2020): 1–19. https://doi.org/10.1080/1535685x.2020.1721197

Browne, Kath, Jason Lim, and Gavin Brown. *Geographies of Sexualities: Theory, Practices, and Politics*. Aldershot, Hampshire: Ashgate, 2012.

Chatterjee, Shraddha. "Transgender Shifts: Notes on Resignification of Gender and Sexuality in India." *Transgender Studies Quarterly* 5, no. 3 (2018): 311–320.

Chicu. "Soliloquy." In *Close, Too Close*, edited by Meenu and Shruti, 88–96. New Delhi: Tranquebar, 2012.

David, Emmanuel. "Capital T: Trans Visibility, Corporate Capitalism, and Commodity Culture." *Transgender Studies Quarterly* 4, no. 1 (2017): 28–44.

Deshpande, Satish. "The Centrality of the Middle Class." In *Contemporary India: A Sociological View*, 125–150. New Delhi: Penguin Books, 2003.

Dutta, Aniruddha, and Raina Roy. "Decolonizing transgender in India: Some reflections." *Transgender Studies Quarterly* 1, no. 3 (2014): 320–337.

Dutta, Aniruddha. "Claiming Citizenship, Contesting Civility: The Institutional LGBT Movement and the Regulation of Gender/Sexual Dissidence in West Bengal, India." *Jindal Global Law Review* 4, no. 1 (2012): 110–141.

254 P. SUBRAMANIAN

England, Marcia R. *Public Privates: Feminist Geographies of Mediated Spaces.* Lincoln: University of Nebraska Press, 2018.

EP, Rahmath. "Why Not Janeu Under My Kurta?" Round Table India, August 10, 2017. https://roundtableindia.co.in/index.php?option=com_content&view=article&id=9150:lipstick-under-my-burkha&catid=120&Itemid=133

Gossett, Reina, Eric A.Stanley, and Johanna Burton. *Trap Door: Trans Cultural Production and the Politics of Visibility.* Cambridge, MA: The MIT Press, 2017.

Hinchy, Jessica. *Governing Gender and Sexuality in Colonial India: The Hijra, C.1850–1900.* Cambridge: Cambridge University Press, 2019.

Johnston, Lynda, and Robyn Longhurst. *Space, Place, and Sex: Geographies of Sexualities.* New York: Rowman & Littlefield, 2010.

Jyoti, Dhrubo. "Section 377: The Fight for LGBT Rights Has Just Begun." *Hindustan Times,* September 7, 2018. https://www.hindustantimes.com/india-news/section-377-the-fight-for-lgbt-rights-has-just-begun/story-odLFyR0eOctAuIJELMMOxL.html

Lefebvre, Henri. *The Production of Space.* Translated by Donald Nicholson-Smith. Malden: Blackwell Publishers Ltd., 1991.

Low, Setha M. "Spatializing Culture." In *The People, Place, and Space Reader,* edited by Jen Jack Gieseking and William Mangold, 34–38. New York: Routledge, 2014.

Massey, Doreen. "Power-Geometry and a Progressive Sense of Place." In *Mapping the Futures: Local Cultures, Global Change,* edited by John Bird, Tim Putnam, Lisa Tickner, and Barry Curtis, 60–70. London: Routledge, 1996.

———. "Some Times of Space." In *Olafur Eliasson: The Weather Project,* edited by Susan May, 107–118. London: Tate Modern, 2003.

Meenu and Shruti. Introduction to *Close, Too Close: The Tranquebar Book of Queer Erotica, xi–xvi.* Edited by Meenu and Shruti. New Delhi: Tranquebar, 2012.

McNally, David. *Bodies of Meaning: Studies on Language, Labor, and Liberation.* Albany, NY: State University of New York Press, 2001.

Phadke, Shilpa. "Unfriendly Bodies, Hostile Cities: Reflections on Loitering and Gendered Public Space." *Economic and Political Weekly* 48, no. 39 (2013): 50–59.

Roy, Ananya. *City Requiem, Calcutta: Gender and the Politics of Poverty.* Minneapolis: University of Minnesota Press, 2003.

Shrivastava, Alankrita, dir. *Lipstick Under My Burkha.* 2017; India: Prakash Jha Production.

Tally Jr., Robert T. *Topophrenia: Place, Narrative, and the Spatial Imagination.* Indiana University Press, 2018.

Ung Loh, J. "Representation, Visibility, Legibility: The 'Queer' Subject in Contemporary India." *Scholar and Feminist Online* 14, no. 2 (2017): np. http://sfonline.barnard.edu/queer-religion/representation-visibility-legibility-the-queer-subject-in-contemporary-india/

Unnithan, N. Prabha. *Crime and Justice in India*. New Delhi: SAGE, 2013.

Williams, Raymond. "Dominant, Residual, and Emergent." In *Marxism and Literature*, 121–127. Oxford: Oxford University Press, 1977.

———. "Hegemony and the Selective Tradition." In *Language, Authority and Criticism*, edited by Suzannede Castell, Allan Luke, and Carmen Luke, 56–60. London: The Falmer Press, 1989.

Wilson, Ara. "The Infrastructure of Intimacy." *Signs: Journal of Women in Culture and Society* 41, no. 2 (2016): 247–80. https://doi.org/10.1086/682919

Wilson, Helen F. "Passing Propinquities in the Multicultural City: The Everyday Encounters of Bus Passengering." *Environment and Planning A* 43, no. 3 (2011): 634–649.

———. "On Geography and Encounter: Bodies, Borders, and Difference." *Progress in Human Geography* 41, no. 4 (2016): 451–71. https://doi.org/10.1177/0309132516645958

CHAPTER 12

Anti-capitalism and the Near Future: In Mohsin Hamid's *Exit West* and Louise Erdrich's *The Future Home of the Living God*

Jessica Maucione

Walking into one of Argentinian contemporary artist's, Tomás Saraceno's,[1] exhibits at a museum or encountering a Saraceno at a gallery, one enters into a three-dimensional visual representation of a possible, habitable, beautiful future. In Saraceno's words, he is positing "a three-dimensional era of social engagement" and "a planetary feeling of belonging."[2] Saraceno sees his art as the necessary work of the human being: "to imagin[e] a world free from carbon, extractivism, capitalism, patriarchy,

---

[1] A note of gratitude to Claudia Rankine whose immediate response to my brief description of this article was to ask me if I was familiar with Saraceno's work—which turns out to embody a visual artistic expression of precisely my reading of these two novels.

[2] Emily Hall, "Tomás Saraceno: Tonya Bodaker Gallery," *Artforum*, 2012, https://www.artforum.com/print/reviews/201208/tomas-saraceno-38835

J. Maucione (✉)
Gonzaga University, Spokane, WA, USA
e-mail: maucionej@gonzaga.edu

© The Author(s), under exclusive license to Springer Nature Switzerland AG 2021
C. Beck (ed.), *Mobility, Spatiality, and Resistance in Literary and Political Discourse*, Geocriticism and Spatial Literary Studies, https://doi.org/10.1007/978-3-030-83477-7_12

258   J. MAUCIONE

and fossil fuel, or what he calls CECPF" by positing vistas of interconnect-edness and solidarity inspired in part by species, such as spiders, whose attuned habitation of the planet Saraceno studies as an aspirational para-digm for future human habitation.[3] As Slavoj Zizek asks in *In Defense of Lost Causes*, "The only *true* question today is: do we endorse th[e] 'natu-ralization' of capitalism, or does contemporary global capitalism contain antagonisms which are sufficiently strong to prevent its indefinite reproduction?"[4] (Fig. 12.1).

Since the endgame of white supremacist, neo-liberal, imperialist, patri-archal capitalism is destruction through extraction of resources and increasing disparity in access, begetting violence—sanctioned and crimi-nalized—against the earth and its inhabitants, many have come to under-stand, believe, or fear that capitalism, at least as practiced currently, is unsustainable.[5] With interdisciplinary artists like Saraceno as a guide, we must now ask: what is the role of literature in our collective future? In her article, "Unsettling the Coloniality of Being/Power/Truth/Freedom: Towards the Human after Man, its Overrepresentation-An Argument," Sylvia Wynter[6] argues that Western and westernized epistemologies have divided the human world into two categories, "Man" and its "human Others" thereby relegating racialized subjects, for example, to subaltern, even subhuman, status.[7] With the rise of renaissance humanism, Wynter explains, "the 'idea of order' on whose basis the coloniality of being, enacted by the dynamics of the relation between Man—overrepresented as the generic, ostensibly supracultural human—and its subjugated human Others was … brought into existence as the foundational basis of

---

[3] Hall, "Tomás Saraceno."

[4] Slavoj Zizek, *In Defense of Lost Causes* (London and New York: Verso, 2008), 421.

[5] As Anand Giridharadas articulates in *Winners Take All: The Elite Charade of Changing the World*: "a successful society is a progress machine. It takes in the raw material of innovations and produces broad human advancement. America's machine is broken" because "[w]hen the fruits have fallen on the United States in recent decades, the very fortunate have basketed almost all of them." Giridharadas argues that this extreme and worsening disparity explains "the spreading recognition on both sides of the ideological divide, that the system is broken and has to change." Anand Giridharadas, *Winners Take All: The Elite Charade of Changing the World* (New York: Vintage, 2019), 4, 5.

[6] Deep thanks to David Polanski, whose chapter also appears in this section, for bringing Wynter's work to my attention and for his thoughtful edits and suggestions.

[7] Sylvia Wynter, "Unsettling the Coloniality of Being/Power/Truth/Freedom: Towards the Human after Man, its Overrepresentation—An Argument," *The New Centennial Review* 3, no. 3(2003): 271, 262.

12 ANTI-CAPITALISM AND THE NEAR FUTURE: IN MOHSIN HAMID'S... 259

Fig. 12.1 Tomás Saraceno, "Cloud Cities/Air-Port-City" Tonya Bonakder Gallery, 2012 https://www.artforum.com/print/reviews/201208/tomas-saraceno-38835

modernity."[8] In keeping with Wynter's argument that since humans are "narratively inscribed," that "one cannot 'unsettle' the 'coloniality of power' without a redescription of the human outside of the terms of our present descriptive statement of the human, Man, and its overrepresentation," it follows that literary narratives that posit future imaginaries may be doing this discursive work of "unsettling the coloniality of power" by narratively and imaginatively moving beyond them.[9] I argue that literary texts that imagine future anti- or post-capitalist beings and spaces are important not only in preparing readers to enter into them, but in making them possible. As Daniel Heath Justice argues, "[a]s humans, we are storied creatures and we're constantly working to restore and re-story our being in the world" (2020). I argue, therefore, that literary texts that imagine future anti- or post-capitalist beings and spaces are important not only in preparing readers to enter into them, but in making them possible.[10] Here I juxtapose twenty-first-century near-future-set novels *The*

[8] Wynter, "Unsettling the Coloniality of Being," 262.
[9] Wynter, "Unsettling the Coloniality of Being," 268.
[10] Daniel Heath Justice, "'Our stories give us a lot of guidance': Daniel Heath Justice on why Indigenous literature matter" by Zoe Tennant, CBC Radio, April 09, 2020, https://

Future Home of the Living God by Louise Erdrich (Ojibwe) and *Exit West* by Mohsin Hamid (British-Pakistani) in order to explore the sociopolitical significance of the futures they manifest.

While Ruth Franklin writing for *The New York Times* describes *The Future Home of the Living God* as an "anti-progress novel,"[11] *Exit West* is decisively "not apocalyptic."[12] Erdrich's novel takes the shape of her twenty-six year-old pregnant protagonist's letter to her unborn child—a meta-text bent on imagining an alternative future to the future the novel posits in which evolution (ostensibly) reverses, martial law has been declared, and women are being captured and detained, their reproductive capacities utilized in service to the police state. *Exit West* imagines a possible desirable future, subverts capitalist myths of inevitability, and implicitly relegates the current apocalyptic narrative trend to a failure of imagination. Those whose bodies have been minoritized and commoditized by global white supremacist capitalist patriarchy in both novels prove more able to navigate a new world order, whether through revolutionary rejection of the colonial State or embrace of a decolonized world order, such that Erdrich's and Hamid's works suggest an inverse relationship between privilege and survival or adaptability, respectively. I argue that these future-set novels register the savagery of late capitalism and at the same time extend radical hope in their characters' forging of interdependence in the place of individualism and their respective worlds' rewarding of communitarian rather than capitalist values. *Future Home of the Living God* and *Exit West* suggest, furthermore, that the notion that "the revolution will be intersectional," is more than a progressive slogan, but perhaps the only pathway by which humans will effectively resist the total destruction built into the capitalist system and inhabit a future at all.

Erdrich's *Future Home of the Living God* maps a near future in which climate change has rendered winter a memory[13] and a hyper-patriarchal,

---

www.cbc.ca/radio/unreserved/why-stories-matter-now-more-than-ever-1.5526331/our-stories-give-us-a-lot-of-guidance-daniel-heath-justice-on-why-indigenous-literatures-matter-1.5527999

[11] Ruth Franklin, "A Timely Novel of Anti-Progress by Louise Erdrich," *The New Times*, November 21, 2017, https://www.nytimes.com/2017/11/21/books/review/louis-erdrich-future-home-of-the-living-god.html

[12] Mohsin Hamid, *Exit West* (New York: Riverhead Books, 2017), 217. All further citations to this novel will be parenthetical.

[13] An "unusually cool day for August" in Minnesota is "only ninety degrees." Louise Erdrich, *Future Home of the Living God* (New York: HarperCollins Publishers, 2017), 55.

12 ANTI-CAPITALISM AND THE NEAR FUTURE: IN MOHSIN HAMID'S...   261

hyper-evangelical-Christian, authoritarian, white supremacist, militarized regime rules the United States, justifying itself as a necessary response to the dominant culture's conception that evolution is "running backward."[14] Because Erdrich employs the narrative form of a diary, readers only understand as much as Cedar Hawk Songmaker does as the novel unfolds and she becomes targeted, detained, freed, subsequently recaptured and detained again as a pregnant woman and a woman with reproductive capacity. In *Future Home*, no one knows precisely what is going on—environmentally, biologically, governmentally, or socio-politically—including Cedar as the novel's sole narrator.[15] In her journal, Cedar reports: "People are out in the streets, demonstrating against not knowing what they should be demonstrating about. The signs are question marks of every color and size ... the people interviewed say, *I just wanna know. Is it a big deal to wanna know? We'll be okay, right?*" (52, original emphasis). Through bits of rumors circulated among detained women, it becomes apparent that the authoritarian government's proof of evolution's reversal lies in babies being born with features associated with human ancestors at a great risk to the life of their mothers. Cedar's half-sister warns, for example, "your baby's gonna be a monkey" (36). Yet some, Cedar included as it turns out, are able to produce what authorities ironically label "Originals"—a term which, again through implication, becomes synonymous with the contemporary understanding of "normal." But Cedar takes issue with the notion of backwardness posited by authorities (and popularized among citizens) in her pregnancy journal addressed to her unborn child: "We would not see the orderly backward progression of human types that evolutionary charts are so fond of presenting. Life might skip forward, sideways, in unforeseen directions. We wouldn't see the narrative we think we know. Why? Because there never was a story moving forward"

[14] Erdrich, *Future Home of the Living God*, 3. All further citations of the novel will be parenthetical.

[15] Erdrich tends to use multiple narrators in her novels, so that the same story is told from many, variably reliable, viewpoints and subject locations. Notably, her two novels that appear to respond to specific political catalysts—*The Round House* which was published just as the Violence Against Women Act was due to either expire or be extended to include more protections for Native American women and *Future Home of the Living God*, about which Erdrich says although she feels "shock" at the speed with which it was rushed into print, "[she] only ha[s] to look at photographs of white men in dark suits deciding crucial issues of women's health to know the timing is right"—both employ single, arguably limited narrators. *The Round House* is narrated by a child, while *Future Home*'s twenty-six year-old narrator spends much of the novel detained. Franklin, "A Timely Novel."

(55); she insists further, "I am not at the end of things, but the beginning" (92). Whether Cedar realizes it or not, these assertions not only denounce the authoritarian regime's and dominant culture's conceptions of linear time and linear progress, but Cedar's reasoning further aligns with Indigenous epistemologies grounded in cyclical temporality. Although her gender, Indigenous Ojibwe heritage, and pregnant status combine to render Cedar a prime target for detention and total governmental control—as the regime apparently[16] intends to sustain its power and build its future upon its ownership of the reproductive capacity and the resultant "Original"/"normal" mixed race children of women like her—she narrates her pregnancy journey against the grain of the sociopolitics of the white supremacist patriarchal regime.

Additionally, there is a sociopolitics to the novel's cast of characters and their relationships to Cedar's trajectory. While the novel comprises a collective of characters who fight for Cedar's freedom through various means, the white father of her child, Phil, betrays Cedar in layered ways, including providing her name and location to the government's hunters of pregnant women. Phil's soft-spokenness and affection for Cedar make his displays of white male entitlement and patriarchal control appear subtle at first. When Cedar demands, however, that they leave right away to head north with her newly acquired stepfather, Eddy, pleading, "Please, I *know* we'll get caught here," Phil steps in and prevents her from making what he considers a rash decision, telling Cedar to "[t]ake it easy" (119, original emphasis). Because he prevents her from leaving then and because, under pain of government-sponsored torture, he turns her in, Cedar is caught and detained. After she frees herself from this initial detention—with the aid of characters I understand as revolutionaries—Phil shows up again, repentant, but still anachronistically operating within a white supremacist patriarchal capitalist paradigm. Because he learns from his torturers that due to her Indigenous ancestry, Cedar may be carrying an "Original," valued by the government for its "normalcy" and partial whiteness, Phil fantasizes his own empowerment narrative, a distinctly capitalist narrative of upward mobility that allows them to capitalize on their "normal" baby. Excitedly, Phil instructs, "The thing is … you have a treasure, Cedar, if our

---

[16] The novel reveals very little about the authoritarian regime in charge and Cedar does not hypothesize about the government's character or intentions, but moments of interaction with characters who are relatively "in the know" (such as the ultrasound doctor) lend themselves to this interpretation.

baby is normal. We would be in charge of things. Rich. Super rich! We'd be safe … the sky's the limit for us" (246). When she responds, "We could seize power and found a dynasty" (247), he mistakes her sarcasm for shared enthusiasm for world domination built upon supposed genetic superiority.

Phil's insistence on exercising capitalist property rights on both his whiteness and the Indigenous ancestry of the baby Cedar carries proves both anachronistic and counter to the novel's revolutionary bent as suggested by its celebration of characters who resist the authoritarian regime. The state of the world remains unclear throughout the novel—for which Erdrich is criticized by some reviewers[17]—and yet there are hints that what characters feel is "the end of the world" may signal instead the crumbling of capitalism (47). In a long line at Wells Fargo bank, Cedar comes to understand that, no, they cannot honor her request to withdraw her "eight thousand dollars [she has] in an old-fashioned savings account" (46), after which she uses the money she does have to obtain items for barter. Readers never again bear witness to money exchanging hands. Functionally Cedar moves through what could be a liminal phase of struggle between the authoritarian regime and the underground collective bent on subverting it following what could be capitalism's demise, while its counterpart, white supremacy, is doubling down its self-preservation efforts. Phil remains relatively free as a white man. Though he is tortured as someone having given aid to pregnant women (191), his combination of maleness and whiteness grants him options, at least to choose between serving the government and feigning to do so as a double agent. Despite the unknowns, Phil's character provides evidence of the authoritarian government's intention to preserve the continuity of white supremacist capitalism. Phil may not be able to retrieve the money he had in now empty banks, but he does seem to maintain what Cheryl Harris describes as the property value of whiteness. In "Whiteness as Property" Harris writes:

> Slavery linked the privilege of whites to the subordination of Blacks through a legal regime that attempted the conversion of Blacks into objects of property. Similarly, the settlement and seizure of Native American land supported

---

[17] Michael Schaub calls Erdrich's *Future Home of the Living God*, a "rare stumble from a great writer," for example, charging that the novel is "too often unclear" to the point of being "inexplicable" Michael Schaub, "Future Home of the Living God is a Rare Stumble from a Great Writer," *NPR*, November 14, 2017, https://www.wfae.org/npr-arts-life/2017-11-14/future-home-of-the-living-god-is-a-rare-stumble-from-a-great-writer

white privilege through a system of property rights in land in which the "race" of the Native Americans rendered their first possession rights invisible and justified conquest. This racist formulation embedded the fact of white privilege into the very definition of property, marking another stage in the evolution of the property interest in whiteness. Possession—the act necessary to lay the basis for rights in property—was defined to include only the cultural practices of whites. This definition laid the foundation for the idea of whiteness—that which whites alone possess—is valuable and is property.[18]

In other words, Phil occupies the position of "Man" in Wynter's thinking. Cedar's successive detentions juxtaposed with Phil's mobility and freedoms seems to be a holdover product of what Wynter describes as the over-representation of Man at the expense of its human others. As Wynter argues, the "post-sixties vigorous discursive and institutional re-elaboration of the central over-representation ... enables the interest, reality, and well-being of the empirical human world to continue to be imperatively subordinate to those of the now globally hegemonic ethnoclass world of 'Man.'"[19] Although Phil gains insight into the authoritarian regime's endgame, as well as its instability, through his experience of being tortured for Cedar's and other pregnant women's names and locations—women he had been helping hide to prevent their capture—he nevertheless adopts the regime's approach as seen in his advocacy for Cedar to join him in using their (mostly her) reproductive capacities to take "charge of things" (246). From Cedar's observations recorded in her diary, readers have clues as to the regime's aspirational quest for the continuity of white supremacy, however counter to the realities of the apparent devolution of the human species. Watching television before her first detainment, Cedar notes: "There are no brown people, anywhere, not in movies not on sitcoms not on shopping channels or on the dozens of evangelical channels up and down the remote" and "The women are fewer, the ones who appear seem awkward, all in their twenties, white with white teeth, yellow or brown

---

[18] Cheryl I. Harris, "Whiteness as Property," *The Harvard Law Review Association* 106, no. 8(1993): 1721.

[19] Wynter, "Unsettling the Coloniality of Being," 262. Eduardo Bonilla-Silva echoes this in *Racism Without Racists* in which he instructs that "race relations acquired ... a new character since the 1960s" and that an "increasingly covert nature of racial discourse and racial practices" works to sustain racial inequity after this point. Eduardo Bonilla-Silva, *Racism Without Racists: Color-Blind Racism and the Persistence of Racial Inequality in America*, 5th edition (Lanham, Maryland: Rowman and Littlefield Publishers, 2017), 23.

hair, sparkling eyes" (44). This can be read as both irony and continuity: the new white supremacy, like what has come before, intends to build itself upon racial and ethnic exclusion, minoritization, and subordination. This new white supremacy, however, seems to scientifically require racial mixing. Readers begin to gain insight into this piece of the evolutionary puzzle (which remains enigmatic throughout the novel) in the ultrasound scene. Knowledge of what the doctor refers to as Cedar's "special ethnicity"—meaning her Ojibwe heritage—mixed with Phil's whiteness, coupled with what the doctor sees on the ultrasound screen gives him cause to think Cedar is carrying an "Original," or "normal," baby. As such, he is required to detain her and turn her over to the government. While Phil intends to bank on what Harris's research uncovers—that "the property interest in whiteness has proven to be resilient and adaptive to new conditions" in that "[o]ver time it has changed in form, but it has retained its essential exclusionary character"—Cedar invests in alternative notions to possible futures, along with a group of characters that in their own ways challenge the State's authority.[20]

In contrast to Phil, *Future Home* also presents white male characters who wholly refuse to capitulate to the new authoritarian regime. There is the unnamed doctor—whose blue eyes remind Cedar of her white father (51)—who has been called in to view her ultrasound, despite the fact that she is scheduled to see a midwife. "We've got one" (50), he announces to the attendants, feigning that he will comply with the government program and detain her. In private, the doctor asks Cedar "if [she has] any special ethnicity," learning that she is Ojibwe and that the father of her child is white, upon which he orders, "with desperate authority": "'Then get the hell out of here'" (51). The doctor has her bind him to the chair with tape and gives her instructions on how to escape the building disguised as a delivery-person (51). Cedar never understands, and so it is not revealed to readers, the supposed science behind which women might carry "Originals." In my reading, the authoritarian regime intensifies its efforts to preserve white supremacy as the white majority becomes threatened by their inability to bear "Originals," unless they are mixed race or multiracial, having what Cedar's doctor refers to as some "special ethnicity."

The diverse group of characters that lend hope to, if not Cedar, then her child, are suggestive of a livable future beyond the novel's conclusion that is makeshift, de-centralized, and intersectional. Readers learn of these

[20] Harris, "Whiteness as Property," 1778.

revolutionary figures' counteractions to the government at the moments of their paths crossing with Cedar, as with the doctor who reads her ultrasound. The novel invests, then, in Cedar's unborn child as representative not just of a vessel of hope for the white supremacist fantasy of domination but also a source of hope for a possible post-revolution, alternative future. Explicitly through Cedar's predictions and fantasies in her journal and implicitly through the intersectional characters' efforts to provide him safe passage, *Future Home*'s unborn child—a single, unborn, body signifying hope for both sides of the novel's ideological space—the hegemonic force as well as the counter-hegemonic resistance. Upon escaping her initial detention, Cedar discovers that there are undercover revolutionaries everywhere—police officers, postal workers, delivery truck drivers. Notably, the revolutionary actions of these characters depend on less developed—and purposefully invisible—characters that risk their freedoms under the current regime to serve the greater good.

A set of relatively developed characters lend insight into Erdrich's novel's suggestion that the future depends upon intersectional collaboration. First there is Sera, Cedar's white adoptive mother, whose character at first simply embodies white liberal stereotypes; one of Cedar's diary entries mocks Sera for "being annoyingly phobic about food additives," for example (4). Although Sera initially invites readers' ridicule as well, the novel reveals her strength and complexity.[21] During Cedar's first detention at a hospital-turned-prison, Sera shows up disguised as a nurse. There Sera discovers that Cedar has already been collaborating with her roommate, Tia to fashion a rope in order to escape out the window and repel down the side of the building. Notably, Tia is a Chinese American woman who pretends to not speak or understand English and who blames her lack of diligence in avoiding capture on the presumption of safety she associates with wealth, saying "that's the problem with privilege, money, in this sort of situation. False sense of security" (170). If Cedar and her baby represent the survival of the oppressed, the revolutionary nature of Sera's sacrifice is further emphasized when Sera and Cedar are taken to the reservation after escaping the hospital to stay with Cedar's biological mother, with whom (Sera has always known and Cedar newly discovers) Sera's husband had an affair. Cedar thus grew up with her biological father, Glen, but always knew him as her adoptive father. Despite Sera's discomfort and

---

[21] As a redeemed white female character who initially annoys characters and readers alike, Sera recalls Polly Elizabeth in Erdrich's 2009 novel, *Four Souls.*

sense of displacement in Cedar's biological mother's home on the reservation, she remains there for her daughter. Sera might best be termed a conservative revolutionary, in that she apparently wishes to return to the "normal" state of things—which she was critical of, but from the privileged position of race, class, and sexuality. She admits to Cedar, "'I know you want me to lie. ... Well, tough. I can't. I wish the baby had never happened'" (207). Yet she is there, using her white body as an instrument to help orchestrate Cedar's escape and safety, in contrast to Glen who disappears from the narrative entirely, presumably having escaped to Canada.

The novel's most prominent revolutionary figure, Eddy, wishes to establish the tribal sovereignty and treaty rights negotiated but never honored by the U.S. government as a way of laying a foundation for, presumably (as the novel does not clarify Eddy's goals), a post-capitalist, post-white supremacist future. Eddy explains his revolutionary action plan simply: "'We're just taking back the land within the original boundaries of our original treaty'" (214). An Ivy League educated Ojibwe man running a gas station on the reservation at the novel's outset, Eddy—Cedar's new stepfather and husband of her biological mother Cedar meets as an adult—comes out of depression and into himself as a revolutionary leader. Eddy is unperturbed by what many characters are experiencing as and naming "the end of the world" (47). He and Cedar have the following exchange:

[Eddy]:   'Indians have been adapting since before 1492 so I guess we'll keep adapting.'
[Cedar]: 'But the world is going to pieces.'
[Eddy]:   'It is always going to pieces.'
[Cedar]: 'This is different.'
[Eddy]:   'It is always different. We'll adapt.'(28)

Cedar's recorded first impression of Eddy relates that "Eddy talks, but Eddy also listens" (31)—distancing him from Phil's expressions of masculinity on the one hand and at the same time laying out an important leadership attribute that may make the survival of the world, or the next world order, possible.

Eddy is a writer working on a manuscript and thus a possible stand-in for Erdrich as revolutionary figure/imaginer of new worlds, pointing as well to the importance of narratives in revolution. He pens coded letters to Cedar during her detention in the first hospital-prison advising her of

268   J. MAUCIONE

escape plans, letters that easily pass through attentive surveillance and are ultimately delivered by another member of the novel's intersectional cast of revolutionary figures, Hiro.[22] Having escaped her initial detention, Cedar experiences the reservation as a protective haven. She discovers that "Eddy has tasked our fastest kids and rehabbed gang members as runners," who like "the old town criers" deliver the news twice daily (223). Thus the minoritized space of the reservation, in part due to Eddy's leadership, acts as the novel's space of refuge, the space of the future. This representation of the reservation echoes Michel Laguerre's insistence upon the complexity of the power dynamics designed to disenfranchise minoritized spaces. While the dominant/majority culture may intend to wholly enervate its inhabitants, Laguerre nevertheless recognizes that a minoritized space can become "the site where the possible is contemplated"—where the collective organizes its efforts at emancipation.[23] In making the reservation a site of refuge and community organizing, Erdrich's novel embodies Henri Lefebvre's claim in *The Production of Space* that "what came earlier continues to underpin what follows" and that "[n]o space disappears in the course of growth and development: the worldwide does not abolish the local."[24] Alongside its subversion of linear time, therefore, *Future Home* also inverts the Western conception of progress, fueled by still-operative beliefs such as Manifest Destiny, that assumes the inferiority of all that came before simply for having occurred earlier in time.

Just as the novel declines to reveal Eddy's endgame, *Future Home*'s revolutionary vision remains indeterminate. Although the novel gestures toward imagining sovereign Indigenous lands as humans' potential "future home," Erdrich does not allow her protagonist to remain on the expanding reservation for long. Cedar is captured a second and final time—her whereabouts apparently discovered by the government, again, due to Phil and his ostensible efforts to help her. In the new higher security detention center, escape is impossible. Yet Cedar continues to imagine, and hope for, a better future for her child. And she continues to write. "Dear baby,"

---

[22] Cedar's mail carrier at her home (which gets seized by the government when she is captured) Hiro, continues to deliver Cedar's mail to her, secretly, after she is detained; Cedar writes, "Hiro has casually risked his life for me because I am on his mail route" (211).

[23] Michel Laguerre, *Minoritized Space: An Inquiry into the Spatial Order of Things* (Berkeley: Institute of Governmental Studies Press, 1999), 161.

[24] Henri Lefebvre, *The Production of Space*, trans. Donald Nicholson-Smith (Oxford: Blackwell Publishers, 1974), 229, 86.

Cedar writes, "I want you to see this world, supernal, lovely" (159). Part of what allows for hope is the reappearance of Jessie—a nurse from her initial institutionalization whom Cedar had underestimated. Cedar initially describes her as "a pale, skinny, chinless, nerdy type of woman ... mousey, bland, limp-haired and cave-chested," and later discovers that she has "the nerves of an outlaw," and that "Jessie was not a nurse, she was an OB-GYN posing as a nurse in order to get women out of the hospital, disguising and hiding them, past security" (262–3). Cedar discovers that the women Jessie has saved include her first roommate at the first hospital-prison, Agnes Starr. It is Agnes who instructs Cedar to flush her daily "vitamins" that give her "a comfortable feeling of peace and order" (127) and who insists that she is the great-great-granddaughter of Belle Starr, the famous outlaw "and that she's going to break out" (12). As it turns out, Jessie faked Agnes's death and smuggled her out of the morgue "in a body bag punched with breathing holes" (263). When Cedar's baby is born healthy, holding her gaze and gripping her finger, Cedar is immediately injected with something that renders her unconscious and the child is taken from her (264). Yet Cedar sustains hope and continues to imagine engaging with him, writing, "My dear son. I know you're going to read this someday" (265). This hope rests in large part on Jessie's direct revolutionary actions and the fact that she has promised Cedar to "keep track of where they take [her] baby" (263). Cedar reflects "I don't know what happened to Jessie, if she's still here ... (I dream she has taken you away. That she's keeping you safe for me)" (266).

When the novel's movement toward revolution seems to halt with Cedar's final capture, the idea that Jessie may have saved her baby symbolizes new hope in rebellion and the future it may manifest. Cedar writes, "instead of the past, it is the future that haunts us now" (63). While theorists such as Van Wyck Brooks have discussed the importance of a "usable past," being able to imagine, and therefore make possible, a plausible future is the revolutionary imperative of the twenty-first century.[25] And this future will be won in large part by those disenfranchised in and by the present. Cedar muses in her journal, "For it shall be as it was. ... The meek shall inherit the earth, the undone shall take it over, the backward shall take it back, the unformed and ancient shall form it new" (144)—a line that powerfully evokes Frantz Fanon's contention in *The Wretched of the Earth*: "In decolonization, there is therefore the need of a complete

---

[25] Van Wyck Brooks, "On Creating a Usable Past," *The Dial* (1918): 337.

calling into question of the colonial situation," Fanon writes, "[i]f we wish to describe it precisely, we might find it in the well-known words: 'The last shall be first and the first last.' Decolonization is the putting into practice of this sentence."[26] Although Erdrich's *Future Home* eschews conjecturing a decolonized future imaginary, I argue that it advances the decolonial narrative beyond cautioning against the endgame of white supremacist patriarchal capitalism. However shrouded in mystery or lacking in clarity and in envisioning an intersectional collective of characters actively orchestrating complex, interdependent actions designed to emancipate the most "wretched of the earth" in an all-too-familiar near future, *Future Home* contributes to the narrative re-inscription, or redefinition of human beings that Wynter calls for in "Unsettling the Coloniality of Being/Power/Truth/Freedom."

While Erdrich's *Future Home of the Living God* cautions readers about where we are and where we are headed while also hinting at the possibility of a post-revolutionary future made possible by leaders such as Eddy along with several characters contributing to possibility through coordinated, collectivist efforts, Mohsin Hamid's *Exit West*, instead, delivers an imaginary in which he invites readers into the kind of post-capitalist, post-patriarchy future Saraceno's Cloud Cities predict. A 2018 article in *The Economist*, "Open Borders: the case for immigration," opens with a discussion of Hamid's *Exit West*. The way that "the world settles into an uneasy equilibrium" toward the end of the novel "reflects what many believe the world would look like if people were free to move wherever they wanted: fairer, freer, with more opportunities for a larger number of people. But it also nods to the fears many people have about unfettered migration: uncertainty, disorder, violence."[27] It goes on to explain the economic and moral arguments for and against open borders. Economists have long predicted, for example, that the world's GDP would increase, even double, in a borderless world, where workers would be free to move away from exploitation and toward opportunity.

What The Economist article does not address, however, is that not only is there a direct relationship between overall wealth and location, but also that wealth is located in and a result of empire. Economies that are "working well" now belong to nation states that were or are currently colonizers

---

[26] Frantz Fanon, *The Wretched of the Earth* (New York: Grove Press, 2005), 2.

[27] L.S. and E.H, "Open Borders: The Case for Immigration," *The Economist*, April 16, 2018, https://www.economist.com/open-future/2018/04/16/the-case-for-immigration

and those that suffer so-called underdevelopment belong to countries that are or have been colonized. Noam Chomsky's body of work maps this cause-and-effect relationship. In *Hopes and Prospects,* Chomsky states, "[i]n general, with extensive state intervention and violence at home, and barbarism and imposed liberalization in conquered areas, Europe and its offshoots were able to become rich developed societies, while the conquered regions became the 'third world,' the South."[28] Works like John Perkin's 2005 *Confessions of an Economic Hit Man* and his updated 2016 version, *The New Confessions of an Economic Hit Man,* disclose some of the exploitative methods used by the U.S. superpower to maintain economic supremacy. But they are not the only ones to recognize that the level of disparity the world is holding now is unsustainable. Even the world's wealthiest are quoting Pope Francis's unabashedly anti-capitalist environmentalist tract, Laudato Sí and Marx and Engles's The Communist Manifesto at their exclusive summits while discussing the future of capitalism. As I began this article, I noticed in the airport a 2019 special issue cover of Forbes, with the affable-looking Kind Bar billionaire, Daniel Lubetsky and the following headline: "REIMAGINING CAPITALISM: How to make the greatest system ever invented more authentic, more accessible and more accountable."[29] Obviously and inevitably, things must change.

In a New Yorker interview on his new book, *Exit West,* Hamid warned, "if we can't imagine desirable futures for ourselves that stand a chance of actually coming to pass, our collective depression could well condemn humanity to a period of terrible savagery."[30] Alongside what Hamid terms "violently nostalgic visions" (including, presumably, white supremacist backlash) is the twenty-first-century's popular genre of apocalypse. Might the white (shrinking) majority be attracted to the notion that apocalypse is upon us now precisely because white supremacy appears to be threat-

---

[28] Noam Chomsky, *Hopes and Prospects* (Chicago: Haymarket Books, 2010), 6–7.

[29] Randall Lane, "Reimaging Capitalism: How the Greatest System Ever Conceived (And Its Billionaires) Need to Change," *Forbes,* March 31, 2019, https://www.forbes.com/sites/randalllane/2019/3/4/reimagining-capitalism-how-the-greatest-system-ever-conceivedand-its-billionairesneed-to-change/?sh=61304b7e64c8

[30] Cressida Leyshon, "This Week in Fiction: Mohsin Hamid on the Migrants in All of Us," *The New Yorker,* November 7, 2016, https://www.newyorker.com/books/page-turner/this-week-in-fiction-mohsin-hamid-2016-11-14

ened? Like Erdrich's *Future Home of the Living God*, Hamid's future-set novel imagines possibilities that subvert myths of inevitability associated with late capitalism; but unlike Erdrich, Hamid brings the novels' protagonists fully into an alternative future that operates differently, yet functionally, with decisively creative and liberatory effects.

While Hamid's *Exit West* side-steps the physical hardships endured by refugees in their movements by way of its employment of magical realist doorways that, once discovered, allow for almost immediate passage between countries, it does vividly register the psychosocial imperatives and costs of displacement. Hamid's *Exit West* suggests also, though with compassion rather than judgment, a future that inverts margins and centers, outsiders and insiders. In their unnamed, eventually besieged home country, where the protagonists, Saeed and Nadia, first meet and are introduced to readers, Nadia wears a full-length black robe, "'so men don't fuck with [her]'" (17), whereas Saeed finds comfort in prayer as a rite of masculinity, considering prayer "about being a man, being of the men, a ritual that connected him to adulthood and to the notion of being a particular sort of man" (201). As their joint migrations take them to Greece, England, and the United States, Nadia proves the more prepared to embrace change, and more specifically, a post-capitalist world, while Saeed's discomfort with change and his indulgence of nostalgia seem to hinder him personally as well as contribute to a growing rift between the two lovers.

It's not that Hamid or the narrative wholly favors Nadia, instead her trajectory reads as realism within the magical realist novel. The narrator explains that "Nadia had long been, and would afterwards continue to be, more comfortable with all varieties of movements in her life than was Saeed, in whom the impulse of nostalgia was stronger, perhaps because his childhood had been more idyllic, or perhaps because this was simply his temperament" (94–5). Indeed, before their city had begun to fall into civil war, Nadia had already lost her family—not by physical violence but because "after finishing university, Nadia announced, to her family's utter horror … that she was moving out on her own, an unmarried woman" (22) and "Nadia and her family both considered her thereafter to be without a family" (22). As the narrator instructs, "when we migrate, we murder from our lives those we leave behind" (98), but due to gendered cultural constraints Nadia had already in a sense committed these murders before migrating through the decision to rent her own apartment.

12 ANTI-CAPITALISM AND THE NEAR FUTURE: IN MOHSIN HAMID'S... 273

Living solo as a woman, "[s]he learned how to dress for self-protection, how best to deal with aggressive men and with the police, and with aggressive men who were the police, and always to trust her instincts about situations to avoid or to exit immediately" (23)—but this doesn't stop everything. Hamid includes a scene in which at a crowded line at the bank in their home city, Nadia gets sexually assaulted through her layers of clothing and robe. The story that follows Saeed and Nadia's departure describes a sort of balance between grave dangers, mostly from "nativist" popular and governmental violence, and impressively organized humanitarian workers and aid. In London, Saeed asks Nadia "why she still wore her black robes, since here she did not need to, and she said that she had not needed to wear them even in their own city ... before the militants came, but she chose to, because it sent a signal, and she still wished to send this signal" (114). Hamid suggests that the situation of being a woman in a patriarchal world, then, allows Nadia to experience a relative continuity. The narrator explains, "in life roughness had to be managed. Nadia thought it madness to expect anything else. For Saeed existence in the [London] house was more jarring" (132). In the refugee communities, particularly in Greece and Britain, Nadia tends to gravitate toward empowering connections and opportunities, while Saeed is left often "feeling emasculated" (151)—which Hamid's novel connects with a collective performance and posturing around masculinity and its intersections with capitalism and religion. A believer in property rights, for example, Saeed feels "guilty that they and their fellow residents were occupying a home that was not their own" (132) and, as solace for his discomfort, he often seeks out people from his own country with whom to pray.

Notably, in Nadia and Saeed's discussions about their desires to travel during their courtship, the first place Nadia declares she would choose to go is Cuba—the western hemisphere's only socialist country and one that has been fending off U.S. imperialism since 1959. Saeed wants to travel, but "in his imagination he had thought he would leave [his city] only temporarily, intermittently, never once and for all" (94). After the couple emerges out of their first globally transporting door, Nadia sees "Saeed pivot back to the door, as though he wished maybe to reverse course and return through it" (105). In the experiences that follow, Saeed seems increasingly immersed in nostalgia and the need to recreate what he can from his homeland while Nadia is relatively weightless and open.

By the time the couple transports themselves through their third door and arrive in Marin in the United States, they have grown apart but are individually strengthened by the realization that "[t]he apocalypse appeared to have arrived and yet it was not apocalyptic" (217). It is here that Hamid locates the most hope by describing a collective resilience that seems to draw upon the dying out of "nativism" and the cooperation of people embracing a post-capitalist, diverse community. It's a new America and yet something like a decolonized, and, importantly, post-imperial, version of the future John F. Kennedy imagined in *A Nation of Immigrants*, where he wrote not only that "[i]mmigration is by definition a gesture of faith in social mobility. It is the expression in action of a positive belief in the possibility of a better life," but also that xenophobia and nativism— "the policy of keeping America 'pure' (that is of preferring old immigrants to new)"—through "the national origins quota system [that] has strong overtones of an indefensible racial preference" were unsustainable.[31] In Marin, Hamid writes, "there were almost no natives, these people having died out or been exterminated long ago, and one would see them only occasionally" (197). Following that description, Hamid immediately disrupts the whole notion of nativism by recognizing that "nativeness [is] a relative matter" and by describing a myriad of ways people might claim nativeness in this space (197). While those "who claimed the rights of nativeness most forcefully, tended to be drawn from the ranks of those with light skin who looked most like the natives of Britain" (198), there were also people whose habitation on this land was not a result of any of their ancestors having migrated—whose citizenship had been disrupted by politics rather that movement. Finally Hamid describes a "third layer of nativeness" that is "composed of those ... descended ... from the human beings who had been brought from Africa to this continent centuries ago as slaves" (198). "While this layer of nativeness was not vast in proportion to the rest," Hamid's narrator continues to explain, "it had vast importance, for society had been shaped in reaction to it" (198). Hamid contrasts the bitterness and nostalgia of white nativism with the leadership and communitarian impulse of these other ways of claiming or experiencing nativeness in Marin—ways that help provide leadership and structure in the emergent new world order. Black leadership in Marin, and presumably across the (former?) United States, signals the fulfillment of Fanon's measure of the first sign of success of decolonization wherein "the

---

[31] John. F. Kennedy, *A Nation of Immigrants* (New York: Harper & Row, 1964), 98, 102, 114.

minimum demand is that the last become first."[32] Thus while Erdrich's *Future Home* communicates a sense of urgency for decolonization, Hamid's *Exit West* concludes in a decolonized space.

The shift away from de facto or de jure colonial power is both local and global in *Exit West* and in most places decolonization is in-process rather than achieved. Hamid interrupts Nadia and Saeed's migration/love story with intermittent vignettes of unnamed characters as they move through and across far-flung destinations, since the magical realist paradigm of the novel has removed not only the arduous travel and extensive barriers and screening processes forced upon refugees and migrants, but also the receiving countries' ability to determine which people and how many they will grant asylum. In contrast to the collectivist, communitarian, and decolonized space of Marin in Northern California, for example, one vignette briefly transports readers to La Jolla in San Diego, which appears to be under military occupation in an attempt to control migrant influx. Here an "old man ask(s) [an] officer whether it was Mexicans that had been coming through, or was it Muslims"—a question the officer declines to answer (50). *Exit West* thus registers decolonization as a process that recalls Fanon's claim that "[t]o dislocate the colonial world does not mean that once the borders have been eliminated there will be a right of way between the two sectors."[33]

If "[t]o destroy the colonial world means nothing less than demolishing the colonist's sector," it will take more than magic doorways that eliminate the physical barriers to mobility and migration.[34] As such, *Exit West* operates on the psychosocial level of coloniality as well. Earlier in the novel, before readers become aware of the magical doors, the narrative cuts to a bedroom in which "a pale-skinned woman was sleeping alone" in an upper-class neighborhood in Sydney, Australia (7). As she sleeps, the narrator describes the entrance in the dark of a man "with dark skin and dark, woolly hair" (9). Here Hamid activates assumptions, fears, biases, remembrances of trauma, perhaps, too, in the minds/bodies of readers. But it shifts mid-sentence, to telling a moment of the unnamed[35] man's story, the would-be intruder: "His eyes rolled terribly. Yes terribly," Hamid

---

[32] Frantz Fanon, *The Wretched of the Earth* (New York: Grove Press, 2005), 10.

[33] Fanon, *The Wretched of the Earth*, 6.

[34] Fanon, *The Wretched of the Earth*, 6.

[35] All characters except the two protagonists, Saeed and Nadia, remain unnamed in *Exit West*.

writes, followed by "Or perhaps not so terribly" (9). Readers learn that the man grew up in "perilous circumstances" and that "he was aware of the fragility of *his* body" (9, emphasis added), before he slips out the bedroom window. Not until several pages later, does Hamid's narrator introduce the doorways that show up seemingly randomly—one may enter through, say, a bathroom door in New York and exit through a closet door in Sydney. The collection of vignettes tracks multifarious encounters, moments that dominant narratives would have erupt into violence, and insist upon readers' imagining otherwise by becoming aware of their own fears and biases, their own assumptions about who belongs where, about who poses a threat to whom.

This disruption of the constructed binary between "Man" and its "human Others" in Wynter's words, makes a new world order possible. "It has been said that depression is the failure to imagine a plausible desirable future for oneself," Hamid writes in *Exit West*, and "[n]ot just in Marin, but in the whole region ... and in many other places too ... plausible desirable futures began to emerge, unimaginable previously, but not unimaginable now" (217). Instead of apocalypse, Hamid describes a "great creative flowering" (217). Just as the apocalypse turns out to be unapocalyptic after all, Hamid also refuses to lament Saeed's and Nadia's romantic trajectory as tragedy. Nadia falls in love with a woman—a talented chef who feeds Nadia beautiful meals in a world where ingredients are often scarce. Saeed falls in love with a woman whose father is African American and whose mother was from his home country and whose religiosity mirrors but helps expand his own. And the two protagonists remain friends, meeting up for coffee years later in their city of origin. This "settling into ... equilibrium" as described in The Economist, seems to represent a global sociological level of what psychologists say about individuals—that after facing great loss, perhaps suffering what an individual feared most in life, that person will return to their previous level of happiness or contentment after about three months.[36]

This is a radical move on Hamid's part. By imagining a future that brings about relative peace by demanding interdependence rather than individualism and rewarding communitarian rather than capitalist values, Hamid helps us put current disasters—the global rise of white nationalism and the certainty of increasingly disruptive environmental catastrophes—in perspective. *Exit West* along with *Future Home* function, then, as

---

[36] L.S. and E.H., "Open Borders."

fictional counterparts to Rebecca Solnit's nonfiction text, *A Paradise Built in Hell: The Extraordinary Communities That Arise in Disaster*, in which she explores the beauty of the interdependence borne of, or perhaps revealed by, disaster. Solnit argues that "[d]isaster doesn't sort us out by preferences; it drags us into emergencies that require we act, and act altruistically, bravely, and with initiative in order to survive or save the neighbors, no matter how we vote or what we do for a living."[37] Solnit adds that while the "positive emotions that arise in those unpromising circumstances demonstrate that social ties and meaningful work are deeply desired, readily improvised, and intensely rewarding," unfortunately, the "very structure of our economy and society prevents these goals from being achieved."[38] White nationalists and the arbiters and beneficiaries of white supremacist global patriarchal capitalism want us to believe that on the other side of the current world order is doom. But we don't need to time travel into the future to know that is not so, since there are contemporary counter-examples that survive despite every effort to disenfranchise or destroy them. There is Cuba. As Chomsky also points out in *Hopes and Prospects*, "throughout the hemisphere and elsewhere there are [I]ndigenous movements seeking to gain land rights and other civil and human rights that have been denied them by repressive and often murderous states."[39] As embodied by Eddy's character in *Future Home of the Living God*, "[t]his is happening," Chomsky (2010) adds, "even where the [I]ndigenous communities barely survived the conquest, as in the United States, where the pre-contact population of perhaps seven million or more was reduced to a few hundred thousand by 1900."[40] I characterize Eddy from *Future Home* as a revolutionary figure largely because he transforms from a depressive adaptivity for the sake of survival to answering the call for revolutionary leadership through rehabilitative engagement with a decolonized, sovereign future.

Erdrich's *Future Home of the Living God* and Hamid's *Exit West* invite readers to consider that not only are there countless ways of anticipating the future, but that it is imperative that we engage our imaginations in order to make "plausible desirable futures" possible. In this way, literary

---

[37] Rebecca Solnit, *A Paradise Built in Hell: The Extraordinary Communities that Arise in Disaster* (London: Penguin Books, 2010), 6.

[38] Solnit, *A Paradise Built in Hell*, 6.

[39] Chomsky, *Hopes and Prospects*, 5.

[40] Chomsky, *Hopes and Prospects*, 5.

278 J. MAUCIONE

narrative space can become one space of resistance, much as Sophie Nield ascribes to the theater and protest as theater. In her article, "There is Another World: Space, Theatre, and Global Anti-capitalism," Nield claims that:

> Authority produces space precisely by cutting it up, marking it with borders and controlling and regulating movement. The tactics of resistance must therefore be to intervene in the illusory homogeneity of abstract space, expose its weaknesses and contradictions, and materialise an alternative space, for however temporary a moment.[41]

Implicit in the logic of Erdrich's and Hamid's speculative fiction is a refusal, in Zizek's words, to "endorse th[e] 'naturalization' of capitalism,"[42] combined with an impulse to simultaneously, as in Justice's words in his interview with Zoe Tennant, "restore and re-story our being in the world" by implicitly rejecting what Wynter calls the "over-representation of 'Man'"[43] and embracing the opportunity to engender representations of space "for the purpose of emancipation."[44] The literary work of imagining nonapocalyptic futures furthermore recognizes that there is a politics to hope as well as to despair. Cornel West argues that the:

> dominant tendencies of our day are unregulated global capitalism, racial balkanization, social breakdown, and individual depression. Hope enacts the stance of the participant who actively struggles against the evidence in order to change the deadly tides of wealth inequality, group xenophobia, and personal despair.[45]

---

[41] Sophie Nield, "There is Another World: Space, Theatre, and Global Anti-capitalism," *Contemporary Theatre Review* 16, no. 1(2006): 61.

[42] Slavoj Zizek, *In Defense of Lost Causes* (London and New York: Verso, 2008), 421.

[43] Daniel Heath Justice, "'Our stories give us a lot of guidance': Daniel Heath Justice on why Indigenous literatures matter," Zoe Tennant, CBC Radio, April 09, 2020, https://www.cbc.ca/radio/unreserved/why-stories-matter-now-more-than-ever-1.5526331/our-stories-give-us-a-lot-of-guidance-daniel-heath-justice-on-why-indigenous-literatures-matter-1.5527999

[44] Michel Laguerre, *Minoritized Space: An Inquiry into the Spatial Order of Things* (Berkeley: Institute of Governmental Studies Press, 1999), 16.

[45] Cornel West, "Prisoners of Hope," in *The Impossible Will Take a Little While: Perseverance and Hope in Troubled Times*, ed. Paul Rogat Loeb (New York: Basic Books, 2014), 346.

West adds that "[t]o live is to wrestle with despair yet never allow despair to have the last word."[46] If, as Michel de Certeau writes in *The Practice of Everyday Life*, "stories 'go in a process' ahead of social practices in order to open a field for them," then future-set literary spaces such as those posited in *Future Home of the Living God* and *Exit West* provide necessary apparatuses for the decolonization and emancipation revolutionary projects.[47] Whether or not the future rendered possible by writers and storytellers like Erdrich and Hamid will resemble one of Saraceno's aspirational cloud cities, its potential is borne at the moment of its narration.

WORKS CITED

Bonilla-Silva, Eduardo. *Racism Without Racists: Color-Blind Racism and the Persistence of Racial Inequality in America*. 5th edition. Lanham, Maryland: Rowman and Littlefield Publishers, 2017.

Brooks, Van Wyck. "On Creating a Usable Past." *The Dial* (1918): 337–341.

Chomsky, Noam. *Hopes and Prospects*. Chicago: Haymarket Books, 2010.

DeCerteau, Michel. *The Practice of Everyday Life*. Berkeley: University of California Press, 1984.

Erdrich, Louise. *Future Home of the Living God*. New York: HarperCollins Publishers, 2017.

Fanon, Frantz. *The Wretched of the Earth*. New York: Grove Press, 2005.

Giridharadas, Anand. *Winners Take All: The Elite Charade of Changing the World*. New York: Vintage, 2019.

Franklin, Ruth. "A Timely Novel of Anti-Progress by Louise Erdrich." *The New York Times*, November 21, 2017. https://www.nytimes.com/2017/11/21/books/review/louis-erdrich-future-home-of-the-living-god.html

Hall, Emily. "Tomás Saraceno: Tonya Bodaker Gallery." *Artforum*. 2012. https://www.artforum.com/print/reviews/201208/tomas-saraceno-38835

Harris, Cheryl I. "Whiteness as Property." *The Harvard Law Review Association* 106, no. 8 (1993): 1707–91.

Hamid, Mohsin. *Exit West*. New York: Riverhead Books, 2017.

Kennedy, John F. *A Nation of Immigrants*. New York: Harper & Row, 1964.

Laguerre, Michel. *Minoritized Space: An Inquiry into the Spatial Order of Things*. Berkeley: Institute of Governmental Studies Press, 1999.

Lefebvre, Henri. *The Production of Space*. Translated by Donald Nicholson-Smith. Oxford: Blackwell Publishers, 1974.

---

[46] Cornel West, "Prisoners of Hope," 346.

[47] Michel de Certeau, *The Practice of Everyday Life* (Berkeley: University of California Press, 1984), 125.

Leyshon, Cressida. "This Week in Fiction: Mohsin Hamid on the Migrants in All of Us." *The New Yorker*, November 7, 2016. https://www.newyorker.com/books/page-turner/this-week-in-fiction-mohsin-hamid-2016-11-14

L.S. and E.H. "Open Borders: The Case for Immigration." *The Economist*, April 16, 2018. https://www.economist.com/open-future/2018/04/16/the-case-for-immigration

Nield, Sophie. "There is Another World: Space, Theatre, and Global Anti-capitalism." *Contemporary Theatre Review* 16, no. 1 (2006): 51–61.

Schaub, Michael. "Future Home of the Living God is a Rare Stumble from a Great Writer." NPR, November 14, 2017. https://www.wfae.org/npr-arts-life/2017-11-14/future-home-of-the-living-god-is-a-rare-stumble-from-a-great-writer

Solnit, Rebecca. *A Paradise Built in Hell: The Extraordinary Communities that Arise in Disaster*. London: Penguin Books, 2010.

Justice, Daniel Heath. "'Our stories give us a lot of guidance': Daniel Heath Justice on why Indigenous literatures matter." By Zoe Tennant. CBC Radio, April 09, 2020. https://www.cbc.ca/radio/unreserved/why-stories-matter-now-more-than-ever-1.5526331/our-stories-give-us-a-lot-of-guidance-daniel-heath-justice-on-why-indigenous-literatures-matter-1.5527999

West, Cornel. "Prisoners of Hope." *The Impossible Will Take a Little While: Perseverance and Hope in Troubled Times*, edited by Paul RogatLoeb, 293–297. New York: Basic Books, 2014.

Wynter, Sylvia. "Unsettling the Coloniality of Being/Power/Truth/Freedom: Towards the Human after Man, its Overrepresentation-An Argument." *The New Centennial Review* 3, no. 3. (2003): 257–337.

Zizek, Slavoj. *In Defense of Lost Causes*. London and New York: Verso, 2008.

CHAPTER 13

Frantz Fanon, Chester Himes, and a "Literature of Combat"

David Polanski

When Frantz Fanon described the process of decolonization as the literal "putting into practice" of Jesus's prophecy that "the last shall be first and the first last" (adding that such a radical reorganization of the social order "will only come to pass after a murderous and decisive struggle"),[1] he was not merely disabusing us of the delusion that decolonization could be achieved through non-violent means, he was reminding us of how deeply embedded the narratives of the Hebrew and Christian bibles were within the foundations of Western colonialism and Western humanism, as well as how dependent decolonization would be on the replacement of those narratives with ones that encourage more inclusive and more compassionate conceptions of time, space, and of the "human" itself.

Recent developments in regard to the dating and purpose of the composition of the Hebrew Bible have greatly bolstered Fanon's argument. Since the 1970s, scholars associated with the "minimalist" perspective of

---

[1] Frantz Fanon, *The Wretched of the Earth*, trans. Constance Farrington (London: Penguin, 2001), 28.

D. Polanski (✉)
Independent Scholar, Salem, MA, USA

© The Author(s), under exclusive license to Springer Nature
Switzerland AG 2021
C. Beck (ed.), *Mobility, Spatiality, and Resistance in Literary and Political Discourse*, Geocriticism and Spatial Literary Studies,
https://doi.org/10.1007/978-3-030-83477-7_13

Near Eastern studies[2] have employed archeological and epigraphical means to demonstrate conclusively that the texts of the Hebrew Bible are "literary constructs"[3] whose authors repurposed themes and motifs from a millennia-old African, Mediterranean, and Near Eastern tradition,[4] and whose historical claims (from enslavement in Egypt to David's kingdom to the return from Babylon) are unable to withstand critical scrutiny.[5] More specifically, a parade of scholarship has situated the construction of the Hebrew Bible's "Primary History"[6] within the Hellenistic period,[7] and illuminated the extent to which its structure and ethos were directly influenced by Plato's blueprints for the utopic state—in particular, his recommendation of state-sponsored narratives as a means to "systematically [program] the beliefs and emotions of the citizenry"[8] and invest state law with "an aura of antiquity, divine authority and unchangeability."[9] The purpose of the construction of the Hebrew Bible, in other words, was the creation of a Platonic "national literature"[10] that would encourage settlers

[2] For an overview of developments associated with the "minimalist" tradition, see Ingrid Hjelm, "History of Palestine verses history of Israel? The Minimalist-Maximalist Debate" in *A New Critical Approach to the History of Palestine: Palestine History and Heritage Part I,* eds. Ingrid Hjelm, Hadman Taha, Ilan Pappe, and Thomas L. Thompson, (London: Routledge, 2019), 60–79; Thomas L. Thompson, "Without Evidence or Method" in *Far from Minimal: Celebrating the work and Influence of Philip R. Davies,* eds. Duncan Burns and John W. Rogerson, (New York: Bloomsbury, 2012), 429–458; Philippe Wajdenbaum, *Argonauts of the Desert – Structural Analysis of the Hebrew Bible* (Sheffield: Equinox, 2011), 22–38.

[3] Thomas L. Thompson, *The Mythic Past: Biblical Archaeology and The Myth of Israel* (London: Basic Books, 1999), 263.

[4] Thomas L. Thompson, *The Messiah Myth: The Near Eastern Roots of Jesus and David* (London: Basic Books, 2005), 25.

[5] Niels Peter Lemche, "Exile as the great divide," in *Myths of Exile: History and Metaphor in the Hebrew Bible,* eds. Anne Katrine de Hemmer Gudme and Ingrid Hjelm, (New York: Routledge, 2015), 14–16.

[6] The "Primary History" is commonly understood as representing Genesis through Kings.

[7] See Russell E. Gmirkin, *Berossus and Genesis, Manetho and Exodus: Hellenistic Histories and the Date of the Pentateuch* (New York: T&T Clark, 2006) and Russell E. Gmirkin, *Plato and the Creation of the Hebrew Bible* (London: Routledge, 2016); Niels Peter Lemche, "The Old Testament – a Hellenistic Book?" in *Did Moses Speak Attic? – Jewish Historiography and Scripture in the Hellenistic Period,* ed. Lester L. Grabbe (Sheffield: Sheffield Academic Press, 2001), 287–318; Bruce Louden, *Homer's Odyssey and the Near East* (Cambridge: Cambridge UP, 2011); Wajdenbaum, *Argonauts.*

[8] Gmirkin, *Plato and the Creation,* 254.

[9] Gmirkin, *Plato and the Creation,* 262.

[10] Gmirkin, *Plato and the Creation,* 250–1.

13 FRANTZ FANON, CHESTER HIMES, AND A "LITERATURE OF COMBAT"   283

in Palestine to view themselves as "a pure race, under threat of contamination from the indigenous population,"[11] with a historical claim to "the land of their fathers."[12] The result of these efforts was nothing less than "a textbook for colonialism,"[13] argues Niels Peter Lemche, "a very specific program for conquest"[14] that promotes systematic dehumanization, land theft, and genocide as divinely sanctioned colonial tactics.

Recent studies have similarly illuminated the extent to which the narratives of the early Christians—whose authors were fluent in Near Eastern literary traditions, urban-oriented,[15] and highly protective of "newfound wealth, powers, and vitality"[16] (many of them slave owners, including Paul)[17]—were *counter*-revolutionary in nature, designed to reinforce, rather than overturn, existing economic and social hierarchies. By positing the fictional ministry of Jesus[18] within an imagined Palestinian "wilderness" (one teeming with "demons, Satan, wild beasts," and bandits),[19] and by having Jesus offer its crudely depicted inhabitants[20] wealth and salvation in the next life in exchange for their subservience here on earth, the authors of the Gospels sought to redirect the increasingly militant impulses

---

[11] Philip R. Davies, *Scribes and Schools: The Canonization of the Hebrew Scriptures* (Louisville: Westminster John Knox Press, 1998), 64.

[12] Niels Peter Lemche, "The History of Israel," in *A New Critical Approach to the History of Palestine*, eds. Ingrid Hjelm, Hamdan Taha, Ilan Pappe, and Thomas L. Thompson, (London: Routledge, 2019), 349.

[13] Niels Peter Lemche, *The Old Testament between Theology and History* (Louisville: Westminster John Knox Press, 2008), 314.

[14] Niels Peter Lemche, "Joshua and Western Violence," in *Far from Minimal: Celebrating the work and Influence of Philip R. Davies*, eds. Duncan Burns and J. W. Rogerson, (New York: Bloomsbury, 2013), 277.

[15] Michael Mann, *The Sources of Social Power, Volume 1: A History of Power from the Beginning to AD 1760* (New York: Cambridge University Press, 2012), 322.

[16] Mann, *Sources of Social Power*, 309.

[17] Roland Boer and Christina Petterson, *Time of Troubles: A New Economic Framework for Early Christianity* (Minneapolis: Fortress Press, 2017), 168–178. As Boer and Petterson demonstrate, the success of early Christianity (especially its missionary work) was dependent on slave labor, just as its ideological perspective was influenced by the status of its founders as slave owners (i.e. class-based resistance is labeled as "wicked rebellion," and the ideal followers of God are depicted as either "tenants who must pay the appropriate due" or slaves who must accept their fate with humility).

[18] Thompson, *The Messiah Myth*, 108.

[19] Boer and Petterson, *Time of Troubles*, 162.

[20] Boer and Petterson, *Time of Troubles*, 160–162.

284   D. POLANSKI

of Palestine's rural majority[21] toward the mere *preparation* of a revolution, rather its earthly *realization*.[22] Additionally, Paul's implementation of Platonic forms of institutional organization,[23] along with his rejection of the Hebrew Bible's fixation on Palestine and his broadening of the terms for church membership (replacing the Hebrew Bible's behavioral codes with a form of kyriarchal subservience available to all),[24] set in motion Christianity's colonization of Europe, and (in tandem with the Hebrew Bible) provided the blueprint for the Western colonial practices Fanon would later deconstruct.[25]

These scholarly developments not only bolster Fanon's description of decolonization as the earthly realization of the post-apocalyptic revolution promised by the early Christians, they reinforce his call for the production of "a national literature"[26] designed to unleash the long "canalized" impulses of the colonized masses[27] and to counteract the narrative tactics employed by the West. Accordingly, Fanon depicted this "literature of combat"[28] in terms reminiscent of the Platonic tactics employed by the authors of the Bible. First, Fanon encouraged colonized artists to "use the

[21] Richard A. Horsley and John S. Hanson, *Bandits, Prophets, and Messiahs: Popular Movements in the Time of Jesus* (Harrisburg: Trinity Press, 1999), 48–87.

[22] Petterson likens this tactic to an "iron cage" wherein "resistance is generated by the system in question and is thereby contained within the system." Boer and Petterson, *Time of Troubles*, 186.

[23] Such tactics included the development of "a network of trained leaders ... who could ensure brand consistency through regular teaching events, liturgical reinforcement and systematic guards [including threats of violence] against defection from the approved teachings and behaviours." K.L. Noll, "Investigating Earliest Christianity without Jesus" in *"Is this not the Carpenter?" The Question of the Historicity of the Figure of Jesus*, eds. Thomas L. Thompson and Thomas S. Verenna, (Durham: Acumen, 2013), 236–259.

[24] I became aware of the use of the term "kyriarchy" to describe Paul's vision for social order by way of Christina Petterson, *Apostles of Revolution? Marxism and Biblical Studies* (Leiden: Brill, 2020).

[25] For further documentation of the manner in which the themes and tropes of the Bible were invoked to justify Western capitalist and colonial development, see Marimba Ani, *Yurugu: An Afrikan-Centered Critique of European Cultural Thought and Behavior* (Baltimore: Africa World Press, 1994), 29–197; Roland Boer and Christina Petterson, *Idols of Nations: Biblical Myth at the Origins of Capitalism* (Minneapolis: Fortress, 2014); Jorge Cañizares-Esguerra, *Puritan Conquistadors: Iberianizing the Atlantic, 1550–1700* (Stanford: Stanford University Press, 2006); J. Martin Evans, *Milton's Imperial Epic: Paradise Lost and the Discourse of Colonialism* (Ithaca: Cornell University Press, 1996).

[26] Fanon, *Wretched*, 193.

[27] Fanon, *Wretched*, 44.

[28] Fanon, *Wretched*, 193.

13 FRANTZ FANON, CHESTER HIMES, AND A "LITERATURE OF COMBAT"   285

past with the intention of opening the future,"[29] injecting new life into the "stories, epics, and songs … which formerly were filed away as set pieces," and replacing the "formula" of "this all happened long ago" with it "happened here today, and it might happen tomorrow."[30] Furthermore, Fanon did not believe (nor did the authors of the Bible) that artists should adhere to contrived distinctions between "fiction" and "history," declaring "the real *leap*" to be the introduction of "invention into existence,"[31] and deriding art intended to portray a "detailed representation of reality" as "evocative not of life but of death."[32] Most importantly, just as the Hebrew Bible is designed to encourage the kind of exilic identity that empowers adherents to pursue radical social reorganization,[33] Fanon saw the creation of such "literature of combat" as the "responsibility"[34] of the "fugitives, outcasts, [and] hounded intellectuals who flee to the countryside"[35] and seek out the "zone of occult instability where the people dwell"[36] and "the conditions necessary for the inevitable conflict are brought together."[37]

Although the only specific example of a "literature of combat" noted by Fanon in *The Wretched of the Earth* is Fodéba Keïta's poem "African Dawn,"[38] Greg Thomas argues that the works of Fanon and author Chester Himes "frequently and profoundly converge in the most identical of terms,"[39] and Fanon himself singled out Himes's nine-volume Harlem-based detective series (of which Fanon lived to see the publication of five)

[29] Fanon, *Wretched*, 187.

[30] Fanon, *Wretched*, 193.

[31] Frantz Fanon, *Black Skin, White Masks*, trans. Charles Lam Markmann (New York: Grove, 1991), 229.

[32] Fanon, *Wretched*, 181.

[33] Philip R. Davies, *The Origins of Biblical Israel* (New York: t&t Clark, 2007), 32.

[34] Fanon, *Wretched*, 193.

[35] Edward Said, *Culture and Imperialism* (New York: Vintage Books, 1994), 272–273.

[36] Fanon, *Wretched*, 183.

[37] Fanon, *Wretched*, 196.

[38] Fanon, *Wretched*, 187.

[39] Greg Thomas, "On Psycho-Sexual Racism & Pan-African Revolt: Fanon & Chester Himes," *Human Architecture: Journal of the Sociology of Self-Knowledge* 5 (2007): 219. It should be noted that this chapter on Fanon and Himes represents both an expansion and a reconsideration of a paper that I first composed in Greg Thomas's 2018 graduate seminar "Fanon and Chester Himes: Psycho-Sexual Racism and Pan-African Revolt" at Tufts University (a seminar that was based on Thomas's 2007 paper on the subject, one that broke new ground in our understanding of the relationship between Fanon and Himes). I am greatly indebted to Thomas for my experiences in his seminar, and I consider this chapter, in part, to represent an extension and an expansion of his previous work on these subjects.

as a vital exploration of the aggressive tendencies and "predominate nervous tension" that colonialism produces in its subjects.[40] Although Himes claimed to have never read Fanon, he was nonetheless aware of Fanon's interest in his work (once claiming that Fanon had written an "unpublished essay concerning the use of violence in his novels"),[41] and Himes frequently made the Fanonian claim that the overarching theme of his Harlem series was the necessity for Black America to transition from unorganized to organized/revolutionary states of violence. The remainder of this paper will argue that Himes's Harlem series—most notably its final installments, *Blind Man with a Pistol* and *Plan B*—represents precisely the type of literature that Fanon declared as necessary for the process of decolonization to unfold: that which unsettles and repurposes (with decolonial intent) the themes, tropes, and narrative tactics employed by the colonizer, encourages the development of new forms of expression and new spatial and humanistic conceptions, and illuminates the numerous pitfalls and endless possibilities associated with violent decolonial action.

"Harlem" and "Palestine"

"I didn't really know what it was like to be a citizen of Harlem," Himes declared, "I had never worked there, raised children there, been hungry, sick or poor there," and "had been as much of a tourist as a white man from downtown changing his luck." However, he clarified, "the Harlem of my books was never meant to be real; I never called it real; I just wanted to take it away from the white man if only in my books."[42] Like the various Palestines invented by the authors of the Hebrew and Christian bibles, the "Harlem" of Himes's novels—a realm marked by "loud voices," "sudden laughter," and "violent gestures"[43] set against a backdrop of "cults and con men," "fake sisters of mercy, nuns in disguise,"[44] and the presence on "every corner, every evening" of "self-appointed prophets" shouting

---

[40] Frantz Fanon, *Alienation and Freedom*, trans. Steven Corcoran (London: Bloomsbury, 2018), 524–525.

[41] Thomas, "Psycho-Sexual," 219.

[42] Chester Himes, *My Life of Absurdity* (New York: Thunder's Mouth Press, 1976), 126.

[43] Chester Himes, "Harlem: An American Cancer," *Présence Africaine: English Edition* 17, no. 45, (1963): 51.

[44] Chester Himes, *Conversations with Chester Himes* (Jackson: University Press of Mississippi, 1995), 128–129.

"Jesus is coming VERY SOON"[45]—was not intended to document a present or historical reality, but to imagine a community engaged in a process of social and spatial reorganization, one whose depiction might encourage readers to reconceive their own reality in similarly radical terms.

To this end, the characters of Himes's Harlem frequently reimagine the stories of the Hebrew and Christian bibles in ways that wildly contradict their original context or intent. In one instance, the parable of the "Prodigal Son" is rewritten so that when the son returns he is promptly killed and eaten by his relatives[46]; in another, Jesus's transformation of the "Legion" of demons into hogs (and his subsequent driving of them into the sea) is reinvented as a revenge fantasy against the white race[47]; and in several instances the citizens of Harlem use the book of Revelation (which the community collectively sees not as the product of divine-inspiration, but of insanity or epilepsy)[48] as a source for numbers with which to gamble, or else cite Revelation's most absurd passages as a tactic to confound the authorities.[49] Such reinventions, however, are not merely the acts of individual citizens, but are woven into the community's organized forms of worship. Reverend Short, for example, models his ministry after the image of an opiate-addicted John the Revelator[50] (declaring upon his arrest, "I'm not insane ... I'm holy"),[51] and Reverend Sam (who lives with his flock in a literal wilderness within Harlem's "concrete jungle," one nearly impenetrable by the police who seek to question him) mimics the evasive rhetorical tactics employed by Jesus during his interrogation by Pilate, then declares himself (as did Jesus) to be unbound by the laws and social codes of humankind.[52]

Likewise, there is a notable absence within Himes's Harlem of the bureaucratic structures that typically regulate behavior within organized Christian churches (and that serve to reinforce the "aura of antiquity, divine authority and unchangeability" that Plato thought was necessary to maintain social control).[53] Not only are *all* of Harlem's clergymen self-appointed,

---

[45] Himes, "Harlem," 49.

[46] Chester Himes, *Cotton Comes to Harlem* (New York: Vintage Books, 1988), 17.

[47] Himes, *Cotton*, 35.

[48] Chester Himes, *The Crazy Kill* (New York: Vintage Books, 1989), 46.

[49] Himes, *Crazy*, 36–37; Chester Himes, *A Rage in Harlem* (New York: Vintage Books, 1991), 36–37, 77–78.

[50] Himes, *Crazy*, 36–46.

[51] Himes, *Crazy*, 158.

[52] Chester Himes, *Blind Man with a Pistol* (New York: Vintage Books, 1989), 7–14.

[53] Gmirkin, *Plato*, 262.

288   D. POLANSKI

but they also display minimal allegiance to sanctioned rituals (in one instance, baptism by water and baptism by fire are combined into baptism by fire-hose!),[54] and many engage in thinly veiled corruption as a means to fund lavish lifestyles.[55] This breakdown within Harlem of any formal Christian order is so apparent that its citizens openly comment on it (a gambler declares that "if Christ knew what kind of Christians He got here in Harlem He'd climb back up on the cross and start over,"[56] and Detective Gravedigger Jones observes that in Harlem it is "everybody to their own Jesus").[57] As a result, there exists no clear distinction between the preachers of Harlem's churches and drug dealers like "Sister Heavenly" (who calls herself a "faith healer," guides her flock through a process of "de-incarnation," and labels her opiates as medicinal "heavenly dust")[58] or con-artists like "Sister Gabriel" (who quotes from Revelation, sells printed tickets to heaven, and is, in fact, a man).[59]

Consequently, these novels depict a causational relationship between the delegitimization of the biblical narrative, the breakdown of ecclesiastical order, and the willingness of Harlem's citizens to consider or attempt the use of violence for anti-systemic ends. In *Blind Man with a Pistol*, Himes makes this connection explicit. A preacher named "General Ham" (self-named after the cursed son of Noah, whom Western colonists later declared to be the ancestor of the indigenous populations of Africa[60] and the Americas)[61] tells his followers that Moses was a coward for having fled instead of overthrowing the Pharaoh,[62] then informs them that the purpose of the Gospels was not the salvation of the wretched of this earth, but rather their pacification ("the philosophy of forgiveness and love," Ham declares, is "the white Jesus's philosophy … whitey's con. Whitey invented it, just like he invented the white Jesus").[63] Ham concludes his sermon by ordering his parishioners/

---

[54] Chester Himes, *The Big Gold Dream* (New York: Pegasus Books, 2008), 7.

[55] Himes, *Big Gold Dream*, 5–15. Sweet Prophet Brown, for example, uses the money he receives from parishioners (in exchange for non-metaphorical breadcrumbs tossed on the floor for them to fight over) to purchase silk robes, diamond rings, and a Rolls Royce.

[56] Himes, *Rage*, 14.

[57] Himes, *Rage*, 45.

[58] Chester Himes, *The Heat's On* (New York: Vintage Books, 1988), 33–35.

[59] Himes, *Rage*, 26–37.

[60] Sylvia Wynter, "Unsettling the Coloniality of Being/Power/Truth/Freedom: Towards the Human, After Man, Its Overrepresentation – An Argument," *CR: The New Centennial Review* 3, no. 3 (2003): 302–303.

[61] Evans, *Imperial Epic*, 24.

[62] Himes, *Blind Man*, 76.

[63] Himes, *Blind Man*, 77.

13 FRANTZ FANON, CHESTER HIMES, AND A "LITERATURE OF COMBAT"   289

soldiers to force-feed the "indigestible" flesh of the Black Jesus to white people until they die,[64] then leads them through Harlem's streets carrying a statue of a bloody Black Jesus with a white noose around its neck and a sign reading "THEY LYNCHED ME."[65] Later, when Ham and his singing, dancing flock unexpectantly cross paths with two other marches—a Black Power march, and one intended to "solve the Negro Problem" by promoting interracial "brotherhood"[66]—a violent conflict ensues that openly targets the authorities sent to quell it and pushes Harlem to a brink that it will soon (courtesy of a blind man with a pistol, of course) tumble over.[67]

When such examples are considered alongside numerous references to Near Eastern mythology/history peppered across all nine of these novels (from characters named "Homer," "Ulysses,"[68] and "Roman Hill,"[69] to comparisons between Harlem and Gethsemane[70] and between the Jersey shoreline and the walls of Rome),[71] it is apparent that Himes intended his imagined "Harlem" as a variant of the various "Palestines" depicted in the biblical narrative, each "Palestine" representing an economically precarious, politically unstable realm primed for a radical reorganization. In a key passage, Himes uses the narrator of *Blind Man with a Pistol* to explain why Harlem, as a social space, has been pushed past the point in which the old order can be re-established, and why its citizens are so willing to embrace novel conceptions of time, space, and the "human" itself:

> Everything else had failed ... what did they have to lose? And they might win. Who knew? The whale swallowed Jonah. Moses split the Red Sea. Christ rose from the dead. Lincoln freed the slaves. Hitler killed six million Jews. The Africans had got to rule – in some parts of Africa, anyway. The Americans and the Russians have shot the moon. Some joker has made a plastic heart. Anything is possible.[72]

[64] Himes, *Blind Man*, 77–78.
[65] Himes, *Blind Man*, 99.
[66] Himes, *Blind Man*, 21.
[67] Himes, *Blind Man*, 105–108.
[68] Chester Himes, *The Real Cool Killers* (New York: Vintage Books, 1988), 39–40.
[69] Chester Himes, *All Shot Up* (New York: Penguin, 1965), 6.
[70] Chester Himes, *Blind Man*, 73.
[71] Chester Himes, *Heat's On*, 6.
[72] Himes, *Blind Man*, 47.

290   D. POLANSKI

Violence and Organization

However, as Fanon reminds us, the delegitimization of the narratives used to justify the Western order and the willingness to use violence to further destabilize that order are insufficient to realize true decolonization unless such violence is organized and tactical, and unless it is accompanied by the development of a more compassionate, more communal form of humanism (one supported by programs designed to meet the material needs of the dispossessed). In his non-fiction writings and interviews, Chester Himes openly embraced these Fanonian prescriptions, rejecting the "sadistic" core of the Christian worldview,[73] and dismissing the form of Christian pacifism espoused by Martin Luther King as a "godsend" to white America.[74] "There is no reason," Himes declared, "why 100,000 blacks armed with automatic rifles couldn't literally go underground, into the subways and basements of Manhattan, and take over,"[75] and "if American blacks could put up an organized resistance," he added, "America would find them as difficult to deal with as the Viet Cong."[76] Accordingly, he infused his Harlem series with these Fanonian sentiments, arguing that its penultimate installment, *Blind Man With a Pistol*, represented a "statement" about the necessity to practice organized/revolutionary forms of violence,[77] and using the series' final novel, *Plan B*, to explore the possibilities and pitfalls associated with violent revolution.

In *Plan B*, Tomsson Black aims to initiate an insurrection against white America by distributing high-powered rifles to thousands of Black Americans and asking them to wait for his signal. Echoing Fanon, along with numerous biblical characters, Black embraces a kind of exilic identity by fleeing to the countryside and developing his plan far from the prying eyes of the established order (choosing an abandoned farm in the southern United States whose untamed landscape had frightened off other buyers, including the United States military).[78] Likewise, Black's plan involves the

---

[73] Chester Himes, *The Quality of Hurt: The Early Years, the Autobiography of Chester Himes* (Boston: De Capo Press, 1995), 73.

[74] Himes, *Conversations*, 62. In a discussion with John A. Williams (and in response to Himes's dismissal of Christian pacifism), Williams stated that King was a "godsend to the American white people," to which Himes replied "Absolutely. There's no question about it."

[75] Himes, *Conversations*, 102.

[76] Himes, *Conversations*, 94.

[77] Himes, *Conversations*, 93.

[78] Chester Himes, *Plan B* (Jackson: University Press of Mississippi, 1993), 35–39.

exploitation of the West's dependence on the themes and tropes of the biblical narrative—in particular, the missionary ethos of the early Christians, and the Hebrew Bible's strict dichotomy between the "chosen" people of Israel and the inhuman, expendable "Canaanites" (that which would serve as the basis for the West's rhetorically universal, yet historically hierarchical form of humanism).[79] In an interview with the Hull Foundation (akin to the present-day Gates Foundation), one intended to procure funding for the front-company Black created to conceal his revolutionary activity, Black impresses his benefactors by playing the part of a humbled, reformed "Canaanite" who desires nothing more than to promote the integration and assimilation of Black Americans into white society. After denouncing Malcom X and declaring that "white people are the only true Christians on earth,"[80] Black proclaims his devotion to the Western order in language that echoes Paul's call for God's chosen people to deliver salvation to the wretched of the earth:

> It is true, you brought us here as slaves and worked us as slaves and profited by our sweat ... but we learned things from you we would never have learned in Africa. We learned trade, we learned Christianity, we learned English, we learned to grow food and build shelter, and eventually we were freed. Now we have acquired more of the blessings of civilization than any other black people of comparable numbers on earth. We American blacks are better fed, better clothed, better housed, better educated, and are more devout Christians than any other blacks on earth.[81]

Black knows that the West's self-identification as the rational, ethical descendants of the Hebrew Bible's idealized Israelites has not only left them vulnerable to such appeals to their vanity, it has produced a profound fragility within the Western psyche whereby it is difficult for Westerners to process any situation in which their various "Others" behave *otherwise*. As such, not only is he successful in procuring enough money to send rifles to thousands of Black Americans, but when white America becomes aware that the "Canaanites" among them are now well-armed and willing to strike, a

---

[79] For a comprehensive analysis of the historical process through which the human/inhuman dichotomy inherent to the biblical narrative was transformed into the ostensibly "secular" terms of Western humanism, see Sylvia Wynter, "Unsettling the Coloniality," 263–283, among other essays by Wynter.

[80] Himes, *Plan B*, 162.

[81] Himes, *Plan B*, 163.

collective, self-destructive panic sets in: the police deploy tanks and drop bombs that leave America's cities cratered "like the face of the moon"[82] (and, in the process, unintentionally kill thousands of white people),[83] panicked mobs of white Americans begin roaming the streets hunting and castrating any and all Black Americans they find (after consulting Hemingway novels for pointers, of course),[84] the stock market crashes and the panic spreads globally, and by novel's end "the very structure of capitalism" has begun "to crumble."[85] Throughout it all, white Westerners across the globe are plagued nightly by dreams that feature "the enlarged sexual organs of black males" attacking and killing them,[86] and the novel concludes with thousands of armed Black Americans having taken over the "sewers and conduits" that "honeycombed the areas beneath the buildings of every large city"[87] in a guerrilla struggle with no end in sight.

The fact that *Plan B* has been largely erased from the critical conversation surrounding Himes's Harlem series is best understood within the context of a long-standing discomfort within academia (as documented by Greg Thomas) toward the radical implications of Fanonian decolonization.[88] Kevin Bell and Jonathan P. Eburne's introduction to a Himes-themed issue of the *African American Review*, for example, dismisses *Plan B* (unpublished at the time of Himes's death in 1984, but "substantially finished by 1971")[89] as little more than a "novelistic sketch,"[90] and Lawrence P. Jackson insinuates the novel was something Himes composed solely for the money.[91] More damningly, Stephen F. Soitos declares *Plan*

[82] Himes, *Plan B*, 186.

[83] Himes, *Plan B*, 63–66, 124–128.

[84] Himes, *Plan B*, 187–189.

[85] Himes, *Plan B*, 182.

[86] Himes, *Plan B*, 139.

[87] Himes, *Plan B*, 185.

[88] Greg Thomas, "The Complete Fanon," May 2018, Department of African Studies, University of Vienna, Vienna, Austria, video, 1:18:59, https://www.youtube.com/watch?v=RialYYb90Os&t=526s

[89] Kalí Tal, "'That Just Kills Me': Black Militant Near-Future Fiction," *Social Text* 20, no. 2 (2002): 83. Tal notes that "only minor changes" to the novel occurred between 1971 and 1984 (i.e., it is misleading to depict the novel's unfinished status as akin to an unrealized vision).

[90] Kevin Bell and Jonathan P. Eburne, "Introduction: A special section on Chester Himes," *African American Review* 43, no. 2–3 (2009): 229.

[91] Lawrence P. Jackson, *Chester B. Himes* (New York: W.W. Norton and Company, 2017), 476. Jackson justifies this interpretation by badly misquoting a letter Himes wrote to John A. Williams. In truth, the quote in question—"I'm certain you know that the main thing in

B's predecessor, *Blind Man with a Pistol*, to be "the final message of the Harlem detective series,"[92] while Thomas Heise labels *Blind Man* the series' "final installment."[93] Even within Christopher Raczkowski's tantalizingly titled "Chester Himes, Frantz Fanon and the Literary Decolonization of Harlem" (a paper that openly explores the relationship between Himes's Harlem and Fanon's *Wretched*), *Plan B* is relegated to a brief footnote, while the unorganized riots that occur at the end of *Blind Man* are depicted as the liberatory conclusion of a Fanonian process of decolonization.[94] Not only do such readings directly contradict Himes's stated purpose for these novels, they imply that Himes intended his imagined "Harlem" to remain nothing more than a wild, untamed, pre-Jesus "Palestine," trapped in what George Jackson described as "the riot stage" within which colonized subjects "think they don't need ideology, strategy or tactics," and are brought down by a violence that lacks "discipline or direction."[95]

It is, in fact, just such a self-destructive "stage" of revolution that Himes intended *Blind Man with a Pistol* and *Plan B* to critique. As James Yaki Sayles reminds us, those who read Fanon's *Wretched* and "come away with little more than a belief in the need to pick up the gun" have badly misread that text. "The underlying aim of social revolution," Sayles argues, "is to promote a change in people," and to that end, revolutionaries must develop "a comprehensive social platform that addresses issues of mental and physical health, education, social services of all kinds, economic welfare" and other "responsibilities beyond those of wanting to vent your frustration or act out your ideal conception of the heroic guerrilla."[96] As

---

this game is to keep putting books out. Even if you have to put out a lot of fillers"—was quite clearly intended not as a reference to *Plan B*, but as advice for Williams's career in the publishing industry. See Chester Himes and John A. Williams, *Dear Chester, Dear John: Letters Between Chester Himes and John A. Williams* (Detroit: Wayne State University Press, 2008), 55–56.

[92] Stephen F. Soitos, "Chester Himes, NWA: The Audacity of Blackness in Himes and His Harlem Detectives," *Clues* 28, no. 1 (2010): 66.

[93] Thomas Heise, "Harlem is Burning: Urban Rioting and the 'Black Underclass' in Chester Himes's *Blind Man with a Pistol*," *African American Review* 41, no. 3 (2007): 487.

[94] Christopher Raczkowski, "Chester Himes, Frantz Fanon and the Literary Decolonization of Harlem," *Lit: Literature Interpretation Theory* 23, no. 1, (2012): 21–22.

[95] George Jackson, *Blood in My Eye*, (Baltimore: Black Classic Press, 1990), 3.

[96] James Yaki Sayles, *Meditations on Frantz Fanon's Wretched of the Earth: New Afrikan Revolutionary Writings.* (Montreal and Chicago: Kersplebedeb and Spear & Shield Publications, 2010), 183–184.

such, when judged by Fanonian standards for true decolonization, Tomsson Black's revolution is not a success. Not only does he fail to provide his revolutionary army with any kind of organizational structure or strategy (resulting in little more than erratic attacks against the police), Black neither models nor encourages the development of the kind of inclusive, compassionate conceptions of time, space, and the "human" that true decolonization requires. While the events of *Plan B* most certainly reinforce Fanon's observation that even poorly organized anti-colonial violence can be "a cleansing force,"[97] both Fanon and Himes are adamant that true decolonization must go beyond merely destabilizing the Western order or unsettling Western/biblical narratives. "For ourselves and for humanity," Fanon declared, "we must turn over a new leaf, we must work out new concepts, and try to set afoot a new man."[98]

Final Reflections

The events that unfolded in the wake of George Floyd's murder (influenced not only by that and other acts of police brutality, but by a series of destabilizing factors including the election of Donald Trump and the COVID-19 pandemic) were infused with what Russell Rickford deems "a decolonial ethic" that transcended mere objections to "police terror, vigilante violence, and the public emblems of racial subjugation," and was directed instead at "producing an alternative framework of knowledge" to replace "the reigning ideological apparatus."[99] Yannick Giovanni Marshall adds that those events must not be viewed (as America's corporate media has framed them) as fleeting, reactionary expressions of grief and outrage, but as a chapter within a broader "uprising" against the Western order, indicative of the uniquely "revolutionary" period in history within which we find ourselves.[100] However, as Marshall and Rickford both warn, the transformation of this uprising into a Fanonian process of decolonization will depend not only on the continued education and organization of participants and allies alike, but on our ability to resist attempts by the ruling class to placate us with superficial "rituals of racial enlightenment" (that

[97] Fanon, *Wretched*, 74.
[98] Fanon, *Wretched*, 255.
[99] Russell Rickford, "Toppling statues as a decolonial ethic," *Africa Is a Country*, July 28, 2020, https://africasacountry.com/2020/07/toppling-statues-as-a-decolonial-ethic.
[100] Yannick Giovanni Marshall, "The racists' peace," *Al Jazeera*, June 7, 2020, https://www.aljazeera.com/opinions/2020/6/7/the-racists-peace.

which will allow them time and space to replace "the old frameworks of power with more refined patterns of domination"),[101] and to wholly reject the Liberal premise that a non-violent engagement in the political process represents the only practical, ethical, and historically justified means by which the dispossessed can seek relief.[102]

It is here wherein the ongoing value of Fanon and Himes is located, offering (among so many other things) strategies for the construction of counter-narratives that promote novel forms of social and economic relations, as well as offering their very lives as models for how those who seek a newer world may introduce "invention into existence."[103] Although the adoption of the tactics of Fanon and Himes among present-day activists will not hinge on the production of academic papers such as the one I am presently concluding, there is nonetheless value in casting light upon aspects of their work not previously or commonly discussed, as well as refuting scholars whose analysis serves to deny or deradicalize the relevance of their work in relation to ongoing events. It is toward such ends that this paper is directed.

Works Cited

Bell, Kevin and Jonathan P. Eburne. "Introduction: A special section on Chester Himes." *African American Review* 43, no. 2–3 (2009): 225–231.

Boer, Roland and Christina Petterson. *Time of Troubles: A New Economic Framework for Early Christianity.* Minneapolis: Fortress Press, 2017.

Davies, Philip R. *The Origins of Biblical Israel.* New York: t&t Clark, 2007.

———. *Scribes and Schools: The Canonization of the Hebrew Scriptures.* Louisville: Westminster John Knox Press, 1998.

Evans, J. Martin. *Milton's Imperial Epic: Paradise Lost and the Discourse of Colonialism.* Ithaca: Cornell University Press, 1996.

Fanon, Frantz. *Alienation and Freedom.* Edited by Jean Khalfa and Robert J.C. Young. Translated by Steven Corcoran. London: Bloomsbury, 2018.

———. *Black Skin, White Masks.* Translated by Charles Lam Markmann. New York: Grove Press, 1991.

———. *The Wretched of the Earth.* Translated by Constance Farrington. London: Penguin, 2001.

---

[101] Rickford, "Toppling."
[102] Marshall, "The racists' peace."
[103] Fanon, *Black Skin*, 229.

296   D. POLANSKI

Gmirkin, Russell E. *Plato and the Creation of the Hebrew Bible.* London: Routledge, 2016.

Heise, Thomas. "Harlem is Burning: Urban Rioting and the 'Black Underclass' in Chester Himes's *Blind Man with a Pistol.*" *African American Review* 41, no. 3 (2007): 487–506.

Himes, Chester. *All Shot Up.* New York: Penguin, 1965.

———. *The Big Gold Dream.* New York: Pegasus Books, 2008.

———. *Blind Man with a Pistol.* New York: Vintage Books, 1989.

———. *Conversations with Chester Himes,* edited by Michel Fabre and Robert E. Skinner. Jackson: University Press of Mississippi, 1995.

———. *Cotton Comes to Harlem.* New York: Vintage Books, 1988.

———. *The Crazy Kill.* New York: Vintage Books, 1989.

———. "Harlem: An American Cancer." *Présence Africaine: English Edition* 17, no. 45 (1963): 46–75.

———. *The Heat's On.* New York: Vintage Books, 1988.

———. *My Life of Absurdity: The Autobiography of Chester Himes, Volume II.* New York: Thunder's Mouth Press, 1976.

———. *Plan B.* Jackson: University Press of Mississippi, 1993.

———. *The Quality of Hurt: The Autobiography of Chester Himes, Volume I.* Boston: De Capo Press, 1995.

———. *A Rage in Harlem.* New York: Vintage Books, 1991.

———. *The Real Cool Killers.* New York: Vintage Books, 1988.

Horsley, Richard A. and John S. Hanson. *Bandits, Prophets, and Messiahs: Popular Movements in the Time of Jesus.* Harrisburg: Trinity Press, 1999.

Jackson, George L. *Blood in My Eye.* Baltimore: Black Classic Press, 1990.

Jackson, Lawrence P. *Chester B. Himes.* New York: W.W. Norton and Company, 2017.

Lemche, Niels Peter. "Exile as the Great Divide." In *Myths of Exile: History and Metaphor in the Hebrew Bible,* edited by Anne Katrine de Hemmer Gudme and Ingrid Hjelm, 89–97. New York: Routledge, 2015.

———. "The History of Israel." In *A New Critical Approach to the History of Palestine,* edited by Ingrid Hjelm, Hamdan Taha, Ilan Pappe, and Thomas L. Thompson, 341–352. London: Routledge, 2019.

———. "Joshua and Western Violence." In *Far from Minimal: Celebrating the Work and Influence of Philip R. Davies,* edited by Duncan Burns and J. W. Rogerson, 272–282. New York: Bloomsbury, 2013.

———. *The Old Testament between Theology and History.* Louisville: Westminster John Knox Press, 2008.

Mann, Michael. *The Sources of Social Power. Volume 1: A History of Power from the Beginning to AD 1760.* New York: Cambridge University Press, 2012.

Marshall, Yannick Giovanni, "The racists' peace." *Al Jazeera,* June 7, 2020. https://www.aljazeera.com/opinions/2020/6/7/the-racists-peace

Noll, K.L. "Investigating Earliest Christianity without Jesus." In *"Is this not the Carpenter?" The Question of the Historicity of the Figure of Jesus*, edited by Thomas L Thompson and Thomas S. Verenna, 233–266. Durham: Acumen, 2013.

Petterson, Christina. *Apostles of Revolution? Marxism and Biblical Studies*. Leiden: Brill, 2020.

Raczkowski, Christopher. "Chester Himes, Frantz Fanon and the Literary Decolonization of Harlem." *Lit: Literature Interpretation Theory* 23, no. 1 (2012): 1–25.

Rickford, Russell. "Toppling statues as a decolonial ethic." *Africa Is a Country*, July 28, 2020. https://africasacountry.com/2020/07/toppling-statues-as-a-decolonial-ethic

Said, Edward W. *Culture and Imperialism*. New York: Vintage Books, 1994.

Sayles, James Yaki. *Meditations on Frantz Fanon's Wretched of the Earth: New Afrikan Revolutionary Writings*. Montreal and Chicago: Kersplebedeb and Spear & Shield Publications, 2010.

Soitos, Stephen F. "Chester Himes, NWA: The Audacity of Blackness in Himes and His Harlem Detectives." *Clues* 28, no. 1 (2010): 61–67.

Tal, Kalí. "'That Just Kills Me': Black Militant Near-Future Fiction." *Social Text* 20, no. 2 (2002): 65–91.

Thomas, Greg. "The Complete Fanon: African Revolution, Black Power Movement, and Neo-Colonial Imperialism (Beyond the Academic Myths of Post-Coloniality)." Filmed May 2018 at Department of African Studies, University of Vienna, Vienna, Austria. Video, 1:18:59. https://www.youtube.com/watch?v=RialYYb90Os&t=526s

———. "On Psycho-Sexual Racism & Pan-African Revolt Fanon & Chester Himes." *Human Architecture: Journal of the Sociology of Self-Knowledge* 5 (2007): 219–230.

Thompson, Thomas L. *The Messiah Myth: The Near Eastern Roots of Jesus and David*. London: Basic Books, 2005.

———. *The Mythic Past: Biblical Archaeology and the Myth of Israel*. London: Basic Books, 1999.

Wynter, Sylvia. "Unsettling the Coloniality of Being/Power/Truth/Freedom: Towards the Human, After Man, Its Overrepresentation – An Argument." *CR: The New Centennial Review* 3, no. 3 (2003): 257–337.

PART IV

Conclusion

CHAPTER 14

Resisting a Wilting Society: *To Blossom*

Christian Beck

This volume explored the ways mobility, spatiality, resistance, literature, and politics intersect and inform each other. At various points of contact, these concepts can be seen to open up new spaces, highlight possibilities of new becomings, and create new approaches to reading movement. While literature serves as the primary means to discuss these ideas throughout this volume, I would like to end by reflecting on an image that encapsulates all of these ideas and embodies what I believe is at the heart of this collection. While Tatyana Fazlalizadeh's mural on Public School 92 in Harlem, NY may appear to simply depict a young Black woman reading, there is much more occurring in this piece, with much greater implications and relevance to the discussions found in this collection. My concluding remarks, therefore, will be directed toward Fazlalizadeh's mural, but will also be a means to reflect back on the various topics and themes that comprise the volume.

I believe the best way to end this collection is to look toward the future. The image of a hopeful future is going to (and ought to) look different than previous images of our history, as Walter Benjamin did with Paul

---

C. Beck (✉)
University of Central Florida, Orlando, FL, USA
e-mail: christian.beck@ucf.edu

© The Author(s), under exclusive license to Springer Nature
Switzerland AG 2021
C. Beck (ed.), *Mobility, Spatiality, and Resistance in Literary and Political Discourse*, Geocriticism and Spatial Literary Studies,
https://doi.org/10.1007/978-3-030-83477-7_14

302   C. BECK

Klee's painting "Angelus Novus." Klee's painting, a 1920 oil transfer drawing with watercolor, depicts an unorthodox and rather disproportionate angel facing the viewer. Benjamin, the painting's first owner, declares that "This is how one pictures the angel of history."[1] Benjamin extrapolates on this idea, reading beyond the painting itself but affording greater meaning to the "angel of history": the angel "sees one single catastrophe which keeps piling wreckage upon wreckage" and a storm "propels him into the future to which his back is turned, while the pile of debris before him grows skyward."[2] We need a new perspective, a new way to conceptualize the future, a new image of the future that does not leave us with piles of debris and wreckage. The image we need both reflects and portends our organic becoming. Fazlalizadeh's mural *To Blossom* offers this, in addition to the immediate relevance to the ideas in this volume.

Fazlalizadeh's piece sits on a wall at a public school and shows a Black girl reading a book. This image could be viewed as innocuous, apolitical, and purely decorative. However, this work, like so many of Fazlalizadeh's projects, makes a very clear statement.[3] Fazlalizadeh's art becomes, as Stephen Zepke writes:

> a kind of bio-politics, an experimentation with life as it is lived, a contestation in the realm of experience with everything that seeks to prevent us from affirming our power of composition. Art is a mechanism to increase our power, to liberate ourselves from the limits of representation (and the political operation of these limits is a constant subtext of Deleuze and Guattari's discussion). Art is the freedom to experiment on our conditions of existence, and is the ethical condition of any revolution. Art as ethics, and as bio-politics, serves to emphasise the fact that art is always concerned with very practical problems.[4]

To Blossom's content does not necessarily speak to an "experiment on our conditions of existence" (though, its placement and engagement with viewers might), as much as it makes an ethical and biopolitical demand. Completed in 2016, the biopolitical demands of *To Blossom* seem to resonate even more

[1] Walter Benjamin, "Theses on the Philosophy of History," in *Illuminations*, ed. Hannah Arendt, trans. Harry Zohn (New York: Schocken Books, 1968), 257.

[2] Benjamin, "Theses on the Philosophy of History," 257–8.

[3] For a complete, up to date list of all of Tatyana Fazlalizadeh's projects see her website: http://www.tlynnfaz.com/

[4] Stephen Zepke, *Art as Abstract Machine: Ontology and Aesthetics in Deleuze and Guattari* (London: Routledge, 2005), 9.

in the wake of the #MeToo movement, the murder of Breonna Taylor—as well as the numerous other unarmed Black men, women, and children killed by police—Black Lives Matter (BLM), and the openly racist opposition to the BLM protests. *To Blossom* is a mechanism to increase the power of Black girls, and the Black community more generally, by addressing the practical problems of education and the social (and literal) mobility of young Black women (Fig. 14.1).

Fig. 14.1 Tatyana Fazlalizadeh, *To Blossom* (2016). Located at PS 92 in Harlem, NY. (Used with permission of the artist.)

In Fazlalizadeh's image we are presented with various small sites of resistance, which when put together become not only an image of resistance to the historical injustices of sexism, racism, and classism, but also a gesture to the future where literature, the environment, and education itself belong in the hands of those who resist. More than just a resistance, this image participates in and creates a mobile geography: "a new way of relating to the earth and marking one's position on it in a way that does not presuppose a fixed, sedentary writer or reader."[5] The very nature of graffiti and street art contains an implied mobility on the part of both the writer/artist and the reader/viewer. In viewing the image, you find yourself in a space that is not the sanitized, constructed space of a gallery; rather, the image and space speak to and mark one another and at the same time the spatial awareness of the viewer becomes paramount to the image itself.[6] The space simultaneously constructs the viewing experience and participates in conveying meaning onto the piece itself.[7] While *To Blossom* might be classified as street art rather than "graffiti" as such, Fazlalizadeh's piece is a form of what David Fieni refers to as nomad grammatology. He writes, "Nomad grammatology is not a theory of walls, graffiti, mobility, illegality, or sovereignty; instead, it is a practice of reading and a form of experimental cooperation between different kinds of writing. Nomad grammatology does not claim to speak for the subaltern; rather, it sees the positioning of subalternity and attempts to think in relation to this positioning."[8] Additionally, as Luca Visconti posits, "street art can aim more specifically to leverage social and market inequalities afflicting people. In this light, street art constitutes a form of political intervention via aesthetic activism."[9] What, then, is the political intervention? What are the biopolitical demands? And how is subalternity positioned in Tatyana Fazlalizadeh's *To Blossom*?

[5] David Fieni, "What a Wall Wants, or How Graffiti Thinks: Nomad Grammatology in the French Banlieue," *Diacritics* 40 (2012): 79.

[6] Tracey Bowen, "Graffiti as Spatializing Practice and Performance," *Rhizomes* 25 (2013): np. http://www.rhizomes.net/issue25/bowen/

[7] While the space is notably absent in the presentation of the image and thus not affecting the viewing in precisely the same manner, we can discuss the place(ment) of the image and the effects of its location.

[8] Fieni, "What a Wall Wants," 75–6.

[9] Luca M. Visconti et al., "Street Art, Sweet Art? Reclaiming the 'Public' in Public Place," *Journal of Consumer Research* 37 (2010): 525.

14 RESISTING A WILTING SOCIETY: *TO BLOSSOM*   305

The placement of the image of a young Black girl reading on the side of PS 92 in Harlem already announces the public nature of the piece. As a public school, the space is state controlled and is largely accessible to a general population. As Sergio García-Doménech notes, "The purpose of a public space—apart from its urban function—is to be fully identified by their users, achieve its own character, be accepted by citizens, and that they consider it an essential part of the city itself. The success in achieving this objective is the result of a complex set of social, historical, political, economic and cultural variables."[10] More specifically, this is a place where children will pass through regularly and engage with the image in some fashion; for many students, they will see a representation of themselves on the side of a building, not a common experience for young Black women in America. The piece writes over the bricks and conveys the aim of the space—a reminder to all of the possibilities this place can and should offer to those within its walls. The regulations of walls and of the institution of education that control this space recede, much like the bricks of the wall, to reveal the animus of the space. This space vis-à-vis the placement of the image *animates* the mind, inspires growth and continued becomings, and brings to the surface the underrepresented power, creativity, and aspirations of young Black women. From this space comes both resistance and mobility through education and Fazlalizadeh's piece marks this potentiality by showing viewers an "interior": both who is inside the building and what is inside the individuals themselves. The artwork makes visible what many don't (want to) see—it's easier to defund education, especially in underrepresented, struggling communities, if you can't see who you are affecting. This piece transgresses the limitations of the walls and as Fieni concludes, "A wall wants to move. It wants mobility. It wants the mobility denied to those it contains. [...] If walls want our mobility, then graffiti demonstrates that another kind of mobility is possible."[11] The young Black woman inscribed on the wall of PS 92 articulates the desire for socioeconomic, racial, and gender equality by entering and exceeding the walls of educational institutions.

---

[10] Sergio García-Doménech, "Urban Aesthetics and Social Function of Actual Public Space: A Desirable Balance," *Theoretical and Empirical Researches in Urban Management* 10 (2015): 63. Also see, Kim Dovey, Simon Wollan, and Ian Woodcock, "Placing Graffiti: Creating and Contesting Character in Inner-city Melbourne," *Journal of Urban Design* 17 (2012): 21–42.

[11] Fieni, "What a Wall Wants," 88.

306   C. BECK

While the image's placement articulates the potentiality of young Black women, the subtleties of the image speak to more than education. Note, for example, the girl's hair: it is her natural hair pulled back out of her face. Leaves and flowers emerge from her hair but are set behind her face. Pairing the natural imagery with the girl's natural hair gestures toward a "natural" behavior of young Black women's desire to grow, learn, branch out, and also reflects the beauty of nature with what is natural. This detail merges the natural desire to learn with the identity of the individual pictured. While the young woman's hair is an important element of the work and allows for this idea of "naturality" to become manifest within the image, it is not and ought not to be a central discussion point of the image. In a similar vein, if we shift our gaze below the girl's face there are simple lines of black paint that merely outline the collar of a shirt and the girl's shoulders. By using unembellished lines, the image puts under erasure any material site of gender (i.e., a color or cut of a top) and class (new/name brand top or threadbare t-shirt), in favor of the femininity of the face and the resolve for knowledge. Furthermore, there is no emphasis on *the body*, but rather the focused mind: the face of determination. The materials, accessories, and cultural identifiers of gender, class, ableness, and monikers of social/group affiliation are absent, which allows us to bear witness to "what the wall wants," to use Fieni's phrase. These peripheral artistic decisions serve as frames for the primary content of the work and at the same time are subtle acts of resistance: many images of women displayed in public are advertisements and our attention is directed to the material objects that adorn the female body—which is decidedly exploited in many cases as a means to create desire (sexual and consumerist) for a particular object. The woman—her body, her image, her appearance—is secondary to the product, but always first as an object. Fazlalizadeh's piece creates agency and meaning in the face of the girl precisely through the absence of material objects on the girl's body at the bottom of the image and merging nature with the natural at the top of the image.

While the image of the girl is the object of our sight, thought, and consideration, her agency remains visible and intact. The girl's eyes remain cast down at the book in front of her. Yet, at the same time, there is the sense that she is casting her eyes down on the viewer. The positionality of the image above the viewer not only portrays the magnitude and certainty of the girl's task but also gives a sense that the girl is aware of being looked at, that she is the object of our gaze. Nevertheless, precisely at this moment she remains undeterred and refuses to meet the gaze of the viewer in favor of her reading/education. Her focus, her concentration, her determination are signaled by her eyes, but also her mouth. The closed mouth not only speaks to her fortitude and resolve, but is also a message to "stop telling women to smile"—the title of another project by Tatyana Fazlalizadeh, which coalesced into a book with the same title.[12] Unlike the unsmiling faces of models selling products, the girl's face reveals her own desire, her unimpeded avenue to empowerment, the hunger for knowledge. Through her head and eye position, our line of sight follows hers to the object before her: the book that engulfs the entire bottom of the wall—decidedly not "wreckage upon wreckage." The blue binding looms large, but does not distract from the central image of the girl's face. While the book might be the largest aspect of the piece, it acts as an "eccentric center" that both pulls our eyes upward to the girl's face and constructs meaning with and for the girl.[13] In other words, the face is the focus of the work of art, but the book is the focus of the girl; therefore, it is the book, or more specifically its unseen writing, that generates the purpose and meaning for the girl and, without viewing the contents of the book, we are witness to the event of learning. Fazlalizadeh artfully shows this connection. The dominant color of the book is blue—it expands the entirety of the wall and the deepness of the color serves as a grounding, an earthy tone of neutrality. However, the darkness of the blue cover serves as a distinct contrast to the white pages of the text. This high contrast pulls the image from the wall, makes itself known, and creates a fracture between the book and the girl's face: these are two separate entities. The white pages afford greater contrast to the dark skin of the girl's face, which only further highlights that this is a *Black* girl reading. However, the white/black contrast is not divisive, but rather connective and reflective. Look again at the girl's face. We can see the light shading of her face as a result of the light reflecting off the pages and illuminating her face, *not whitening or lightening her, but giving her the glow of knowledge and education.* Importantly, the whiteness of the pages creates a significant parallel with the whiteness of the girl's eyes. This is the connection between the text and the girl; the whites of her eyes create a visual link to the text in front of her, but it is the dark irises that absorb, reflect, and connect to the

---

[12] See Tatyana Fazlalizadeh, *Stop Telling Women to Smile: Stories of Street Harassment and How We're Taking Back Our Power* (New York: Seal Press, 2020).

[13] Jacque Derrida, *Mémiores: For Paul de Man*, trans. and ed. Avital Ronell and Eduardo Cadava (New York: Columbia University Press, 1989), 73.

308   C. BECK

words on the page. Fazlalizadeh's portrait captures the event of reading, of the power of knowledge, of the beauty of learning and reading for oneself. But most importantly, Fazlalizadeh's visual contrast and signification of the event reveal the biopolitical demand and most important message of the image: *witness a young Black woman becoming.*

Fazlalizadeh's *To Blossom* encapsulates everything that this collection seeks to do: find connections and lines of flight, make central those voices—and faces—that have been pushed to the periphery, see the possibility of mobility in the seemingly static, show the radical and transformational effects of spatiality, and identify resistance to hegemonic norms, oppression, and capitalist forms of capture. Much like the mural, in these seemingly singular texts, a multiplicity is found. From buses in India to internment camps in America, from an imaginary Harlem to dystopian displacement in U.S. cities, and from mapping a city to bringing backgrounds into the foreground, these chapters span peoples, centuries, and continents. Yet, they are brought together in their ability to show representations of becoming. The literary texts and associated discourses discussed in the volume are about becoming, overcoming, and transforming. At their core, these chapters embody re-readings, re-thinkings, and the profound possibilities contained in both new and well-trod narratives. In the texts on mobility, we see the ways movement serves as a basis for identity construction and ideological frameworks. A focus on mobility and movement opens new avenues to think about alternative ways of engaging with the world. As Mimi Sheller writes, "A mobile ontology, in which *movement is primary as a foundational condition of being,* space, *subjects, and* power, helps us imagine the constituent relationality of the world in a new way."[14] In this way, mobility and movement play important roles in chapters throughout the collection (see, e.g., Subramanian's and Hulsey's chapters) and the crosscurrents of mobility and spatial analysis of literature create "new cartographic approaches, new forms of representation, and new ways of imagining our *place* in the universe."[15] But just as mobility reaches into other areas of the collection, so do does spatiality or geocriticism (see, e.g., Gleyzon's and Khan-Thomas's essays). As Foucault pointed out at the end of the twentieth century, "the present epoch will perhaps be

---

[14] Mimi Sheller, *Mobility Justice: The Politics of Movement in an Age of Extremes* (London: Verso, 2018), 9. Emphasis original.

[15] Robert T. Tally Jr., *Spatiality* (New York: Routledge, 2013), 42–3. Emphasis original.

14 RESISTING A WILTING SOCIETY: *TO BLOSSOM* 309

above all the epoch of space."[16] Our current epoch is witnessing all types of positive spatial disruptions: protests, autonomous zones, squatting, radical gardening, and organization of political activism in the streets on scales and with frequency never before seen—I gesture toward leftist movements only, because the far-right groups (III percenters, QAnon, Proud Boys, and other overt white-supremist groups) have oppression, hierarchy, and dominance as their goal, not liberty, equality, and solidarity. These disruptions or nodes of resistance are directly challenging the inequality and unjust practices of the dominant culture that have, for too long, maintained control (explicit and interpellated) over large numbers of the global population.

An undercurrent of resistance runs through all of the chapters found in this volume. As I argue in the introduction, resistance is not simply a visible act of defiance; it is a frog on the chessboard, a moment of unprecedented and unexpected creation. Each of these chapters, and the literature that they discuss, is an example of an act of creation that, if they do not present something completely new and unexpected, they contain the *possibility* of realizing the unexpected within their language: "Every act of resistance is not a work of art, even though, in a certain way, it is. Every work of art is not an act of resistance, and yet, in a certain way, it is."[17] These chapters, like so many essays, articles, books, short stories, novels, plays, and poems, exceed their linguistic trajectories and make possible (and permissible) new forms of biopolitical production. "The ultimate core of biopolitical production," Antonio Negri and Michael Hardt write in their Preface to *Commonwealth*, "is not the production of objects for subjects, as commodity production is often understood, but the production of subjectivity itself. This is the terrain from which our ethical and political project must set out."[18] Indeed, the project they are referring to is their own work, but I think we can read "our ethical and political project" more broadly to include this volume, if not all scholarship, writing, and art that seeks to produce subjectivities that resist control and oppression. They continue, "Biopolitics is a partisan relationship between subjectivity and history that is crafted by a multitudinous strategy, formed by

---

[16] Michel Foucault, "Of Other Spaces," trans. Jay Miskowiec, *Diacritics* 16 (1986): 22.

[17] Gilles Deleuze, "What is the Creative Act?," in *Two Regimes of Madness: Texts and Interviews 1975–1995*, ed., David Lapoujade, trans. Ames Hodges and Mike Taormina (New York, NY: Semiotext(e), 2007), 328.

[18] Michael Hardt and Antonio Negri, *Commonwealth* (Cambridge: The Belknap Press of Harvard University Press, 2009), x.

events and resistances, and articulated by a discourse that links political decision making to the construction of bodies in struggle. [...] Events of resistance have the power not only to escape control but also to create a new world."[19] The chapters in this volume engage with biopolitics and biopolitical production as a part of a "multitudinous strategy" and clearly articulate or gesture toward the relationship between subjectivity and history. Consider all the various characters and contexts addressed in this collection, when paratactically placed together, they show a narrative history of classed, racialized, and variously sexed "bodies in struggle" in diverse places around the world. At all points, these chapters, through their biopolitical production, enter the fray of the production of subjectivity, history, and a "discourse that links political decision making to the construction of bodies in struggle." When brought together through parataxis, the "and ... and ... and" creates an urgency, an image that cannot be ignored, and must be addressed through a concerted, intersectional resistance to the "wreckage upon wreckage" that is piling up at the feet of Klee's angel. In this assessment, then, biopolitical production, which is crafted by resistance to control and oppression, also becomes a production of the future.

Let's return to Klee's "Angelus Novus": "His eyes are staring, his mouth is open, his wings are spread. This is how one pictures the angel of history. His face is turned toward the past."[20] This angel of history, with his back turned to the future and debris piling up at his feet, is propelled into the future by a storm, which Benjamin identifies: "This storm is what we call progress."[21] Bleak as it may be, this is not a predetermined trajectory.[22] There are alternatives and change can occur. Tatyana Fazlalizadeh has provided us with a new image of both how to shift the trajectory of the angel of history and of the future itself. Progress can be imagined and treated as something different than the neoliberal techno-capitalist vision. Progress can be based on biopolitical production through interactions between people, nature, and ideas. One does not just blossom as an individual: in Fazlalizadeh's mural, the book implies that our "progress" comes from the work/ideas/help of others not only before us (temporal

---

[19] Hardt and Negri, *Commonwealth*, 61.

[20] Benjamin, "Theses on the Philosophy of History," 257.

[21] Benjamin, "Theses on the Philosophy of History," 258.

[22] While Benjamin states that the storm is "blowing from Paradise," I think we can think this paradise as utopic moment free of all oppression, imminent climate collapse, and divisive political discourse. Benjamin, "Theses on the Philosophy of History," 257.

and spatial), but of those all around us: the girl could pick her head up at any point to ask a question, to tell us what she has learned, to use the knowledge she has gained, to extrapolate on the ideas she has read, to build new concepts from the those she has just learned, to expand our own knowledge and world in ways we could not have imagined. *To Blossom* is and ought to be the vision of the future. To go further: *To Blossom* supplants "Angelus Novus" as an image that speaks to history because, in so many ways, the subject of Fazlalizadeh's work has had her history put under erasure, her history has been revised, her history is traumatic, or, as is so often the case with people of color, there is no history at all. Therefore, *To Blossom* is the aspirational vision of the future, but until this future is made a reality, this art work is an event of resistance that possesses the ability to generate "power to create a new world."

Works Cited

Benjamin, Walter. "Theses on the Philosophy of History." In *Illuminations*, edited by Hannah Arendt and translated by Harry Zohn, 253-264. New York: Schocken Books, 1968.

Bowen, Tracey. "Graffiti as Spatializing Practice and Performance." *Rhizomes* 25 (2013): np. http://www.rhizomes.net/issue25/bowen/

Deleuze, Gilles. "What is the Creative Act?" In *Two Regimes of Madness: Texts and Interviews 1975–1995*, edited by David Lapoujade and translated by Ames Hodges and Mike Taormina, 317–329. New York: Semiotext(e), 2007.

Derrida, Jacques. *Mémoires: For Paul de Man*. Translated and edited by Avital Ronell and Eduardo Cadava. New York: Columbia University Press, 1989.

Dovey, Kim, Simon Wollan, and Ian Woodcock. "Placing Graffiti: Creating and Contesting Character in Inner-city Melbourne." *Journal of Urban Design* 17, no. 1 (2012): 21–42.

Fazlalizadeh, Tatyana. *Stop Telling Women to Smile: Stories of Street Harassment and How We're Taking Back Our Power*. New York: Seal Press, 2020.

Fieni, David. "What a Wall Wants or How Graffiti Thinks: Nomad Grammatology in the French Banlieue." *Diacritics* 40, no. 2 (2012): 72–93.

Foucault, Michel. "Of Other Spaces." Translated by Jay Miskowiec. *Diacritics* 16, no. 1 (1986): 22–27.

García-Doménech, Sergio. "Urban Aesthetics and Social Function of Actual Public Space: A Desirable Balance." *Theoretical and Empirical Researches in Urban Management* 10, no. 4 (2015): 54–65.

Hardt, Michael and Antonio Negri. *Commonwealth*. Cambridge, MA: The Belknap Press of Harvard University Press, 2009.

Sheller, Mimi. *Mobility Justice: The Politics of Movement in an Age of Extremes.* London: Verso, 2018.

Tally Jr., Robert T. *Spatiality.* New York: Routledge, 2013.

Visconti, Luca M., John F. Sherry Jr., Stefania Borghini, and Laruel Anderson. "Street Art, Sweet Art? Reclaiming the 'Public' in Public Place." *Journal of Consumer Research* 37, no. 3 (2010): 511–529.

Zepke, Stephen. *Art as Abstract Machine: Ontology and Aesthetics in Deleuze and Guattari.* London: Routledge, 2005.

INDEX[1]

NUMBERS AND SYMBOLS
#MeToo, 303

A
Abstract space, 157, 190, 278
Adorno, Theodor, 106, 107
Affirmative geography, 30
Agency, 13, 16, 30, 31, 34, 120, 127,
 145, 167, 170, 183, 306
Ahmed, Sara, 119, 123, 129,
 250, 251
Alienation, 25n4, 26n6, 31, 52,
 79, 80
American Indian Movement, 147
Angelus Novus, 302, 310, 311
Animus, 305
 of space, 305
Antebellum, 164, 166, 179, 182
Anti-capitalism, 17, 18, 257–279
Antonioli, Manola, 225

Art
 and the body, 198
 and Deleuze, 8, 9, 94, 302
 and desire, 180, 198
 and the environment, 9, 304
 and Fanon, 285
 and mourning, 103
 and Palestine, 92–95, 103
 production, 103
 and resistance, 8–10, 14, 94,
 103, 309
 street/graffiti, 304
 subjectivities, 309
Assemblage, 212n11, 224
Assimilation, 138, 141, 145, 147,
 154, 291
 and interior, 138
Augmented Reality (AR), 204
Auschwitz, 98, 106, 107
Authoritarian, 261–265, 262n16
Autoscopia, 221

---

[1] Note: Page numbers followed by 'n' refer to notes.

© The Author(s), under exclusive license to Springer Nature
Switzerland AG 2021
C. Beck (ed.), *Mobility, Spatiality, and Resistance in Literary and
Political Discourse*, Geocriticism and Spatial Literary Studies,
https://doi.org/10.1007/978-3-030-83477-7

313

314 INDEX

B

Bakhtin, Mikhail, 240, 241, 243
Ballet, 188, 202
Baramki, Andoni, 98, 99
Barker, Robert, 198
Bataan Death March, 141, 148
Beckett, Samuel, 211
Becoming
  and Benjamin, 199
  and Deleuze, 215, 225, 226,
    228, 230n97
  and geography, 53, 224, 225
  ontology, 308
  and power, 228
  and race, 308
  and space, 18, 226, 238, 301, 305
Benjamin, Walter, 199, 201, 301, 302,
  310, 310n22
Berlant, Lauren, 240
Bhabha, Homi, 38, 100
Biopolitics, 309, 310
Black geographies, 164
Black Jesus, 289
Black landscape, 167, 168, 171, 173
Black Lives Matter (BLM), 303
Black Power, 289
Black representational spaces, 169
Bloomsbury Group, 188
Bransky, Robert, 92, 92n2
Bubbled mobility, 126
Butler, Judith, 102

C

Camelot, 62–64, 68
Canaanites, 291
Capitalism, 11, 18, 35, 80, 140, 257,
  258, 260, 263, 270–273, 277,
  278, 292
  and masculinity, 273
Caribbean, 24, 25n4, 26, 28, 31–33,
  33n15, 38, 46–48, 53, 54,
  54n52, 74–78

Carroll, Lewis, 223
Cartography, 210, 227,
  227n84
Centre of Architectural
  Conservation, 96
Césaire, Aimé, 35
Chivalry, 61, 63, 65, 66, 68
Chomsky, Noam, 271, 277
Choreography, 202
Chronotope, 236, 240–243, 252
Cinema, 198, 200
  and distance, 198, 200
Ciné-relief, 198
Civilization, 33–35, 48, 49,
  64, 291
Civil liberties, 179
Class, 2, 10, 13, 24, 47, 59,
  143, 174, 194, 246, 247,
  247n39, 267, 283n17,
  294, 306
  and sexuality, 10, 247
Coetzee, J. M., 35
Cold subjectivity, 94
Colonialism, 11, 48, 91–95, 97, 99,
  101, 106, 110, 236, 281,
  283, 286
  and oppression, 11
The Communist Manifesto, 271
Confinement
  and control, 8, 147, 148
  and Deleuze, 8
  domestic, 124
  and gender, 117
  and identity, 116, 148, 156
  and imperialism, 144,
    148, 156
  of Japanese Americans, 16, 140,
    148, 156
  and memory, 142
  and race, 16, 140, 144
Consciousness
  and becoming, 18
  collective, 83

INDEX   315

and geography, 30, 31, 45
and memory, 82, 160
national, 160
and phenomenology, 190, 195
and space, 18, 27, 30, 188, 190
and toggling, 189–191, 197
Conservative revolutionary, 267
Consumerist, 306
Counter-hegemony, 95
Counter-narrative, 80, 295
Covid-19, 294
Crary, Jonathan, 200
Cresswell, Tim, 3

D
de Certeau, Michel, 279
Decolonization, 269, 270, 274, 275,
    279, 281, 284, 286,
    290, 292–294
Deleuze, Gilles, 5, 5n15,
    6n19, 7–9, 11, 12, 94, 209,
    211–216, 212n11, 212n12,
    215n31, 215n34, 218–221,
    223–230, 227n84,
    230n97, 230n98
Derrida, Jacques, 307n13
Desire
    and becoming, 42, 53, 225
    and Benjamin, 199
    and cinema, 198
    and class, 13
    and control, 2, 8, 12, 204
    and Deleuze, 224
    and difference, 75
    and distance, 198, 204
    and gender, 242, 305
    and geography, 53, 224
    and identity, 40, 125
    and immigration, 74, 81, 85
    individual, 12, 81, 204
    and landscapes, 200, 224
    and movement, 12

object of, 42
and Orientalism, 33, 43
and production, 228
shared, 244
Deterritorialization, 17, 211–213,
    215–217, 220n53, 221
Difference, 5n15, 13, 14, 25, 27, 29,
    31, 34, 35, 37, 41n25, 74, 100,
    154, 165, 238, 248, 249
Digital distance, 204
Digital space, 204
Domesticity, 115–117, 121–123,
    128–130, 132, 174, 177,
    181, 182
Double-consciousness, 43n31

E
The Economist, 270, 276
Edward, the Black Prince, 59, 65
Empire
    American, 147, 151, 157
    British, 27, 139
    and geography, 24
Equality, 180, 247n39, 305, 309
Ethnoclass, 264
Executive Order 9066, 148
Exploitation, 34, 38, 270, 291
Exterior, 15, 17, 119, 142, 144,
    160, 201

F
Fanon, Frantz, 18, 41, 42, 81, 102,
    269, 270, 274, 275, 281–295
Fazlalizadeh, Tatyana, 301–308,
    302n3, 310, 311
Fieni, David, 304–306
Forbes, 271
Foucault, Michel, 2–6, 3n5, 8, 9,
    230n98, 308
Francis, Pope, 271
Freedmen's Bureau, 172, 175

316 INDEX

G

Gender variant bodies, 244, 246
Gentrification, 249
Geocriticism, 308
Geography
and becoming, 53, 224, 238
and colonialsim, 26, 36,
43, 95
and consciousness, 30, 31
cultural, 1, 26n6
and Deleuze, 224, 226
and desire, 53, 224
and the encounter, 26
and gender, 2
and identity, 1, 23
and imagination, 26
and mobility, 26
and narrative, 26, 205
social, 166
and social relations, 237, 253
Gibson, James, 189
Gilroy, Paul, 43n31
Gordon, Gavin, 188
GPS
and art, 205
Grant, Duncan, 188
Greek drama, 189
Guattari, Félix, 11, 211–213, 212n11,
215, 215n34, 226, 227, 227n84,
229, 302

H

Hardt, Michael, 309
Harper's Magazine, 151
Hemingway, Ernest, 292
Heteronormativity, 121,
123, 126
Homestead Act, The, 165, 172
Huhtamo, Erkki, 198,
200, 204

I

Icarian Perspective, 220
Identity
colonized, 156
construction, 42, 308
and environment, 4, 129
exilic, 285, 290
formation, 160
gender, 116, 117, 234n2
and imperialism, 16, 23
individual, 138
national, 58–60, 66, 68, 160
racial, 24, 40, 41
spatial, 16
transnational, 53
III Percenters, 309
Immigrant
Black, 73–75, 77–83, 86, 88, 89
European, 165
Jewish, 97, 99
Nation of Immigrants, 274
Immigration, 74, 75, 79, 82,
85, 270
Imperialism, 16, 23, 35, 37, 38,
46n33, 48, 81, 108,
137–161, 273
and confinement, 142, 148, 156
Inequality, 242n21, 278,
304, 309
Interconnected imperialism, 149
Interior
Gulf, 105, 106
and power, 16
Interiorized imperialism, 16,
137–161
Internalized imperialism, 144,
152, 156
Interpellate, 119, 309
Intersectional, 74, 260, 265, 266,
268, 270, 310
and resistance, 266, 310

INDEX **317**

J
James, C.L.R., 53
Jefferson, Thomas, 172
  and property, 172
Jouissance, 191, 222, 223, 226

K
Kafka, Franz, 214
Kanafani, Ghassan, 93–95, 93n7,
  94n10, 95n13
Keynes, John Maynard, 188
Klee, Paul, 302, 310

L
Labor
  and death, 58
  forced, 151, 177
  free, 150, 181
  global, 54
  and hands, 146
  as payment, 58, 59
  physical, 181
  and race, 24, 181
  sex work, 54
  slave, 283n17
  "Statute of Laborers," 59
  and travel, 49, 54
Lamming, George, 53
Landownership, *see* Ownership
Laudato Sí, 271
Law
  and authority, 224, 282
  and colonization, 97, 100
  martial, 260
  and Pilate, 287
  and politics, 183
  and race, 154, 175, 178
  and the State, 282
  and transgender, 233

Lefebvre, Henri, 2, 2n3, 3, 165, 166,
  238, 248, 268
Liberty
  individual, 12, 13
  social, 11
Liminality, 18, 24
Line of intensity, 222
Lines of flight, 10, 215, 216, 225,
  226, 228, 308
Lopokova, Lydia, 188, 202
Lovelace, Earl, 54
Lynching culture, 164, 181

M
Manifest Destiny, 268
Marcuse, Herbert, 30
Masculinity, 37, 267, 272, 273
Massey, Doreen, 25, 28,
  238, 240
Massumi, Brian, 122
McClintock, Anne, 36
McGreevy, Thomas, 188
McNally, David, 241
Mediterranean, 48, 108n53, 282
Memoir
  Danticat, 74, 76, 77, 82, 83
  Houston, 139, 151
  Woolf, 185, 187, 192,
    193, 196
Merleau-Ponty, Maurice,
  194–198
Metropolitan, 13, 32, 35, 45,
  53, 75, 80, 235, 243
Milton, John, 218
Minoritization, 265
Minoritized space, 268
Morrison, Toni, 76, 77, 85
Movement
  between object, 190
  and cinema, 198

318 INDEX

Movement (*cont.*)
  and deterritorialization, 211,
    215, 216
  foreground/background, 189, 190,
    197, 204
  and gender, 117, 234n2
  and perception, 192
  in poetry, 70
  and race, 168
  and sexuality, 197
  of thought, 2, 189, 192
  and toggling, 189, 191, 192,
    197, 204
  of vision, 202
Muzak, 202

N
Naipaul, V. S., 31, 32, 32n13, 54
Nationalism
  nationalist, 13, 60, 61, 64,
    65, 68, 70
  white nationalists, 277
Native American Renaissance, 16
Native Americans, 16, 137–161,
    261n15, 263, 264
  seizure of land, 140
Nativeness, 274
Nativist, 273
Navajo Code-Talkers, 137
Negri, Antonio, 309
New Yorker, 271
Nietzsche, Friedrich, 214, 220
Nijinsky, Vaslav, 188
Nonmovement
  and gender, 124
  and resistance, 126

O
Other/others, 42, 43, 138–140, 153,
    158, 258, 276, 291
Ownership
  and citizenship, 172, 177, 181

and community, 164
house/home, 96, 98, 128, 129,
    132, 171–178
and prosperity, 177
and reproduction, 260
and rights, 172, 177
and transgression, 144

P
Palestine, 18, 92–94, 92n2, 93n7,
    94n10, 96, 97, 100–102, 107,
    111, 283, 284, 286, 289, 293
  and Harlem, 286–289
Panopticon, 6
Panoramic vision, 194, 204
Patriarchy
  and the environment, 122
  and exchange, 180
  heteropatriarchy, 234n2,
    246, 248n39
  and ideology, 115, 118–120
  and oppression, 116, 120, 122
  and place, 118, 121
  and race, 262
Pearl Harbor, 150
  bombing of, 151, 159
Peasants' Revolt, 60–62
Perkin, John, 271
Phenomenology
  of place, 121
  queer, 119
Pity
  emotion, 244
  and truth, 244
Postcolonial, 23, 24, 26, 26n6, 35,
    236, 242, 247
Poverty
  and labor, 177
  War on, 147
Power, 1–19, 28, 32, 32n13, 43n31,
    61, 75, 84, 87, 93, 94, 97, 103,
    105, 106, 108, 121, 122,
    145–148, 196, 204, 213, 215,

218, 228, 236, 238, 252, 259, 262, 263, 268, 275, 283, 295, 302, 303, 305, 308, 310, 311
and literature, 213
Privilege, 13, 53, 172, 260, 263, 264, 266
white male, 263
Proud Boys, 309
Public School 92
Harlem, NY, 301
Public transport, 249

Q

QAnon, 309

R

Racism, 11, 36, 304
Regionalist, 60, 64, 65, 68, 70
Renaissance
and humanism, 258
(translation), 220
Representational black spaces, 168
Rescinded land, 175
Reterritorialization, 211–213, 217
Rilke, Rainer Maria, 209–210, 210n2

S

Said, Edward, 100, 139
Saraceno, Tomás, 257–259, 257n1, 270, 279
School-house, 173, 174
as place, 173
Selvon, Sam, 53, 54
Sexuality, 197, 223, 224, 234, 241, 245, 248, 249, 252, 267
and space, 248
Sex work, 234, 245
Shakespeare, William, 187
Sheller, Mimi, 3, 308
Signifyin(g), 78, 87, 167, 225, 266
Social construction

of gender, 117, 123
of home, 128
of identity, 117
of space, 164
of womanhood, 123, 125
Socialist, 86, 273
Solidarity, 28, 111, 183, 258, 309
Solnit, Rebecca, 277
Southern economy
post Civil War, 176
Southern violence, 179
Space, 1–19, 25, 27–32, 36, 38, 45, 65, 74, 78, 80, 81, 94, 98, 100, 101, 103–112, 116–119, 122–124, 129, 130, 138–143, 138n3, 145, 147, 148, 151, 152, 155, 157, 164–171, 173, 174, 176–179, 181–183, 186–191, 193–196, 198–205, 212, 216, 217, 220, 226–228, 234–244, 248, 249n43, 250, 251, 259, 266, 268, 274, 275, 278, 279, 281, 289, 294, 295, 301, 304, 305, 308, 309
constructed, 2, 164, 304
Spatial relativity, 203
Spatial reversibility, 203
Spivak, Gayatri, 23
Stiegler, Bernard, 213
Subjectivity
and biopolitics, 309
female, 118
global, 26
production, 309, 310
transient, 118
Surveillance
of black bodies, 168
of bodies, 237

T

Tally Jr., Robert T., 3n5, 10n35, 242n22, 308n15
Toggling, 187, 189–193, 196–198, 204

320 INDEX

Topography, 18, 221, 223, 225
Tournier, Michel, 223
Transgender, 233, 234,
    234n2, 237, 243, 244,
    248, 251, 252
  and representation, 237
Transgression
  of boundaries, 130
  and erotica, 235
  of identity, 220
Trauma
  and confinement, 156
  and empire, 138
  generational, 132
  and immigration, 79, 82, 85
  of immobility, 24
  individual, 142, 145
  individual and collective, 140
  individual and ecological, 144
  and memory, 77
Trump, Donald, 294
Tuan, Yu Fi, 138, 138n3

V
Valéry, Paul, 196, 212n12, 223
Virtual Reality (VR), 204
Voloshinov, Valentin, 241

W
Walker, Alice, 87
Warburg, Aby, 210
West, Cornel, 278, 279
White culture, 141, 145
White supremacy, 43n31, 183,
    263–265, 271
Will to power, 214, 228
Wynter, Sylvia, 258, 259, 264,
    264n19, 270, 276, 278

Z
Zepke, Stephen, 302
Zionism, 107
Zizek, Slavoj, 258, 278

Printed in the United States
by Baker & Taylor Publisher Services